SEMEIA 69/70

INTERTEXTUALITY AND THE BIBLE

Editors: George Aichele and Gary A. Phillips

©1995
by the Society of Biblical Literature

SEMEIA 69/70

Copyright © 1995 by the Society of Biblical Literature

All rights reserved. No part of this work may be reproduced or transmitted in any form or by any means, electronic or mechanical, including photocopying and recording, or by means of any information storage or retrieval system, except as may be expressly permitted by the 1976 Copyright Act or in writing from the publisher. Requests for permission should be addressed in writing to the Rights and Permissions Office, Society of Biblical Literature, 825 Houston Mill Road, Atlanta, GA 30329, USA.

ISSN 0095-571X
ISBN 1-58983-156-X

Printed in the United States of America
on acid-free paper

Contents

Contributors to this Issue v

Introduction:
    Exegesis, Eisegesis, Intergesis
        George Aichele and Gary A. Phillips 7

1. Sifting For Cinders: Leviticus 10:1–15
        Tod Linafelt and Timothy Beal 19

2. Resistance to the Carnivalization of Jesus:
    Scripture in the Lucan Passion Narrative
        Robert Brawley 33

3. Figure, Knowledge and Truth:
    Absence and Fulfillment in the Scriptures
        Jean Calloud 61

4. Imaginings at the End of an Era: Letters as Fictions
        William Doty 83

5. "What is Written? How are you Reading?" Gospel,
    Intertextuality and Doing Lukewise: Reading
    Lk 10:25-42 Otherwise
        Gary A. Phillips 111

6. Multiple Signs, Aspects of Meaning, and Self as Text:
    Elements of Intertextuality
        James Voelz 149

7. Christological Slippage in Schwarzenegger's *Terminator*
        Roland Boer 165

8. Intertextual Trekking: Visiting the Iniquity
    of the Fathers Upon the Next Generation
        Susan Graham 195

9. Jezebel Re-Vamped
        Tina Pippin 221

10. 'The Getting of Names': Anti-intertexuality and the Unread
     Bible in Toni Morrison's *Song of Solomon* and *Beloved*
        Nicole Wilkinson 235

11. Texts, More Texts, a Textual Reader, and a Textual Writer
    Peter Miscall 247

12. Jesus' Frankness
    George Aichele 261

Response: "When Jesus Rewrote the Corn Mothers:
Intertextuality as Transnational Critical Practice"
    Laura E. Donaldson 281

Response: "Issues for Further Discussion"
    Daniel Boyarin 293

Glossary 299

Selected Bibliography... 303

CONTRIBUTORS TO THIS ISSUE

George Aichele
  Department of Religion
  & Philosophy
  Adrian College
  Adrian, MI 49221

Timothy Beal
  Letters Collegium
  Eckerd College
  4200 54th Avenue S.
  St. Petersburg, FL 33711

Roland Boer
  United Theological College
  16 Masons Drive
  North Parramatta, NS 2151
  Australia

Daniel Boyarin
  Department of Near
  Eastern Studies
  250 Barrow's Hall
  University of California at Berkeley
  Berkeley, CA 94720

Robert L. Brawley
  McCormick Theological Seminary
  5555 S. Woodlawn Avenue
  Chicago, IL 60637

Jean Calloud
  Centre Pour L'Analyse du
  Discours Religieux
  Université Catholique, Lyon
  25 Rue du Plat
  Lyon 69288
  France

Laura E. Donaldson
  English, Women's Studies, and
  American Indian/Native Studies
  University of Iowa
  202 Jefferson Building
  Iowa City, IA 52242-1418

William Doty
  Department of Religious Studies
  University of Alabama
  Tuscaloosa, AL 35487

Susan Lochrie Graham
  15 Barwell Cres
  Etobicoke, ON M9W 2W4
  Canada

Tod Linafelt
  1507 Lamont Court
  Chapel Hill, NC 27514

Peter D. Miscall
  St. Thomas Seminary
  1300 S. Steele
  Denver, CO 80210

Gary A. Phillips
  Department of Religious Studies
  College of the Holy Cross
  Worcester, MA 01610

Tina Pippin
  Department of Religion
  Agnes Scott College
  Decatur, GA 30030

James W. Voelz
  Concordia Seminary
  801 DeMun Avenue
  St. Louis, MO 63105

Nicole Wilkinson
  Department of Religious Studies
  Vanderbilt University
  Nashville, TN 37235

INTRODUCTION:
EXEGESIS, EISEGESIS, INTERGESIS

George Aichele
Gary A. Phillips

WHAT IS INTERTEXTUALITY?

The aim of this volume of *Semeia* is to explore the issue of intertextuality, which has recently gained wide and varying attention especially within comparative literature and cultural criticism circles (Kristeva, Mai, Plett, Clayton and Rothstein) and among a growing number of biblical scholars of quite different stripes (Boyarin, Brawley, Buchanan, Delorme, Draisma, Fewell, Hartman and Budick, Hays, Sternberg). Set over against a traditional, restrictive notion of "literary influence," intertextuality has emerged as a fertile concept that, for many scholars, has expanded the ways of accounting for the complex relationship of texts to texts, to interpretive traditions, to writers and readers, and to institutional contexts. Intertextuality serves as a critical gateway that opens out onto matters of ideology, subjectivity, the material production of meaning, and accountability.

As a concept intertextuality cuts across different methodological and theoretical borders (including those of formalism, semiotics, discourse analysis, narratology, poststructuralism, deconstruction, and other postmodern approaches), as well as widely varying disciplinary fields (including literature, film, architecture, ethnography). It would be a mistake, however, to limit intertextuality to the domain of literary relationships. For as the following essays illustrate, intertextuality is very much concerned with a range of social practices and cultural expressions, including but not limited to literary texts. In the language of the anthropologist Clifford Geertz, a "thicker" notion of intertextuality circulates in this volume. This is required, we feel, in order to challenge the tendency especially among certain biblical scholars to employ intertextuality (along with other theoretical concepts) as a restrictive tool for nailing down authorial intent and literary influence (for example, see Buchanan, Draisma and Hays). Thinly veiled in such efforts are conservative ideological and theological interests in maintaining the primacy of certain (usually Christian) texts over against secondary (usually Jewish) precursors. The aim of this volume is, in part, to open up the discussion of intertextuality and its importance for reading the Bible in a two-fold way: first, to provide readers with an entrée into the wide-ranging theoretical discussions of intertextuality in literary and cultural critical fields; and, second, to illustrate many of the diverse and fruitful ways intertextuality is *already being employed* as a critical lever in the work of biblical scholars today.

First systematically developed by Julia Kristeva in 1967, the concept of intertextuality has been employed vigorously within poststructuralist circles by Roland Barthes, Jacques Derrida, Umberto Eco, Michel Riffaterre, and Paul de Man, among others. Barthes has given intertextuality special visibility through his now classic metaphor of text as "tissue" or "weaving" as viewed from a semiotic, discourse analysis, and psychoanalytic point of view. As texts are read by individual readers and reading communities who enter into conversation with them, they are rewoven or rewritten out of the threads of innumerable other texts. From this perspective, texts acquire meaning to the extent that they are situated in relation to other texts in a web of mutual interference and illumination. Relationships between reading and writing, text and corpus, authorial intent and textual meaning are to be thought in terms of pressure, interference, and systemic change rather than linear development, authorial design, and textual influence. Intertextuality raises important questions about the dynamic and systemic nature of texts, of writing, of reading, indeed of the material production of meaning within communities of readers. Intertextuality underscores the role of interference in the social setting where texts, subjects, and meaning are constructed.

As is often the case with important theoretical terms, intertextuality has generated a bevy of associated terms: "inter-semioticity," "inter-contextuality," "intratextual rewriting," "Interautorialité," "interdiscursivité," and "autotexte," to name but a few (cf. Mai: 31). Intertextuality enjoys an expansive, even contradictory, range of meanings: at times it is used to designate an allusion or interconnection between texts (Mailloux), at other times the specific quality of relation between literary texts (Tallis); some critics take it broadly as a synonym for deconstruction or poststructuralism (Leitch), while others limit it narrowly to traditional text linguistics (Beaugrande and Dressler). Although critics differ on how direct a bearing the early twentieth century Russian critic Mikhail Bakhtin's concept of "dialogism" had upon Kristeva's notion of intertextuality (contrast Mai: 33 and Pfister: 212), most do agree that in Kristeva's view this concept operates at the intersection of several eclectic discourses—including semiotics, deconstruction, ideological criticism, feminist critique, linguistics, and psychoanalytic critique. For this reason Kristeva insists upon drawing a very sharp distinction between intertextuality defined as a structural-semiotic and psychoanalytic *process* and intertextuality defined pejoratively as little more than "banal" source-hunting and allusion-counting (cf. Barthes, 1977:160–1, with Buchanan: 4-5).

For Kristeva, intertextuality has little to do with matters of influence of one author upon another, or of one literary source upon another literary work. Rather, intertextuality signals foremost systemic relationships and process: "the transposition of one (or more) system(s) of signs into another" (Kristeva, 1984:59–60) and the cultural production of subject positions. As Jonathan Culler puts it, "Intertextuality . . . [is] less a name for a work's relation to prior texts than a designation of its participation in the discursive space of a culture" (103). For Kristeva, intertextuality, therefore, has two dimensions: the inner play, namely "'the web of relations that produce the structure of the text (or the subject),' and the outer play, 'the web of relations linking the text (subject) with other discourses.'"[1] Intertextuality encompasses those forces that give structure and shape not only to texts but to reading and writing subjects as well.

The historical context of Kristeva's work is significant for understanding the importance of the systemic and transformative character of intertextuality. The concept as Kristeva came to employ it emerged in the 1960s in France at a time of profound social upheaval and change similar to the way Bakhtin's notion of dialogism arose in the context of the Soviet cultural revolution of the twenties. It was in the setting of the *Tel Quel* circle, a radical social-literary cell that sought revolutionary change in French political and cultural life, that Kristeva coined this term as a means of revolutionizing notions of art, literature, text, and subjectivity (Pfister: 211). Building upon Bahktin's notion of the literary word, she "textualized" and "socialized" Bahktin's "word": intertextuality is the "*intersection of textual surfaces* rather than a *point* (a fixed meaning)" (Kristeva 1980:65, emphasis hers).

Intertextuality is not some neutral literary mechanism but is rather at root a means of ideological and cultural expression and of social transformation.[2] This makes the narrow, conservative use of the term by cer-

---

[1] Cited in Barzilai: 297. Kristeva's critique of Lacan focuses in one way upon an overdependence upon a Saussurian dyadic model of the sign, in contrast to the triadic model of the sign of C. S. Peirce, which lends itself to thinking about meaning as a signifying *process* rather than as a *system*. Kristeva's *semanalysis* is designed precisely as the means to study signifying processes. See Kristeva, in Moi: 24–33.

[2] The transformative role of intertextuality is most visible in the range of postmodern intertextual writers who foreground intertextuality as both the form and substance of postmodern writing. See Pfister. The term can also be compared in some respect to Derrida's notion of deconstruction as "event," that is, as a process out of the control of an individual author or subject. Deconstruction "takes place" (*à lieu*) by

tain biblical critics all the more ironic and ideologically contradictory. In an effort to critique the prevailing "bourgeois" ideology that expresses itself in the West in the form of a belief in "the autonomy of individual consciousness and the self-contained meaning of texts" (Pfister: 212), Kristeva expanded Bahktin's notion of dialogism beyond the literary text to encompass *all* cultural formations: she "semioticizes" and socializes the concept and along with it the notions of text, subject, and history. On this view subject, history, and society are not to be conceived as objective realities lying somewhere outside of the text but as part of that larger textuality that Derrida refers to as the "general text." "We will call 'intertextuality' this textual interaction which is produced within the text itself. . . . intertextuality is a notion which will be an index for the way a text reads history and inserts itself within it" (Kristeva, 1969b:443). In the dynamic interplay of a textuality that knows no fixed boundaries, responsibility for productivity and creativity shifts from author to literary text to the general text: "The text is therefore a *productivity*, and this means: (1) that its relationship to language in which it is situated is redistributive (destructive-constructive) . . . ; (2) that it is a permutation of texts, an intertextuality: in the space of a text several utterances drawn from *other texts intersect and neutralize one another*" (Kristeva, 1969a:113, translation and emphasis ours).

The element of *neutralization* is pivotal for Kristeva; it underscores intertextuality's ideological and cultural-critical edge. As a productivity each and every text (e.g. literary text, film, social practice, cultural object) must be seen as a conflict of surfaces.[3] This means that the intersection of texts is the battleground not just of conflicting texts and authorial intentions but of competing semiotic systems and ideologies. It is no surprise then that the notion of "intertextuality" has proven to be a contested arena of ideological debate itself. Intertextuality from this view signals the process of structural-semiotic transposition of *textual systems* (understood as systems of signs) by one or more systems. Furthermore, following the lead of the European linguists Benveniste and Jakobson, this transposition denotes a new articulation of enunciative positions within critical discourse. Subject and object positions are ever-shifting and reconstituted or "remade" in the turbulence of structural change. Translation: readers are constantly made and remade in and through the intertextual process;

---

finding a textual place to do its work (Derrida: 6). Just as deconstruction "happens," so too intertextuality "happens."

[3] In this respect Kristeva appears to share a popular semiotic view of culture that sees it "as a minimal condition for social existence, and to regard it as the domain of social conflicts and struggle for collective memory" (Rewar: 375; cited in Mai: 40).

worlds are remade as well. There is little closure and fixing of textual boundaries associated with Kristeva's notion of intertexuality.

For Kristeva, then, intertextuality is concerned foremost with the act of cultural production and reproduction (a "signifying practice" following Barthes, a "writing" following Derrida) in which the text (be it linguistic, somatic, visual, etc.) can be envisioned spatially as a field traversed by lines of force in which various signifying systems undergo transposition of varying sorts and in varying degrees of magnitude.[4] Laura E. Donaldson's response in this volume underscores the cultural character of intertextuality and its inherent link to ideology in a strategic way. Traditional "banal" source critical ("intertextual") explanations of citation, allusion, allegoresis and the like, which claim a concern for history, prove exceedingly thin by comparison because they fail to take into account the historical and cultural nature of textual productivity and the implicature of readers and readings in the production of culture (Kristeva, 1984:60). Critical reading as intertextual production defines "the specificity of different textual arrangements by placing them within the general text (culture) of which they are part and which is in turn part of them" (Kristeva, 1980:36). The intertextual procedure would "by studying the text as intertextuality, conside[r] it within (the text of) society and history" (37), which includes the procedure's own place and the place of the *reader* in history.

By this measure, reading the Bible intertextually ought to be disturbing in so far as it leads to determining "the specificity of textual arrangements" by "studying the text as an intertextuality within society and history," today's and yesterday's. This means nothing less than a deconstructive search for the inherent conflicts, tensions, and aporias in the transposition of systems and subjectivities, in the violent juxtaposing, to borrow the Gospel of Matthew's words, what is new and what is old from the treasure room (13:52). It also means a close scrutiny of the roles readers—especially critical readers—play in perpetuating these systems, as subjective agents engaged in the violent acts of neutralization. To repeat, intertextuality is not a matter of allusion or source tracking; it is a matter of transformation.

BIBLICAL ALLUSIONS AND INTERTEXTUAL ILLUSIONS

When biblical scholars attempt to explain phenomena like allusion, citation, and allegorical interpretation as forms of intertextuality, what they are really concerned with is agency and influence. Typically they

---

[4] See Leon Roudiez's helpful discussion in his introduction to Kristeva's *Desire in Language. A Semiotic Approach to Literature and Art* (1980:15).

have in mind historicist models of agency as a way to account for "influence."[5] For modern biblical scholarship, the concept of "influence" has been historicized as a linear, agentive process. A narrow sense of "influence" can be traced to the mid-eighteenth century concern for authorial originality and genius. This sense of influence was bolstered and extended by the comparativist efforts of nineteenth century historicism to include notions of context and tradition (cf. Clayton and Rothstein: 4–6). Because authorial consciousness and historical context are said to determine meaning, the critical task of explaining the meaning of a text in its modern forms reduces to a charting of what-leads-to-what. Set up then as an epistemological problem, the effort to explain influence translates into an enormous project to develop a stable of critical methods; in fact it is this methodological orientation to texts, history, and meaning that largely defines the success as well as the limits of modern biblical scholarship (The Bible and Culture Collective: 1–2).

Pressure coming from feminist, poststructuralist, and postmodernist quarters has catalyzed change in the dominant critical paradigm, which has succeeded for the most part in excluding ideological and cultural considerations from the critical reading of the Bible (so Alter and Kermode: 4; although for an alternative position see The Bible and Culture Collective: 7–8). While the collapse of the "old historicist paradigm" and the transformation of "literary into cultural studies" that Anthony Easthope argues is overtaking literary studies is hardly imminent in biblical studies, there are clear signs that the modern view that promotes "intertextuality as influence" is superficial and suspect. In eschatological tones that should make traditional biblical scholars flinch, Bloom says that the "wearisome industry of source-hunting, of allusion-counting, an industry that will soon touch apocalypse anyway when it passes from scholars to computers" (31) is about to be booted, or in the terminology of information science, rebooted.

Our contention is that the concept of intertextuality proves pivotal at this time because it provides critical readers of biblical texts an avenue for clarifying not only textual mechanisms and processes but also for transforming destructive disciplinary and cultural practices. For example, in the case of an explicitly anti-Pharisaic text such as Matthew's Gospel, in-

---

[5] The prevailing approach to these intertextual matters is to treat them as discrete and essentially unrelated phenomena, and further to explain them in theological terms. For example, the Pauline appropriation of Hebrew Scriptures in the Letters to the Galatians and Romans is read with a view toward explaining a Christian theological purpose rather than as an instance of Rabbinic-style intertextual practice. In the Gospels, the theological inclination to read the narratives as realistic story obscures the complex intertextual weaving of these texts. Ironically, the impetus to read the biblical texts in non-theological ways has come from outside the field. See Hays; Fewell.

tertextuality has important ramifications for contemporary readers of the Gospel concerned about the ethics of reading a violent biblical text which portrays Jews as "hypocrites," as "killers of children"—especially so in this the fiftieth anniversary of the liberation of the child-death camps in Nazi Germany. Do we accept or reject the narrative roles established for us as readers? What are our responsibilities to the text as critics? And what will be our obligation to those who are portrayed in biblical texts and traditions as repugnant? Engagement with the theoretical question of intertextuality, we argue, has the potential for opening up cultural and ethical issues in a field and in a culture that continues to be marked by virulent, theological anti-Semitism. Except for the effort of a small cohort of biblical critics, there is a conspicuous absence of sustained theoretical reflection upon the phenomenon of intertextuality as a cultural and ethical matter, although the essays in this volume in varying degrees suggest that change is at hand. Theoretical reflection upon intertextuality is demanded to help explain and to engage the complexities and power of biblical texts within culture, both past and present, and to expose the narrative unconscious that shapes a West in which the Bible functions as a primary sub-text that legitimates hatred not only of Jews but of women, gays and lesbians, the poor, and any marginalized other.

One important point of overlap between poststructuralist and postmodern engagement with the Bible and intertextual theory has been the explicit attention given to the ideological forces at work in the production *and* reception of texts. For too long the privileged theological reading of the Bible has masked ideological interests well hidden behind its critical methods of interpretation. Challenging traditional exegesis to a critical accountability that seeks disclosure of its ideological interests (e.g., regarding gender, race, sex, ethnicity, religious privilege, etc.) has provoked outright hostility and a ready condemnation of theory in general as an imposition upon "the text." But as Terry Eagleton points out, "hostility to theory ... [usually] means an opposition to *other* people's theories and an oblivion of one's own" (1983:viii, emphasis ours). Which means we must take Althusser's warning seriously when he says, "As there is no such thing as an innocent reading, we must say what reading we are guilty of" (14). Reflection on the intertextual nature of reading and writing the Bible, a text which is frequently identified as a strategic resource for theological anti-Semitism, can provide a lever for exposing the ideological formation of the text and its critical readers, who in Matthew's case feel perfectly at home assigning the blood of the children (2:16) and Christ to the Jews and their children (27:25).

In this broader ideological and cultural critical setting attention to intertextuality compels a rethinking of the privileged notions of authorial consciousness and intentionality, as well as any theory of meaning which would seek to isolate meaning at a safe distance "inside" the text. Furthermore, intertextuality poses a challenge to a unidirectional and linear understanding of literary history, indeed to a "flat" understanding of history altogether. The prevailing metaphysics, which Derrida and other poststructuralist critics argue underlies the modern understanding of both the sources and the limits of the self-identity of the literary work, may be exposed and interrogated as a result of and by means of intertextual investigation.

In this regard, intertextuality poses a special challenge to a certain view of the relationship between text and "outside-of-the-text" current among traditional biblical critics. In the critical practice that still dominates modernist biblical scholarship, the gap between what is inside and what is outside is wide and deep. The hallmark of modern critical scholarship has been one of preserving the integrity of the inside and the outside by ensuring that the one does not contaminate the other. Hence, the rigid dichotomy between exegesis and eisegesis, between text and reading, between author and text, between text and reader. Yet, the interference between outside and inside is all but impossible to ignore. As that quintessential modern biblical critic, Rudolf Bultmann, points out in his famous "Is Exegesis Without Presuppositions Possible?": "The question whether exegesis without presuppositions is possible must be answered affirmatively if 'without presuppositions' means 'without presupposing the results of the exegesis.' In this sense, exegesis without presuppositions is not only possible but demanded" (1960:289). The process of critical reading remains essentially open. Bultmann's argument undermines the notion that the biblical text contains a truth which the skillful reader discerns and must extract more or less intact, all the while being careful not to impose upon it. In a non-interference view the text is set apart from reality—a material reality that lies outside of the text (the extratextual)—which grounds the proper meaning of the text. At a distance too stands that self-sufficient, technically trained, expert reader who operates on the text. At a further remove yet is the question of responsibility and accountability.

From an intertextual perspective, however, the traditional opposition between exegesis and eisegesis proves unstable; intertextuality displaces the reductive binary opposition of exegesis/eisegesis with "intergesis," the term that Gary Phillips proposes for reading that is the act of rewriting or inserting texts within some more or less established network. Meaning does not lie "inside" texts but rather in the space "between" texts. Meaning is not an unchanging ideal essence but rather variable, fluid, and contextual depending upon the systemic forces at work that bind texts to one another. On this view meaning can no longer be thought of as an objective relation between text and extratextual reality, but instead it arises from the subjective, or ideological, juxtaposing of text with text *on behalf of* specific readers in specific historical/material situations in order to produce new constellations of texts/readers/readings. Intertextual readings in turn cannot finally be justified except in terms of the readers' interests or desires to find or give meaning and the impossibility of doing this in any other way. What this suggests is that every interpretive method, no matter how rational, systematic, and scientific, is in an important way the expression of desire and of broader socio-cultural interests. Making these investments public and holding readers accountable to them then is one of the benefits of intertextual reading.

Contents of This Volume

However, like the closely related "concepts" of narrative, genre, and linguistic structure, the meaning of intertextuality is not univocal; it acquires different nuances and meanings in the hands of different readers of literature and culture. So it is the case in this volume. Our aim here is to situate the range of uses that the concept currently enjoys within literary critical circles especially, to present the efforts of certain biblical critics who draw from these diverse resources, and to explore the extent of their distinctive application in the reading and rewriting of biblical texts.

This volume gathers together essays that focus upon historical, theoretical, and applied issues. Some essays, such as those by Jean Calloud, William Doty, Peter Miscall, and Tina Pippin, have a primarily historical or institutional focus in an effort to situate the history and use of the term "intertextuality" currently within the literary and biblical studies fields, with special attention to the relationship to traditional "influence" views of textuality and textual relationship. Other essays, such as those by James Voelz, George Aichele, and Gary Phillips, focus on explicitly theoretical concerns in that they describe the intertextual phenomenon through the prism of different methodological approaches. A third group of essays, including those of Tod Linafelt and Timothy Beal, Roland Boer, Robert Brawley, Nicole Wilkinson, and Susan Graham, stress exegesis (or intergesis) and focus upon the reading of specific biblical and non-biblical "texts" (including film and television). Yet this tripartite division admittedly does not do full justice to intertextual readings; classically clear borderlines between theory and application, historical development and present statement blur and dissolve in the general field of the intertextual.

Our intent is not to be exhaustive but illustrative; i.e., to display the diversity of understandings, approaches, readers, and texts addressing this issue as a reflection of the diverse state of affairs within biblical studies itself. The volume offers an array of theoretical perspectives (semiotic, deconstructive, ideological, feminist, narratological, poststructuralist) and a range of biblical texts (Hebrew narrative, Gospel narrative, Pauline letters) as well as a wide variety of contemporary literary, cinematic, video, and other texts. Each essay attempts to be self-reflexive about its own intertextual and theoretical "location," and also to address the question of implications of the concept of intertextuality for biblical studies. The articles and the responses by Laura Donaldson and Daniel Boyerin reflect in turn a different range of style, content, and foci regarding the variety of contexts and ways intertextuality is currently being deployed. Importantly, these responses challenge the authors to further engagement, transformation, and accountability.

Finally, the essays by Aichele, Phillips, Pippin, Boer, Graham, Linafelt and Beal, and Voelz were originally presented as papers at the 1992 SBL meeting in San Francisco. All have been rewritten for this volume. Calloud's essay was translated by Gary A. Phillips with the assistance of Nicole Wilkinson.

WORKS CITED

Alter, Robert and Frank Kermode, eds.
    1987   *The Literary Guide to the Bible*. Cambridge: Harvard University Press.

Althusser, Louis and Etienne Balibar
    1970   *Reading Capital*. Trans. Ben Brewster. London: Verso.

Barthes, Roland
    1977   *Image Music Text*. Trans. Stephen Heath. New York: Hill and Wang.

Barzilai, Shuli
    1991   "Borders of Language: Kristeva's Critique of Lacan." *PMLA* 106:294–305.

Beaugrande, Robert and Wolfgang Dressler
    1981   *Introduction to Text Linguistics*. London: Longman.

The Bible and Culture Collective
    1995   *The Postmodern Bible*. New Haven: Yale University Press.

Bloom, Harold
    1975   *The Anxiety of Influence: A Theory of Poetry*. New York: Oxford University Press.

Buchanan, George Wesley
    1994   *Introduction to Intertextuality*. Lewiston, NY: Edwin Mellen Press.

Bultmann, Rudolf
    1960   "Is Exegesis Without Presuppositions Possible?" Pp. 289-96 in *Existence and Faith: Shorter writings fo Rudolph Bultmann*. Cleveland: World.

Clayton, Jay and Eric Rothstein
    1992   "Figures in the Corpus: Theories of Influence and Intertextuality." Pp. 3–36 in *Influence and Intertextuality in Literary History*. Ed. Jay Clayton and Eric Rothstein. Madison: University of Wisconsin.

Culler, Jonathan
    1981   *The Pursuit of Signs: Semiotics, Literature, Deconstruction*. Ithaca: Cornell University Press.

Derrida, Jacques
    1982   *Margins of Philosophy*. Trans. Alan Bass. Chicago: University of Chicago Press.

Draisma, Sipke, ed.
    1989   *Intertextuality in Biblical Writings. Essays in Honour of Bas van Iersel*. Kampen: J. H. Kok.

Eagleton, Terry
    1976   *Criticism and Ideology*. London: New Left Books.
    1983   *Literary Theory: An Introduction*. Minneapolis: University of Minnesota Press.

Easthope, Anthony
    1991   *Literary Into Cultural Studies*. London: Routledge.

Fewell, Danna Nolan, ed.
    1992   *Reading between Texts. Intertextuality and the Hebrew Bible*. LCBI. Louisville: Westminster/John Knox.

Hays, Richard
    1989   *Echoes of Scripture in the Letters of Paul*. New Haven: Yale University Press.

Kristeva, Julia
    1969a   *Semeiotiké. Recherches pour une sémanalyse*. Collections Tel Quel. Paris: Le Seuil.
    1969b   "Narration et transformation." *Semiotica* 1:422–48.
    1980   *Desire in Language. A Semiotic Approach to Literature and Art*. Trans. Thomas Gora, Alice Jardine and Leon S. Roudiez. Ed. Leon S. Roudiez. New York: Columbia University Press.
    1984   *Revolution in Poetic Language*. Trans. Margaret Waller. New York: Columbia University Press.
    1986a   "Semiotics: A Critical Science and/or a Critique of Science." Pp. 75–88 in *The Kristeva Reader*. Ed. Toril Moi. New York: Columbia University Press.
    1986b   "The System and the Speaking Subject." Pp. 24–33 in *The Kristeva Reader*. Ed. Toril Moi. New York: Columbia University Press.

Leitch, Vincent
    1983   *Deconstructive Criticism: An Advanced Introduction*. New York: Columbia University Press.

Mai, Hans-Peter
    1992   "Bypassing Intertextuality: Hermeneutics, Textual Practice, Hypertext." Pp. 30–59 in *Intertextuality*. Ed. Heinrich Plett. Untersuchungen zur Texttheorie 15. New York: de Gruyter.

Mailloux, Steven
    1982   *Interpretive Conventions: The Reader in the Study of American Fiction*. Ithaca: Cornell University Press.

Pfister, Manfred
    1991   "How Postmodern is Intertextuality?" Pp. 207–24 in *Intertextuality*. Ed. Heinrich Plett. Untersuchungen zur Texttheorie 15. New York: de Gruyter.

Phillips, Gary A.
    1985   "History and Text: The Reader in Context in Matthew's Parables Discourse." *Semeia* 31:112–138.
    1991   "Sign/Text/Différance. The Contribution of Intertextual Theory to Biblical Criticism." Pp. 78–100 in *Intertextuality*. Ed. Heinrich Plett. Untersuchungen zur Texttheorie 15. New York: de Gruyter.

Rajan, Tilottama
    1991   "Intertextuality and the Subject of Reading/Writing." Pp. 61–74 in *Influence and Intertextuality in Literary History*. Ed. Jay Clayton and Eric Rothstein. Madison: University of Wisconsin.

Rewar, Walter
    1976   "Notes for a Typology of Culture." *Semiotica* 18:361–77.

Tallis, Raymond
    1988   *Not Saussure: A Critique of Post-Saussurean Literary Theory*. London: Macmillan.

West, Gerald
    1993   *Contextual Biblical Studies*. St. Petermaritzburg: Cluster Publications.

White, Stephen
    1991   *Political Theory and Postmodernism*. Modern European Philosophy. Cambridge: Cambridge University Press.

SIFTING FOR CINDERS:
STRANGE FIRES IN LEVITICUS 10:1–5

*Timothy K. Beal, Eckerd College,
and Tod Linafelt, Emory University*

ABSTRACT

Western literary history is a history of fire and ash. The white and black fire of the Torah and the fire of Auschwitz both command us to write against death. Here the threat of erasure becomes the threat of all-burning. But never without remainder, never without a trace. Cinders remain, resisting oblivion, leading one to ask what was there, rekindling—perhaps—a memory. At an impure meeting-place between the story of Nadab and Abihu's "strange fire" and their incineration by fire from YHWH (Lev 10:1–5) on the one hand, and Derrida's most recent interrogation of the cinder (1991) on the other hand, we are compelled to fan the embers into flames once again. Among the ashes of this strange fire, we find traces that lead us into the realm of child sacrifice. In the process, our reading and writing must inevitably transgress the borders of this text—and perhaps the borders of Derridean orthodoxy as well—confirming Kristeva's assertion that all writing is intertextual and therefore transgressive.

> When ashes turn into a posthumous book, the words are
> reborn from their first sound.
> Audible post-mortem. Have we made it legible?
>
> —Edmond Jabès, *The Book of Shares*

> Off he gone then singing:
>   Seed of the littl
>   Seed of the wyld
>   Seed of the berning is
>   Hart of the chyld
>
> —Russell Hoban, *Riddley Walker*

The force of intertextuality is to problematize, even spoil, textual and interpretive boundaries—those lines of demarcation that allow a reader to talk about *the* meaning, subject, or origin of a text.[1] If every text is, as

---

[1] For a more extensive discussion of poststructuralist theories of intertextuality as they relate to biblical studies, see the collection edited by Danna Nolan Fewell (1992), to which we have both contributed essays. For a treatment of the theoretical issues, especially as they relate to ideological criticism, see Beal (27–39). For an intertextual

Kristeva puts it (1980:65), an "intersection of textual surfaces," then there can be no such thing as *"the* point" of a text; and since there is no single point, there can be no clear lines of influence or origin drawn from one text to another (for a line needs two points). Thus the "dialogical space of texts" (Kristeva, 1980:66) explodes the autonomy and univocality of any particular text, making its subject profoundly ambivalent and its meaning fundamentally undecidable.

In reflecting on a "semiotic approach to intertextuality,"[2] the word that has planted itself in our minds is *dissemination.* As Derrida writes,

> one of the theses ... inscribed within dissemination is precisely the impossibility of reducing a text as such to its effects of meaning, content, thesis, or theme. Not the impossibility, since it is commonly done, but the resistance—we shall call it *restance* [remainder]. . . . (1981:7–8)

Dissemination suggests the inherent intertextuality of all writing. No reader can ever successfully comprehend every element of a text, without remainder, without the trace of a remainder. No text can be hermetically sealed off from other texts. Seeds of signification (*semeia*) are always spilling over—disseminating—into the margins and off the page and out of the book, engendering meaningful relationships in other (con)texts.

> To try to resist the removal of a textual member from its context is to want to remain protected against the writing poison. It is to want at all costs to maintain the boundary line between the inside and the outside of a context. (Derrida, 1981:316)

A semiotic approach to intertextuality begins by presuming the inherent intertextuality of every text.[3] Every text is a "field of transpositions" (Kristeva, 1984:60); and the rickety old fences that separate one field from

---

reading which is particularly concerned with the character of God, see Linafelt (99–113).

[2] This is the phrase that was used in the call for papers for the Semiotics and Exegesis Section at the 1992 annual meeting of the Society of Biblical Literature, where an earlier version of this paper was presented. We are thankful to Gary A. Phillips, David Penchansky, and the other participants in that section for invaluable comments and suggestions. We also thank S. Brent Plate, Brian McCormick, and Clay Beal for dendrological comments pertaining to the last section.

[3] While we are aware that there is always overlap, we wish to make a rough distinction between theory and methodology (see Beal: 27–39). The theory of intertextuality sketched in these first few pages is intended to frame and expose the limits of our reading of Lev 10:1–5. In this sense, our understanding of theory falls in with the tradition of negative dialectics, best championed by Theodor W. Adorno and Max Horkheimer, who make strong distinctions between technology/technique and theory/negativity. As they write: "But true revolutionary practice depends on the intransigence of theory in the face of the insensibility with which society allows thought to ossify. . . . The spirit of this kind of unrelenting theory would turn even the mind of relentless progress to its end" (41, 42).

another do not prevent seeds from blowing over and being planted—accidentally or intentionally—elsewhere.

The reader of dissemination, then, will attend to (and tend) traces—traces of the other who has been erased from the text, but who leaves, if nothing more, erasure marks; traces of the other who has been incinerated, but whose cinders, or perhaps only scattered ashes, remain there. For traces there are, leading readers to jump fences, and to venture outside the camp, following the priests at a distance, in order to sift through the scattered ashes in search of a still-glowing ember.

I. Reading Derrida Reading Derrida

This is the exegesis of the cinder. And this is the sort of work we wish to do in Leviticus 10:1–5, the story of Nadab and Abihu's "strange fire" (or, as we shall propose later, "seed fire"), and their subsequent incineration by YHWH.

In a recent translation (*Cinders*, 1991) of a fairly recent article (*Feu la Cendre*, 1987), Derrida has reflected on the trace in terms of *cinder* and *ash*—words that he finds recurring throughout his own writing (almost in spite of himself) since he first wrote them on the last page of *Dissemination* (1981 [1972]:366).

> Moving off of itself, forming itself wholly therein, almost without remainder, writing denies and recognizes its debt in a single dash. The utmost disintegration of the signature, far from the center, indeed from the secrets that are shared there, divided up so as to scatter even their ashes.

> Though the letter gains strength solely from this indirection, and granted that it can always not arrive at the other side, I will not use this as a pretext to absent myself from the punctuality of a dedication: R. Gasché, J. J. Goux, J. C. Lebensztejn, J. H. Miller, others, *il y a là cendre*, will recognize, perhaps, what their reading has contributed.

> And near the end, at the bottom of the last page, it was as though you had signed with these words: "Cinders there are." I read, reread them; it was so simple, and yet I knew that I was not there; without waiting for me the phrase withdrew into its secret. (Derrida, 1991:31)

> ...the sentence in question imposed itself upon me with the authority, so discreet and simple it was, of a judgment: "cinders there are." (Derrida, 1991:21)

Here, as elsewhere, we lean over the page to find Derrida reading Derrida, sifting through the cinders of his own writings, which are no longer totally within his grasp.

> I would prefer *ashes* as the better paradigm for what I call the trace—something that erases itself totally, radically, while presenting itself. (1987b:177)

> For nearly ten years, this specter's comings and goings, unforeseen visits of the ghost. The thing spoke all on its own. I had to explain myself to it, respond to it—or for it. (1991:22)

We find in Derrida's reflections on cinder and ash an eerily suggestive antiphonal for our reading of Lev 10:1–5. Or vice-versa. The outcome will no doubt be impure—a dissemination that can be neither purely Derridean (a loaded phrase, to say the least), nor purely exegetical in any common or orthodox sense.

II. "The Cinder in a Sentence Here No Longer Is…"

In his *Speculations* (1924), T. E. Hulme wrote that "the world is finite … and that it is yet an infinitude of cinders" (in Derrida, 1991:n.59). In *Cinders*, Derrida erases the L in *world* in order to reflect on the undecidability and indeterminacy of meaning in the written *word*. He constantly reminds himself that the written word is finite:

> "You well know how solid a sentence is" (1991:55).

Yet he persists in tracing what hides between the lines. To transpose Hulme: The word is finite, and it is yet an infinitude of cinders.

> … the innumerable lurks beneath the cinder. Incubation of the fire lurking beneath the dust. (1991:59)

> The sentence is adorned with all of its dead. (1991:55)

As is often noted, meaning for Derrida is endlessly deferred along the chain of signification. There are but traces (or cinders) left from the presence of a meaning that has always already absented itself. So it is not surprising when Derrida (rather wistfully) seems to subvert his own project of reflecting on the recurrent cinder in his own work.

> Who would still run the risk of a poem of the cinder? One might dream that the word "cinder" was itself a cinder in that sense, "there," "over there," in the distant past, a lost memory of what is no longer here. And thereby its phrase would have meant, without holding anything back: the cinder is no longer here. Was it ever? (1991:31)

The cinder no longer is. It has been incinerated, crushed into ashes perhaps, and taken with the breeze. How indeed can one still run the risk of a poem of the cinder? How indeed can one hope to fan the ashes once more into flames? (Were there ever flames?)

> It remains from what is not, in order to recall at the delicate, charred bottom of itself only non-being or non-presence. (Derrida, 1991:39)

These words—ashes, flames, cinders, presence—all intersect in our reading of Leviticus 10. Here we find the story of the incineration of Nadab and Abihu (the sons of Aaron). Following the inaugural sacrifice of Lev 9:22–4, in which the presence of YHWH is manifested in a great consuming fire, this story intrudes without warning, disrupting the entire cultic order. Thus it presents what Edward L. Greenstein has called "a model of undecidability" (56). We have in Leviticus 10 "the story of what looks to most readers like a punishment in search of a crime" (Greenstein: 56).

> Why cinders "there"? The place of burning, but of what, of whom? (Derrida, 1991:37)

This is the question put to our text again and again, beginning with Moses' own cryptic theodicy in verse 3: "This is what YHWH meant when he said, 'Through those near to me I make myself holy, and gain glory before all the people.'" Who or what was burned at this place, in this strange fire? Derrida's inquiry into the no-longer-available-(was it ever?)-presence-of-meaning in language becomes an inquiry into the similarly no longer available-(were they ever?)-incinerations. For there were two burnings, one tindered by mortals and one by God. We know the second one was savage. What about the first?

> . . . a remnant that must no longer remain, this place of nothing that may be, a pure place was marked out. (Derrida, 1991:37)

A pure place was marked out, a place from which the ashes of the burning were to be removed. "And Moses called Mishael and Elzaphan, sons of Uzziel the uncle of Aaron, and said to them, 'Come forward and carry your kin away from the front of the sanctuary to a place outside the camp'" (Lev 10:4). The ashes have become a remnant that must no longer remain. The presence of what has remained from the incineration is under erasure. The cinders of the burning have been scattered outside the borders of the camp, even as the cinders of significance have been scattered outside the borders of the text. Are we to believe that this is the end of them?

> But the urn of language is so fragile. It crumbles and immediately you blow into the dust of words which are the cinder itself. . . . In this sentence I see the

> tomb of a tomb, the monument of an impossible tomb—forbidden, like the memory of a cenotaph, deprived of the patience of mourning. (Derrida, 1991:53)

In this story we see the tomb of a tomb, twice-removed ashes of cremated bodies with no urn to hold them other than the fragile urn of language. Deprived even of a cenotaph, having been displaced beyond the borders of the camp, the only grave marker for those cremated at this place is the story itself. And we have seen that in the story meaning is likewise banished outside the borders. Who indeed would risk writing yet another poem of the cinder?

> ... writing in the passion of non-knowledge rather than of the secret. (Derrida, 1991:75)

> The sentence avows only the ongoing incineration, of which it remains the almost silent monument: this can be "there," *là*—. (Derrida, 1991:37)

Doomed as ever to failure, we must nonetheless try again. For cenotaph there is, and cinders there are—even though "there" is wholly elsewhere. Can the one lead (or defer) us to the other? Sifting through the cinders of this strange fire, we find traces that compel us to risk a reading.

III. "... But Cinder There Is"

> It is the threat of an absolute crypt: the non-return, the unreadability, the amnesia without remainder, but the non-return *as* return, *in* the return itself. (Derrida, 1986:83; in Lukacher: 14)

It is the threat of an absolute crypt against which we read. And we know that the threat of non-return is ever-present. But a trace, or the trace of a trace, remains there. Scarcely visible, altogether unreadable, this is what makes reading a necessary impossibility.

> Trace destined, like everything, to disappear from itself, as much in order to lose the way as to rekindle a memory. (Derrida, 1991:57)

> No doubt the fire has withdrawn, the conflagration has been subdued, but if cinder there is, it is because the fire remains in retreat. (Derrida, 1991:61)

It is the very trace, always already under erasure, that sparks a distant memory of loss (or maybe lack) in language. It is the very absence of the fire that allows the cinder to exist. Only with the flames absent may we sift for cinders, and perhaps kindle another fire (a *third* burning).

No cinder without fire.... That is what is owed to the fire, and yet, if possible, without the shadow of a sacrifice, at noon, without debt, without the Phoenix. (Derrida, 1991:37)[4]

Sifting through the cinders of Lev 10:1–5, we find traces that suggest to us the possibility of child sacrifice, an "almost silent monument" (Derrida, 1991:37) to the children of another Holocaust, buried within the ashes of this text; a sacrificial incineration of Nadab and Abihu's *seed*.

> ... someone vanished but something preserved her trace and at the same time lost it, the cinder. (Derrida, 1991:34–35)

Virtually all interpreters break up the phrase in Lev 10:1 אש זרה אשר לא צוה ("strange fire which he had not commanded"), focusing more narrowly on the meaning of אש זרה, and issues of cultic malpractice.[5] But what if we shift our attention to the commonly ignored relative clause אשר לא צוה ("which he did not command")? Some investigation reveals that it is not a common phrase in the Hebrew Bible. Outside Leviticus 10, it occurs with YHWH as the subject of the verb only in the books of Deuteronomy (once) and Jeremiah (four times).[6] Strikingly, three of the four occurrences in Jeremiah deal explicitly with child sacrifice: "... to burn their sons and their daughters in the fire which I did not command, nor did it come into my mind [Jer 7:31] ... to burn their sons in the fire as burnt offerings to Baal which I did not command or decree, nor did it come into my mind [Jer 19:5] ... to offer up their sons and daughters to Molech, which I did not command them, nor did it enter my mind [Jer 32:35]."[7]

---

[4] "Ah no, above all not Phoenix (which for me, moreover, is first of all, in my fundamental language, the mark..." (Derrida, 1987:254).

[5] Kirschner (382) identifies the following ten justifications in rabbinic literature: (1) Nadab and Abihu presume to decide the Law in the presence of Moses; (2) they approach too close to the divine presence; (3) they bring an improper offering; (4) they bring fire from an oven rather than from an outer altar; (5) they neglect to consult first with one another (or with Moses); (6) they drink wine before approaching the altar; (7) they approach with unwashed hands and feet; (8) they lack the prescribed number of garments; (9) they have fathered no children; (10) they are arrogant.

Among modern interpreters, Morgenstern (6) holds that the two priests offered "fire kindled by ordinary means," rather than fire taken from the altar. Clements (29–30) suggests that Nadab and Abihu offered a "pagan incense," such as that prohibited in Exodus 39. Laughlin (563–65) identifies their offering more specifically with Zoroastrian practices. In his recent and very impressive commentary on chapters 1–16, Jacob Milgrom (595–635) argues that they offered "unauthorized coals" which were not taken from the altar in the sanctuary (like Morgenstern), and that the text reflects a polemic against burning incense at private altars.

[6] The verbal phrase occurs with Moses as the subject in Deut 17:3.

[7] The fourth use of the phrase is found in Jer 29:23: "They have spoken lying words in my name, which I did not command them." While not dealing directly with

Unlike the cryptic reference in Leviticus 10, the transposition of the phrase in Jeremiah makes clear that what YHWH did not command was child sacrifice.[8]

> Holocaust of the children ... God himself had only the choice between two crematory ovens.... (Derrida, 1987a:143)

Is there a filial relation to be drawn between the strange story in Leviticus 10 and the practice of child sacrifice?[9] Are they the ashes of children that we find in this fragile urn of language?

> [The cinder] ... is what remains without remaining from the holocaust, from the all-burning, from the incineration the incense. (Derrida, 1991:43)

The sacrifice performed at this place has remained without remaining. Cinders there are, but they are so fragile, and call for "yet another voice" (Derrida, in Lukacher:14) to make their story readable, their cries audible. We have, in heeding the cenotaph, already transgressed the borders of this text, and of the history of its interpretation.[10] In light of our reflections so far, we offer a less innocent evaluation of the relationship between Leviticus 10 and Numbers 3 as well. Num 3:4 contains one of the few explicit references in the Hebrew Bible to the burning of Nadab and Abihu: "And Nadab and Abihu died before YHWH when they offered strange fire אֵשׁ זָרָה before YHWH in the wilderness of Sinai; and they had no children."

---

child sacrifice, even in this reference we find a strong connection with the other passages above. Here the phrase refers to the false prophets Zedekiah and Ahab, who, we learned in 29:22, were "roasted in the fire."

[8] The one Deuteronomic occurrence is found in 18:20, and concerns prophets whom YHWH "did not command to speak, and who speak in the name of other gods." Interestingly, this phrase is very near yet another rare reference to child sacrifice (18:10, "the passing over of his son or daughter in fire").

[9] By filial, we do not mean to suggest genealogical. We do not wish to speculate on familial *origins*. See our introductory discussion above.

[10] The only precedent we have found for our reading here is offered in a medieval Hebrew poem by Isaac bar Shalom, published in Jakob J. Petuchowski's study of the *Piyyut* (78). The poet compares the people to priests, burning their children so that they would not be subjected to an imminent pogrom. These lines include a direct quotation from Lev 10:6:

> They made ready to slay the children, ...
> As priests for the slaughter of their holocaust,
> They bound the children and their mothers;
> And, in the fire, they burned their skins, ...
> *All Israel weeps for the burning....*
> Do not keep silence!

In the context of this passage, the mention of childlessness apparently serves to show why the line of Nadab and Abihu died out.¹¹ But "no text is an island" (Miscall: 45), and with the intersection of the phrase אשר לא צוה in Leviticus 10, this statement of childlessness takes on more ominous tones. Could it be that the crime of Nadab and Abihu in Leviticus 10 is the sacrifice of their own children to YHWH, and that this is why Num 3:4 remembers them as childless?

> At present, here and now, there is something material—visible but scarcely readable—that, referring only to itself, no longer makes a trace, unless it traces only by losing the trace it scarcely leaves. (Derrida, 1991:43)

This discussion may also lead us to reevaluate the phrase אש זרה. זרה in Lev 10:1 is invariably read as a feminine participle from the root זור (thus "foreign" or "strange"). זרה as a verb, however, is synonymous with זרא, and is typically rendered as "to sow" or "scatter seed." The noun form of זרא, in turn, means "seed" or "offspring" (also "semen"). Here again, in the strangeness of Nadab and Abihu's fire, there are traces of their burning seed—a dis-semination of another kind.

Finding ourselves in the realm of child sacrifice by way of the phrase אשר לא צוה we cannot help but expand the semantic field of אש זרה to include traces of "seed fire," understood as the sacrifice of offspring. The play of meaning between "seed" and "strange" need not finally be settled.¹² The "seed fire" of Nadab and Abihu is certainly a "strange fire."

> ... can you not feel the step into the burning sand? In the place of others, plural already, of their names and not of themselves, cinder there is, "of others, cinder there is." ... *like burning semen* .... (Derrida, 1991:73–74)

There is yet another way of reading the ashes in Leviticus 10. Interpreters have often noted similarities between this text and 1 Kings 14–15, where Jeroboam's sons, Nadab and Abiyah, are presented as dying for the improper action of their father, who erected a golden calf. Both Gradwohl (294–95) and Damrosch (71) exploit this connection to great effect, bringing out the reference to Aaron's golden calf at Sinai and the negative response of the tradition. While the Sinai incident is not explicitly mentioned in our text, the connection with Jeroboam raises the possibility that

---

¹¹ This verse is also the basis for rabbinic speculation that Nadab and Abihu died because they had no children. See *Pesiq. Rab Kah.* 26:9–10.

¹² The sense of "foreign" or "strange" for זרה may not be unrelated to the sense of "winnowing" or "scattering" seed, since foreigners are often scattered members of another nation (e.g. "diaspora Judaism").

Nadab and Abihu in Leviticus 10 are also presented as dying for the sins of their father Aaron.

> No, the phrase does not say what it is, but what it was [*fut*], and ... do not forget that it remains in memory of the departed..., "the late so and so," the bereaved. (Derrida, 1991:35)

With this possibility before us, the trace we read as child sacrifice takes a new course. Here, it is not the offspring of Nadab and Abihu that are understood to be sacrificed, but the sons of Aaron, that is, Nadab and Abihu themselves. In this reading, the play between זרא and זרא evokes the punishment for Aaron's sin (like Jeroboam's) by the burning of his offspring.

> Holocaust of the children ... God himself had only the choice between two crematory ovens.... (Derrida, 1987a:143; 1991:62)

This reading resounds with Moses' statement to the Levites in Exodus 32 as well: "Today you have ordained yourselves for the service of YHWH, each one at the cost of his son." The ordination here of the Levites conflates with the ordination of Aaron in Leviticus 8 and 9, emphasizing the cost of his sons involved in this whole ordination process. In this regard, YHWH's response in Exod 33:34 is also suggestive: "In the day when I visit them, I will visit their sin upon them." This may suggest a belated punishment of Aaron in Leviticus 10, a punishment for which Gradwohl and Damrosch have found evidence elsewhere. The reference to the "day I will visit them" thus evokes the setting of our story, which, as we may recall, falls immediately after the inauguration of the cult in 9:24. Here, then, we may arrive on the day when YHWH visits the people, the day on which Aaron's sins are visited upon him at the cost of his sons.[13]

---

[13] We are concerned that either of our readings might be construed as an apology for YHWH's burning of Nadab and Abihu, and thus might serve to "blame the victim." This would be inexcusable, especially after the Holocaust. Like the "fire of God" in Job 1:16 (following the sinister wager), YHWH's incineration in this text is savage, no matter how the first strange fire may be read. Indeed, there is no hint of retribution or just cause in the theodicy of verse 3. On the contrary, YHWH's words ("through those near to me I make myself holy, and gain glory before all the people") do not even acknowledge Nadab and Abihu's strange fire. The second half of that utterance, moreover, with its use of על־פני (lit., "upon the faces of") and אכבד (from כבד, lit., "I will make myself heavy") can easily carry an oppressive connotation. Note, e.g., the Hiphil use of הכביד in 1 Kgs 12:10-14; 2 Chr 10:10-14; Isa 9:1; Lam3:7. Cf. also Exod 14:4, 17, and 18, where a similar pronouncement is made by YHWH over Pharaoh and his army.

IV. INCONCLUSION

We have traced out this cryptic tale in two different, mutually incompatible, directions, in a sense, writing with an erasure. Of course, the dissemination does not stop here, for the cinder is always the trace of a trace. The process of deferral is endless, and one can never finally arrive at self-evident, self-present meaning.

> ... the innumerable lurks beneath the cinder. Incubation of the fire lurking beneath the dust. (Derrida, 1991:59)

No, the dissemination does not stop here. Rather, one might say that our readings have petered out. Is this not the way of all readings?

> I hear well, I hear it, for I still have an ear for the flame even if a cinder is silent, ... seeing in order not to see, writing in the passion of non-knowledge rather than of the secret. (Derrida, 1991:75)

Sifting through the cinders of this story, we alighted on traces suggesting the sacrificial burning of children. Are the children of Nadab and Abihu burned? Or are Nadab and Abihu the children sacrificed for Aaron's sin? Or is it finally our own childlike yearning for the absolute Presence of the Father that is sacrificed?[14] We find ourselves unable to write the ending, for "the sentence is adorned with *all* of its dead" (Derrida, 1991:55; our emphasis).

There is a tree, known mainly in the Pacific Northwest, called the lodgepole pine (*pinus contorta*), which disseminates by fire. While some of its cones release their seeds during the first two or three years, many remain closed and attached to the tree for over 15 years, during which time they amass more and more seeds. These cones open and disseminate by the heat of a fire. This *pyrogenesis* is dramatically illustrated by the following account from the *Textbook of Dendrology*.

> A camping party in the Rocky Mountains once built a fire against a solitary lodgepole pine. The tree was killed, as shown by the subsequent loss of its needles. Four years later, a long, tattered green pennant, formed by thousands of lodgepole pine seedlings, showed on the mountainside. This pennant, varying in width from 10 to 50 ft, began at the tree and streamed out for more than 700 ft from its base. (Harlow, Harrar, and White: 112)

Three burnings have swept across these pages: the strange fire of Nadab and Abihu, the fire from YHWH, and our reading ("make allowance for fire where writing spreads" [Jabès: 99])—a third burning, a fanning of cinders, a rekindling from ashes, a tindering of the trace, *pyrogenesis*. There is a

---

[14] On the other hand, perhaps the cinder is what Levinas has called "protection against the madness of direct contact" with absolute presence (219).

certain risk in this, both for thin-barked lodgepole pines and for fragile urns of language like Lev 10:1–5. Perhaps the dendrologists put it best: "fire is always a serious menace even though heavy new stands result through this agency" (Harlow, Harrar, and White: 112).

> ... light counter-fires to stop the progression of a blaze, avoid a holocaust. (Derrida, 1987a:222)

We have lit our counter-fires. It is too late to avoid a Holocaust. But perhaps we can still "take sides with the mothers of the children" (Fackenheim: 32), and prevent yet another all-burning, lest the memory of the children preserved in this fragile urn of language is forever consumed.

> And do not lie, you well know how solid a sentence is. By its very disappearance it resists so very many eclipses, it always has a chance of returning, it incenses itself to infinity. (Derrida, 1991:55)

WORKS CONSULTED

Adorno, Theodor W.
    1973   *Negative Dialectics*. Trans. E. B. Ashton. New York: Continuum (1966).

Beal, Timothy K.
    1992   "Intertextuality and Ideology: Surplus of Meaning and Controlling the Means of Production." Pp. 27–39 in *Reading Between Texts: Intertexuality and the Hebrew Bible*. Ed. Danna Nolan Fewell. LCBI. Louisville: Westminster/John Knox.

Clements, R.
    1970   "Leviticus." *The Broadman Bible Commentary*. Nashville: Broadman.

Damrosch, David
    1987   "Leviticus." In *The Literary Guide to the Bible*. Ed. Robert Alter and Frank Kermode. Cambridge: Harvard University Press.

Derrida, Jacques
    1981   *Dissemination*. Trans. Barbara Johnson. Chicago: University of Chicago Press (1972).
    1986   *Schibboleth: Pour Paul Celan*. Paris: Galilee.
    1987a   *The Postcard*. Trans. A. Bass. Chicago: University of Chicago Press.
    1987b   "On Reading Heidegger: An Outline of Remarks to the Essex Colloquium." *Research in Phenomenology* 17.
    1991   *Cinders*. Trans. and Ed. Ned Lukacher. Lincoln: University of Nebraska Press.

Fackenheim, Emil L.
   1990   *The Jewish Bible after the Holocaust: A Re-reading.* Bloomington: Indiana University Press.

Fewell, Danna Nolan, ed.
   1992   *Reading Between Texts: Intertextuality and the Hebrew Bible.* LCBI. Louisville: Westminster/John Knox.

Gradwohl, R.
   1963–4   "Das Fremde Feuer von Nadab und Abihu." *ZAW* 75–76.

Greenstein, Edward L.
   1989   "Deconstruction and Biblical Narrative." *Prooftexts* 9.

Harlow, William M., Ellwood S. Harrar, and Fred M. White
   1979   *Textbook of Dendrology.* New York: McGraw-Hill.

Hoban, Russell
   1980   *Riddley Walker.* New York: Washington Square Press.

Horkheimer, Max and Theodor W. Adorno
   1972   *Dialectic of Enlightenment.* Rev. ed. Trans. John Cumming. New York: Continuum (1969).

Jabès, Edmond
   1989   *The Book of Shares.* Trans. Rosemarie Waldrop. Chicago: University of Chicago Press (1987).

Kirschner, Robert
   1983   "The Rabbinic and Philonic Exegesis of the Nadab and Abihu Incident." *JQR* April.

Kristeva, Julia
   1980   *Desire in Language: A Semiotic Approach to Literature and Art.* Trans. Leon S. Roudiez. Chicago: University of Chicago Press (1969).
   1984   *Revolution in Poetic Language.* Trans. M. Waller. New York: Columbia University Press (1974).

Laughlin, J.
   1976   "The Strange Fire of Nadab and Abihu." *JBL* 96.

Levinas, Emmanuel
   1979   "To Love the Torah More Than God." Trans. H.A. Stephenson and R. I. Sugarman. *Judaism* 28.

Linafelt, Tod
   1992   "Taking Women in Samuel: Readers/Responses/Responsibility." Pp. 99–113 in *Reading Between Texts: Intertexuality and the Hebrew Bible.* Ed. Danna Nolan Fewell. LCBI. Louisville: Westminster/John Knox Press.

Lukacher, Ned
   1991   "Introduction: Mourning Becomes Telepathy." Pp. 1–18 in *Cinders* by Jacques Derrida. Lincoln: University of Nebraska Press.

Milgrom, Jacob
    1991   *Leviticus 1–16*. AB. New York: Doubleday.

Miscall, Peter D.
    1992   "Isaiah: New Heavens, New Earth, New Book." Pp. 41–56 in *Reading Between Texts: Intertexuality and the Hebrew Bible*. Ed. Danna Nolan Fewell. LCBI. Louisville: Westminster/John Knox Press.

Morgenstern, J.
    1963   *The Fire Upon the Altar*. Chicago: Quadrangle Books.

Petuchowski, Jakob J.
    1978   *Theology and Poetry: Studies in the Medieval Piyyut*. London: Routledge & Kegan Paul.

RESISTANCE TO THE CARNIVALIZATION OF JESUS: SCRIPTURE IN THE LUCAN PASSION NARRATIVE[1]

Robert L. Brawley
McCormick Theological Seminary

EARLY ON, LUKE TIES KNOWING TO BEARING FRUIT. By a norm that Jesus himself establishes, trees are known by their fruit (Luke 6:44). John adds a prior qualification that the tree that does not bear good fruit is cut down and consumed by fire (3:9), and further, that Jesus will gather the fruit of the harvest and sift the chaff into an unquenchable fire (3:17). Along the way, the interpretation of the parable of the sower anticipates that Jesus' sowing of God's word will bear fruit among those who hear it, and hold it fast (8:15). Readers traveling these tracks expect to know that Jesus is the spirit-filled prophet and messiah by the fruits of his mission. What better occasion for these expectations to come to fruition than festival—unleavened bread—ancient reminiscences of the fruits of barley harvest—passover—divine deliverance from oppressors.[2]

Moderately astute readers, however, may ponder which tree gets cut down and thrown into the fire. Do readers know who Jesus is by his fruits? When his life draws to its end, the multitudes have dwindled to a paltry band of the eleven and those with them (Luke 24:33), and this group has been riddled with satanic enticement, betrayal, and denial (22:3, 35, 47, 54–62; 24:21). With the gathering this meager, never mind the sifting. If Jesus is a tree known by his fruits, is he cut down and thrown into the fire? Instead of acclaiming Jesus messianic king at the festival—reminiscences of the fruits of barely harvest and all—two of his disciples reluctantly locate their dream completely in the past: "We had hoped that he was the one to redeem Israel" (24:21). In this case knowing linked with bearing fruit appears to indicate that Jesus is not the Spirit-filled prophet and messiah.

---

[1] A revised version of this article appears in Robert L. Brawley, *Text to Text Pours Forth Speech: Voices of Scripture in Luke-Acts*. Indiana Studies in Biblical Literature, Indiana University Press, 1995.

[2] E.g. Luke 1:52–55, 71–74; 4:18–19 raise such expectations. On harvest, Passover, and liberation themes see Senior: 42–43, 56–57, 162–63. Senior notes the orientation toward future hope in the Passover celebration that lies under the setting of Luke's passion.

Such an impression comes across to readers particularly through the mockery of Jesus by his opponents. They clearly state the problem of the passion: "If you are the Messiah, tell us" (Luke 22:67). Three times, opponents of Jesus catch the sardonic twist of the crucifixion of God's messiah. Leaders scoff: "He saved others; let him save himself if he is the Messiah of God, his chosen one!" (Luke 22:35). Soldiers mock: "If you are the King of the Jews, save yourself!" (22:37). And one of the malefactors crucified alongside Jesus jeers: "Are you not the Messiah? Save yourself and us!" (22:39). In fact, opposite opinions about Jesus clash in the Lucan passion (cf. Neyrey, 1985:133), and the two opinions are constitutive of two different constructs of world. On the one side, antagonists perpetrate a mockery that introduces elements of the carnivalesque into the passion narrative, a mockery that attempts to deflate Jesus' messianic identity. That is, antagonists attempt to convert the sacred festival into frivolous absurdity.³ On the other side, Jesus wins unexpected support from several corners—including the God to whom he commits himself. But direct resistance to the carnivalesque comes primarily through hermeneutical allusions to scripture.

"Carnivalesque" is a modern term that Mikhail Bakhtin uses for an age-old phenomenon. Carnival is a representation of established values so absurd as to undermine established values. It creates an inverted world alongside the norm, inside out, top to bottom. The inverted world comes to expression particularly in mockery and the grotesque body.⁴ The corresponding literary idiom is the carnivalesque, and the process of transposing the phenomena of carnival into the language of literature is the carnivalization of literature. Though Bakhtin includes parody within the carnivalesque, Julia Kristeva carefully distinguishes the two. Parody is humorous because it ridicules itself as absurd. But with all its comical effects, the carnivalesque is virulently serious—it is murderous, cynical, revolutionary (Kristeva: 78–85). Parody is itself ridiculous; the carnivalesque portrays established culture as ridiculous. Bugs Bunny performing his variation on the "Barber of Seville" is parody. Voltaire's *Candide* is a cynical undermining of Leibniz's "best of all possible worlds."

Peter Stallybrass has proposed a tentative morphology of the carnivalesque that includes: (1) replacement of fast by feast, (2) transgression of spatial barriers (e.g. town people abandon their private homes for open places), (3) transgression of bodily barriers, (4) inversion of hierarchy—

---

³ Senior speaks of a similar agonistic struggle as finally triumphant over chaos and death (43–44).

⁴ Bakhtin, 1984b: 5–17; 1984a: 108, 120–76. Garcia-Treto produces an intriguing reading of the fall of the House of Ahab using Bakhtin's analysis of the carnivalesque (153–71).

the servant rules the master, (5) degrading of the sacred, and (6) violation of linguistic norms.[5] Further, he challenges Kristeva's view that the carnivalesque is necessarily a viciously serious rebellion against the social order. Stallybrass argues rather that the carnivalesque can occur within the social order. Both have a point. If by the carnivalesque, one intends a thoroughgoing construct of world, it is viciously rebellious. On the other hand, if one means carnivalesque as features of the morphology, the carnivalesque may occur within the social order.

Though Bakhtin and Stallybrass analyze the carnivalesque from the Renaissance and the Middle Ages, it derives from ancient agrarian festivals and has antecedents in the Saturnalias and related festivals of antiquity. May was Flora's month in ancient Rome, a month for inversions in the social order.[6] More graphic, however, was the Saturnalia, spectacular for its unruly, unrestrained carousing. Celebrated as a temporary return of the golden age over which Saturn once ruled, it reduced the social hierarchy to temporary egalitarianism so that masters and slaves ate together even in the imperial court, and social relationships could be reversed with masters serving slaves.[7] Further, true to Stallybrass's morphology, the Saturnalia occurred after the Caesarian fast (Nilsson: 201, 205–6).

The view that Jesus' opponents in Luke introduce the carnivalesque into the passion may be sharply differentiated from a hypothesis a century old that on first glance appears to be similar. In 1898 Paul Wendland saw resemblances between the mockery of Jesus and the Saturnalia, but explicitly only in Mark and Matthew, and claimed that the soldiers made Jesus a carnival king (175-79).[8] His hypothesis was an attempt to move behind the narrative to reconstruct a historical event fossilized in the nar-

---

[5] Stallybrass: 113–14. Modern Mardi Gras in New Orleans closely approximates the morphology. (1) Feasting replaces fasting in anticipation, although the true fast of Lent has all but vanished. (2) People transgress spatial barriers by taking to the streets in massive proportions. (3) Exposed breasts and potbellies transgress normal bodily barriers. (4) Crowning of mock queens and kings is reminiscent of inversion of hierarchy. (5) The contrast between Mardi Gras and Lent is an element of the degrading of the sacred. (6) Vulgar language is the violation of linguistic norms. But Mardi Gras in New Orleans has reinverted the social order of carnival. Rather than invert the normal social order, the socially elite dominate the crews in New Orleans and exclude the socially marginal.

[6] Bakhtin, 1984b:7–8; Stallybrass: 123.

[7] Seneca mentions an established holiday in which masters and slaves eat together, slaves have honors in the household, pronounce judgment, and the household is considered a miniature republic (*Epistles* 47.14).

[8] Wendland depended heavily on Philo's report of the mockery of Agrippa I in 38 C.E. (when he visited Alexandria on his way back to Palestine from Rome) as analogous to the mockery of Jesus (Philo *Flaccus* 29–39). Moreover, he thought that the account of Jesus before Herod preserved a reminiscence of the Saturnalia but dismissed it as unhistorical.

rative. James Frazer engaged Wendland on the same terms and argued against a historical Saturnalia performed by the soldiers. Frazer then made extensive, and far less likely, conjectures to associate the crucifixion of Jesus with the ceremonial hanging of Haman in the Jewish festival of Purim (345-418).[9] In contrast to these efforts to reify history, I am suggesting that in the narrative itself antagonists attempt to carnivalize the passion—a literary feature. Further, I digress momentarily to report something of the development of my own connections between the Lucan passion and the carnivalesque. I take it that Wendland and Frazer caught the relationship from the perspective of the Saturnalia and its kind in antiquity. My experience was quite the opposite. I began to catch the relationship as I read Kristeva and Bakhtin on the carnivalesque in literature. Nevertheless, as distinct as my approach may be from Wendland and Frazer, there is some element of confirmation in that we made related, even if different, connections with the carnivalesque.

But if the carnivalesque infiltrates Luke's passion, the narrative evokes the cultural repertoire. Therefore, the interest here is not to claim a direct relationship with something such as the Saturnalia but to claim that the passion narrative invokes the cultural code. That is, it draws on a bank of common knowledge. The carnivalesque is part of the unformulated text. Though Wendland and Frazer made conjectures that cannot be substantiated, their instincts served them well, and they caught the vital relationship with the carnivalesque in the cultural repertoire.

There is broad-based evidence, both chronologically and geographically, for the carnivalesque in the cultural repertoire of Luke-Acts; that is, in the cultural repertoire of antiquity. From Rome to Persia, in a period antedating and postdating the NT, there were festivals of indulgence, clowning, and social inversion like the Saturnalia. Ancients celebrated the Saturnalia on December 17, but in fact often designated the festival simply as December. The Saturnalia is well attested for the New Testament period. Livy mentions an observance of a Saturnalia with sacrifices at the temple of Saturn in the month of December (22.1.19). Tacitus gives some indication of the reversal of hierarchy by mentioning the custom of drawing lots for the king of the feast of Saturnalia. Once the lot fell on Nero to be mock king of the Saturnalia. He played the part by giving amusing orders but became irate at Britannicus who insisted an playing his role seriously. According to Tacitus, Nero ordered, in entire seriousness, that Britannicus be poisoned to death (*Annals* 13.15.2). Obviously, the egalitarianism was temporary. With similar irony, Cicero mentions in passing that some prisoners were sold on the third day of the festival of

---

[9] Frazer also speculated that Barabbas played the part of Mordecai.

Saturn during a military campaign in Syria (*To Atticus* 5.20). Unfortunately, the social inversion was invalid for the prisoners.

In order to synchronize lunar and solar calendars, many cultures in antiquity intercalated extra days at the end of the year. For example, Egyptians inserted five days which they considered alien to both the lunar and solar calendars, and thus a curious interval dissimilar to ordinary time (Frazer: 338–41). Further, the Hebrews celebrated the New Year not at the beginning but at the end of the year (Exod 23:16), or at the turn of the year (Exod 34:22) (Widengren: 197). The extraordinary character of time in these periods likely fed the indulgence and social inversion of the festive seasons.

But there were other occasions as well—springtime effervescence to invoke fertility or fall debauchery to celebrate the vintage (Bakhtin, 1984b: 5). A case in point is the feast of Matronalia, a female celebration held on the first of March in which socially elite women feasted their slaves (Frazer: 346). A more sensational example is the Syrian cult of Attis that spread especially in Asia Minor in connection with the Magna Mater cult—the cult of Cybele in Syria—which also found its way to Rome. When Attis, intrigued with a water nymph, lost the chastity he had promised Cybele, Cybele became enraged. She wounded the nymph by cutting down a fir tree, the fate of the nymph being, according to one version, bound to the fate of the tree (Ovid *Fasti* 4.215–46). In remorse, Attis emasculated himself. Another version attaches the significance of the fir tree not to the nymph but to Attis himself who put off his human form and solidified into the trunk of the tree (Ovid *Metamorphoses* 10.103–5). Cybele instituted a feast of mourning in which priests (Galli) searched for Attis in the mountains. When they found his image (the fir), they broke out in wild exuberance, even to the point of inflicting wounds on themselves and castrating themselves.[10] In antiquity the remorse and emasculation of Attis was taken to correspond to the wilt of vegetation, and his fresh love to the rebirth of vegetation in spring.

Yet another example further demonstrates the geographical extent. Dio Chrysostom relates a conversation in which Diogenes tells Alexander the Great about the Sacian feast of the Persians against whom Alexander is massing for war. According to Diogenes, the Persians set one of their condemned prisoners upon a king's throne, clothe him in royal apparel, let him give orders, drink, carouse, and have his way with royal concubines. Then they strip and scourge him and hang him to show how the

---

[10] "Attis," *Der kleine Pauly* 1, 1964: 725–26.

wicked and foolish acquire royal power and then after a time of impudence come to a shameful and most evil destruction (*Discourses* 4.66–69).[11]

With this sort of unformulated text in the cultural repertoire, when Luke sets the passion against the feast (23:1), the carnivalesque begins to emerge according to Stallybrass's morphology. But immediately the morphology fails from the perspective of Jesus and his disciples because Passover is a family feast celebrated in the privacy of homes. In fact, Jesus moves from the open out on the Mount of Olives (21:37) into the confining boundaries of a house, and an upper room in the house—the reverse of Stallybrass's second category of the morphology. Nevertheless, there is a leak in the dike, because the chief priests divert their energies from the solemn sacred celebration of Passover to the execution of Jesus—from the perspective of the norms of the narrative, an aspect of what Stallybrass calls "degrading the sacred."

Luke's report of the last supper juxtaposes feast and fast as the morphology anticipates. The account of the supper is fraught with ambiguity. Does Jesus eat the Passover with his disciples or refrain from it? It is possible to read Jesus' desire to eat the Passover in Luke 22:15 as unfulfilled. Further, should the text follow the manuscripts that omit 22:19b-20?[12] Neither ambiguity should detain this discussion long. The ambiguity of fulfilled or unfulfilled desire cannot finally be resolved, though the preparations in 22:7–13 generate expectations of fulfillment, expectations that readers are not likely to revise apart from specific indications otherwise. Quite apart from the ambiguities, Jesus proclaims a fast: "I will not eat it [Passover] until it is fulfilled in the kingdom of God"; "From now on I will not drink of the fruit of the vine until the kingdom of God comes" (22:16, 18).[13]

In any case, the disciples keep the feast.[14] Further, they appear to be headed for carnival. A didactic saying from Jesus gives explicit expression

---

[11] Cf. Frazer: 412–14. In his argument against Wendland (see note 9), Frazer conjectured that the Jewish practice of hanging an effigy of Haman at Purim was an extension of the Babylonian Sacian feast. He also cited the parallel from Philo (see n. 8) where an unruly mob jeers at Agrippa I and then mockingly enthrones a madman named Carabas, putting a sheet of papyrus on his head for a crown, draping a rug around his shoulders as a royal robe, giving him a rod of papyrus for a scepter, and hailing him as lord (*Flaccus* 29–39).

[12] Vööbus: 459; Talbert: 210; Fitzmyer: 1387–89.

[13] In Luke 13:29, Jesus describes a messianic banquet in which people from all points on the compass will sit at table in the kingdom of God. This indicates that the abstinence of Jesus in 22:16, 18 refers to the parousia when the messianic banquet will be fulfilled.

[14] One of the things this feast does is to recall covenant traditions. The new covenant (Luke 22:20) echoes Jer 31:31–34. But it also picks up references to Abrahamic, Sinaitic, and Davidic covenants, which are collapsed into one in Luke 1:55; 69–73. See

to the inversion of hierarchy (Luke 21:24–27), Stallybrass's fourth category. Jesus then confers a kingdom on the twelve, and installs them on thrones (21:28–30)—reminiscences of the Saturnalia or the Sacaea. But the remainder of the morphology does not follow. Jesus and the twelve remain in private space for the time being. There is no violation of bodily barriers, no degrading of the sacred, no transgression of linguistic norms. In addition, in contrast to the temporary character of social inversions in carnival, so ironically evident in Nero's execution of Britannicus, or in the eventual hanging of the condemned prisoner in the Persian Sacian festival, Jesus espouses a permanent social inversion and installs the twelve on thrones in seriousness rather than in jest.[15] The key is that carnival is an absurd representation of established values. Two worlds stand juxtaposed (Bakhtin, 1984b: 6, 11). The carnivalesque is an absurd replication of norms—here the norms established by the narrative—in an attempt to undermine them. Thus, readers should expect to find elements of Stallybass's morphology on the side of established values because the carnivalesque side will repeat them in a preposterous form.

Even when Jesus and his disciples abandon the private boundaries of walls for the open territory of the Mount of Olives, the space remains private. In fact, Jesus withdraws farther from the disciples (21:39–41). Although lamentation can mix with exuberance in the carnivalesque,[16] the disciples do not frolic in exhilaration in the open-air but sleep, out of deep grief (22:45). Two worlds are emerging. The one represented and reflected by Jesus carries the sanction of the narrative. There have been hints of the other—priests abandoning sacred for profane, Satan violating the bodily barriers of Judas.

A far more forceful indicator, surfaces in Jesus' advice to the disciples to take up swords and in his prediction that he will be reckoned among the lawless (Luke 22:35–38). The history of interpretation of this passage is characterized by dilemma. But the carnivalesque may shed some light. The carnivalesque inverts inlaw and outlaw, a dramatic case of which is Dio Chrysostom's account of the Persian Sacian festival. Jesus predicts just such an inversion from his opponents by citing scripture—a portion of Isa 53:12. Jesus identifies the citation as scripture by an introductory formula. Further, he provides it with a christological hermeneutic—the

---

Senior: 62–63. Fitzmyer catches only the echoes of Jer 31:31 and the Sinai covenant Exod 24:3–8 (1391).

[15] The seriousness of Jesus' promise can be seen in its realization within Luke-Acts. On the realization of Jesus' promise in the context of Luke-Acts see Senior: 74–75, 176.

[16] Fowler: 117; Nilsson: 203.

words of scripture are to be fulfilled in him.[17] The passive ἐλογίσθη enables Jesus to formulate his opponents' construct of the world for them. They are the agents who do the reckoning.

To digress momentarily, the citation both recognizes and violates the boundaries of canon (τὸ γεγραμμένον). There is a presumption that an authorial audience recognizes scripture from the cultural repertoire—canon is a shared assumption. But the text of the past is taken to have meaning for the present. Because the Lucan passion narrative takes part of its meaning from texts from the past, it perpetrates what Harold Bloom calls a "lie against time."[18] Diachrony, the historical separation of Luke-Acts from scriptures, gives way to synchrony, the consonance of the two in meaning. The claim of fulfillment violates the boundaries of canon at the same time that it recognizes them.

When by Jesus' inference the opponents drive toward a carnivalesque construct of world, the world sanctioned by the narrative resists it primarily by a citation from scripture. This citation may be classified as hermeneutical, that is, it provides understanding of the baffling event of the arrest of the messiah. This answer comes as part of the world that stands in contrast to the carnivalesque. In the construct of world advanced by the norms of the narrative, the answer is fulfillment of scripture: "He was reckoned with the transgressors" (Luke 22:37).

Part of the difficulty of interpreting the citation is that it falls in the middle of the enigmatic instructions of Jesus to the apostles to buy swords. The conflict with readers' expectations is so sharp as to constitute what Michel Riffaterre calls an "ungrammaticality," that is, an incongruity that forces interpretation to a figurative level[19]—here the figure is the interplay of a revisionary citation of scripture. Significantly Jesus contrasts his instructions to take up purse, sack, and sword with his previous instructions when he sent out the seventy(-two) (Luke 10:4).

Conzelmann takes the ἄλλα νῦν of 22:36 as an indicator of a new major epoch of history in which the danger of persecution replaces the security of the itinerant disciples (16, 81-2, 150).[20] In direct rebuttal, Paul Minear makes a more coherent interpretation when he argues that the period to which 22:36 refers is the immediate future, and the disciples are the transgressors, the ἄνομοι.[21] According to Minear, the apostles are confused and

---

[17] This is not an exclusively christological interpretation. The text could also be fulfilled in others.

[18] Bloom, 1982b:passim. Cf. Bloom 1975b:112.

[19] An ungrammaticality is a feature of the text that resists interpretation on a literal level and drives it to a figurative level (Riffaterre, 1983:51).

[20] This is part of Conzelmann's well-known thesis that Luke-Acts divides time into three major epochs.

[21] Cf. Neyrey. Contra Minear, see Marshall: 826.

obtuse, distanced from Jesus, quarrelsome over their status, under threat of being sifted by Satan. Thus, Jesus' prediction finds immediate fulfillment in the passion narrative itself, and as a matter of fact, the present tense of τέλος ἔχει in 22:37 indicates that the citation from Isaiah *is being fulfilled*. The collapse of the disciples in grief is a confirmation that the disciples are the transgressors. In the cultural repertoire, to sleep in grief is a disorder associated with sin and punishment with verbal parallels in Isa 50:11.[22] Their grief is a part of the fulfillment out of the Isaianic context.

In order to make things fit, however, Minear forces Jesus' command into the category of an artificial literary device to provide for fulfillment of scripture and to expose the apostles who have already disobediently taken up swords against Jesus' teaching. Minear apparently fails to realize that this implies that Jesus is at least partially one of the agents behind the passive ἐλογίσθη—he reckons the apostles to be the outlaws among whom he will be reckoned. H.-W. Bartsch takes another tack, proposing that Jesus uses the citation to predict his crucifixion between two outlaws.[23] But Bartsch's proposal runs into the difficulty that the vocabulary is altogether different. In Luke 22:37 Jesus speaks of the ἄνομοι whereas he is crucified between two κακοῦργοι. Further, the citation implies a reckoning contrary to fact, and Luke presents the crucifixion of Jesus between two malefactors as factual.

The carnivalesque provides a far less strained construal of the text. The phrase ἀλλὰ νῦν does introduce a special time but not from that moment forward.[24] Like the Egyptian intercalation of days, the passion is a curious period set off from ordinary time as a time of inversion. From the perspective of the norms of the narrative, it is a time of satanic testing (Luke 22:31-32) and a curious time of inversion when the sun's light fails in the middle of the day (23:44-45). In contrast to Minear's claim that the Lucan Jesus portrays the apostles as outlaws, in the absurd world of the carnivalesque, it is the antagonists hidden behind the passive ἐλογίσθη

---

[22] Neyrey argues from a redactional critical point of view based on alleged Lucan alterations of Mark (1980). But his argument still holds from the point of view of the literary features of Luke and the cultural repertoire.

[23] Bartsch is also concerned with establishing the saying as based in a historical logion of Jesus and with its meaning for a post-70 audience split over the flight of some Jewish Christians from Jerusalem to Pella while others remained to face persecution. Neyrey extends the ἄνομοι to include Satan, Barabbas, and the two malefactors crucified alongside Jesus (1985:38).

[24] Agreeing with Conzelmann, conventional interpretations take Jesus's command to take purse and bag, and to buy a sword (Luke 22:36) as predicting a new situation from that time forward. Cf. Moo: 132-35; Soards: 243.

who portray them as outlaws.²⁵ To be sure, the disciples play the role, but only partially. They produce two swords.

This astounding shift again pushes the disciples toward a carnivalesque reversal. On the one hand, they stand by Jesus in his trials (Luke 22:28). On the other hand, Satan is sifting them (22:31). Even the phraseological plane is an indicator of a shift from one world to another. Because Jesus confers the name Peter on Simon, its use indicates a special relationship with Jesus. Thus, when Jesus addresses Peter as Simon (22:31), he reverts to a perspective outside the special relationship (Brawley, 1990:142–43), an indicator that Simon threatens to exchange the construct of world mediated by Jesus for the carnivalesque. Further, the disciples do partially play the part of the carnivalesque reversal. One of them takes up the sword, and cuts off the ear of the high priest's slave. It should come as little surprise that they really do play the part. The reversals of the Saturnalia were quite real even if temporary (Bakhtin, 1984b:7–8). Slaves really did eat with their masters. The prisoner of the Sacian festival really did carouse. Cybele's priests really did wound themselves, sometimes irreversibly (reminiscences of Kristeva's notice that the carnivalesque is deadly serious).

Two things in particular prevent the apostles from a complete carnivalesque reversal. The first is the prayer of Jesus for Simon in order that he might play a role in the restoration of his companions (Luke 22:32). The second is the command of Jesus to put an end to the swordplay (22:51). Significantly, the swordplay is the first event involving the disciples after Jesus warns them about the time of trial. The swordplay is part of the satanic sifting, and Jesus himself puts an end to it.²⁶ On the other hand, Judas becomes a permanent part of the opponents' construct of world with repercussions in Acts 1.

Against the unformulated text of the carnivalesque, the narrative also keeps evoking the unformulated text of scripture. The citation of Isa 53:12 openly relates the narrative to scripture, but there are subtle allusions rippling out from it to the Isaianic context. Acknowledging these allusions is

---

[25] Senior is in agreement that enemies do the reckoning (80-81). He, does not, however, identify the ἄνομοι with any specific character or set of characters.

[26] It bears noting that Jesus' command to stop the swordplay, ἐᾶτε ἕως τούτου (Luke 22:51) stands in continuity with his reply to the disciples' possession of two swords in 22:38: ἱκανόν ἐστιν. There are three basic interpretations of the latter: (1) an ironic "this is sufficient" implying the overwhelming odds of combat and future persecution, (2) "enough of that" as a injunction against the possession of swords, and (3) a symbolic demand for commitment of disciples unto death. See Rengstorf: 248. The third interpretation is patently the superimposition of ecclesiastical tradition. The first is grammatically weak. For this meaning one would expect ἱκανά εἰσίν. The grammatical form and the continuity with ἐᾶτε ἕως τούτου in 22:51 are strong clues that Jesus gives a charge against the possession of swords. See Fitzmyer: 1434, 1451.

a significant revision for me. I have argued elsewhere that citations from Isaiah 53 here and in Acts 8:32–33 break off without reference to the remainder of the context. I based my argument only on the phraseological plane of what Richard Hays calls "volume"—the degree of verbatim repetition (29–32). But when I pressed Hays's criterion of volume beyond the phraseological plane to include such things as plot and setting, the volume of the Isaianic context increased conspicuously.

The setting in Isaiah is the perplexing event of the exile. In that setting, Isaiah plays two constructs of world off against each other—the world of idolatry and the world of the God of Israel. The setting in Luke is the baffling event of the crucifixion of God's messiah. In that setting, Luke-Acts plays the carnivalesque construct of world off against another construct mediated by Jesus. But it is especially the Lucan plot that evokes the Isaianic context. Hays's criterion of availability strengthens the case. To what degree was the context of Isaiah 53 available for the author and authorial audience? There is ample evidence that it was readily accessible. In the larger environment, *1 Enoch* 48 is dependent on Isa 49:1–8; *1 Enoch* 49:4 on Isa 42:1, and perhaps *1 Enoch* 38:2 on Isa 53:11. Both *1 Enoch* 62–63 and Wis 5 are expansions of Isa 52–53 (Nickelsburg).[27] Further, Luke-Acts clearly cites texts throughout Isaiah 40–66. From the use of Isaiah 40:3–5 to identify John the Baptist as a voice crying in the wilderness (Luke 3:4–6), to Stephen's quotation of Isa 66:1–2 to make the point that God does not dwell in habitations made by human hands (Acts 7:49–50), Luke-Acts demonstrates the availability of the Isaianic context. Significantly, Jesus delineates the nature of his mission with direct reference to Isa 61:1–2 (Luke 4:18–19), but the inclusion of Isa 53:6d in the alleged reading demonstrates the availability of the context. In close proximity to the passion narrative, Jesus makes a claim on the temple with words from Isa 56:7: "My house shall be called a house of prayer." Further, though one or two words hardly comprise a fair sample against which to test verbatim repetition, the designation of Jesus as God's chosen one (Luke 9:35; 23:35 [in the mouths of opponents]) and references to him as παῖς (Acts 3:13, 26; 4:27, 30) do repeat terms that frequently occur in tandem to designate the Isaianic servant.[28]

A vivid example of how Luke-Acts can cite a text and allude to the context is the account of the Ethiopian eunuch in Acts 8. The narrative re-

---

[27] The use of the Isaianic context in intertestamental tradition may mean that some of the NT allusions were mediated through other traditions such as *1 Enoch* and *4 Ezra* (Schaberg: 216, 222 n. 48).

[28] E.g. Isa 41:8, 9; 42:1, 43:10; 44:1, 2, 21; 45:4; 49:6; 50:10; 52:13. Cf. Acts 1:2. Karabidopoulou suggests that the designation of Jesus as the "chosen one" derives from Isa 42:1 (190). To designate a single text may be too precise. But there is a bank of tradition within which the designation of Jesus as the chosen one is at play.

peats the passage of scripture that the eunuch was reading—Isa 53:7–8. But readers who know the Isaianic context can scarcely fail to catch that the plot of Acts 8:26–38 reiterates Isa 56:3–5—the inclusion of foreigner and eunuch in the people of God.[29] This is not to say that Isa 56:3–5 provided the source for the story any more than Isa 40:3–5 provided the source for the account of John the Baptist but that the story nevertheless reverberates with the Isaianic text.

Therefore, the criteria of availability and volume (including reiteration on the level of setting and plot) indicate a high probability of allusions to the Isaianic context beyond explicit citations. Thus, when Jesus' opponents mock him and beat him (Luke 22:63), readers who recall Isaiah may hear echoes of 50:6 LXX: "I gave my back to the whips and my jaws to slaps, and I did not turn my face away from the dishonor of spittings" (author's trans.). But this is not merely a direct allusion to Isaiah. The reverberation is mediated through Jesus' previous predictions of his passion (Luke 9:22, 44–45; 18:31–33). When those who mock Jesus demand that he prophesy (22:64), they make an ironic analeptic reference to 18:32–33 where he had already prophesied precisely what his mockers are doing. Unwittingly, they are themselves fulfilling prophecy. Curiously, although 18:33 forecasts that Jesus will be spat upon,[30] in the passion account itself no detail corresponds to this prediction. Nevertheless, the passion narrative as mediated through the predictions repeats the plot of Isa 50:6— there is some repetition of the cognates μάστιξ, ἐμπτύσμα (Isa 50:6); μαστιγόω, ἐμπτύω (Luke 18:33),[31] and close readers can pick up the spitting as an ellipsis in the mockery of Luke 22:63.

The plot of the passion narrative coincides with the disdain and rejection of Isa 53:3: "But his appearance was dishonorable, abandoned more than all others, he was a man of calamity and he knew what it was to bear weakness" (LXX, author's trans.). There is also correspondence between the verdict of innocence in Isa 53:8 and declarations of Jesus' innocence in Luke 23.[32] The narrator points out to readers before the crucifixion that Pilate declares Jesus innocent three times (Luke 23:22, cf. 23:4, 14). In addition, Pilate appeals to Herod for the same verdict (23:15). In symmetry with these declarations, three incidents after the crucifixion affirm Jesus'

---

[29] Some additional clear allusions to portions of Isaiah 40–66 are: Isa 42:6; 49:6 = Luke 2:32; Acts 13:47; 26:23; Isa 43:5–6 (cf. 49:12; 59:19) = Luke 13:29; Isa 56:7 = Luke 19:46.

[30] Spitting is a particular manifestation of the carnivalesque—transgressing bodily barriers, inside becomes outside (Bakhtin, 1984b:26, 317; Stallybrass: 114).

[31] Ἐμπτύω and its cognate ἐμπτυσμα appear only three times in the LXX. Only the verb ἐμπτύω appears in the NT, and only in connection with Jesus' passion. See Moo (88).

[32] So Karabidopoulou (202–3, 210–11).

innocence. The repentant malefactor gives the verdict that Jesus has done nothing wrong (23:41). The centurion declares, "Certainly this man was innocent" (δίκαιος, 23:47). And when the curious crowd withdraws, they beat on their breasts as a sign of remorse over the injustice (23:48).[33] Readers who know the verdict of Isa 53:8 will be unlikely to miss the same verdict in the Lucan passion narrative.[34]

One element of Luke's account of the crucifixion stands in sharp relief against the context of Isaiah 53. In contrast to the servant of Isa 53:7, the Lucan Jesus does not maintain silence in the face of abuse. True, he remains silent before Herod (Luke 23:9), but he briefly engages both the council and Pilate, and these encounters bear marks of the carnivalesque. On the heels of the mockery of those who arrested Jesus, the council demands, "If you are the Messiah, tell us" (22:67). But Jesus deals with this interrogation as an absurd subversion of a genuine judicial inquest. They will not regard his answer soberly. Nevertheless, in competition with the cultural repertoire of the carnivalesque potentate, Jesus speaks to them of his genuine enthronement at the right hand of the power of God (22:67–69). Though in his claim he makes no mention of his identity as son of God, that is precisely what his examiners ask. But again they operate on the level of the carnivalesque. Like the prisoner enthroned for the Sacian festival, in the carnivalesque he is whatever they say: ὑμεῖς λέγετε ὅτι ἐγώ εἰμι (22:70).[35]

The absurd subversion of an inquest continues with Pilate, and the same logic holds. Jesus' accusers put a claim to messianic kingship on his lips. But Pilate extends the question of identity: "Are you the king of the Jews?" Jesus' answer stands in continuity with his response to the council. In the carnivalesque, he is whatever Pilate says: σὺ λέγεις (Luke 23:3). The carnivalesque is all the more explicit in the mockery of Herod and his soldiers—they dress Jesus in an exquisite robe—carnival king (23:11).[36]

---

[33] Brawley, 1987:141. Karris claims that the centurion declares Jesus "righteous" rather than "innocent." Karris fails to notice the symmetrical architectonic structure in which Pilate's three declarations find their counterpart in the malefactor, the centurion, and the people. Further, the Greek δίκαιος denotes both righteous and innocent without implying the dominance of one over the other.

[34] Karabidopoulou claims correspondence between the Lucan passion narrative and Isaiah 53 in Jesus' prayer for those who crucify him = Isa 53:12 (190, 193, 199). Text critical questions concerning the authenticity of the prayer aside, it does not appear in the LXX of Isa 53:12.

[35] Senior is correct that this cannot be taken as a denial of the messianic identity of Jesus that is asserted throughout the context of Luke-Acts (n. 8). The irony of their question is that it is true on one level and undermines the carnivalesque mockery.

[36] Bakhtin explicitly refers to the crowning of Jesus as a king as direct carnivalization (1984a:135).

Suddenly there is a street scene. The people have transgressed the spatial boundaries of the walls of privacy and have taken to the open streets—Stallybrass's second category. Carnivalization continues in the release of Barabbas—outlaw for inlaw. In Luke the impetus for the release of Barabbas is a ground-swell of sentiment. Here the carnivalesque helps to explain to some extent the role of the Jewish populace in the death of Jesus. The populace does not observe carnival as a spectacle—they live it.[37] As a matter of fact, the inversion of outlaw and inlaw has already come to light in Luke 22:52 where Jesus asks those who arrest him: "Have you come out with swords and clubs as if I were a bandit [λῃστής]?"[38] Further, as leader of an uprising, perhaps with aspirations for social and economic liberation for the populace, Barabbas may have been a Robin Hood figure. Thus, the people call for the carnivalesque inversion—outlaw for inlaw (Luke 23:18–25).[39]

Again, biblical allusions are among the principal features that resist the carnivalesque. But whereas Isaiah 53 and its context dominate the arrest of Jesus, a new battery of allusions comes into play at the crucifixion. First, in response to the women who mourn (Luke 23:27), Jesus cites Hosea 10:8.[40] As is the case with the context of Isaiah 53, the setting of Hosea is also the juxtaposition of two worlds—the world of idolatry and the world of the God of Israel. The death wish of Hosea 10:8 is the destiny of people who live out of the idolatrous construct of the world. Jesus anticipates a similar destiny for those who live out of the carnivalesque construct of world in Luke 23:30—an anticipation that becomes tangible in the death of Judas Iscariot (Acts 1:16–26).

True to a stock element of carnival (Stallybrass: 117), the populace ridicules Jesus as his opponents parade him through the streets. Here again reading the Lucan passion narrative through the lenses of the carnivalesque constrains me to revise my former reading. I had argued that the women seriously lament Jesus (1987:140).[41] Even when I argued that, I was nevertheless perplexed by Jesus' caustic remarks to the daughters of Jerusalem. From the point of view of the carnivalesque, the role of the

---

[37] Bakhtin, 1984b:7; 1984a:122.

[38] On banditry as social resistance see Theissen (35–38, 49–51, 61, 806); Horsley (138–9); and Crossan (168–224).

[39] On the inversion of inlaw and outlaw see Stallybrass (120).

[40] The order of καλύψατε ἡμᾶς and πέσετε ἐφ' ἡμᾶς is reversed in Luke 23:30 in comparison with Hosea 10:8 LXX.

[41] On the women as favorable to Jesus see Senior (122). I still maintain that Jesus' reply, though anticipating judgment, does not indict the women or the populace in their entirety. Rather, the reply resists the carnivalesque construct of world. Neyrey takes the women to be professional mourners and Jesus' response as a prophetic judgment oracle (112, 119). Cf. Untergassmair (16–17) and Stählin (844–46).

women is part of the exuberance of carnival that included weeping. Kristeva points out that the carnivalesque mixes the comic and the tragic, and even if there is laughter, it is serious, murderous laughter (80, 82).[42] Geo Widengren documents just such a characteristic double emotional climax in Ugaritic texts—laughter associated with the resurrection of the deity, and weeping associated with the death of the deity.[43] Remarkably, it is precisely this kind of weeping that is going on in the Hosea passage from which the Lucan Jesus cites the death wish. The people of Samaria weep over the departure of the calf of Beth-aven (Hos 10:5–8). Such carnivalesque weeping makes all the more sense if the green wood to which Jesus refers has to do with spring festivals. The devotees of Cybele ran into the hills in search of green trees in spring. In England during the Middle Ages May was a time when people romped in the woods breaking boughs and trees of green wood.[44] Jesus' remark in Luke 23:31 indicates the tragedy of his death in spite of the carnivalesque—reminiscent of the case of Britannicus when Nero ordered his death seriously.

Second, the battery of allusions shifts to the Psalms. Ioannou Karabidopoulou claims that there are five allusions to the psalms in Luke 23:33–49 (1972:194–96). Two of these, however, are weak at the most. Karabidopoulou detects an allusion to Ps 37:12 LXX in Luke 23:49: "But all of his acquaintances, including the women who had followed him from Galilee, stood at a distance, watching these things."[45] The volume here is extremely low. The verbal correspondence hangs on the phrase ἀπὸ μακρόθεν ("at a distance"). Further, the Lucan plot does not play out the psalm in that Jesus has already died—no longer the suffering one—and unlike the

---

[42] Cf. the mourning followed by cynical laughter in the raising of Jairus' daughter (Luke 8:52–53).

[43] Widengren: 179. Cf. Hos 10:58; Ps 126:4–6.

[44] Stallybrass 1985:126. Stallybrass claims some continuity of the practice with ancient Rome. Fitzmyer (1498–99) notes four possible interpretations for the green wood/dry wood: (1) If the Romans treat an innocent person thus, how will they treat rebels? (2) If Jews so treat one who came to save them, how will they be treated for destroying that one? (3) If people behave in this fashion before their cup of wickedness is full, what will they do when it overflows? (4) If God has not spared Jesus, how much less impenitent Judaism? Jewett associates the dry wood with "burning zeal" and the green wood with Jesus' rejection of the Zealot option (105–21). Many interpreters associate the contrast between green and dry wood with a contrast between two epochs of time. See Soards (243). Neyrey treats the green wood as a popular aphorism that means if the Jews deal thus with one sent to save, what will they receive for killing him (74–86). His references to rabbinic parallels are stretched. Marshall assumes that the wood is associated with fire as a sign of judgment (865). Similarly, Untergassmair thinks the wood is to be burned with fire as a sign of judgment, and the contrast between green and dry reflects the situation of the destruction of Jerusalem and the final judgment respectively (31–32, 142). No fire is mentioned, and the act associated with the green wood is taking place as Jesus utters the saying.

[45] So also Bachele (56) and Untergassmair (106).

case of the groaning psalmist, the voice is the narrator's rather than the suffering one's.

The other weak case is an alleged allusion to Ps 68:22 LXX in the soldiers offer of sour wine to Jesus (Luke 23:36). Ὄξος is the only word the two texts have in common. Again, rather than a complaint on the lips of Jesus, as in John 19:28–29, the reference to sour wine is in the narrator's voice who gives readers the clue to its function as mockery. What is more, the offer of sour wine is a part of the carnivalesque. Notably, the soldiers are mocking Jesus as a king—carnival king—and they offer him sour wine instead of the superior beverage appropriate for a king (Danker 1988:376). Then Jesus dies under an inscription: "This is the king of the Jews"—carnival king (23:38).

Things are different with the mockery of the leaders in Luke 23:35. The narrator gives readers notice of the mockery, but the words of mockery are on the leaders' lips. On the verbal plane, the volume of repetition is considerable. There is repetition of the verbs θεωρέω and μυκτηρίζω from Ps 21:8 LXX, though Luke differentiates those who watch from the leaders who mock. There is also repetition of the nuclear word σωσάτο from 21:9,[46] though in distinction from the psalm where it means "Let [the Lord] save him," here it means "Let him save himself." Two more of Hays's criteria come into play at this point—availability and repetition. The availability of Psalm 21 LXX is clear from its prominence in the passion narratives of all four Gospels. The repetition is clear because the previous verse is an unambiguous citation of Ps 21:19 LXX.

In contradistinction to the typical allusions to scripture in the Lucan passion narrative that resist the carnivalesque, the leaders use a revisionary allusion to boost the carnivalesque. They twist the hypogram of Ps 21:8–9 and play an absurd mimicry off of it.[47]

Two other allusions to the psalms resist the carnivalesque and point to an alternative construct of world. The first has to do with dividing Jesus' clothing, including apparently the exquisite robe that Herod put on him. Luke 23:34 abbreviates Ps 21:19 LXX and stylizes it to fit grammatically, but reproduces it with high volume. A crucial issue for understanding it is the textual authenticity of Jesus' prayer for his opponents. Its absence from prominent early manuscripts with a wide geographical

---

[46] Nuclear words stimulate readers to conceive of related networks (Riffaterre: 39). Dillon suggests that the case for nuclear words is stronger when the settings of precursor and successor are similar (431 n. 3).

[47] Bakhtin mentions parodically reinterpreted citations as part of the carnivalesque (1984a:108). Significantly, for Bakhtin this contributes to the plurality of voices in the text.

dispersion is difficult to explain as an omission by copyists.⁴⁸ Nevertheless, a somewhat persuasive argument for its authenticity is the parallel with Acts 7:60 among a number of parallels between the deaths of Jesus and Stephen and the agreement with Lucan motifs.⁴⁹

One way out of the conundrum is to consider the text in both forms, with and without Jesus' prayer. Without the prayer, the allusion to the dividing of Jesus' garments establishes a straight reading of Ps 21:19 before the leaders make their own absurd mimicry of it in Luke 23:35. Like the ones who arrested Jesus in 22:64, those who cast lots for Jesus' clothing unwittingly fulfill prophecy, and the first straight allusion to the Psalm sets off the second as an absurd mimicry.

With the prayer, not only does Jesus carry out the theme of forgiveness of sinners, he also makes a clear distinction between the two constructs of world. This makes it even more explicit that dividing Jesus' clothing and mocking him are a part of the carnivalesque. Thus, this is another case where allusion to scripture resists the carnivalesque construct of world.

Psalm 21 falls into two contrasting parts—lament for Godforsakenness (vv. 1–21) and thanksgiving for divine deliverance (vv. 22–31).⁵⁰ For readers who know Psalm 21, the division of Jesus' clothes and the ensuing mockery of the leaders call to mind the lament. Is there also reason to recall the divine deliverance? One end of the spectrum of opinions takes the allusions as atomistic associations that carry nothing of their context.⁵¹ The other end takes the part, particularly the opening lines, as representing the whole.⁵² Luke, however, does not record the opening lines so prominent in Mark and Matthew: "My God, my God, why have you forsaken me?" Further, by the standard of verbatim repetition, Luke gives readers little reason to recollect the divine deliverance. But when the setting and plot come into play, the Lucan passion strongly reiterates the full psalm.

The setting of Psalm 21 is the contrast of a carnivalesque vision of world and a theocentric vision of world. In the carnivalesque inversion, the victim is considered a worm rather than human, scorned and de-

---

⁴⁸ Metzger: 180. On consideration of the text as an interpolation see Ehrman and Plunkett: 401–16. On consideration of the text as authentic see Neyrey 1985:56–57.

⁴⁹ Houlden: 56–57. Karabidopoulou argues similarly and also suggests that the prayer completes the theme of Jesus' love for outcasts and sinners (199). Talbert strongly supports the authenticity of the prayer on the basis of its congruity with Lucan language and themes (219–20). On the prayer as consonant with Lucan motifs see Schweizer, 1984:340. Cf. Schneider: 483.

⁵⁰ See e.g. Kraus: 323.

⁵¹ Cf. Hahn: 54.

⁵² So e.g. Gese: 180; Fisher: 20–38. Cf. Moo: 33.

spised, mocked. The mouth of opponents opened like a lion's mouth (21:14) is a violation of bodily barriers—typical of the carnivalesque (Bakhtin, 1984b:26, 317). The taunt, "He hoped in the Lord, let him deliver him; let him save him, because he cares for him" (21:9, author's trans.), profanes the sacred in carnivalesque fashion.

Further, biblical scholarship has developed some fascinating hypotheses about the relation of Psalm 22 (21 LXX) to the carnivalesque. In the wider environment, part of the Babylonian New Year festival involved an intriguing ritual in which the king entered Nebo's chapel, followed by the high priest. The high priest proceeded to remove the king's royal attire and to take away his scepter, ring, weapon, and crown. The priest then buffeted his cheeks, tugged his ears, and compelled him to bow before Marduk and assert that he had not been derelict in his duties to Babylon. After the ritual the king resumed his normal status (Gadd: 53–54). Aage Bentzen argues for a parallel carnivalesque inversion of the king's status in Israel, and specifically sees it as a feature of royal Psalms of lament including Psalm 22 (21 LXX).[53] Though echoes of the ritual humiliation may linger in NT times, its memory is not mandatory in order for Luke-Acts nevertheless to pick up the carnivalesque setting as a literary feature. But the hypothesis does support the presence of the carnivalesque precisely as a literary feature.

Beyond the carnivalesque setting, however, the narrative of the Lucan passion plays out the plot of Psalm 21. Immediately before the passage in Psalm 21 that Luke splices into the passion narrative, the details parallel details of the crucifixion uncannily: "Many dogs encircled me, an assembly of those who do evil surrounded me, they pierced my hands and my feet" (author's trans.). Luke mentions nothing of the piercing of Jesus' hands and feet as details of the crucifixion. But the risen Jesus explicitly shows his hands and his feet to the eleven and those with them (Luke 24:39, 40), though he makes no mention of the wounds.[54] With these multiple touch points between the Lucan passion and Psalm 21, readers who know the Psalm may also begin to sing the song of deliverance, salvation, and rescue from its second half. In fact, because they allude to the Psalm, the leaders who mock unwittingly call to mind the power of God to save.

But not too fast! Jesus dies in the midst of a curious time of inversion. The sun's light fails, the temple curtain is torn.[55] Day becomes night, sa-

---

[53] Bentzen: 25–28. Similarly, Johnson: 228. This hypothesis has received support from Eaton: 71–2, and Anderson: 184.

[54] See Moo: 283. Dillon conjectures that the psalm entered the passion tradition in an early Aramaic stage so that there is no reference to the piercing of hands and feet, details that only the LXX of the psalm relates, in the passion narrative itself (431 n. 3).

[55] Senior interprets these events as ominous signs of chaos and doom (141–43). On the separation of carnivalesque time from normal time see Bakhtin, 1984a:175–76.

cred becomes profane, inlaw is swapped for outlaw, God's messiah is killed. The carnivalesque threatens to eclipse Jesus' construct of world in a deadly serious way. In the jaws of such jeopardy, Jesus casts himself in utter dependence upon God: "Father, into your hands I commend my spirit" (Luke 23:46).[56] Conventionally, the saying has been understood from the perspective of the dichotomy of body and soul, so that at this moment of death, Jesus' spirit leaves his body.[57] There is some basis for such an interpretation elsewhere in Luke-Acts. When Jesus heals Jairus's daughter, her πνεῦμα returns (8:55). When the risen Jesus appears to the eleven and those with them, they think they are seeing a πνεῦμα, and Jesus makes a distinction between his risen nature and a πνεῦμα (24:37, 39). To be sure, in the cultural repertoire of Luke-Acts, spirit and body can exist in a dichotomy.[58] But πνεῦμα can also be the seat of life, the corporeal matter and its life-giving force together, and as such it can refer to the totality of human existence.[59] Thus, it is in this last sense that at the moment of his final extremities, Jesus commits his life to God's care: "Father, into your hands I commend my spirit."

B. *Talmud Ber.* 4b-5a gives some evidence that in citing the Psalm Jesus was also reciting a Jewish bedtime prayer.[60] The talmudic discussion begins with the opinion of R. Joshua b. Levi that one ought to recite the *Shemaʿ* at bedtime even if it has already been recited in the synagogue. R. Nahman gives the opinion that it is not necessary for a scholar. But Abaye is reported to have said that even a scholar should recite at least one verse, as for instance: "Into Thy hand I commit my spirit. Thou hast redeemed me Lord." *Midrash Rabbah* on Numbers 20:20 and *Midrash Tanhuma* B VII.23 on Numbers distinguish Israelites from other people by the evening (and therefore characteristic) prayer: "Into Thy hand I commit my spirit" (Ps 31:6). The problem is that the talmudic scholars date from the third and fourth centuries of our era, and the recension of the Midrashim is much later. Thus there is insufficient evidence to show how

---

[56] Jesus' final words are a verbatim repetition except that the verb παρατίθημι appears in the present to reflect the moment of Jesus' death rather than in the future as in Ps 30:6 LXX.

[57] E.g. Schweizer, 1968:6.415.

[58] Sjöberg: 6.376–79.

[59] Bieder: 6.368–69; Baumgärtel: 6.360-61, 364; Kleinknecht: 6.334–35. On the meaning of πνεῦμα as life in Luke 23:46 see Grundmann: 435; Ernst: 639; Kremer: 233; Fitzmyer: 1514. Anderson takes the meaning of this text to be the preservation of the life of the psalmist though he understands the Lucan use of it conventionally as Jesus' impending death (248). According to Senior, Jesus entrusts "his entire being to God" (168). See Untergassmair: 88–89.

[60] Psalm 31:5 = 30:6 LXX is still used in Christian liturgy as an evening prayer including the remainder of the verse not cited in Luke 23:46: "Thou hast redeemed me, o Lord, thou God of truth." *The English Hymnal* (Oxford University Press, 1906) 648.

far back the tradition goes. But notably Abaye's tradition recalls divine redemption as well as the committal to God.

Whether the Lucan Jesus recites a bedtime prayer or not, he casts himself in dependence upon God. Does the authorial audience know Psalm 30:6 (LXX)? And when Jesus says, "Father, into your hands I commend my spirit," do they also hear, "You have redeemed me, Lord, God of truth. You have hated those who guard vanities carefully to no purpose. But I have hoped in the Lord" (Ps 30:6–7 LXX, author's trans.)? The explicit and implicit hope in God is a key to the allusions to scripture in the passion narrative. The allusions resist the carnivalesque by juxtaposing another world to it. But what kind of world? It is a world that centers on God. It is conventional to speak of messianic or christological interpretation of scripture in Luke-Acts.[61] The point is well taken, as references in Luke 24:27, 44–46 show. Further, in Luke 22:37 Jesus himself implies a christological perspective for interpreting Isa 53:12: "It is necessary for this that is written to be fulfilled in me." On the other hand, Luke 22:37; 23:30, 34 refer equally to opponents. But if Jesus is the key to understanding the scriptures, he gives another key—God. That is, both explicitly and implicitly, allusions to scripture make the understanding of the crucifixion of Jesus dependent on the power of God to rescue. The Lucan appropriation of scripture is primarily theocentric.[62]

The interplay between the Lucan passion narrative and scripture is a kind of repetition that exhibits what Riffaterre calls overdetermination. Overdetermination is an overlapping of synonymous systems that helps to leverage a "correct" reading. Allusions are a particular case in which one text is superimposed on another, and the text that alludes to another is a variant on the allusion.[63] Recall of scripture in the Lucan passion places Jesus in continuity with a tradition dominated by hope in God for deliverance.

This theocentric appropriation of scripture is a figuration. Luke views the crucifixion of Jesus indirectly through scripture. But Luke equally views scripture through the crucifixion of Jesus. The juxtaposition of the

---

[61] E.g. Longenecker: 104–5. Juel suggests that the major focus of scriptural interpretation for early believers was Jesus as the crucified and risen messiah (1).

[62] Theocentric readings of Psalms 22 and 31 are typical. See Gese: 191–93; Anderson: 184–93, 245–48; Eaton: 75–76, 93–95; Kraus: 327, 396. But a theocentric reading of Lucan allusions to Scripture has usually been obscured by a christological or messianic reading. Although he emphasizes a christological hermeneutic in Mark, Joel Marcus interprets the christological hermeneutic in terms of God's way. Similarly, Suhl: 46–47. Similarly, on Mark but also Luke, Hultgren: 61–63, 85.

[63] M. Riffaterre, 1978:7–11; 1983:44–46.

two relocates the center of each[64]—crucifixion shifts off the center of senselessness; scripture shifts off its center in Israel's past to relocate on the crucifixion of Jesus.

But what kind of figure is the refiguration? In spite of their multiplicity and complexity, it is possible to give some indication of the refigurations through what Harold Bloom calls revisionary ratios. One case is the twist that the leaders who mock give to Ps 21:8–9 (Luke 23:35). Like the scoffers in the psalm, they make deliverance a criterion of authenticity, but the new mockery bends the criterion from divine deliverance to Jesus' deliverance of himself. Bloom terms the bending of the precursor "clinamen," that is, a twist that in its relationship to the precursor produces irony.[65] The leaders imply the absence of the power to deliver. Ironically, they locate the absence of power in God's messiah himself. But to the chagrin of the scoffers the plots of both Psalm 21 and the Lucan passion locate the presence of the power of deliverance in God. Thus, even in the allusion of opponents, readers may overhear hope in God.

Jesus' direct appeal to Isa 53:12 (Luke 22:37) makes a claim to be a fulfillment, a completion. This is "tessera" in Bloom's terminology.[66] Completion means both continuity and discontinuity. Jesus' citation does not overthrow Isa 53:12. Rather, it depends on it. On the other hand, there is an implicit claim that Isaiah is unfinished, and as such it takes on a meaning that prior to its use in the passion narrative it did not have. Completion is not merely like the tesserae of a mosaic, distinct and yet when viewed together forming a whole. Rather, it is like the broken fragments of an urn pieced back together to compose a whole (Bloom, 1976: 17–18). By itself Isa 53:12 centers on the history of Israel. By itself Jesus' passion centers on senselessness. Together, the two texts relocate on new centers. The history of Israel extends to Jesus' passion, Jesus' passion takes its meaning from the God of the history of Israel.

Mere completion, however, does not do justice to the revisionary relationship between Jesus' passion and Isa 53:12, as if an arc continues until it traces a full circle back on itself. Completion comes about when the revisionary relationship raises a new level of discernment, a gain in meaning, like a coil spring turning back over itself at a higher level—in Bloom's terms, "daemonization" or hyperbole. But the gain in meaning occurs at the expense of a loss of meaning of the precursor, a "kenosis."[67]

---

[64] Bloom, following Nietzsche, uses the spatial metaphor of de-centering to speak of the way in which figuration provides a new perspective. The change in perspective is what is meant by de-centering (1975b:120).

[65] Bloom, 1973:14; 1975a:71, 84; 1975b:79; 1976:16–17; 1982a:137, 201.

[66] Bloom, 1973:14, 66–91; 1975a:71–72, 84, 95–96.

[67] Bloom, 1973:87–91, 96–114; 1975a:72, 84, 95–96; 1982a:238–39; 1982b:17, 24.

Viewed through the Lucan passion narrative, Isa 53:12 is no longer part of Israel's hope of the restoration of the nation after exile but the hope of the restoration of Jesus as messiah.

Because the citations of Hos 10:8, Ps 21:19, and Ps 30:6 are markers that attract readers' attention to their contexts, they also correspond to Bloom's category of tessera. That is, the explicit citations are synecdochical in that the part stands for the whole. In addition, the allusive texts fit with the passion narrative to form a new whole—the broken fragments of an urn pieced back together. As with Isa 53:12, Hos 10:8 recalls the juxtaposition of two constructs of world—the world of idolatry and the world of the God of Israel. The revisionary use of these texts shifts the center historically but also substantively. The historical shift is to the event of Jesus' death. The substantive shift is from the juxtaposition of the world of the God of Israel with the world of idolatry to its juxtaposition with the world of the carnivalesque.

The figuration with all these texts is also metonymic. Not only does the part stand for the whole, the allusions also stand for the power of God. In each of the above cases, even when scoffers play off of scripture, the allusion represents the power of God to rescue—Bloom's categories of "kenosis" and "daemonization."[68] On the one hand, the metonymy is limiting. It reduces the power of God to rescue to its representation in a few allusions to scripture—kenosis. On the other hand, the metonymy leads to daemonization, hyperbole, that is, a gain in meaning over the precursor.

Because there is such a gain in meaning, allusions to scripture in the Lucan passion break off from their precursors. Bloom refers to this as "askesis," a rift between precursor and successor because the successor claims an efficacy which the precursor does not possess.[69] The successor de-centers the precursor; that is, it provides a new perspective toward the precursor so that readers see what has not been seen before, namely, the power of God to rescue the messiah from the scandal of crucifixion. On the other hand, the only way readers gain the new perspective in Luke is to hear the voices of Isaiah, Hosea, and the psalmists. The precursor returns and overcomes the tension created by the new perspective and the merits of the new meaning—Bloom's "apophrades," metalepsis, or transumption.[70] When Luke speaks in the voice of Isaiah, Hosea, and the psalmists, these figures of the past come to the present to speak. But when they speak, they speak in Luke's voice.

---

[68] Bloom, 1973:14–15; 1975a:72, 84; 1975b:120; 1976:18; 1982a:132, 238.

[69] Bloom, 1973:15; 1975a:73, 84; 1975b:120; 1976:19; 1982a:134.

[70] Bloom, 1973:15–16, 141; 1975a:74, 84; 1976: 19–20; 1982a:135; 1982b:74–75.

Allusions to scripture in the Lucan passion narrative form a hendiadys, two in one. There are two voices, precursor and successor, in one. This hendiadys resists the carnivalesque construct of world that comes from Jesus' adversaries, and it keeps reminding readers that beyond the machinations of the opponents something about the story is the Lord's doing.

So, do readers know who Jesus is by his fruits? If Jesus is a tree known by its fruits, is he cut down and thrown into the fire? The perspective of the carnivalesque in the Lucan passion narrative presses on readers the notion that he is. But the passion is a part of the anticipations of readers that they must revise as the narrative develops. Against their expectations that Jesus is like a flourishing tree planted by streams of water which yields its fruit in its season, Luke's passion narrative offers a revision of messianism. The messiah is crucified. But the revision of messianism is also a revision of the God of the messiah. "He hoped in the Lord, let him deliver him; let him save him, because he cares for him" (Ps 21:9 LXX, author's trans.).

WORKS CITED

Anderson, A.
    1972   *The Book of Psalms. Introduction* and *Psalms 1–72*. NCB. Vol. 1. London: Oliphants.

Bachele, A.
    1978   *Der Tod Jesu im Lukasevangelium: Eine redactionsgeschichtliche Untersuchung zu Lk 23*. Frankfurter theologische Studien 26. Frankfurt: Josef Knecht.

Bakhtin, M.
    1984a   *Problems of Dostoevsky's Poetics*. Manchester: Manchester University Press.
    1984b   *Rabelais and His World*. Bloomington: Indiana University Press.

Bartsch, H.-W.
    1974   "Jesu Schwertwort, Lukas XXII. 35–38." *NTS* 20:190-203.

Baumgärtel, F.
    1968   "πνεῦμα." *TDNT*. Vol. 6.

Bentzen, A.
    1955   *King and Messiah*. Lutterworth Studies in Church and Bible. London: Lutterworth.

Bieder, W.
    1968   "πνεῦμα." *TDNT*. Vol. 6.

Bloom, H.
  1973   *The Anxiety of Influence: A Theory of Poetry*. New York: Oxford University Press.
  1975a   *A Map of Misreading*. New York: Oxford University Press.
  1975b   *Kabbalah and Criticism*. New York: Seabury.
  1976   *Poetry and Repression: Revisionism from Blake to Stevens*. New Haven: Yale University Press.
  1982a   *Agon: Towards a Theory of Revisionism*. Oxford: Oxford University Press.
  1982b   *The Breaking of the Vessels*. Chicago: University of Chicago Press.

Brawley, R.
  1987   *Luke-Acts and the Jews: Conflict, Apology, and Conciliation*. Atlanta: Scholars.
  1990   *Centering on God: Method and Message in Luke-Acts*. LCBI. Louisville: Westminster/John Knox.

Conzelmann, H.
  1961   *The Theology of St. Luke*. New York: Harper & Row.

Crossan, J.D.
  1991   *The Historical Jesus: The Life of a Mediterranean Jewish Peasant*. San Francisco: Harper.

Danker, F.
  1988   *Jesus and the New Age: A Commentary on St. Luke's Gospel*. Philadelphia: Fortress.

Dillon, R.
  1987   "The Psalms of the Suffering Just in the Accounts of Jesus' Passion." *Worship* 61:430-40.

Eaton, J.
  1967   *Psalms: Introduction and Commentary*. Torch Bible Commentaries. London: SCM.

Ehrman, B. and M. Plunkett
  1983   "The Angel and the Agony: The Textual Problem of Luke 22:43–44." *CBQ* 45:401-16.

Ernst, J.
  1977   *Das Evangelium nach Lukas: Übersetzt und erklärt*. RNT. Regensberg: Pustet.

Fisher, L.
  1964   "Betrayed by Friends: An Expository Study of Psalm 22." *Int* 18:20-38.

Fitzmyer, J.
  1985   *The Gospel According to Luke (X-XXIV): Introduction, Translation, and Notes*. Garden City, NY: Doubleday.

Fowler, W.
  1899   *The Roman Festivals of the Period of the Republic*. London: Macmillan.

Frazer, J.
 1913 *The Scapegoat. The Golden Bough.* Part 6. London: Macmillan.

Gadd, C.
 1933 "Babylonian Myth and Ritual." Pp. 40-67 in *Myth and Ritual: Essays on the Myth and Ritual of the Hebrews in Relation to the Cultural Pattern of the Ancient East.* Ed. S. Hooke. London: Oxford University Press.

Garcia-Treto, F.
 1992 "The Fall of the House: A Carnivalesque Reading of 2 Kings 9 and 10." In *Reading Between Texts: Intertextuality and the Hebrew Bible.* Ed. Danna Nolan Fewell. LCBI. Louisville: Westminster/John Knox.

Gese, H.
 1974 "Psalm 22 und das Neue Testament: Der älteste Bericht vom Tode Jesu und die Entstehung des Herrenmahles." In *Vom Sinai zum Zion: Altestamentliche Beiträge zur biblischen Theologie.* BEvT 64. München: Chr. Kaiser.

Grundmann, W.
 1961 *Das Evangelium nach Lukas.* ThHNT 3. Berlin: Evangelische.

Hahn, F.
 1969 *The Titles of Jesus in Christology: Their History in Early Christianity.* London: Lutterworth.

Hays, R.
 1989 *Echoes of Scripture in the Letters of Paul.* New Haven: Yale University Press.

Horsley, R.
 1989 *Sociology and the Jesus Movement.* New York: Crossroad.

Houlden, J.
 1984 "The Purpose of Luke." *JSNT* 21:53-65.

Hultgren, A.
 1987 *Christ and His Benefits: Christology and Redemption in the New Testament.* Philadelphia: Fortress.

Jewett, R.
 1979 *Jesus Against the Rapture: Seven Unexpected Prophecies.* Philadelphia: Westminster.

Johnson, A.
 1958 "Hebrew Conceptions of Kingship." In *Myth, Ritual, and Kingship: Essays on the Theory and Practice of Kingship in the Ancient Near East and in Israel.* Ed. S. Hooke. Oxford: Clarendon.

Juel, D.
 1988 *Messianic Exegesis: Christological Interpretation of the Old Testament in Early Christianity.* Philadelphia: Fortress.

Karabidopoulou, I.
  1972   "To pathos tou doulou tou theou epi tou staurou kata ten diegesin tou euaggelistou Louka." *Deltion Biblikon Meleton* 1.

Karris, R.
  1986   "Luke 23:47 and the Lucan View of Jesus' Death." *JBL* 105:65-74.

Kleinknecht, H.
  1968   "πνεῦμα." *TDNT*. Vol. 6.

Kraus, H.-J.
  1978   *Psalmen*. 1. Teil, *Psalmen 1–59*. Neukirchen: Neukirchener.

Kremer, J.
  1988   *Lukasevangelium*. Die neue Echter Bibel. Wüzburg: Echter.

Kristeva, J.
  1980   *Desire in Language: A Semiotic Approach to Literature and Art*. Trans. Thomas Gora, Alice Jardine, and Leon S. Roudiez. New York: Columbia University Press.

Longenecker, R.
  1975   *Biblical Exegesis in the Apostolic Period*. Grand Rapids: Eerdmans.

Marcus, J.
  1992   *The Way of the Lord: Christological Exegesis of the Old Testament in the Gospel of Mark*. Louisville: Westminster/John Knox.

Marshall, I.
  1978   *The Gospel of Luke: A Commentary on the Greek Text*. NIGTC. Exeter: Paternoster.

Metzger, B.
  1971   *TCGNT*. London: United Bible Societies.

Minear, P.
  1964   "A Note on Luke xxii.36." *NovT* 7:128-34.

Moo, D.
  1983   *The Old Testament in the Gospel Passion Narratives*. Sheffield: Almond.

Neyrey, J.
  1980   "The Absence of Jesus' Emotions—The Lucan Redaction of Lk 22,39–46." *Bib* 61:153-71.
  1983   "Jesus' Address to the Women of Jerusalem (Lk. 23.27–31)—a Prophetic Judgement Oracle." *NTS* 29.
  1985   *The Passion According to Luke: A Redaction Study of Luke's Soteriology*. Theological Inquiries. New York: Paulist.

Nickelsburg, G.
  1962   "Enoch, Book of." *IDB*.

Nilsson, M.
  1923   "Saturnalia." *PW* 2.A.

Rengstorf, K.
1952   *Das Evangelium nach Lukas: Übersetzt und erklärt.* Göttingen: Vandenhoeck & Ruprecht.

Riffaterre, M.
1978   *Semiotics of Poetry.* Bloomington: Indiana University Press.
1983   *Text Production.* New York: Columbia University Press.

Schaberg, J.
1985   "Daniel 7, 12 and the New Testament Passion-Resurrection Predictions." *NTS* 31.

Schneider, G.
1977   *Das Evangelium nach Lukas Kapitel 11–24.* Gütersloh: Mohn.

Schweizer, E.
1968   "πνεῦμα." *TDNT.* Vol. 6.
1984   *The Good News According to Luke.* Atlanta: John Knox.

Senior, D.
1989   *The Passion of Jesus in the Gospel of Luke.* Wilmington: Glazier.

Sjöberg, E.
1968   "πνεῦμα." *TDNT.* Vol. 6.

Soards, M.
1987   "Tradition, Composition, and Theology in Jesus' Speech to the 'Daughters of Jerusalem' (Luke 23,26–32)." *Bib* 68:221-24.

Stählin, G.
1965   "κοπετός." *TDNT.* Vol.3.

Stallybrass, P.
1985   "Drunk with the Cup of Liberty: Robin Hood, the Carnivalesque, and the Rhetoric of Violence in Early Modern England." *Semiotica* 54 1/2.

Suhl, A.
1965   *Die Funktion der altestamentlichen Zitate und Anspielungen im Markus-Evangelium.* Gütersloh: Mohn.

Talbert, C.
1982   *Reading Luke: A Literary and Theological Commentary on the Third Gospel.* New York: Crossroad.

Theissen, G.
1978   *Sociology of Early Palestinian Christianity.* Philadelphia: Fortress.

Untergassmair, F.
1980   *Kreuzweg und Kreuzigung Jesu: Ein Beitrag zur lukanischen Redaktionsgeschichte und zur Frage nach der lukanischen "Kreuzestheologie."* Paderborner theologische Studien 10. Paderborn: Schöningh.

Vööbus, A.
1969   "A New Approach to the Problem of the Shorter and Longer Text in Luke." *NTS* 15:457-63.

Wendland, P.
   1899   "Jesus als Saturnalien-Koenig." *Hermes: Zeitschrift für classische Philologie* 33.

Widengren, C.
   1958   "Early Hebrew Myths and Their Interpretation." In *Myth, Ritual, and Kingship: Essays on the Theory and Practice of Kingship in the Ancient Near East and in Israel*. Ed. S. Hooke. Oxford: Clarendon.

FIGURE, KNOWLEDGE AND TRUTH: ABSENCE AND FULFILLMENT IN THE SCRIPTURES

Jean Calloud
Centre Pour L'Analyse du Discours Religieux
Université Catholique, Lyon

THE SEMIOTIC THEORY DEVELOPED by A.J. Greimas and others who make use of his work has clearly shown for some time now how the notions of "figure" and "figuration" account for a distinctive feature of certain discourses, which incorporate within their signifying mechanisms elements of a semiotic of the natural world.[1] My aim here is neither to lay out in detail this theoretical point nor to recount the debates it has generated.[2] Rather, I hope to show why and how semiotic studies of biblical texts have particularly benefitted from these theoretical developments and are now in a position to contribute by way of certain arguments to an advance in knowledge. The question of intertextuality, around which the present volume of *Semeia* is constituted, seems to me to find its clarification here.

I proceed in three stages: first, I will show what, in my view, is the primary question posed by the biblical corpus (Old and New Testaments), and why and how the figurative dimension demands the most attention. Second, I will show the interpretive perspective or reading point of view to which the privilege accorded the notion of "figure" responds and what practical use can be made of it. Finally, I will ask about the consequences of this figurative choice and the shifts that we can expect in the field of semiotic study of the Bible.

THE FIGURATIVE DIMENSION OF SCRIPTURE

By Scripture I mean, of course, the collection of texts in the Bible that we sometimes call the "biblical corpus." I have purposefully chosen the term "Scripture."[3] It directs us away somewhat from the question of "intertextuality," but the detour will prove useful. The term "Scripture" (*graphei* or *graphai*—literally, "writings") is frequently encountered in

---

[1] A.J. Greimas published the first article related to the "figure" as "Les actants, les acteurs et les figures" (1973). See also A.J. Greimas and J. Courtès, for entries on "figurative," "figurativization," "figure," and "configuration".

[2] On this question see the work of Jacques Geninasca. For works by CADIR (Centre pour l'Analyse du Discours Religieux) see the journal *Sémiotique et Bible*. In particular, see Panier; Delorme 1992, 1987 and Genuyt.

[3] The French *"écriture,"* which can mean both "scripture," and also simply "writing," functions throughout this essay in a way that neither English word can. The reader is requested, however, to keep in mind the now neglected root meaning of the English word "scripture"—i.e. "writing"—in what follows.

New Testament texts where it designates what was written prior to fulfillment and in view of this "fulfillment." It offers the advantage of focussing attention less on an object to be read (available to us as information or for purposes of confirmation), and more on the effect of an act (the act of writing), on the trace left behind or the sediment deposited in the field that we call "literature" by the activity of speaking human beings. It is on this horizon of writing, one that is opened up by the word at work in human beings, and on its widening ripples that we will focus our questions in order to locate in both its source and its functions the notions of "figure" and figurative practice.

"Figure" as Anticipation

The unity of the biblical corpus, at least as Christian readers or interpreters perceive and present it, lies in the fact of a centering or a recentering on the advent and event of Jesus. Thus, the biblical collection acquires a very particular arrangement; it organizes what precedes and follows in a concentric pattern around a unique moment. The signifying value of this pattern is incomprehensible within the categories of succession or linear development. For many centuries this phenomenon has been described as a move from "figure" to "fulfillment."

When the word "figure" appears in this context of traditional interpretation, it does not possess the precise meaning it enjoys in contemporary semiotic theory. "Figure" translates the word *typos*, for which the English equivalent "type"[4] is used and that we find again in the more frequently used term "typology." It designates more the phenomenon of "prefiguration" or anticipation than that of "figurativity." But the intersection of vocabulary has interested semioticians, and we are keen not to lose this opportunity to reflect further on this lexical content and what motivates it (Calloud, 1993).

---

[4] The term "figure," when used in the field of biblical studies, can refer to two Greek words and their different Latin equivalents: (1) *Typos* (from *tuptein*, meaning "strike"): imprint, mark, trace, image, effigy, example, model, type; often translated by *figura* (1 Cor 10:6) and more frequently by *forma* (Acts 7:43–44; Rom 5:14; Phil 3:17), or *exemplar* (Heb 8:5). (2) *Tropos* (from *trepein*, meaning "turn"): demeanor, manner, way, conduct, character, comportment; translated by *mores* (Heb 13:5), *modus* (Rom 3:2), and *locus* (2 Thes 3:16). The French term "trope," which designates "a tendency of style," a manner of self-expression, derives from this Greek word. On "typology," which examines the phenomenon of "prefiguration" in Scripture consult the articles by Paul Beauchamp and Francis Martin.

Consistency and Inconsistency of the Figure

Strictly speaking, we have a figure (in the sense of prefiguration) only to the extent to which a trace has been preserved up to the moment of fulfillment. We have here a written trace, a truly detailed picture of the past about which we could ultimately ask questions regarding the status the trace might have during this waiting period and how it maintains its signifying potential and capacity to subsist and to grow. In other words, is the fulfillment-figure mechanism not merely suspended until the future event it announces? In such a case, who manages it, or what secret knowledge is in charge of its allocation or its economy?[5] And for those persons who do not have the opportunity to live at the time of fulfillment, what knowledge do they acquire? Is it, by its very nature, articulated around what we need to understand or what is necessary in order to indicate presence and operativity? In this case the meanings of the term "figure" tend to move toward one another in order to say or to try to say something about the enigma of the human condition and the paradox of the path followed by successive generations, between knowledge of the trajectory and lack of knowledge of the future.

Forwards and Backwards: The Insistence of the Figure

It is not enough to say there is a time for the figure and a time for the fulfillment. We need to recognize in the figure a genuine mode of signification which is not content to announce what will be but which actually speaks now, in concealed terms and for the person who knows how to listen. The originality of the figure lies less in forecasting what will take place or in anticipating the future as a form of knowledge, than in signaling—as the events unfold—another scene, other stakes, a work in progress that takes us back to the public place. A going forwards and backwards, an unfolding of actions and operations distributed over time and a unique work that is never interrupted, a multitude of actors who succeed one another and the one who comes: this is what speaking and writing are all about; that which is entrusted to speech and that which, because of its complexity, demands the work of writing. In other words, the figure is necessary so that the outline of real novelty waited for as an effect of

---

[5] The term "economy" is used by ancient Christian authors in order to designate the wise apportioning of time of forms of revelation in history and in the Scriptures which precede the time of fulfillment. We frequently encounter it in the work of Ireneus, for example *Adversus Haereses*, I,10,3; II,4,1; IV,26,1. This word does not imply that there is revelation only at the time of fulfillment or that "economy" manages only delay and waiting. I suggest that the very fact of the progressivity of revelation, and therefore the passage by means of the time of the "figures," is indicative of the nature of what later on will be manifested and of its presence from the beginning.

speaking might be maintained in the changing course of the reported events or situations described, a novelty which is already audible in past narratives. In the figurative insistence we find both "the hope for things we do not as yet see" (a paraphrase of Heb 11:1; cf. 1 Cor 13:8–12) and the evidence of their actual reality.

Figure and Scripture

A necessary link thus appears to tie figure and scripture together. It is a connection that binds in a text or a unique tissue of signifying elements the discourse of knowledge about the world and its changing states with the effort to approach its center of gravity and that unknowable vanishing point which organizes the perspective. Insofar as knowledge of what happens and how on the changing surface of the world is required, language as a system knows only this domain. But the painful and burning obligation to anchor the written work beyond the veil (Heb 6:18–19), or to articulate the question that holds the successive actors in suspense is imposed upon the witness who writes. We see this in the Scriptures as a whole as in the military logistics described in Exodus 17:8–16; as Joshua and his men do battle on the plain, Moses lifts up his arms toward heaven. This is a good example of the figure articulating two scenes in a single mechanism, with an eye toward revealing in the present and a fulfillment yet to come. See also Numbers 21:4–9: poisonous snakes threaten the people, the serpent of bronze erected on a standard saves those who look upon it. So it goes with scripture, in the text of our Bible: attention to what takes place among people and attention directed elsewhere, the ear straining toward that obscure point where the truth can finally speak.

In sum, the question posed by the biblical corpus for purposes of its reading and interpretation may be formulated as follows: How do we do justice to what is deposited in this secular literature (i.e. knowledge of the world, its practices, and intrigues) without silencing an obstacle to the witness rendered to speaking humanity inscribed between its lines? What kind of reading is appropriate for this double-edged scripture (see Heb 4:12, Ps 149:6, Rev 1:16 and 19:15) that says what it knows while at the same time announcing figuratively that toward which it strains, a Scripture that knits together the threads of knowledge and of revelation?

The notion of "figure," which Christian interpretive tradition has retained in order to define its manner of reading, answers this question as far as possible. It defines the direction or the tendency on the part of this double-edged scripture to articulate knowledge and truth, to signal at precise points along its trajectory an echo, a depth, a genuine weight, which is always distinct from what is said or known but given or promised there as supplement to what is known, what is said, what is told. If biblical authors write less to say what they know than to give a chance to what speaks through their humanity, then their engagement in writing combined with this withdrawal before speech must be figured in their work. This is none other than the question of the "style" of writing, and it is in this domain of style that the notion of "figure" needs to be repositioned, along with its temporal and semiotic dimensions. Starting from this point and taking into account the diversity of authors and the extremely wide range of truth effects in the domain of knowledge, we should be able to define a new approach to "literary genre." This study remains to be pursued. In what follows, we should also see the notion of "figure" intersect with that of "theme" so often employed in the commentaries on biblical texts and in the elaboration of what we call biblical theology. For its part this intersection has theoretical and methodological value to the extent that the initial semiotic propositions offered by A.J. Greimas in the area of discursive semantics link the figurative and thematic levels, the "figurative trajectory" with the "thematic role."

Figure and Figurative Practice

The figure is an essential element of style. It is first of all a "figure of discourse" or "figure of style." It particularizes the style and marks its originality while at the same time indicates how and on what grounds each has to do with language use. Figure gives us an outline of what we altogether expect from our hardworking apprenticeship with the language in which we speak and write. It brings us in snatches, in pieces or fragments, nourishment for the body, something like a modest feast and a discrete rejoicing that is compatible with the laws that govern speaking beings. Certainly it is to our mind nothing but a compensation for abandoning Eden, whence we were excluded upon gaining access to language, but it is an effective and proper compensation. It is genuine gratification which is sufficient to assure life to the woman's descendants, from generation to generation, and one day to crush the serpent's head. Understand by this that figure and style do not designate simple ornaments of discourse or unfortunate obstacles to transparent communication, but salutary representations of what, having been lost at the start, never ceases to be given to us along the way: Hansel and Gretel's stones which mark the way back to the cottage,[6] salutary purchases by Tobit during the

---

[6] This well-known story is found in Charles Perrault (1628–1703). The process of laying down a path to follow is for him as well a figurative element present in different forms in other texts.

course of his travels in Medea with his companion and guide Raphael,[7] bread multiplied in the desert and distributed to the crowd by Jesus and his disciples (Matt 14:13-21; 15:32-38 and parallels).

These few allusions show that it is indeed possible to grasp figures in the text and what perspectives facilitate the passage from the notion of "theme" to that of "figure." But I wish to be more precise. For this reason I want to return to two stories: one taken from the Book of Genesis (4:1-16) that deals with the episode of Cain and Abel, and the other from Luke's Gospel (9:7-45) that deals with the healing of the epileptic boy.[8] I will not offer a detailed study but will content myself with trying to illustrate what I call a figurative practice.

THE BROTHER

Genesis 4:1-16 is a story that obeys the laws of narrativity in as much as it presents itself as the transformation of an initial situation into a final one. It is integrated within a larger story that spills over before and even more after this passage. The logic of transformation, which can be studied on different scales, enables us to grasp the connections and correlations and to approach the question of intertextuality in a straightforward way. My goal, however, is different: I hope to show that by approaching this text from an angle that focuses on figurativity (in all of the senses indicated above), we will better perceive the textual effects of this story, the resurgence of a source to which it first bears witness, and the resonating capacity that it carries. We need to exercise caution in two ways. The first is a matter of prudence. When dealing with a text as enigmatic as this one, we need to pay close attention to the way things are told us and not allow ourselves to be mesmerized by our customary models. The second is a matter of discernment: we must not confuse information transmitted as such with practical information, namely instructions about how to read.

A Single Begetting for Cain and Abel

Let us pay attention to the way things are said in Gen 4:1. "Adam (or man) knew his wife Eve. She conceived and gave birth to Cain, and she said `Qaniti (I have gotten) a man with the help of the Lord.' And again

---

[7] The Book of Tobit, where Raphael appears, is particularly interesting for studying the figure of the voyage, of its different stages, and what is acquired along the route. It permits us as well to ask about what links the Angel to the question of the "figure" and, indirectly, about what opposes the angel and demon.

[8] The study of this healing story would have to include the examination of all healing and resurrection stories concerning children. Cf. Jairus' daughter, the centurion's servant, the son of the widow of Nain, etc.

she gave birth to a child, his brother Abel. . . ." Translators are divided over the concern to stay as close as possible to the text and the desire to make it clearly understood that a second child is born to Adam and Eve. We immediately grasp the difficulty in resisting the natural inclination to understand and to make understandable, and in being content to register what I have called instructions about how to read, whose relevance will become apparent later on. It seems to me that there are four instructions: Abel enters the picture in the most discrete way possible, namely without any mention being made of an encounter between Adam and Eve or of the conception (which is, however, mentioned in 4:25 in connection with Seth); Abel is not named by his mother and his name is not the object of any pronouncement; he is called "brother" to Cain before he is even named; and his arrival falls under the sign of an addendum, a supplement to a birth which seems clearly to be Cain's. These are the textual details. What are we to make of them?

It is difficult to consider Abel Adam and Eve's full-fledged second child. In no way is he Cain's twin because the biblical text recognizes twin births and identifies them as such. Nor is it helpful to reduce it to some sort of physiological supplement to the birth (like the afterbirth which normally disappears) since he has a place and role as "brother." The fact that his name is interpreted as "vapor, lacking consistency, vanity" is not strong enough to support this. It remains for us to chance a figurative identification. I propose one which takes note but does not exceed the scope of all the instructions furnished by the text: with Cain's birth, the first-born to human parents, comes a supplement that the text attempts to inscribe at a specific place in the texture of the story and concerning which it stages both a processing and a becoming. Obviously, it is not a matter either of giving a definition or of resolving once and for all the whole question of the supplement's identity and function. The text is satisfied to open up a perspective, to begin marking off a line, to sketch out a path to follow. Let us recognize here the features of a figure, of the sort of face given in a provisional way to the one who must appear further on and later on. Let us give a name to this figure since the text permits it: the "brother figure," given as a supplement at every birth, including the first in a given family—the unique and yet manifold face of humanity.

I will explain this text in a more detailed study to follow.[9] But it is sufficient here to indicate the intertextual perspectives that are opened up be-

---

[9] A more complete study of Gen 4:1–16 and the figurative chains linked to one another there will appear in *Sémiotique et Bible*. I don't take up here the question of the provenance of traditions related to Cain considered as ancestors of the Kenites or Canaanites (cf. Judges 1:16 and 4:17), nor the reasons that can explain how this documentation related to Cain and his descendents was linked to Adam and Eve before the history of Seth and his descendents. I attempt a reading of the text in terms of the

fore us by the simple fact that we have not closed the figure of Abel in on itself and that we have not interpreted it as a theme—be it one of jealousy, murder, violence or victim—all of which are legitimate and useful considerations but marginal in relation to our goal.

The familial dimension of the brother figure

I have already hinted at the fact that Abel's coming as "brother" rather than as child or son (since he can never become father) inaugurated the chain of "brothers" which will be amply documented in the biblical corpus. I mention but two famous links: first of all, Joseph, concerning whom Rachel his mother pronounced his name saying, "May the Lord add [Hb. *yoseph*] to me another son" [Gen 30:24], the one whose cohabitation with his brothers proved very problematic and caused a simulacrum of murder that reminds us of the treatment Abel suffered. Second, the first four disciples chosen by Jesus in Mk 1:16–20: ". . . Simon and Andrew, the brother of Simon, were there . . . . A bit further on Jesus saw James the son of Zebedee and John his brother." I do not draw any conclusions here, since I do not possess all of the links in this initial chain, but some useful work can be done on the question of the brother approached in this way. Developments in the First Letter of John concerning the love of the brother, especially in chapter 3, which recalls explicitly the tragic episode of Cain and Abel, should also form a part of this picture.

In the same familial domain I recall two other issues tied as well to this ancient story: the question of the first-born and that of the only child. Both categories appeal each in their own way to the absent brother, which the biblical texts also treat: first-born children for whom special sacrificial rites are established; the several instances in which the evangelists mention the only child. I will say more about this. I leave open for now the question of the first-born, which would take us further afield than we wish to go at this time. Note that Abel is not a first-born, although he brings the first-born of his flock as an offering.

THE BROTHER'S BLOOD

One sentence is all that is needed to report the "murder" of Abel. As Gen 4:8 says: "And it came to pass that while they were in the fields Cain attacked Abel his brother and killed him." At the heart of the conversation which follows between the Lord and Cain is the question of the blood, the voice of the blood which cries out from the ground to the Lord. The ques-

---

place which has been attributed to him in Genesis and the echos which can be heard in the rest of the Scriptures.

tion shifts from what we customarily label the murder of Abel to his blood. This shift has two consequences: first, it diverts the direct condemnation that we expect away from Cain, a condemnation that is further on contemplated with regard to those who lay the blame on Cain himself; second, it opens up a new figurative field, namely that of the blood and the blood's crying out. This figurative appearance is surprising. The story did specify that Cain had shed his brother's blood. But it is only the first link in a very long chain whose final witness we find in the 1 John: "This is he who comes by water and the blood, Jesus Christ, not with water only but by water and blood. And the Spirit is there to bear witness, because the Spirit is the truth: Spirit, water, and blood, and these three agree" (5:6–7); in Revelation: "You are worthy to take the scroll and to break its seals, for you were slain and by your blood did purchase for God men of every tribe and language, people and nation" (5:9); in 1 Peter: "You know that it was no perishable stuff, like gold or silver, that bought your freedom from the futile ways inherited from your fathers, but with precious blood, of that of a lamb without mark or blemish" (1:18–19); and in Hebrews: "But you have come to Mount Zion and the city of the Living God . . . and to Jesus the mediator of a new covenant, and to the sprinkled blood that speaks more graciously than the blood of Abel" (12:21–24).

It would take a very lengthy treatment to present in its full details the scriptural documentation related to blood. I limit myself to a few comments. I want to make it clear that what we have here is a figurative chain and not a theme. The difference between the two matters for the comprehension of the descriptive practice that I am exposing here: the theme gathers up around a specified indicator a set of information or knowledge about a field; the figurative chain consists in the insistence upon a signifying element recognizable simply from its name, or by mention of one or another of its distinctive features; its meaning is held in suspense. Such a chain does not yield an accumulation of information or explanations; it establishes a trajectory, a course, a route. Thus, it designates through its contours and without direct conceptualization a field withdrawn from, yet essential to, knowledge. This is what we call—so as to distinguish it from all other paths of knowledge—revelation.

The blood, whose first inscription is located in this ancient story of the murder of Abel, is one of the principal figures of the Bible. It is found in both testaments where it maintains a solid footing in the enigma of life, human life understood according to Leviticus:

> For the life of the flesh is in the blood; and I have given it for you upon the altar to make atonement for your souls; if it is the blood that makes atonement, by reason of the life. Therefore, I have said to the people of Israel, No person among you shall eat blood, neither shall any stranger who sojourns among you eat blood. (17:11–12)

Could one put the transfer of blood into the order of meaning any better?

Abel's Place: Two Lines of Descent

At the end of chapter 4, Genesis reports the birth of Seth. The text opens up at this point other figurative perspectives which also merit mentioning because of their capacity to clarify the practice I describe. What is clearly at issue here is another child, the second mention of an encounter between Adam and his wife, a conception and a naming. Seth is the real second child. The name he receives records both his position and his place: "God has granted (Sheth) me another son in place of Abel, because Cain killed him" (4:25). It also implies taking into consideration another line of descent characterized precisely by this place that is left wide open. Three observations can be made in this respect: about the place occupied by Abel, the part that Cain takes, and the other descendants.

As one actor among others, Abel is present in only a limited way. He is the shepherd of a small flock, he offers the first-born from his flock, and he then disappears. Thus he leaves no descendants. The story says nothing about the place he vacates nor what will become of this space. Only the figure of the blood can signal that Abel's disappearance leaves a void which is not forgotten and marks as a reserve space a sort of enclosed place within the vastness of the earth "which opened its mouth in order to receive his blood." It is a space around which will turn the circle of men and women springing forth from the one who, born in this place, will tie together the theory of all biblical personages.

It is important to note in effect that, starting with chapter 5, Genesis is exclusively concerned with Seth's descendants, abandoning Cain's family and descendants to their fate. Cain is not only the author of Abel's disappearance—he does not bear the curse of the ground by himself; he is also the ancestor of five generations of human beings. It is small in comparison to Seth's descendants, and to Noah's, but it is adequate enough for the appearance of towns, pastoral life, music, copper-making, and fire, in a word what we call culture. Are we to understand that because of the curse spoken against Cain we should not expect Seth's descendants to be in a position to utter truthfully its discourse about the human condition and the enigma of speaking beings? But we are able to give him credit for having invented science, technology and the arts. To another descendent another side of the legacy. This cleavage within concrete humanity will be referred to in the later well-attested opposition between the just and the wicked, the righteous and the evil ones. See Wisdom 10:3, 1 John 3:12, and Hebrews 11:4. Based on these observations it is possible to go back and examine Cain's very action and to understand it less as a "murder"—because the offense characterized this way will be envisioned only after

Abel's death and for Cain's protection—than perhaps as the worst possible way of objecting to this birth supplement by settling accounts with it and carrying around its after-effects. Another study will be needed to clarify this difficult question.

I have two additional things to say about Seth's descendants. This long list of names, to which the text adds a large number of sons and daughters, unfolds throughout the whole Bible like an immense chain of generations from which emerge here and there certain famous individuals. The whole Bible thus opens up before us. Hebrews 11 offers us a good picture of this procession when it enumerates (as Sirach 44–50 also does) the principal "figures" in history, and adds to them the anonymous crowd of women and men who "wandered about dressed in skins of sheep and goats, destitute, afflicted, and ill-treated. They were too good for a world like this. They were refugees in the deserts and on the hills, hiding in caves and holes in the ground" (11:37–38). This way of introducing the multitude of Seth's descendants (also to be distinguished from the "world") into history and on to a signifying trajectory, draws our attention to the question that they bear and to the line that they constitute. As they are "destitute, afflicted, and ill-treated," we see that their mode of being and style is like that of Abel's, that their wandering about unaware of their fate delimits the contours of this very place and safeguards it as a sanctuary for humanity for the benefit of all.

On these figurative grounds, we also need to take up again the question of the division of descendants. We ought to add the question posed by several specific personages whose existential status was more problematic and more visibly enigmatic: first, Melchizedek (Gen 14, Psalm 110, Hebrews), Isaac, Joseph . . . and the one who is called "high priest according to the order of Melchizedek." They would likely confirm the figurative nature of this line.

Before moving on to another story we must not conclude this partial description of a story without restating its nature and direction. Two factors are worth mentioning in this respect. First, it is a deliberately modest description which neither intends nor pretends to say what the meaning of the text is or to speak directly about the signified of the text, but rather to pinpoint the figurative formations which open up or prolong a chain, which invite and encourage us to follow a certain trajectory. Second, it is a description that is attentive in two senses of the term: on the one hand it demands attention to the way things are said, in detail and as precisely as possible; and on the other it puts on hold what comes later on, so as to reinitiate the movement, to specify the trajectory, to delineate the movement until some prudent hypothesis emerges that permits us to memorize the whole, to recognize a trace, in short, and under the best of circumstances, to risk an interpretation.

The Sick Child: Jesus Heals an Epileptic boy

At quite some remove from the text recounting Cain's birth is a healing story selected from Luke's Gospel (9:37–45). This text captured my attention because of its figurative nature. The little I will have to say about the story will show how, rightly or wrongly, one approaches a text in a "semiotic spirit" and therefore reacts to intertextuality. Three narrative details place themselves in the extension of the figurative chains I mentioned. They provide confirmation of a tentative trace and show here that they meet the minimum requirement for becoming the object of a more careful investigation: the child is an only child (μονογενής), at least in Luke's narrative;[10] before entering the house, Jesus denounces the unbelieving and perverse generation about him; and after the healing Jesus announces that "the Son of Man is going to be betrayed into human hands" (NRSV).

It is not hard to see in the first detail a variant on the status of the child in relation to the question of the brother. The figure brought to mind here is linked to the absence of the brother and, in Mark's text, which omits this detail, to the childhood proximate to birth. "How long has he been like this?" Jesus asks. "From childhood," the father replies to this question of generation. Matthew, Mark and Luke address Jesus' question to this "generation". We have enough in the way of meaningful elements here to examine the case of this poor boy: something appears not to have been given to him at birth, more precisely with birth. The absence of this mysterious supplement does not prevent him from living, even from growing up among people. But he does not truly have his place; he knows neither rest nor peaceful situation; he does not seem to be left with speech. Alive to be sure, he is also "half dead." However, this is not a lack that he suffers but an excessive presence, a demon (an unclean spirit according to Luke, a deaf and dumb spirit according to Mark, simply a demon in Matthew). We are to suppose that the flaw in this supplement not granted at birth frees up space for an occupant, one who occupies places from which he must be expelled, not in order to replace it with another occupant but to keep it empty and to safeguard the interior space where hu-

---

[10] In Matthew's narrative (17:14–21) the sick boy is brought forward by his father, about whom he is simply called "the son" (μου τὸν υἱόν). In Mark's narrative (9:14–29) the sick boy is also brought forward by the father who speaks of his son (τὸν υἱόν μου) and who specifies that he was ill from infancy (ἐκ παιδιόθεν). It is in Luke's text that the father adds: τὸν υἱόν μου, ὅτι μονογενής μοί ἐστιν. The same text speaks of "the child" (τὸν παῖδα) at the moment of the healing.

man beings breathe. It is not difficult to see here that this kind of supplement is not just one among other things, a positive addition, but a portion, a participation, a division which means both deliverance and binding. It is right for the father to ask for his son's sake. As for the disciples to whom the father's request is first directed, perhaps they have not quite fasted or prayed enough to be prepared to make the distinction between a lack that should be filled and the powerlessness of lacking.

Does Jesus perceive how far the disciples whom he has chosen as disciples have yet to come? Does he realize the obstacles lined up in opposition to the act of human birth? Both perhaps. In any event, in a straightforward way he defines the ground on which the question is raised, in which the powerlessness of lacking manifests itself and the healing must intervene. The harshness of his words directed to the unclean spirit (9:82) indicates the determined nature of Jesus' actions; it is the authority of the judge to hand down a sentence without the possibility of appeal. The fact that the child remains as if he were half dead in the Markan story confirms for us that death is present in the break which takes place between the power that possesses the child and the child, even though death must be postponed so that the one who just crossed over the threshold of death and anguish might live.

It would be good for me to say much more about the way the "sick child" belongs to the figurative chain of Cain and Abel's birth. I will recall from the end of the story only its continuation in the form of Jesus' announcement of his own passion, the second announcement that remains obscure to his disciples, and which we must connect with the transfiguration episode that precedes the healing of the child. We are given to understand, and the disciples are clearly invited to get it through their thick heads, both that the one, as man, who bears and guarantees the title "son" must suffer; and that the one whom humanity will reject is indeed the son himself, who is betrayed so that they might be human beings, so that they might play a part in the one humanity about which they know nothing and which remains obscure to them. Should we be surprised that the disciples "did not understand this saying . . ." and also that "they were afraid to ask him about it"? Do we not find ourselves at the heart of the figurative question?

Conclusion

This presentation of the figurative practice, which is too lengthy and perhaps unsatisfactory, has had two goals. First of all, to give an idea in the most precise detail possible of the layout of the figures, the constitution of the figurative chains, and the working out of interpretive hypotheses; and, second, to allow us to compare this way of proceeding and its results with narrative analysis such as has been proposed for some time now by greimassian methodology. It is to this second point I want to add some further remarks.

By defining narrativity as a system of operations performed on the content, more precisely as a sequence of transformations operating on situations or states, semiotics claims to have the means to follow narrative trajectories on different scales, in both micro- and macro-narratives. The basic elements of the descriptive models—narrative statements, subjects, objects, conjunctions and disjunctions—are recurrent and permit us to describe narrative formations that are quite diverse and varying in length. The proof is to be found in the necessity and descriptive efficacy of these models repeatedly honed down over the past years. I am not unaware of its usefulness. Nevertheless, I note a danger or a drift which seems to me to offer more consistency and more drawbacks in the study of biblical texts due to their age, their complexity and our present-day reading habits.

Concretely, this problem has to do with the necessity we very quickly face within the framework of narrative analysis of having to specify the objects, subjects, and all the polarities as well as axiological distributions which order them. We are easily rushed into evaluating the opposing forces, "camps," stakes. This hastiness is accentuated if we work within the very constraining framework of the generative trajectory, which establishes the narrative level on the basis of the oppositional elementary structure. I know the care semioticians take in establishing the constitutive values of objects, in order to distribute subjects into their valorized fields. But biblical texts also obey a logic of expectation, difference, and suspense about meaning itself, which we run the risk of erasing if we decide prematurely and in an irreversible way about the axiology, and, therefore, the meaning.

The proposal I am making here shifts the descriptive center of gravity,[11] and by inviting a careful observation of the figurative details and their organization enables us to progress and to establish useful correlations before drawing conclusions about the overall narrative goals, as well as about the sets of values which are the crystallization of signifieds. I think that I have also shown that figurative units, which are formed in chains, are endowed with capacities of syntagmatic structure that govern

---

[11] In the framework of the greimassian "generative trajectory" the center of gravity is reported rather in the direction of the "narrative structure" and the "elementary structure of signification." In our presentation the "discursive structure" and its figurative level are the principal place for the constitution and recognition of the signification.

the narrative organization rather than are governed by it. It seems that there is an order to follow in the descriptive steps and telescoping them is not without its consequence.

These methodological reasons speak, therefore, in favor of a re-evaluation of the figure and the figurative dimension of texts. There is perhaps little risk if the interests of biblical semioticians are rapidly oriented in this direction. But we have now to ask ourselves other questions, and perhaps to try to formulate additional questions for the future. It is this point I wish to take up in the last part of this study.

Semiotic Perspectives

Interest in the figurative dimension of biblical texts has made possible the proposition to very different groups of a reading directly inspired by figurative practice. We have had enough experience to offer an initial assessment and to contemplate new developments. I will begin with a brief reflection on the path we have covered. Then I will try to make it clear toward what horizons of knowledge and understanding of biblical texts we are headed. Finally, by way of conclusion, I'll return to the question of intertextuality.

Lessons Learned in Recent Years

The fact of placing the figurative dimension at the center of semiotic practice and the collective reading of texts has had an impact—one that appears confirmed—on the way we take up or begin the description. Not that the doubts, perplexities, and confusions that were with us from the start have disappeared, nor that the possible guiding marks in the narrative field are henceforth disregarded, but the effect of actually opening up the semiotic work on a given text is felt the moment participants agree on a detail, an obscure point, an enigma, an index of retreat from the obvious sense, an obstacle to easy reading and to the simple repetition of accepted meanings. Origen has said:

> But if in every detail of this outer covering, that is, the actual history, the sequence of the law had been preserved and its order maintained, we should have understood the scriptures in an unbroken course and should certainly not have believed that there was anything else buried within them beyond what was indicated at a first glance. Consequently the divine wisdom has arranged for certain stumbling-blocks and interruptions of the historical sense to be found therein, by inserting in the midst a number of impossibilities and incongruities, in order that the very interruption of the narrative might as it were present a barrier to the reader and lead him to refuse to proceed along the pathway of the ordinary meaning; and so, by shutting us out and debarring us from that, might recall us to the beginning of another way, and might

> thereby bring us, through the entrance of a narrow footpath, to a higher and loftier road and lay open the immense breadth of the divine wisdom.
>
> Origen, *On First Principles* (Trans. G.W. Butterworth) IV, 2, 9.

Thus engaged on figurative terrain, the manner of speaking, and the style (in the semiotic sense of these terms), the description takes off rapidly in another direction, one that is more concrete, more attentive to the novelty of signification, more amply displayed. We could say that it becomes the entry point to intertextual play since the signifying traits which appear at one point are encountered elsewhere, sometimes at a great distance, and in various configurations, but which are nevertheless recognizable and whose comparison proves extremely enlightening.

The fact of establishing the reading and the description of texts on this figurative terrain has produced this other effect of making the reading of Scripture possible and fruitful for a large number of readers who are more familiar with other literatures or trained in the study of other signifying objects. This broadening of groups coincided with the discovery, or rediscovery, of the human (we could label them "anthropological") interest in Scripture. It is good to see men and women today find relevance in the books of Genesis and Exodus, the oracles of Isaiah, Hosea, Ezekiel, the Gospels, Paul's letters, and Revelation without any feeling that they are outmoded or ill-suited. This is so because the signifying elements such as the figures, even if forgotten or no longer used, are sheltered from the ravages of time and are ever-capable of returning to life. Ezekiel had a vision of this: "Son of Man, can these bones live again?" (Ezek 37:3). What comes close to touching the truth does not suffer the ravages of time.

Toward What Knowledge?

The future will disclose the fecundity of the Scriptures and the kind of reading pleasures toward which we are heading. I am not proposing here a pragmatic program to put us to work. Rather, I question myself and cock my ears in order to hear "what the Spirit says to the Churches"(Rev 2:7, and parallels) for the sole purpose of being less resistant to life and of having the desire and patience to work in the right place. Here is where I find myself today: in relation to the issue of figurativity, I am questioned in three respects—regarding texts, human beings, and biblical revelation. Let me explain.

With respect to texts, I ask myself if the change in perspective enabled by the reading and practice of semiotic description can be exclusively and definitively maintained within the methodological field. The notion of "figure," as I have proposed it here, overflows the framework of discursive semantics properly speaking, where A.J. Greimas first located it.[12] No longer merely a kind of packaging of "thematic" content, and thereby more conceptualized, the figure is now seen as a genuine signifying element of the first order, one that does not simply refer us back to signifying elements of the same sort in a chain. As such, the figure privileges at one point what we have called, ever since F. de Saussure, the signifier, which proves difficult to restrict to the side-effects of change to the signified, the idea, the thought, and thus to the way of contemplating the Scriptures and their reception. We will need perhaps to take note of the fact that once admitted into the field of textual reading, figure and figurativity impose a new vision upon the biblical corpus, one that allows it to be seen as more unified and less dependent on a display of the time of composition, formation, and institution.

By nature both semiotic and theological,[13] this unity is grasped as a continuous thread. We caught a glimpse of this unity in the several figurative chains described above. This unity is a seamless tunic which resists partition and dividing up. It is certainly only one side of the scriptural movement which is nothing less than the product of long centuries of living, of thinking, and of writing, but is also the side of truth and universality, the side opposite that of knowledge and diversity. This cleavage of texts between what we call utterance and enunciation in the strict sense of the term is well-known. It is a matter that must further occupy biblical semioticians.

Beyond the fact that it will be increasingly important to adopt a much larger scale of textual description (the scale of figurative chains, say, as opposed to pericopes or individual sequences), it seems right to envision the theoretical and methodological mechanism adequate to avoid simply returning to a thematic study or to history-of-ideas models. It is urgent, indeed, that semiotics be recognized for its rigor, according to its own models (for models do exist for studying the pattern of figurative chains) and for the explicit and therefore debatable character of its propositions. We are working on both here.

With respect to human beings it is not without interest to note that the movement of figurative chains woven throughout the texts, both biblical and non-biblical, passes over as well into our lives as living and speaking beings. The frequenting of Scripture, when carried out with the requisite

---

[12] We see this in the studies noted n.1 above. "Grasped within the global generative trajectory, the figurative level of discourse appears as an instance characterized by new investments—of installations of figures of content—added on top of the abstract level." See "Figure" in Greimas and Courtès.

[13] The unity of the biblical corpus is semiotic from the point of view of figurative theory because of the capacity of figures to form chains. This unity is theological from the point of view of the inspiration of Scripture, namely the uniqueness of the Author.

seriousness, will intersect in each person with that which slumbers in oblivion for four days or more and awakens the dead for judgment and the great battles of life.[14] But that is not ordained and not proven anywhere except in practice, in the body and in the heart of each one of us. The outcome is positive for human beings, because it is about the person that the Scriptures are spoken, about the person's path through life, the person's place in humanity alongside everyone else. At the same time it is the Glory of God which manifests itself. Are we dealing here with theology, anthropology, the divine sphere, or the earth? Perhaps we are dealing with the celestial Jerusalem that descends from heaven where God dwells among human beings.

I come now to biblical revelation. I have used the term "revelation" purposefully in order to avoid a drift in the interpretation of scripture which sees in this body of texts whose history has demonstrated a progressive formulation over time, a kind of witness to progress in religious thought, although it does not present it as the overdrawn expression of a "message" to receive and to transmit. I prefer to speak of "revelation" as the light which ultimately bears upon the "Glory of God" in its divine and human sides. As Ireneus declared: "The Glory of God is living man; the life of man is the vision of God".[15] John also says this in the Prologue to the Gospel: "And the Word became flesh, and dwelt among us and we have seen his glory . . . ." (1:14).

The figurative perspective avoids this drift because the figure is arranged only in relation to another figure and gradually into a chain of figures whose outline shapes or delimits the figure but without defining it: the burning bush which burns without being consumed, the place where the revelatory word comes. That which is known about the world, things, beings, different situations and events, indeed everything that we can know, comprehend, and understand is reappropriated and reconstituted around this inaccessible center, put back into confrontation with the truth of the face of the other that is governed by the figures. Consequently, we should not expect some kind of perfect or self-sufficient end-product, be it a thought, an idea, a piece of information, a "message" from the passing of time and from the aggregating of texts to other texts. From the point of view of the theological tradition, the corpus is closed; not for

---

[14] In addition to John 11 (story of the death and resurrection of Lazarus), we read the discourse of Jesus after the healing of the paralytic by the pool at Bethsaida in John 5, in particular verses 19–30. Refer as well to Rev 19 and 20.

[15] Ireneus, *Against Heresies* IV, 20, 7. The complete sentence reads as follows: "For the glory of God is living man, and the life of man is the vision of God: if indeed the revelation of God by creation procures life for all beings who live on the earth, how much more will the manifestion of the Father by the Word procure life for those see God."

reasons of cognitive perfection in content or expression but on the basis of time, the fulfillment of time. The one who has come, borne by these figures and called forth by the pattern of the figurative chain, is come. Word become flesh. He attests in himself to the connection between figure, body, glory, and fulfillment. We will no longer go back to what heretofore preceded the figure, that is to what precedes the judgment of the Word.[16]

Conclusion

I return by way of conclusion to the question of intertextuality. I have treated intertextuality here from an atypical point of view in that it is not the point of view of "discourse" and its cultural, ideological or sociological ties, but the point of view of that which in discourse presents itself as complementary or supplementary enunciation. I mean this original component of every use of language, be it oral or written, and therefore of every speech act which, besides the fact that it enunciates objectively, ever-signifies the way in which the subject is self-involved in the act of speaking and ever-expresses the link between the fact of enunciating and the filiation with speaking humanity. Because of the particular work that it demands, Scripture accentuates this reserved portion and leaves it more open for the voice of Abel's blood to cry out. This holds true for literature as well as for the Scriptures. It is the figures and the figurative chains which lend signifying support to this voice and which are organized from text to text as a genuine intertextual phenomenon. This is what I have attempted to speak about.

Attention to this side of discourse does not simplify semiotic practice, especially when it is applied to biblical texts. It challenges all assimilation of the reception of Scriptures to a fact of "communication" and all reduction of the Bible to the expression of a "message." It invites and incites us to elaborate a theory and a methodology which can take responsibility for

---

[16] The question of the figure is linked in two ways to the judgment considered as a speech act: on the one hand, it is by such an act that we are prohibited from returning to a prior phase of language and therefore to a setting in motion of the figurative chain; on the other, it is in this "figurative" trajectory that we have some chance of finding our life and of intersecting with the truth by an act of giving that appears as a judgment. The first act has the value of death; the second is the experience of life. The irreversibility of judgment is original. It is ever recalled and confirmed throughout time. Closure of the Scriptural corpus, to the extent it constitutes them in a "body," signals the primacy of the punctiliar over the durative, from the moment when the speaking body is constituted over the duration and the variations of its history. In Acts 17 we read Paul's discourse to the Athenians, in particular vv. 30-31: "While God has overlooked the times of human ignorance, now he commands all people everywhere to repent, because he has fixed a day on which he will have the world judged in righteousness, by a man whom he has appointed, and of this he has given assurance to all by raising him from the dead."

this original dimension, one that has less to do with discursivity and interdiscursivity than with subjectivitiy and intersubjectivity. The two dimensions are not found one without the other, but we must be careful not to confuse them. They come together but are not complementaries. Like Cain and Abel, brothers and inseparable friends, they make their way by opposing and mutually serving each other. So that living humanity might also be speaking humanity.

-Translated by Gary A. Phillips
and Nicole Wilkinson

WORKS CITED

Beauchamp, Paul
    1992   *La Maison-Dieu* 190/2.

Calloud, Jean
    1993   "Le texte à lire." Pp. 31–63 in *Le temps de la lecture: Recueil d'hommages pour Jean Delorme*. Paris: Cerf.

Delorme, Jean
    1992   "Sémiotique." Pp. 281–333 in *Dictionnaire de la Bible. Supplément*. Ed. L. Pirot, A. Robert, Jacques Brend and Edouard Cothenet. Vol 12. Paris: Letouzey & Ané.
    1987   *Parole, figure et parabole*. Collectif. Lyon: Les presses d'Université Lyon.

Geninasca, Jacques
    1985   "L'identité intra- et intertextuelle des grandeurs figuratives." Pp. 203–214 in *Essays in Honor of A.J. Greimas*. Ed. Vol. 1. Leiden: John Benjamins Publishing Company.
    1985   "Place du Figuratif." *Le Bulletin du Groupe de Recherches sémio-linguistiques* 20:5–15.
    1986   "Sémiotique." Pp. 48–64 in *Introduction aux études littéraires, méthodes du texte*. Ed. Maurice Delcroix and Fernand Hallyn. Paris-Gembloux: Duculot.
    1987   "Pour une sémiotique littéraire." Pp. xx in *Actes Sémiotiques. Documents*. 9/83.
    1991   "Du texte au discours littéraire et à son sujet." Pp. xx in *Littérarité*. Ed. Louise Milot and Fernand Roy. St. Foy: Les presses de l'Université Laval.
    1990   "Le discours en perspective." *Nouveaux Actes Sémiotiques*. 19/11.

Genuyt, F. and J. Calloud
    1982   *La première èpître de Pierre: Analyse sémiotique*. Paris: Cerf.

Greimas, A.J.
    1973   *Sémiotique narrative et textuelle*. Paris: Larousse.

Greimas, A.J. and J. Courtès, ed.
    1982   *Semiotics and Language. An Analytical Dictionary*. Trans. Larry Crist, Daniel Patte, et al. Bloomington: Indiana University Press.

Martin, Françis
    1988   "Parole, Ecriture, Accomplissement dan l'évangile de Matthieu." *Sémiotique et Bible* 50:51–54.

Panier, Louis
    1993   "Le statut discursif des figures." *Sémiotique et Bible* 70:13–23.

Pierre, Jacques
    1993   "Le croire et la bordure inquiète du savoir." Pp. 97–122 in *Le temps de la lecture. Recueil d'hommages pour Jean Delorme*. Paris: Cerf.

IMAGININGS AT THE END OF AN ERA: LETTERS AS FICTIONS

William G. Doty
The University of Alabama/Tuscaloosa

ABSTRACT

At the end of a period dominated by historical-critical reconstructions, we may hope that Wallace Stevens's characteristic of the imagination—"that it is always at the end of an era"—is correct. Revising some goals of the critical imagination, primitive Christian letters are explored as constructs, "fictions," in the same literary frame as Samuel Richardson's *Clarissa*, P. A. Choderlos de Laclos's *Les Liaisons Dangereuses*, and John Barth's *Letters*. Insights from literary criticism of the epistolary novel tradition raise questions about the literary dynamics of early-Christian letters as well as about biblical criticism.

Paul's explicit references to writing letters are explored for his intertextual awareness, and for what he names as epistolary subjects. The recurring references to recommendation (*sustatikē*), his comparison of his personal apostolic presence (*parousia*) to the written Paul, and his metaphoric flight in 2 Corinthians help us comprehend him within the traditions of *fiction*.

It is one of the peculiarities of the imagination that it is always at the end of an era. (Stevens: 22)[1]

[Plato] has installed his name by holding a discourse on installation (question of letters again, of correspondence and of epistole, of stele and of epistole, the Greek lexicon is marvelous in this area: *epistello*, I send, is also "I mandate, order, arrest"—a decision, an order but the idea of arrest or of installation, the *stellen* if you will, the idea of pause or of post, of halt, works upon the entire family; what I prefer: *epistolen luein*, to open a letter, *to unbind* the strings of a letter, even before alleging to analyze. One did not unglue, one did not cut, one did not tear. (Derrida: 165)

---

[1] The thought continues in a vein I will be following only obliquely: "What happens is that it is always attaching itself to a new reality, and adhering to it. It is not that there is a new imagination but that there is a new reality." Wolfgang Iser (1993) engages the history of philosophical arguments for the role of the imagination within the cognitive process. His 1989 book anticipates some of the topoi that are focal in the later volume; both expand reader response criticism helpfully.

Introduction: A Paradigm Shift in Biblical Literary Criticism

In his letter soliciting an earlier version of this paper as part of the celebration of the centenary of the Society of Biblical Literature in 1980, Dan Via suggested that "some scholars" consider that thanks to contemporary linguistic and literary-critical approaches to the Jewish-Christian Bible, "a linguistic paradigm is replacing a historical one in Biblical studies."[2] I agree insofar as those scholars refer to historical and sociological reconstructions spun out from scantily-detailed literary evidence. We have had our fill of form-critical reconstructions that attempted to reconstruct the sociological and economic milieus for periods in which hard data is almost entirely second-hand or lacking—Phil Mullins (39) reminds us that we lack any reference to Christianity in Roman sources until about eighty years after its founding.

We are no less irritated today when analysts ignore literary aspects, or move directly to theology-building without consideration of changes in basic worldview over the twenty-some centuries since the documents first appeared. The analysis likewise rankles that proceeds without considering again the now well-established intertextual aspects according to which Paul's few citations of non-Jewish/Christian writings must count for a great deal in indicating his own level of learning, and hence his probable competence in cross-cultural intertextual referencing. Fortunately, the earlier derivative-rabbinic viewpoint represented by pointers to "Paul's use of Scripture" has become passé, Richard Hays's more instructive search (1989) for scriptural recollections, allusions, or "echoes" having replaced such assumptions of primary and secondary texts, the latter "using" the former. Hays's book is a good indication of attention to the poetics of the texts as part of the biblical scholar's hermeneutical propaedeutic, beginning as it does with an excellent section on intertextuality (14–21). Alert to dangers of misprision, Hays recognizes the need to remain attentive to the historical parameters of epistolary texts (26) while still recognizing that Paul, rather than practicing line-by-line decoding of the Bible, "allows Scripture to echo into the text of his letters in such a way that the echoes suggest patterns of meaning wider than his own

---

[2] The vagaries of unemployment left me unable to attend the celebration, or to complete the essay, which is now taken up again thanks to editors Aichele and Phillips. Some sadness as I find the earlier text typed on the back of the catalogue of books I sold to live on until I was offered my present employment, but also a sense of how brief our tenure on the planet, how easily we overvalue what we have produced/owned, even a sense of the relative miracle that so much of the Pauline and other primitive Christian materials survived, out of what must have been such a mass of rich and tumultuous dialogues. Compare Derrida (6 n.1): "You are right, doubtless we are several, and I am not as alone as I sometimes say I am when the complaint escapes from me, or when I still put everything into seducing you."

overt interpretive claims. Paul's own discourse recapitulates the allusive complexity of his great subtext" (155).

Or "of all the great subjects," perhaps, as the more imaginative authorial leapfrogging that the Argentine writer Jorge Luis Borges thrusts us into in imagining a *universal* literacy/library. Such an activity was practiced by Robert W. Funk, the founding editor of this journal, in *Jesus as Precursor* (1975), when he opened up the Jesus stories by means of the Kafka stories, while nudging the Parable of the Leaven up alongside Henry Miller, John Fowles, and Carlos Casteneda. "Jesus as precursor" to such figures *interprets* differently: no longer as a figure transcendentally originary but now as a link in a chain of eminent fictions whose endless networks of signifying quickly situate meanings beyond the official religious pales. Already Funk saw the importance of moving biblical criticism beyond theology, declaring that otherwise "the immediate prospects" of the discipline "are grim indeed...One appears to be left with the choice . . . of retiring to the monastic ghetto and perpetuating, in cloistered precincts, the now archaic tongue of the Christianized age, or of abandoning the tradition altogether in favor of a secular surrogate" (151).

If the era of theology and historical reconstruction is apparently past, we may hope that Stevens is correct and that a renaissance of critical imaginings is at hand. Indeed new insights from literary critical approaches to biblical materials already have become *de rigeur* in ways I never would have anticipated, given the resistance in biblical studies to such work just a few decades ago.[3] Certainly Jacques Derrida's *The Post Card* (1987) demands an opening up of the religious-epistolary traditions, precisely through his repeated recountings of epistolary terms in the book, but as well by his erasing of the boundaries between types of writing—between, in particular, "writing" writing (fiction, imaginative literature) and philosophical writing (expository prose). I hope here to point

---

[3] I remember one journal repeatedly asking me to review works from literary-critical perspectives, because "no one else in the country could do it"—now, thank heavens, no longer the case at all. Likewise one hopes that writers and literary critics are presently more aware of generic histories and trajectories than was represented in the instance cited by Altman (10): Robert Randall, the author of *The Fan*, a mystery novel consisting of letters, declared in a television interview that he thought he had invented the epistolary novel!

Much of the movement beyond the fiction vs. reality dichotomy, and as well as much of the reliance upon the imaginary, that follows here, are sustained now by Iser's (1993) arguments. Cf. MacArthur (118) on letters as fictional constructions: "Letter writers do not merely reproduce the sentiments they feel and the events they observe; they transform them, whether consciously or unconsciously, into written texts whose organization, style, vocabulary, and point of view generate particular meanings." Letters are more metonymic than metaphoric (272), their position on the borderlines between implied reality and implied fiction being one of the reasons why the reader is reduced to or compelled to interpolate the position of onlooker.

to the non-theological resources of literary criticism on the epistolary novel.

In particular I want to encourage poetic or imaginative approaches in a period labeled poststructuralist or postmodernist, and then to ask about the sorts of questions we might set as our goals as we utilize them. It ought not be necessary to defend the use of the critical imagination in the present context. Even in dictionary definitions of "imagination," negative, pejorative implications of "unreality" and "falsehood" now enter as secondary nuances, while the base meanings remain those of setting out images, picturing to oneself, representing or fashioning something. The stem (*imāgo, imāgin-em*) is apparently, although obscurely, from the same root as *im-itārī*, to imitate. My initial point is simple: in addition to considering literary materials as standing within particular historical trajectories and genre histories, we may broaden our perception of them by considering them as fictions, as creations made, fashioned, or fabricated (*fictio*, from *facere*, to construct) by their writers to convey the existential or religious meanings they drew from their own life-contexts. In this instance I look at such factual fictions as they project forward into a type of writing I find repeatedly to be of important comparative interest for the earlier Christian materials, namely the epistolary novel—a genre that Derrida curiously but perhaps correctly pairs with the detective novel![4]

Primitive Christian and Contemporary Fictional-Factual Epistles

The primitive Christian epistles are fictions in a somewhat different manner than are, say, John Barth's novel, *Letters* (1979), or Pierre Ambroise Choderlos de Laclos's *Les Liaisons Dangereuses* (1782), or Samuel Richardson's *Clarissa* (1747–48). Barth's very title page bears an anagram that indicates some of the themes of fiction and reality that will be engaged here:

---

[4] Iser's incisive survey (1993) of the philosophical status of fiction and the imaginal supports my use of the fictive/factual/imaginal here. According to his definition, the fictive is "an operational mode of consciousness that makes inroads into existing versions of world" (xiv). It is *not* the unreal or nonreal, but a mode of perception best discerned when we look not abstractly at what fiction *is* but at what specific fictions *do* (6), hence avoiding the authorial intention dead end as well as exposing just how fictions work to bridge the known and the imagined, the present and the to-be that arise as boundary factors whenever fictions are called into play. Iser (146) cites Hans Vaihinger's reference to fictions as "expedient patterns of the imagination," and recognizes their semantic instability as the basis for their fertile intertextuality: "The text itself becomes a kind of junction where other texts, norms, and values meet and work upon each other; as a point of intersection, its core is virtual, and only when actualized by the potential recipient does it explode into its plurivocity" (227).

A	NOLD	TIMEE	PISTO	LARY	NO V	E L
B	Y	S	E	V	E N	F I
C	T	I	T	I	O U	S
D	RO	L	L	S&	DRE	A M
E	R	S	E	A	C H	O
F	W	H	I	C	H I	M A
GINE	SHIM	S	E	LFAC	T U	A L

(that is, "an oldtime epistolary novel by seven fictitious drolls and dreamers, each of which imagines himself actual"); similar wordplays extend to the table of contents and each part-title throughout the book, in what might be a literary analogue to the recent text-paintings of artist Mark Tansey. But instead of saying that these later novelists (and I've listed only three of the many epistolary novelists now thoroughly canvassed in the critical literature[5]) were "fictional" or "imaginative," and the primitive Christian writings were not, we may profitably point to the widespread acceptance and use of the primitive Christian letters by religious communities, primarily as informal materials outside the imperial realms of formal literary expression as such, as what distinguishes them.

I want neither to reopen the *Hoch-/Kleinliteratur* distinctions of early twentieth-century German biblical criticism, nor to argue that Paul's letters belonged exclusively to either classification (discussed in the work of Adolf Deissmann and others in Doty, 1969), but rather to recognize the

---

[5] Among the twentieth century novels named by Kauffman (1992: xxv) that are epistolary in style, or heavily indebted to conventions of the epistolary novels are: Manuel Puig's *Heartbreak Tango*, Lee Smith's *Fair and Tender Ladies*, John Updike's *S.*, Saul Bellow's *Herzog*, D. M. Thomas's *The White Hotel*, Kathy Acker's *Great Expectations*, Julian Barnes's *A History of the World in 10 ½ Chapters*, A. S. Byatt's *Possession*, and Michael Dorris and Louise Erdrich's *The Crown of Columbus*. With respect to the critical literature, some of the essential book-length publications include Altman; Gillis; Kauffman (1986 and 1992); MacArthur; and Perry. Although now over a decade old, the bibliography of primary works and of criticism in Altman (217–27) is still very helpful.

That there is much to be gained from an inter- or retrotextual design is evident from the lively intensity, even the diction of analysis, in these works. Merely listing some of the chapter titles or subheads must suffice to encourage further reading: alien discourse; disjointed letters, long farewells; historical background and theoretical coordinates; generic reaccentuation and innovation; "Masculine Writing/Feminine Speech: Atwood's Epistolary Antecedents" [in *The Handmaid's Tale*]; the dynamics of epistolary closure; the parameters and paradoxes of epistolarity; reading letters as narrative; harmony and conflict in the epistolary exchange; the social contexts of letters; modeling the epistolary relationship. My orientation is toward exploring the "filiation about which everything remains to be thought" (Derrida: 263); our most promising agendas entail not how expressive/imaginative molds are transgressed/broken, but how they orient us toward interconnections, holistic intertextualizations we would otherwise ignore.

consequences of such distinctions. What the sociology of knowledge calls "tacit knowledge," the way a culture seems instinctively to treat differing literary materials, changes over time. The recently established New Historicism (or Cultural Poetics) represents changes in such tacit knowledge insofar as new research paradigms bring into focus certain social forms and informal artifacts that were ignored even at the middle of the century, yet now comprise appropriate subjects of literary study. Formerly excluded issues such as racism, sexism, and ideology, are analyzed now, and close readings are devoted to less formal types of literary productions (for an overview, see Montrose).

To be sure, there were Hellenistic guidelines and handbooks for learning how to write letters, but even when Cicero establishes the first "personal" correspondence as a mode of literature—roughly coincident with the primitive Christian period—and the rhetorical schools continued to teach imitation of the Platonic and other epistles, the informal, non-imperial expression found in religious letters was hardly "literature" on the order of the works produced by state poets or chronologists or philosopher-moralists. A New Historical view might attend more adequately to the primitive Christian epistles in their cultural contexts, raising important questions about economies, hierarchies, and gender relationships.

But what if we look at another analogy, a later type of literature? Paul's self-referencing "fictions" are, on the face of it, similar to those of the American novelist John Barth: both writers re-view, re-instate earlier writings, and both refer self-consciously to the process of writing in epistolary form. The early epistolary novelists gave birth to ongoing literary traditions, just as Paul's Christian adaptations of the epistle, in ways that reflected both Greco-Roman correspondence and Jewish religious-interpretive elements, gave rise to literally hundreds of clones and apocryphal transformations. Both writers—if we were to consider all of Paul's writings as a literary whole—provide additions to earlier thoughts and situations (Barth integrates correspondents from several of his earlier novels, echoing the convention established in the eighteenth-century epistolary novel according to which epistolary characters make references to characters in *other* epistolary novels). Both Paul and John Barth refer repeatedly to events outside the fictions and/or representations of contemporary events, developing different perspectives upon them, and granting them more or less validity and importance in different segments. In Paul's case there is more or less adherence to what was originally written, in contrast to the epigones of the Pauline Schools and the conservative correctors who sought to provide what Paul "really ought to have said," alongside what he may well have written originally (although in the canonical perspective all such materials blur together so that I have had many students insist that not only Titus but also Hebrews *must* be Pauline).

What do we gain by recalling Paul and Barth and Choderlos de Laclos in the same instance? Such an exercise may help us recognize the arbitrariness of Paul's diction, the fact that his choices from the available linguistic traditions were doubtless as arbitrary as Barth's, if indeed for what many of my readers would consider a more serious purpose, because a religious one. But what if Paul sought out the genre of the epistolary novel for his purposes, if it already existed, as apparently the pastoral novel genre did?[6] For one thing, he probably would have developed the psychological aspects of his characters and plots in ways that most modern literature finds necessary. An intertextualist approach instructs us in what to expect, and what not to, at various moments in a generic trajectory. Likewise a comprehensive hermeneutics will identify various modes of interpretation and decide which of them are most appropriate to a particular text. J. G. Altman's six types of "distinct generic approaches to epistolary literature" (192) seem to me to mix analytical categories, but they provide a convenient listing of relevant treatments:

1. The *expressive* approach focuses upon the mental attitudes that underlie the author's choice of the letter form.

2. The *pragmatic* approach charts the letter's effect on the reader.

3. The *semantic* studies thematic constants in letter fiction.

4. The *structural* or *syntactic* considers national, historical, or sociological variables affecting the origin, development, and decline of the genre.

5. The *subgeneric* identifies subdivisions of the genre, using the same approaches that are applicable to study of the genre as a whole (compare, in biblical studies, form and redaction criticism).

The list represents a sample; whatever approach/es is/are taken to be most useful in any given case, the critic ought to recall them all and allow them to influence the primary treatment. In the end the method ought to become transparent, as it opens the texts to new dialogues with readers.

---

[6] It must be doubted that Paul or his compatriots would have paid much attention to the literature of Roman high society, nor does there seem to be *any* cross referencing to Ovid's almost-contemporary *Heroides* (Ovid fl. 43 BCE-17 CE), which established the genre of the amorous epistolary novel. The amorous/erotic/friendship issues will be addressed below.

EROTIC INCLUSIONS AND EXCLUSIONS

Hence one imagined model might focus upon the psychological development of Paul and of his characters and plots. Few writers, except for Richard Rubenstein in *My Brother Paul* (1972), have dared such a re-imagining-reconceiving-contemporanizing, especially in psychoanalytical terms. Yet classicists are not afraid to develop psychological readings of Homer or Ovid, and psychohistorians now argue for this or that interpretive position within the pages of their own journal and press. Earlier neither Albert Schweitzer nor Arthur Darby Nock shied away from discussing Paul's inner development and self-understanding (themes central to the later epistolary novels, although usually their authors added erotic episodes that would have made the canonical Paul blush). Nor were the existentialist interpreters reticent on the subject, although their *Selbstverständnis* automatically assumed a more abstract, philosophical tone. I suspect there is something important to be learned from the many popular psychologizings and fictionalizations of New Testament figures in the middle years of this century—such as Lloyd Douglas's *The Robe* or Morris West's *The Shoes of the Fisherman*. There must have been (or must be) a readership whose interests were simply not met by the "What happened when and where?" of traditional biblical criticism.[7]

In the epistolary novel the stage is swept bare except for the two primary correspondents, who often can pursue their love only by bucking social convention (or they wish they *could* do so). But if the epistolary genre *develops* into such personalistic, interiorizing fashions as become evident in European salon literature, why not earlier? Even in different emotional registers, do we not have here an insight into the famous question about the extent to which Paul is a religious mystic? I am not urging the scholar of primitive Christianity to become an epistolary novelist. But I am noting that the time may be ripe for a more moderate psychohistorical account of Paul and other primitive Christian figures than would have

---

[7] Traditionally, biblical criticism has rarely recognized the socioeconomic and historical differences between Episcopalian/Presbyterian and BIOLA/Moody Bible Institute adherents, and never explained why the latter turned their fundamentalist perspectives resolutely against German biblical criticism in the period between the Wars, hence against academic biblical criticism *tout court*. We learn from *Criticism and Culture* by Robert Con Davis and Robert Schleifer that the self-critical component of Enlightenment rationality is still resisted heartily even where logos is the official motto of intellectual inquiry. No wonder "the dead hand of the past" label is so readily attached to religious inquiry, although "the truth shall make you free" is claimed to be suprapositional. As a result of Romanticism and the growth of technology, Western society lost much of its imperative for communal identity and cooperation, largely because of the emphasis upon the artistic and entrepreneurial individual (57); the subsequent Modernist emphasis upon the classics was an (often quite authoritarian) attempt to re-energize the values of the commonweal, and not just the individual.

been possible earlier in schools of psychological-biblical thought. Furthermore, recognitions of the political and material contexts of interpretation, including institutional motivations toward self-preservation, dare not be overlooked.

In particular I am struck by the suppression of so much of human experience in the name of religious criticism, a point repeatedly made in David Freedberg's massive and revisionist *The Power of Images* (1989). Centuries of art criticism have ignored the physiological responses of the human body to art works—attraction, repulsion, etc.—as being somehow inferior to the logical, abstract, "elevated" contents of words/theory/doctrine. Rather, argues Freedberg, we must examine the whole continuum of responses to affective images, and not draw artificial high- vs. low-culture barriers that exclude most of those that a particular period considered inferior or subsidiary. The application of Freedberg's point in this context is to the body's attraction within epistolary fiction: we are drawn by it into the sense of seeing inside a relationship, of overhearing a dialogue between A and B that is likewise a message to the onlooking C. It is a curious characteristic of epistolary literature that it makes aesthetic distance seem to disappear (as Kauffman notes, 1986:45), so that a projected three-cornered relationship becomes a model of *presence* although it is founded on *absence*. It becomes a model of union or satisfaction of desire although it is based upon separation and hiatus (Carson: 91–92; cf. Altman: 135, 140), and it usually models triumph over or submission to an entrapping social (familial or erotic) situation.

Why are we always so impressed with what individuals accomplish as they shatter expectations—à la the modern Capitalist/Social-Darwinian model of progress—as opposed to recognition that doing the familiar *better* is as importantly creative a gesture as bringing about the as-yet unvoiced? Intertextual dimensions point toward the future to which texts give rise; hence the earlier importance of imitating the masters in rhetorical schools, so that one would learn to anticipate the most favorable future (see Melanchthon's *Introduction to Rhetoric*, quoted in Roberts and Good: 50). But literary devices also point backward, as they reprocess, perhaps more elegantly, the received wisdom of the past within the conventions and worldview of the present. Finding the great chains of literary relatedness ought to be more important than discovering just who "invented" which genre or who copied whom, the usual obsessions of literary-historical pedants.[8]

---

[8] I am following what Craige (53) discusses within the context of *holistic thinkers*, those who in particular look beyond the usual definitions of important "literature." "Interest in authorial originality has yielded to interest in the text as the intersection of ideas, ideas of which the text's writer is never fully aware, since the writer's con-

Within the history of religious epistolary literature, the erotic/connective aspects were shunted aside very early on, or they got sidetracked. Instead of looking at the communicative-dialogic aspects of Paul and his correspondents, the tradition came to focus upon Paul and his opponents, and scholars plumbed for information about early Christians hardly mentioned in the texts. More recently scholars have adopted Heikki Koskenniemi's emphasis (1956) upon letters in antiquity being primarily designed *to cultivate friendship*. Of course they did that,[9] but by such an emphasis we miss both the immense significance of the (almost erotic) *immediacy* in which Paul experienced the Spirit, and the similar social immediacy he idealized as *koinōnia*. The epistolary novel tradition reminds us that the letter entails such close communication at the I-You level that, at its most "epistolary," it would be so intensely dialogic that a third party might discern its subject matter only with difficulty (cf. Altman: 120). The same tradition reminds us of the importance of *readers* (Altman): 88: "In no other genre do readers figure so prominently within the world of the narrative and in the generation of the text"). As I have argued for some time (cf. Doty, 1973), ideally the completion of an epistolary gesture is a response, co-responding in one's own context, rather than repeating the terms of the initial letter.

Hence with respect to epistolary exchanges, I am interested in an image encountered in Marcel Detienne's *The Gardens of Adonis*, and in other works by Detienne, Jean-Pierre Vernant, and others within the post-Lévi-Straussian developments of French mythography and classics. The image is that of a cross-referenced matrix or series of *inter-connecting symbol systems*. Vernant's introduction to Detienne's *Gardens* makes explicit how a new comparative hermeneutical method ought to be developed. It would evoke comparisons among the elements of the symbol systems of a single culture, within the range of what has traditionally been considered the "ideological" dimension of cultural expression (today most concisely

---

sciousness is also constructed by social forces." "With the concept of *intertextuality*, the flow of ideas through texts, cultural holists abandon the atomistic consideration of works in favor of analysis, through a variety of texts, of the discursive system. *Literature* gives way, as the object of study, to *culture*, and cultural understanding replaces literary knowledge as the discipline's primary purpose."

Recent arguments treat the instability of texts, their dependence for meaning upon *contexts*. They are similar to Derrida's argument that every "trace" is the trace of a trace, and "any theory . . . another text in an unstable network of texts in which every text bears the traces of all the others" (citing Bennington's summaries in Bennington and Derrida: 90-92). It would be intriguing to pursue this in more detail with respect to Paul's own intertextualizations of rabbinical materials and Tanakh, as well as his citations of Hellenistic philosophical writers.

[9] Letters developing the relationship between correspondents did so either as part of *banausos philotēs*/banal intercourse, or as an attribute of *eleutheras paideias koinōnia*/liberal education, as Plato's seventh epistle indicates (VII.334b).

identified by Michel Foucault's concept of *the discourse* of an era; see now *Semeia* 59 [1992], *Ideological Criticism of Biblical Texts*). To some extent I would want to expand that with the older cross-cultural comparative-symbolic approach, but my point here is that we have few besides Rudolph Bultmann's mappings of Paul's anthropological symbol system/s, as opposed to the many volumes on "Pauline theology." Perhaps the lack of clarity in that respect will be developed by analysis of the "mythological" level in analytics derived from narratological criticism, but the Christian animus against the mythological (the fictive?) retards metaphoric, anti-literalistic readings that might warrant a Nietzschean revisioning across biblical studies. Hence my concern for the imaginative, and ultimately here for the conjunction between the fictions of a European literary genre and the primitive Christian epistles.

Perhaps such an approach must be developed more extensively before we can turn to the relationships of Paul's fictions to those of other contemporary mythic structures, something that Dan Via assays in *Kerygma and Comedy*, and in which Burton Mack engages with respect to Mark. Such construction/fiction on the parts of the critics is necessary before we can make the most of another important analytical model, namely relating primitive Christian thought to the social matrices in which it is sited.[10] That in turn means comprehending both the formal constraints within the surrounding linguistic constructs (how something might be expressed), and the ways in which a theme might be developed *in dialogic interactions*—which is precisely how I understand Paul to have developed most of the contents of his letters.

Here the work of Mikhail Bakhtin is relevant, of course. Bakhtin hardly dared to speak out in Stalinist Russia, yet evangelistically abhorred the monological and monothetic as he exposited the crucial dialogicity of Western classics. Almost as sad, in terms of missed lines of interpretation, is proto-Marxist Walter Benjamin, who notes how seldom translation succeeds if it does not respect the intertextual spacings between referents of the original and the secondary culture. But just those spacings, a problem of distance, are already in the texts, and Benjamin merely points us to what we ought to have focused upon, rather than the reconstruction of something like a seamless Letter to the Philippians (with its putative four major letter fragments, tree of them now rewoven around the fourth).

Note the repeated use of ellipsis points and spacings in Derrida's *Post Card*, and the epistles whose sentences begin with lower case letters

---

[10] I first drafted this before the turn in the 1980s to the socio-political contexts, as explored for instance by Bruce Malina and Wayne Meeks; I discuss the contextual with respect to mythological materials in Doty, 1994.

(especially across pp. 164–70); or those, such as two letters dated 8 July 1979 (202), that consist entirely of sentence fragments:

> during all the time that I spent cutting out these
> two little flowers for you.
> follow the line of my drawing, my life line, my
> line of conduct.
>
> from the same drawing I answer your question, for
> not just anyone who wants to does so: not just any one
> buggers Socrates.

Do they not remind one of the gaps, interruptions, and fragments in the Pauline corpus? Honestly confronting the partial, fragmented texts, we would not look for a consistent Pauline theological corpus, but appreciate even more his contextualism, his refusal to affirm a single gospelizing or to recognize only one of the charismata. Likewise with respect to the post-Paulinist revanchists, there is Derrida's very conceit of the postcard on which Plato dictates to Socrates—so that Derrida posits palimpsest upon palimpsest, even while he is parodying epistolary literature—and hence the problematic of communication raised by Plato's monotonous privileging of the oral over the written.

The elliptical quality of letters is part of their openness toward many possible horizons. Altman (155) notes that: "Whenever we find ourselves wondering what the letter writer would have communicated in his next letter or asking why there is no response to the final letter, we are testifying to a particular potential for continuation implicit in any letter sequence." How hard we strain to figure out whether Clement's remarks about the Corinthian Christian households represents yet another stage of development after Paul! And how useful it is to extrapolate the *next* letter that might have followed receipt of Philemon: was John Knox correct years ago when he suggested that the Onesimus of the letter was the later bishop who both organized one of the first collections of Paul's letters, and insisted on the inclusion of just that letter that had brokered his freedom? Philemon is an unusual letter in the Pauline corpus because of its *particular, individualistic* topic, and we are hard pressed otherwise to see how it might have been considered a letter of the entire Christian community worthy of being preserved for all posterity.

Where these gaps in information take me in particular is to my hoarded shoeboxes of postcards from around the world, some reaching back into the last century: who would dare to connect such isolated fragments? Yet the religious translator-transmitter satisfies the psychological need for closure and fills the gaps repeatedly; look at the rounding off of the church epistles with liturgical elements, claims of authentic Pauline signatures, and the like. As usual Derrida cuts to the chase; *Post Card's en-*

vois are prefaced by a writing that ends (6): "in order to make peace within you [?] I am signing [these *envois*] here in my proper name, Jacques Derrida." A footnote continues the double-entendres: "I regret that you do not very much trust my signature, on the pretext that we may be several"—hardly the reason Paul's signatures were distrusted (there was as yet no tradition of "signing" one's "proper name" to documents), yet the sort of revisionary overlayering of a tradition that we meet in the multiple strands of tradition "signed" by Jesus, Kafka, Borges, Miller, Fowles, and Casteneda. Whose is the "proper" name, The Author/ity? Where are the limits to what might be added and altered in epistolary transmission?

In order to comprehend such issues we need to know more than we do yet about the importance of oral discourse and rhetorics in the Hellenistic period, and their relationships to literary expression. Knowledge about rhetoric in antiquity and about the development of other discourses, among them synagogal, has to be purchased for the tool kit of anyone who intends *to connect* the original-originary with the contemporary—the third element in the classical hermeneutical triad of exegesis (the textual origins), interpretation (how it meant then), and application (how one might apply it in a later context).[11] As contemporary feminist writers have noticed repeatedly, gendered aspects of genres are always to be accounted for (see especially Gerhart; she concludes: "the reader oblivious to gender and genre as framing the text will be framed in one way or another" (226) by that very ignorance). What does it mean in the history of the epistolary novel that Europeans conceived of women as the gender most comfortable with letter-writing (Perry: 68)? Or did that tradition develop as a backlash against the medieval masculinization of Christianity, so that by the Renaissance the woman epistolographer complements the adoration of Mary that forced traditional masculinisms aside before the realities of folk religion?

What seems most astonishing in the context of interpretive moves is the monovision by which the performative plane of Philemon (for example—apparently dictated at an intensity at the level of "Oh my! Here's how to resolve *that* issue quickly") is conflated with those of Galatians and Romans, with their careful rhetorical, legal, and hermeneutical polish. Anyone teaching primitive Christian studies will be aware how strongly Christian students reject suggestions that the Pauline letters incorporate and reflect cultic materials such as benedictions, "epistolary" conclusions, fragments from baptismal liturgies, and so forth: Paul's letters *must* have been originary materials, not reflective, just as Jesus has been regarded even within scholarship primarily as one who *breaks* with his mother re-

---

[11] The responsa literature, after all, is one of the closest parallels we have to the early Christian episcopal letters, and these letters are still issued by chief rabbis.

ligion, rather than augmenting and repristinating Judaism. Perhaps a key hermeneutical litmus test would be to examine not only what have been considered *insertions* and *alterations* to founding documents, but also why the Romantic focus upon outstanding individual artistic and religious leaders (referred to earlier) had such determinative influence upon all following Western religion and poetics. Glancing at something like the long-term literary trajectories of epistolary literature may be but one effective way in which to begin exorcising the selfish narcissistic attitudes that have become a matter of tacit knowledge, to the point where the question of *the communal* and the values of the *common*wealth have become a major topic in conferences and journals. Fantastic, that: just what classical Christianity and previously Judaism emphasized—call it theocracy or not—has returned as a key issue of postmodernist reflection. No longer the individual but the communal becomes problematic for a culture whose roots were nurtured initially by ideals of the *commonwealth*.

Self-Referencing Intertextuality

Returning to the self-referential aspect of epistolary communications mentioned above, I am struck in several of the classics among epistolary novels by the self-consciousness with which their authors refer to their works *as* epistolary novels, although one might say as easily "refer to themselves"—it is intriguing how certain literary genres convey an *agentive* atmosphere, as if they were writing and not merely being written. Hence "today genre replaces authorial motivation [intention] as a key to understanding text" (Gerhart: 3, referring to the *Lettres Portugaises*).[12]

Already Choderlos de Laclos self-consciously stresses the epistolary genre tradition within his putative "Publisher's Note" and "Editor's Preface," and in the literary instance wherein Madame de Tourvel takes only two books from a small library: a volume of *Christian Thoughts* and Richardson's *Clarissa*. Within the span of the NT canon, of course, we already have the sense that the earliest model has become *scripturally generic*: 2 Peter 16 equates Paul's letters, "in which there are some things hard to understand," with "the rest of the Scriptures," and Paul refers to his own earlier letters on several occasions. Above I indicated Derrida's consistent self-reference to the problematic of epistolary conventions,[13]

---

[12] *Lettres Portugaises* was published anonymously in 1669, author's gender unknown, but was supposedly written in French by Mariana Alcoforado and only translated by Gabriel-Joseph de Lavergne de Guilleragues.

[13] *The Post Card* might stand alongside Ronell as imbricating openings for a study of contemporary communicative praxis reflecting: the enormous changes wrought by electronic means of communication, already now, and as we are phased willy nilly into the next millennium. How odd that science fiction projections remain so unre-

and I want to explore here some aspects of Paul's letters, considered as "fictions," in terms of his self-awareness of themes of these letters, and of the epistolary tradition and conventions.

Paul could not have been aware of the future importance of his letters as a collection, or as anything other than eschaton-temporizing patches upon what he would have idealized as the whole cloth of rabbinic Judaism. But at the same time the Pauline letters are more than merely private messages. In fact they are addressed to religious communities, and they even refer—if Colossians is Pauline—to the reading of a particular letter in a particular Colossian neo-Jewish religious household (church) and then subsequently at Laodicea (Col 4:16). In 1 Thess 5:27 Paul commands that his letter be "read to all the brethren," a convention already known from the pseudonymous letters of Plato: "Let this letter be read, if possible, by all three of you gathered together, otherwise by twos, and as often as you can in common" (VI.323d).

As I have argued previously (1973:25–27, 42, 44), the self-consciousness of Paul as a post-Jewish apostle from and for the Christian communities means that we can never quite compare his letters to other "private" letters of whatever tradition. But certainly there is also a great awareness among Richardson, Choderlos de Laclos, and Barth that their novels are addressed not just to individuals, but to communities, even if more literally (fictively?) *fictional* communities. The literary convention demands that each letter within the epistolary novel context must *appear to be* a private letter, or written at most to a household, or enclosed in a letter to a third party before being sent on to the actual addressee. Such mechanics of transmission echo Romantic/Gothic conventions of secrecy and privacy. Just these conventions are what bourgeoisies claim as differentiating themselves from the previous generations; hence, another hermeneutical touchstone: What does the society consider private, what public? At which points do generations consider that their own cultural productions replace earlier norms? Or does the epistolary novel tradition finish with Barth's *Letters* or Alice Walker's *The Color Purple*?

Paul's References to His Own Letter-Writing

What does Paul write about? What does he mention as topics and situations he has written about? If we follow his references to *writing*, almost all of our information will come from the Corinthian correspondence (which will be treated here just as it stands, without attempting to

---

garded as the millennial transition approaches; does the fact that science fiction outsells all other genres today count *against* its imaginative projections as a form of anticipatory knowing?

distinguish between the four or more letter-fragments usually identified, or determining the sequence of their composition). A few other Pauline letters also contain references of this sort.

(1) Paul writes in order to admonish as a father would (1 Cor 4:14), so that he prohibits associating with immoral persons (5:9, 11). Letters testamentary do no less, and hence they become ancillary/intertextual references that we cannot ignore. What the rhetorical schools taught, under the ongoing influence of Cicero, was precisely that speaking or writing is not a neutral enterprise, but that "speech was a God-given faculty to be cultivated and used for the public good, in defense of justice and liberty, against evil and oppression." Indeed a bit later Petrarch would equate rhetoric with ethics (Roberts and Good: 30–31). Paul's own self-consciousness of the power of language (especially in the "word of the world" vs. "word of the cross" opposition, 1 Cor 1–2) is buttressed by such pre-Christian (Cicero) and Christian (Petrarch) intertexts.

(2) Paul writes to avoid pain when he will come in person later. That "painful letter" (2 Cor 2:3–4) initially caused him many tears, although it demonstrated his love for the Corinthians. Letters apparently bridge between immediacy and eschatologically-tinged presences—*parousias*, a term we must heed carefully when regarding Paul, for whom the *epistolē* is only an awkward stand-in for his personal *parousia*—just as one might question Jesus' own relationships to the prospects of having his own ("second") *parousia*/presence or coming. What does it mean, with respect to genre, that *letters carry substitutionary valences*? How can the written word replicate the living presence, whether of normative primitive Christian figures such as Paul or Jesus or of later ecclesial authorities and modes of institutional operation? If the deconstruction of "presence" may be said to have transpired with respect to philosophical-theological claims, how are any religious-scriptural presences now more or less valid than any other?[14]

(3) Paul's letters explore the extent to which a community is obedient to him and to his Kyrios: "I wrote for this reason: to test you and know whether you are obedient in everything" (2 Cor 2:9). In 2 Thess 3:14 the community is put on notice to watch carefully anyone who refuses to obey what is contained in that letter. And it is Paul's "confidence in [Philemon's] obedience" that is the basis of his writing to that Colossian

---

[14] What really happened when the vernacular guitar-strummed Mass replaced the Latin chant? On the other hand, watching the Holy Father blessing couples in Mexico in September 1992, his beaming visage wracked with exhaustion and illness the moment they turned their backs, I saw a televisual "presence" we usually theorize only when discussing the stage presence of presidential candidates. The voice-over chanted the praises of an authoritarian hierarchy that saves "us" from postmodernist relativism.

slave-master (v. 21). Tests, texts, weavings; cross-references to previous times and possible future courses of (liberating) action: *intertexts create history*. They name the ways in which history sorts out those series of meanings through which societies narrate community, selfhood, the eschaton. Hence Galatians finds one of its post-texts in Martin Luther King, Jr.'s "Letter from a Birmingham Jail" (as I conclude in Doty, 1993).

(4) After apparent second thoughts about the severity of his "painful letter," and the sorrow that it caused, Paul subsequently came to feel no regret, because that letter had led to repentance and earnestness. It led to self-vindication, zeal, avenging of wrong, and the proving of innocence (2 Cor 7:8–12). Repentance of this sort leads to change. How else dare one write (after experiencing the sheer presence of an archaic statue of Apollon), as Rilke writes: "*Du mußt dein Leben ändern*/You have to change your life?" The religio-textual weavings of life *hold/ seam/quilt-together* (*religio*, from *religare*);[15] they provide yogas of interpretation by which one religionist codes reality differently from the ways another might. Letters seem both the pieces of the textual quilts and the process of quilting itself, a performative dimension that does not insist so much that one use the old designs and fabrics yet again, but that one learn how to stitch together the bits and pieces of one's own decentered existences in the multiplex theatres of contemporary selfhood and community.

(5) Paul does not intend to frighten the Corinthians by the authority he has from the Lord (2 Cor 10:9), although in 13:10 he indicates that by using severity *in his letter*, he will not have to exercise it *in person*. What is the significance of the fact that letters are primarily *substitutionary*? To what extent ought contemporary interpretation/application of primitive Christian epistles develop the structuralist insight that erases historical particularities?—universal/archetypal situations *subsume* the merely local/historical as humankind begins to understand that its various instantiations remain (archetypally) unique-yet-common. To be sure, Paul's self-consciousness is restricted to his own Hellenistic historicity, yet religious interpreters relentlessly have related "Paul" to their own contemporary ethical sites. At the edge of a whole new e-mail/postcard mentality, interpreters of these epistolary materials now can but question their uniqueness, and their originary qualities—With what "canonical" or universal elements might a range of contemporaries agree? Postmodernist thought begins where old line liberals ended: the relativists of global intertextualism may chant old Lutheran tunes, but their texts are those of Jean Baudrillard and Keith Haring, their visuals not so much stained-glass

---

[15] Following the usual Indo-European etymology, as in the *American Heritage Dictionary*, 3rd edition, 1992, rather than recent suggestions of different Latin roots.

chapel windows as acres of muscled flesh, trim and oh-so-affectless—related, in some bodily dimension, to Paul's athletic metaphors?

(6) Paul writes "nothing other than what you [Corinthians] can read and also understand," 2 Cor 1:13—a passage in which this "understanding" becomes both an occasion for Paul's pride in the Corinthians and a sign of eschatological communion (and of Christian tradition—intertexts secure and solidify the pattern of significations of the discourse, thereby establishing community). Doubtless Paul knew within his own life span that what he had developed as a post-Jesuanic Christianity might indeed replace his earlier fixation upon the Judaism(s) of his fathers. Ever aware of the tension between the weaker/stronger community members, he finds the flex of epistolary dialogue just right as the praxis in which the new world-orientation might be voiced. How we'd love to have his correspondents' views more clearly in sight—what if among them there were many just as dedicated, as religiously insightful as Paul? We do know from his disputativeness that there were many as stubborn as he! Were there also those who treated fragments of his letters like magical papyri—or kissed and stroked them as stand-ins for the writer, as correspondents do in old time epistolary novels (Perry: 101–02)?

(7) Paul *does not* write in order to secure the salary that he could rightfully demand for his church work (1 Cor 9:15). What is the price of a text? A covering for one's spiritual nakedness? What does it mean when tradition is for sale?—as in an ethnography,[16] or a history-of-theology monograph? Who profits from the epistolary exchange, and when? Why is that an awkward question for religionists to face?

(8) Paul writes in connection with the offering to the saints in Jerusalem (whatever its purpose as a *semeion*/sign of the end of time, proof positive of his own brand of Christianity, etc.). In 1 Cor 16:3 he notes that he will accept letters of accreditation for those whom the Corinthians are sending with their contributions. He would find it "superfluous" to write to the Corinthians about this matter—perhaps implying that he *has* had to write to other churches about it. At any rate *control* is the issue here, as in who determines which intertexts get included in the canon. Roberts and Good (55–56) show the care with which the commonplace books whose use dominated the longest segment of Western history were constructed. "It was precisely [a particular poet's] arrangement of intertextual references [in a typical commonplace book, to which he is now adding his own

---

[16] I treat (1990) some of the new dimensions of ethnographic dialogue, with its concomitant problems of not mis-/leading the informant by one's own projections or payments. In a postliterate society there are no singular-canonical texts; what remains is to teach how to determine one or another version that stitches together meanings not trancendent but sufficient unto the fully multicultural day.

work] which enabled him to dominate them and speak with his own voice" (see Castelli, 1991a with regard to the Corinthian situation). The first Bibles without apocrypha came about because commercial publishers realized that they would be cheaper to sell—no theological rationale, merely mercantile. On the other hand Marcion's Bible, for *religious* reasons, omitted most of the Tanakh as pre-, hence non- or anti-, Christian.

How much of the Pauline discourse *presumes* what Martin Heidegger called *dictionary-language*, as the common canonical religious language of post-Jewish Christianity? *Kainē ktisis*/new creation, or no, it would be fascinating to determine the extent to which Paul saw himself breaking with what he considered normative religion within the range of Hellenistic Judaisms. Was Paul's "mysticism" a sort of twentieth-century maverick individualism?—I cannot see how it could have been, given his strict Judaeo-Hellenistic upbringing, his pride at having been a Pharisee. Yet he saw ways of renewing from within that have inspired subsequent generations of Paulinists, whether Christian, Marxist, or Freudian, and/or Jesuanic: that remains the eternal question, but I don't see how Paul could have interpreted Jesus as being conservative, rather than as a partisan in Paul's own liberalizing reform Judaism. His letters are the source of major language recentering; could he have known just how much of the New Creation diction he was determining? Or, alas, how quickly his epigones would tamp down his religious revisions in the name of institutional and indeed canonical stability?

(9) In referring to the letter-writing process, "Paul" attests to his own authenticity: "In what I am writing to you, before God, I do not lie" (Gal 1:20, marked in some translations by parentheses). Nor does it bother him to write on the same subject repeatedly (Phil 3:1 — the content that follows has to do with avoiding the ultraconservative Judaizers). The thematic repetitiveness of many epistolary novels extrapolates this Jakobsonian element to almost unbearable extents, but then the element of danger in transmission never abates: for Paul, the problem of finding a sympathetic traveler; for the romantic heroine, that of locating a loose brick in the wall behind which her maid could secret the *billets doux*. It would be instructive to assemble a sort of *Pauline Parallels* (cf. Francis and Sampley) in which formula elements in the epistolary novels were charted; once again the need for a fully intertextual generic study is evident.

(10) Already in 2 Thessalonians (within Paul's lifetime if it is genuinely Pauline, which I doubt), persons were writing, falsely, in his name (2 Thess 2:2), a practice that will be sanctioned canonically, later, by the Pseudo-Pauline or "Pastoral" Letters. But to ask about the relative "reality" of epistles, to challenge their mimetic fidelity, misses the literary point: "Letters are as much fictional constructions as they are transparent

reflections. Letter writers do not merely reproduce the sentiments they feel and the events they observe; they transform them, whether consciously or unconsciously, into written texts whose organization, style, vocabulary, and point of view generate particular meanings" (MacArthur: 118; on *mimesis* in Paul generally, see Castelli, 1991b).

One (fictional) guarantee that the letters are Pauline is the indication that he tacks on a few lines of greeting in his own handwriting (2 Thess 3:17; 2 Cor 7:12; 1 Cor 16:21; Gal 6:11; Col 4:18)—but do *they* really guarantee authenticity? The Hellenistic world did not share our fetish for chirographic autographs. These references are just what I would expect persons "running scared" before the presence of letters supposedly written in Paul's name to have inserted. Pseudonymous letters (written by persons other than the person named as author) are certainly not rare in Hellenistic antiquity![17]

(11) Two additional themes appear in Paul's own references to letter writing: the recurrent theme of the *epistolē sustatikē*/the formal letter of recommendation, known from many examples other than Paul's, and the apostolic *parousia*/visit issue, in which Paul's letters are contrasted negatively to his personal presence with the epistolary addressees. Most likely the two themes are not disconnected in Paul's mind, since the discussion of the "living letter" or the "letter of Christ" that is what, metaphorically, the Corinthian believers are (contrasted to the merely external, formal written epistolary recommendation) soon turns to a discussion of the other connotation that "writing" must bring into the picture of primitive Christian-Jewish discourse, namely that of the written Law, to which Paul now compares, theologically, that of the unwritten and immediately-present Spirit. (How familiar was he, one wonders, with the Platonic distrust and disparagement of writing mentioned earlier?)

Such a comparison is not far from Paul's remarks about his personal, in contrast to his epistolary, presence. The theme surfaces in 2 Cor 10, in the context of Paul's defense of his apostolic authority and the curious equating of his own personal success with success attributed to the agency of the Kyrios working through him ("*our* gospel"). With respect to his own personal presence, certain numbskulls (who? where?) have remarked that "his letters are weighty and strong, but his bodily presence is weak, and his speech contemptible." Paul responds to such a complaint that "what we say by letter when absent, we will also do when present" (2 Cor 10:11); and in 2 Thess 2:15 Paul admonishes the Thessalonians to

---

[17] As mentioned before, Derrida engages this topic repeatedly in *The Post Card*, and as usual, obliquely; the author/authority issue has been a constant theme in his many writings.

maintain the sacred traditions he has taught them "either by word of mouth or by our letter."

Inescapably determined today by learned analyses of the oral-versus-written dichotomy, we might ignore prematurely their occasional equivalence. Must "a text" be written?—if so, Paul Ricoeur and Clifford Geertz would have to fold up their khaki-hermeneutic tents! *Euangelizesthai* meant, one assumes, spoken/written persuasive activity with words. The issue is not the medium but the message. Just what mid-century structuralists proposed—deep structural paradigms (agentive, like genres, as I guessed earlier), want to be expressed—dare we avert the *desire* of the word itself? And they want to do more than merely replicate the same: certainly Paul is impatient that he has *to write* to his addressees, or to rely upon second-hand information from his associates or from gossip (that theme reappears in the Johannine letters: "Although I have much to write to you, I would rather not use paper and ink; instead I hope to come to you and talk with you face to face, so that our joy may be complete," 2 John 12).

The breakthrough points where the same is transcended occur at the entrances of creative newness: How is this night the same yet *unlike* any other, not only in 0000 BCE but in 0000 CE? The intertext provides the essential frame/substrate, but the specific instantiation of any particular interpretation depends upon breaking the mold that it must nonetheless sustain (at least partly) if it is to remain comprehensible. A completely new ritual is a non sequitur. Intertexts are not "the same"/they are the same/they create the fundaments upon which new re-voicings appear. No individual, not even Friedrich Nietzsche, is privileged to engender autonomously her/his own solipsistic self (see my argument about social ritualization in Doty, 1992). Hence without the generational discourse nothing old/new can be uttered. With it, one's place is recognized as a legitimate starting-point, a benchmark, a launching platform.

Many Greco-Roman references to letter-writing name the *frustration* of the epistolary situation, maintaining the original connections created by shared beliefs, friendship, family, etc. Does that not translate into the *longing* of the later epistolary novels, the sense of possible but not probable fulfillment? In literary terms we are talking not about a genre featuring closure, the fulfillment of a relic impulse, but "a series of present moments of letter writing . . . and the future is yet to be decided"; it is a matter of "interminable desire" or "nonclosural dynamics" (MacArthur: 3, 26, 271). What would the eschatological epistolary moment look like?—Is it any wonder that apocalyptic language returns repeatedly to the dialogic choirs, the symphonic *correspondence* of the saints?

Agentive/Dialogic Letters Building Community

All this is well and good given a healthy epistolarity that retains something of the popularity it had earlier.[18] But what about contemporary suggestions that the postmodern era entails a whole new ballpark? For example, Theodor Adorno's claim that "in the age of the disintegration of experience human beings are no longer subjectively disposed to letter writing. For the present it looks as though technology is eliminating the preconditions for the letter. Because letters are no longer necessary, given the speedier possibilities of communication and the shrinking of spatio-temporal distances, their inherent substance is disintegrating as well" (235, quoted in, Craig: 10). Similarly Linda Kauffman has observed that Derrida's *The Post Card* "sets a death sentence for epistolarity." And yet, Kauffman continues, it "reinscribes all the traits that have marked" the postal epoch; *The Post Card* "is composed of sentences that delay its execution, thus demonstrating that it is both paradigm and exception to the rule (law). Like set theory, which is folded into Derrida's theory of genre, epistolarity is a destabilized and destabilizing concept" (1992:90).

Both paradigm and exception: the question of intertextuality strikes me as the important reactive response to the isolative individualism of our (post-Reagan/Bush/Thatcher) context: it is a political praxis disallowing the rigid customary exclusions (women, persons of color, gays and lesbians, et al.) Asserting the exception, the open-ended futurity of epistolarity, it nonetheless reinscribes *some* elements of the paradigmatic; what does eschatological language look like?—Small wonder that the Apocalypse to John enfolds *heavenly* letters!

Some respite from the historical-formalist approach named at the outset is found in looking beyond the formal contours of the epistle—beyond the content aspects of particular sets of canonical letters; beyond the vast typology of epistolary types. Epistles are *enactive*, as well as content-bearing. If we are truly without effective epistolary exchanges, as Adorno hints, then the a-epistolary situation reflects disastrously upon our lack of effective *communal existence* today. But I'd rather look at the burgeoning capacities of hypertextual interactive novellas as a form of contemporary

---

[18] On the popularity of the genre: Würzbach (ix-x) notes that epistolary novels made up about *one fifth* of the total of 18th century fiction. "The form of the letter was so popular that travel books, political and philosophical treatises, satires and essays on various subjects were written in the form of a 'Letter from . . . to . . . .' It is therefore hardly surprising that fiction too began to make use of this device." Likewise Perry (66): "It is difficult to make generalizations about the subject matter of [letter] collections [in the 17th and 18th centuries], for the letters are usually written on every conceivable subject and in most volumes are discontinuous, each one speaking to a different situation." Cf. Doty (1973:15): "In Hellenism the epistolary mode became so inclusive that almost any type of material could be presented in letters."

communication, or at e-mail and the various dialogic international networks that may well replace the snail-mail epistolarity of the past. Who cares if it is not *written*-textual? It is still and especially interactive-dialogical; it is performative in ways only face-to-face voice conversations have been previously.[19]

Kauffman (1992: xv) notes with respect to Roland Barthes's *A Lover's Discourse* and Derrida's *The Post Card* that these authors stress "the performative aspects of language, using amorous discourse to stage [their] speculations about love, literature, identity, difference. They deconstruct the dichotomies dividing love from scholarship, margin from center, fiction from theory." *Letters as dialogues,* or most frequently half-dialogues, but above all as participatory and projective: "Real and fictional epistolary narratives require the reader's active participation, whether to replace the absent narrator or to share in producing an exchange. The reader necessarily enters into dialogue with the epistolary text, a dialogue that is never resolved and never completed" (MacArthur: 273; and see Kauffman, 1992:261 on the resistance to closure in *The Handmaid's Tale*). Such a text is—as Barthes and Derrida help us to see—a connective, amatory text, a dialogue that resists closure or telic completion. Such a text claims anyone who reads/hears it as a counter-text, an anti-normal performance of the simplistic promises of success and happiness without historical depth or extensive philosophical reflection.

That the sort of "new day" of biblical literary criticism I referred to at the outset may indeed be dawning is evident from Kauffman's comment that "Atwood's contribution to the long tradition of female voices in epistolary literature is to combine epistolary poetics and apocalyptic politics" (262—why did I first think she was describing *Paul*?) A major component of Kauffman's enterprise seeks to determine whether it is legitimate or not to speak of a feminine mode of writing, but I have not been able even to approach gendering issues, not just as they appear from the NT point of view, but how the NT matters of gender look *retrospectively* from the genre of the amorous epistles, in which the role of women is

---

[19] Within a few years the contemporary development of computer hypermedia will demand treatment in the same context as metaphor, ending, library, authorial intention, and readers' responses. Neither MacLuhan nor Ong foresaw how the new morality represented here relativizes utterly, and opens dialogic concepts such as I've stressed, toward a twenty-first-century epistolarity that will be polymorphic and multidimensioned. For instance, in his overview, Landow (70) remarks that the "hypertextual dissolution of centrality, which makes the medium such a potentially democratic one, also makes it a model of a society of conversations in which no one conversation, no one discourse or ideal, dominates or founds the others."

While Coover never mentions epistolary fictions, the works to which he points are clearly templates in which such fictions could be realized with great dialogic power.

central, yet always ambiguous, and usually inferior, over against the male principals.

And with respect to intertextuality I can only note the dialogic quality of Ovid's *Heroides* as that work "counterpoints other letters within Ovid's text and other authors' treatment of the same heroines" (Kauffman 1986:43). Kauffman gives one even more food for thought when she continues: "This intertextuality bears a striking resemblance to the procedure of psychoanalysis, which involves the same effort to interpret, to account for repetitions, to assess the structure of desire. In a sense, no individual letter can be analyzed without considering its status as part of a repetitive structure of seduction, betrayal, abandonment."

Obviously I have not followed the easier path of treating the many examples of intertextuality in the literature of the epistolary novel (Ovid refers to and incorporates material from Sappho [Kauffman, 1986:51]; the 1669 *Lettres Portugaises* influenced all subsequent editions of Heloise's letters to Abelard [and Rilke's development of the Duino Elegies!] and they were in turn influenced by the *Heroides*, as was *Clarissa*). But I have attempted here to devise subtexts and subquestions that challenge, even deconstruct, business as usual. Against the dominant social-Darwinian pressure by which scholars always theorize progress changing from primitive/inferior to more-complex/capitalist, I have asked about *retrospective* historiographic mythography: What happens when we progress not from putative chicken to egg, but from later manifestations to earlier? My historiography is not cyclic. I do not advocate the eternal recurrence of the same; but I do question any "the latest is best" model, and I am old enough to challenge, on the basis of my experience, the going assumption that anything predating Clinton's incumbency is irrelevant. Just because of such experience, I dare to enstate repeated queries about the traditional wisdom that reaches us now within the radical frames of the postmodern, maybe even post-postmodern, contours of the end of the twentieth century.

At the end of an era we look forward to another with some trepidation. We imagine amorously just what might yet provide the connectiveness (eros, philia, *and* agape) that can engender creative repossessions of all our heritages, rather than grinding to a halt in the same old business as usual. We would be truly stupid not to learn from the "unbinding" of letters (my second epigraph, and see again note 1) an effective modus operandi for twenty-first century communication. It will hardly be monotheistic or monological. It *will* clearly be polytheistic (multicultural?) and dialogical.

If I did not believe in that dialogue, in you, Dear Reader, I would not bother to compose this and send it out to you. Do drop me a note and tell me what you think about it.

Collegially,
/s/ William

WORK CONSULTED

Biblical translations, when not my own, are from the New Revised Standard Version.

Adorno, Theodor W.
    1992   *Notes to Literature*. Vol. 2. Ed. Rolf Tiedemann. Trans. Shierry Weber Nicholsen. New York: Columbia University Press.

Altman, Janet Gurkin
    1982   *Epistolarity: Approaches to a Form*. Columbus: Ohio State University Press.

Barth, John
    1979   *Letters*. New York: G. P. Putnam's Sons.

Bennington, Geoffrey, and Jacques Derrida
    1992   *Jacques Derrida*. Religion and Postmodernism. Chicago: University of Chicago Press.

Carson, Anne
    1986   *Eros the Bittersweet: An Essay*. Princeton: Princeton University Press, for the Center for Hellenic Study.

Castelli, Elizabeth A.
    1991a   "Interpretations of Power in 1 Corinthians." *Semeia:* 54:197–222.
    1991b   *Imitating Paul: A Discourse of Power*. Literary Currents in Biblical Interpretation. Louisville: Westminster/John Knox.

Choderlos de Laclos, Pierre Ambroise
    1962   *Les Liaisons Dangereuses*. Trans. Richard Aldington. New York: repr. New American Library. Originally 1782, French text in *Oeuvres Complètes*. Paris: Gallimard, 1943.

Coover, Robert
    1993   "Hyperfiction: Novels for the Computer," "And Hypertext Is Only the Beginning. Watch Out!," "And Now, Boot Up the Computers." *The New York Times Book Review*, 29 January; 1, 8–12.

Craige, Betty Jean
    1992   *Laying the Ladder Down: The Emergence of Cultural Holism: Critical Perspectives on Modern Culture*. Amherst: University of Massachusetts Press.

Davis, Robert Con, and Robert Schleifer
　1991　　*Criticism and Culture: The Role of Critique in Modern Literary Theory*. London: Longman.

Derrida, Jacques
　1987　　*The Post Card: From Socrates to Freud and Beyond.* Trans. and Intro. Alan Bass. Chicago: University of Chicago Press.

Detienne, Marcel
　1977　　*The Gardens of Adonis: Spices in Greek Mythology*. Intro. J.-P. Vernant; Trans. Janet Lloyd. Atlantic Highlands: Humanities Press.

Doty, William G.
　1969　　"The Classification of Epistolary Literature." *CBQ* 31:183–99.
　1973　　*Letters in Primitive Christianity*. Guides to Biblical Scholarship. Minneapolis: Augsburg-Fortress.
　1990　　"Writing the Blurred Genres of Postmodern Ethnography." *Annals of Scholarship: Studies of the Humanities and Social Sciences* 6:267–87.
　1992　　"Wild Transgressions and Tame Celebrations: Contemporary Construals of Ritualization." *Journal of Ritual Studies* 6:115–30.
　1993　　"The Epistles." Pp. 445–57 in *A Complete Literary Guide to the Bible*. Ed. Leland Longman and Tremper Ryken III. Grand Rapids: Harper Collins/Zondervan.
　1994　　"Silent Myths Singing in the Blood: The Sites of Production and Consumption of Myths in a 'Mythless' Society." Pp. 173-220 in *Picturing Cultural Values in Postmodern Society*. Ed. W.G. Doty. Tuscaloosa: University of Alabama Press.

Francis, Fred O., and J. Paul Sampley
　1984　　*Pauline Parallels*. 2nd ed. Foundations and Facets. Minneapolis: Augsburg/Fortress.

Freedberg, David
　1989　　*The Power of Images: Studies in the History and Theory of Response*. Chicago: University of Chicago Press.

Funk, Robert W.
　1975　　*Jesus as Precursor*. Semeia Suppl., 2. Atlanta: Scholars Press.

Gerhart, Mary
　1992　　*Genre Choices, Gender Questions*. Oklahoma Project for Discourse and Theory. Norman: University of Oklahoma Press.

Gillis, Christina Marsden
　1984　　*The Paradox of Privacy: Epistolary Form in Clarissa*. University of Florida Monogr., Humanities, 54. Gainesville: University Presses of Florida

Hays, Richard B.
　1989　　*Echoes of Scripture in the Letters of Paul*. New Haven: Yale University Press.

Iser, Wolfgang
- 1989 *Prospecting: From Reader Response to Literary Anthropology.* Baltimore: Johns Hopkins University Press.
- 1993 *The Fictive and the Imaginary: Charting Literary Anthropology.* Baltimore: Johns Hopkins University Press.

Kauffman, Linda S.
- 1986 *Discourses of Desire: Gender, Genre, and Epistolary Fictions.* Ithaca: Cornell University Press.
- 1992 *Special Delivery: Epistolary Modes in Modern Fiction.* Women in Culture and Society. Chicago: University of Chicago Press.

Koskenniemi, Heikki
- 1956 *Studien zur Idee und Phraseologie des griechischen Briefen bis 400 n. Chr.* Helsinki: Suomalaien Tiedekatemie.

Landow, George
- 1992 *Hypertext: The Convergence of Contemporary Critical Theory and Technology.* Parallax: Revisions of Culture and Society. Baltimore: Johns Hopkins University Press.

MacArthur, Elizabeth J.
- 1990 *Extravagant Narratives: Closure and Dynamics in the Epistolary Form.* Princeton: Princeton University Press.

Mack, Burton
- 1988 *A Myth of Innocence: Mark and Christian Origins.* Minneapolis: Augsburg/Fortress.

Montrose, Louis
- 1992 "New Historicisms." Pp. 392–418 in *Redrawing the Boundaries: The Transformation of English and American Literary Studies.* Ed. Stephen Greenblatt and Giles Gunn. New York: The Modern Language Association of America.

Mullins, Phil
- 1993 "Some Others" [a review essay on three titles]. *Interdisciplinary Humanities* 10:39–44.

Perry, Ruth
- 1980 *Women, Letters, and the Novel.* AMS Stud. in the Eighteenth Cent., 4. New York: AMS Press.

Richardson, Samuel
- 1962 *Clarissa, or The History of a Young Lady.* Ed. George Sherburn. Boston: Houghton-Mifflin.

Roberts, R. H., and J. M. M. Good, eds.
- 1993 *The Recovery of Rhetoric: Persuasive Discourse and Disciplinarity in the Human Sciences.* Knowledge: Disciplinarity and Beyond. Charlottesville: University Press of Virginia.

Ronell, Avital
 1989 *The Telephone Book: Technology, Schizophrenia, Electric Speech*. Lincoln: University of Nebraska Press.

Rubenstein, Richard L.
 1972 *My Brother Paul*. New York: Harper Collins.

Stevens, Wallace
 1951 *The Necessary Angel: Essays on Reality and the Imagination*. New York: Random House.

Via, Dan O.
 1975 *Kerygma and Comedy in the New Testament: A Structuralist Approach to Hermeneutics*. Minneapolis: Augsburg Fortress.

Walker, Alice
 1982 *The Color Purple*. New York: Pocket.

Würzbach, Natascha, ed.
 1989 *The Novel in Letters: Epistolary Fiction in the Early English Novel 1678–1740*. Coral Gables: University of Miami Press.

"WHAT IS WRITTEN? HOW ARE YOU READING?"
GOSPEL, INTERTEXTUALITY AND DOING LUKEWISE: READING LK 10:25-42 OTHERWISE

Gary A. Phillips
College of the Holy Cross

ABSTRACT

Luke's Gospel poses a fundamental question to the reader of this text about reading and writing. It is an issue that preoccupies Luke from prologue to conclusion. Luke seeks to answer this question—"What is written in the Law? How are you reading it?"—and to answer for his reader by imposing a rhetorical strategy upon his many materials and readers so as to make the "many one." This effort to reduce the many to one is part of a controlling narrative effort that binds the Gospel to the Acts and surfaces with a disturbing clarity in Jesus' conversation with the lawyer and with Martha in chapter 10. Using a deconstructive strategy and focusing on the critical concept of intertextuality, the attempt is made to profile (1) Luke's masterful and controlling effort to manage diverse texts and readers and how it is bound to fail for some readings; (2) the inherent difficulty controlling either text or reader; and (3) the nature of a responsible reading that seeks to resist Luke's way of reading by reading otherwise, not Lukewise.

Intertextuality designates the multitude of ways a text has of not being self-contained, of being traversed by otherness.—Barbara Johnson

The text is that *social* space which leaves no language safe, outside, nor any subject of enunciation in position as judge, master, analyst, confessor, decoder.—Roland Barthes

The Gospel of Luke is an extremely dangerous text, perhaps the most dangerous in the Bible.—Jane Schaberg

READING, WRITING, AND THE READER BEWARE

...the Text requires that one try to abolish (or at the very least to diminish) the distance between reading and writing, in no way by intensifying the projection of the reader into the work but by joining them into a single signifying practice.—Roland Barthes

In the complex discursive space carved out for the reader in Luke's narrative, Jesus engages in two well-known conversations, one with a lawyer and the other with a woman named Martha. These are discursive interludes in Luke's narrative presentation of Jesus' long journey to Jerusalem, which is part of a much larger "connective narrative" (1:3). Sandwiched in between conversations between Jesus and his disciples about mission (9:51–10:24) and prayer (11:1–13), the first exchange unfolds in a two-stage movement between a lawyer and Jesus. It starts off in a fairly innocuous way. The lawyer asks, "Teacher, what shall I do to inherit eternal life?" (10:25). Jesus responds by rephrasing the lawyer's question with a two-fold question of his own: "What is written in the law? How are you reading it?" The lawyer answers Jesus' double question with his own doubled speech—a spliced citation of the law (Dt 6:5; Lev 19:18)—to which Jesus responds approvingly once again, this time with a double exhortation: "You have answered right. Do this and you will live."

But the lawyer is not satisfied. He comes back with a second battery of questions. Now his aggressive stance is disclosed to the reader: "... but he wanted to vindicate himself, so he said to Jesus, 'Who is my neighbor?'" Jesus deftly counters once again, this time with a question-prefaced-by-a-story. Jesus' response to the lawyer's question is as before a rewriting and rereading: "Which one of the three did the neighborly thing?" Dutifully, the lawyer answers Jesus' question correctly a second time by identifying the Samaritan as that neighbor. The second round ends as did the first with a double injunction: Jesus says, "Go, and do likewise." With this said, the lawyer disappears from narrative sight, and Jesus moves on to the home of Martha and Mary and to the second exchange.

Like the Lawyer, Martha presses Jesus with her question, actually a two-part question and command. Also designed to put Jesus on the defensive ("don't you care..."), Martha's question barely masks the complaint about her sister Mary's unhelpful, uncooperative behavior; it is a rhetorical move intended to maneuver Jesus to take her side. In contrast to the lawyer, it is Martha who utters the double exhortation: "Tell her to come and lend a hand." But Jesus once again has the last word—a "kind rebuke" or expression of "love patriarchalism" (Schaberg: 289) depending upon how you read it—that twice repeats Martha's name and zeroes in on that "one and only thing necessary" (v.42) to know about Mary's behavior. With Martha effectively silenced she too disappears from the narrative, and Jesus moves on to the next place to resume teaching his disciples.[1]

---

[1] In fact Luke's doubling strategy is carried forward not only into vv. 38–42 but throughout the gospel. The episode is rich rhetorically in this respect. There is a hendiadic pairing of the women; the double vocative (Μάρθα, Μάρθα); the verbal pair of "anxious and "troubled" (μεριμνᾷς καὶ θορυβάδζῃ) (Metzger takes the latter as a gloss

Two characters engage in conversation with Jesus: both want answers to their questions; both maneuver rhetorically in their conversation to get Jesus to respond the way they want; both are trumped by Jesus who reads and rewrites his interlocutors' words; both yield without further contest to the more able Jesus; both are effectively silenced and disappear from the narrative. Read one way, the conversations are straightforward example stories that illustrate the way both characters misread Jesus and their situations: the lawyer misreads Jesus' capacity to read both the law and the lawyer's own vindicating intent and to transform his question and answer into something other than was first intended; Martha misreads Jesus' ability to read the situation between the sisters and to turn the table on the critique of Mary's passive behavior by lifting her up as the favored one among many. Typically read as unambivalent example stories, these texts illustrate Jesus' prescience and interpretive skill and affirm the virtue of love and service.

Read in a more suspicious way, these dialogs disclose something about Jesus' role as a dominating reader of texts and people, and Luke's narrative as an imposing text intent on making its readers see, hear, and act (10:24) in a very directed way. Traditionally, Luke the gospel writer has been acknowledged for his oratory and writing skills (Tannehill). But equally other readers (Schaberg) warn about the coercive power of this text to construct and constrain certain models of Christian conduct. Is it possible that with a first naive reading we too underestimate this Jesus, Luke's skill as a writer and the subtle, yet powerful, effects of this text upon its readers? Put another way, because of the skill of the writer and a history of reading this masterful text are we prone to "misread" the Gospel and our situations as readers? If so, then these stories are "examples" but in an ironic and disturbing way, and our potential identification with the lawyer and Martha/Mary more ambivalent. It is this ambivalence that Jane Schaberg acknowledges in her warning to readers of Luke to beware its palatable style.

What might at first be read as a recounting of two initially quite ordinary stories ("On one occasion a lawyer came forward [10:25]. . . . While they were on their way Jesus came to a village where a woman named Martha. . . ." [10:38]) turns out on closer reading to be substantially other than that. In the economy of this pair of dialogs about writing, reading, and behaving, Luke's reader is presented with structure, balance, clarity, and instruction by way of an elaborate rhetorical use of double questions, double textual citations, multiple double exhortations, textual hendiadys

---

upon the former; [Fitzmyer: 452]) and a disputed textual variant in 10:42 in which the textual witness supports "but of a few things there is need, or of (only) one" (ὀλίγων δέ ἐστιν χρεία ἢ ἑνός); Fitzmyer (894) takes this to be the likely problematic reading.

left and right. In both dialogs we read about citations, readings, writing, scripture and actors paired up and stitched together for reasons that go beyond simply providing two more examples of Jesus' teaching or models of appropriate disciple behavior.

Reading between the lines, we discover an explicit concern in these two dialogs with language, power, and control, one that compels metacritical questions about Luke's narrative design. As an educational text, Luke's narrative is "elegant" in its "structure, style and portrait" of both men and women (Schaberg: 275). But Luke's rhetoric affirms more than service and self-effacement: it is a writing about loving and service that is linked at the same time to the winning, overpowering, silencing, and ordering that we read elsewhere in the Gospel. For example, in the dialogic give-and-take between Jesus and the Lawyer, Jesus bests the lawyer at his own game, namely reading and writing the text of the law. It resonates with the triumphant and exultant return of his disciples in the preceding verses (10:19–21) where Jesus acknowledges that his disciples have power "to tread underfoot snakes, scorpions, and all the forces of the enemy" (10:19). In the exchange with Martha over her sister's inaction, Jesus wrests control of the discourse from her—less subtly than with the lawyer—and by turning complaint into compliance exercises a discursive power that at once responds to and silences his female interlocutor. This ambiguous interaction with a woman anticipates other silences and disappearances to come (cf. 24:49). The textual rhetoric is powerful and mixed at best, especially for women readers (Schaberg: 291–92).

Being a reader and writer in and of Luke's text is the issue: Luke draws the reader's attention at the start. What is less obvious is the extent to which Luke's way of writing and reading proves to be a problem for gospel readers. Furthermore, what Luke says and demonstrates about reading and writing through his own reading and writing is crucial for understanding something else about the biblical text and the readers who read it. Luke's narrative invites us explicitly to ask about reading and writing ("What is written in the Law? How are you reading it?"), specifically Luke's way of reading and writing. At the same time Luke's text poses an acute self-reflexive question to us its readers: what do *we* read in the biblical text, and how are *we* reading it? Jesus' question to us can be turned back upon Luke's own reading and writing in a way that even he cannot dodge: How are we to read Luke's doubling rhetoric and the way he addresses issues of writing, reading, knowledge, power, women, silence, passivity, and discursive control? What are the implications of reading Luke's way as one instructed to read and write (like the lawyer) and act (like Martha) in a trumped fashion? What is our responsibility as critical readers of the gospel text to read and rewrite "otherwise"? In the epigraph above, Jane Schaberg warns her readers—beware the danger lurking in the Lukan text related to the reader's "identity" construction and the "oppressive dynamics" that "pressure" the reader (291) into reading and acting in a certain way, Luke's way. To be aware of Luke's way of reading and writing is to beware.

In this essay I take up Luke's question about reading and writing as a way of focusing self-reflexively on my own status as a reader/writer. Broadly speaking, I employ deconstructive strategies and the poststructuralist concept of intertextuality. The latter serves as a critical lever[2] for clarifying some of the complicated rhetorical interests and gestures of the Lukan text and of the reader's role and response to Luke's writing. Intertextuality—the complex manner in which texts exist as a mosaic of signifying, dialogic, and culturally coded material—is an especially appropriate critical tool because of the Lukan preoccupation with questions about writing and reading, the relationship of one text to many other texts, the dialogic relationship between Jesus and others, the complex issues of convincing readers of mixed cultures about the appropriate way to read and respond to Scripture. In fact I would argue that Luke's two-volume work is framed, prologue to conclusion, by intertextual issues (cf. Lk 1:1–4; Ac 28:23) and that his instruction about reading and writing, which is articulated explicitly in 10:25–42, is written across both volumes for all to read who have eyes to see and ears to hear (Lk 10:23–24; Ac 28:27).

Hendiadys becomes a rhetorical trope of choice for reading and writing Luke's way. From the start of the Gospel Luke announces his overarching writing goal: to narrate that one continuous, complete, and accurate narrative that reduces the many to one (Lk 1:1). The text unfolds with a "hendiadyic" rhetorical strategy that in all sorts of ways seeks to link the one-to-the-many—to submerge the many into one—as a means of mastering not only the narrative text and its complicated literary and reception history, but also to master history and control the reader. But to what end? Ostensibly in order to protect her from "inaccurate" readings (1:3), but we are beginning to suspect that there are other reasons. It is a desire that manifests itself variously in the narrative organization, in textual structure, even figuratively in character interactions as we read in Jesus' words with Martha, "but one thing is necessary" (10:42). Luke's desire to serve and protect means writing for a reader who will accept Luke's writing and reading and do as she is told.

---

[2] The "lever" (μόχλος) is an important concept for Derrida (1988:111–54) in discussing what is needed to move from a certain kind of foundationalist ethical thinking to an alternative way of regarding ethico-political responsibility. See White: 79–81.

However, the reality is that not all readers readily accept Luke's instruction; even Luke acknowledges that his own words sometimes are not effective—some are won over, others remain skeptical he says (Ac 28:24). Reading Luke deconstructively is a particular kind of intervention in the text, a resistant engagement that aims to be responsible not only to Luke's text but to those who read Lukewise or read "otherwise." The resistance to reading and writing Luke's way is fueled ironically by Luke's text itself, in particular that self-reflexive question Jesus poses to the Lawyer (and to whoever has ears to hear) about writing and reading. I read it as a metacritical question that prompts my deconstructive reading. The latter focuses on the tension in the narrative surrounding the figure of the "one and the many": in spite of Luke's "impressive" effort to reduce the many readings, writings and readers to one, the Gospel also has the opposite effect of generating other writings, readings, and readers. A text designed to produce a single, comprehensive, and orderly account of the "events that happened among us" (1:1) produces at the same time an opening for multiple, dys-orderly readings. In Luke's text the suturing and rupturing of reading go hand-in-hand.[3]

Deconstructive reading and intertextuality combine then to give us a way to think about how readers as subjects are constructed in relation to texts and about the responsibility we have to become critical readers and writers of a certain (for example, non-Lukan) sort, to become aware, to beware. In other words, reading Luke's text deconstructively and with attention to its intertextual character opens up important ethico-critical issues that go beyond Luke's text to the very heart of textuality and subjectivity. This text is an invitation to reflect, therefore, on *my* reading strategy, *my* network and production of texts, *my* social context, *my* obligation. Reading deconstructively for Lukan intertextuality is an acknowledgement that reading and writing, especially as it concerns the Bible, is always about "more than" texts; it is ever about reading subjects, cultural positions, ideologies, ethical responsibility, and a "more than," an "otherness," that escapes critical assessment.[4] What deconstruction and intertextuality share is an attention to the excessiveness of text and subject that traverses the Gospel text and therefore makes the reading and rereading of Scripture inherently risky and demanding, as even Luke warns (Ac 28:26). Far from distancing us, then, from important textual, ethical,

---

[3] This is related to Derrida's point about the "undecidability" of reading and writing. His discussion of the notion of *pharmakon*—the medicine is at the same time the poison—is suggestive here. Is writing not Luke's pharmakon? Is it appropos of Luke given his identification within the tradition as a doctor? See Derrida, 1972b:95–134, especially; 1972c:58–59).

[4] See Kristeva, 1995:122 on the limitations of criticism to capture the otherness that Johnson says traverses the text.

and religious matters, reading this way puts us in a position to take Luke and our responsibility as readers seriously by reading the Gospel for what is other, to read otherwise, to read other than Lukewise.

INTERTEXTUALITY AND THE READING SUBJECT

> [The critic-reader's task is to hear] not only through the different figures or spaces made by those signs which resemble linguistic signs, but also through other elements . . . which, although always already caught in the web of meaning and signification, are not caught in the same way as the two-sided units of Saussurean signs. . . . —Julia Kristeva

Julia Kristeva first proposed the term "intertextuality"[5] more than two decades ago; the term-and-concept has since acquired a life of its own and, like "deconstruction," has largely come to stand for a generational difference in the way texts are critically read in relationship to each other and to history.[6] For Kristeva the concept of "intertextuality" denotes a

---

[5] The concept of intertextuality has exploded in literary and cultural critical circles. The historical and ideological relationship of intertextuality to the concept of influence is a complex question. Clayton and Rothstein argue that intertextuality serves as a sort of generational marker for younger critics who end up doing what "elder" critics did with the notion of "influence" and its cognate terms, "context," "allusion" and "tradition" (3). One way to think of the relationship of influence to intertextuality is degree of awareness. "Any given text...filters its substance from the intertextual, and the process of filtration lends itself to the language of influence. An influential work, presumably, is one that changes the components of the intertext and their relative weighting" (30). In general, influence has to do with agency, intertextuality with a more impersonal field of crossing texts. It is ironic that the very discussion of influence is largely anonymous while that of intertextality goes under the name of several "influential" theorists (Bakhtin, Barthes, Derrida, Foucault, Kristeva, Lacan, Riffaterre) (4). See also Plett (3–29). In the area of biblical studies, see the edited essays in Draisma and Boyarin's work on Midrash.

[6] Cited in Barzilai (297). Kristeva's critque of Lacan focuses in one way upon an overdependence upon a Saussurian dyadic model of the sign. While to my knowledge Kristeva does not explicitly employ a Peircean scheme, in part I suspect because of the important categorical distinction she makes between *le sémiotique* and *la sémiotique*, Peirce's triadic model of the sign in fact lends itself to thinking about meaning as a signifying process rather than as a system. "Semanalysis" is designed precisely as the means for studying signifying processes. See Kristeva, 1986:24–33; Phillips, 1991.

Kristeva defines or describes "intertextuality" in a variety of ways: "each word (text) is an intersection of words (texts) where at least one other word (text) can be read" (1980:66); "Any text is constructed as a mosaic of quotations, any text is the absorption and transformation of another. The notion of *intertextuality* replaces that of intersubjectivity, and a poetic language is read as at least double" (1980:66); "in the space of a given text, several utterances, taken from other texts, intersect and neutralize one another" (1980:36); "The term *intertextulty* denotes this transposition of one (or several) sign system(s) into another; but since this term has often been understood in the banal sense of 'study of sources,' we prefer the term *transposition* because it specifies that the passage from one signifying system to another demands a new articulation...of enunciative and denotative positionality" (1974:59–60); "...every text is

complex structural-semiotic and psychoanalytic process[7] to be distinguished sharply from a "banal" source critical conception of intertextuality as "influence." Banal source criticism is a problem for literary studies (especially biblical studies) because critics fail to take into account the structural and systemic character of textual productivity (1974:60). As defined by Kristeva, intertextuality has little to do then with matters of influence by one author upon another, or of one literary source upon another. Rather, intertextuality points primarily to systemic relationships and processes that are always at work in the cultural production and reception of texts: the transformation of one (or more) system(s) of signs into another whose effect, in part, is to shape the subjectivity of the readers of those texts. For Kristeva, then, intertextual relations have two facets: an inner play, namely "the web of relations that produce the structure of the text (or the subject)," and an outer play, "the web of relations linking the text (subject) with other discourses."[8] The influence as well as critique of Saussurean structural linguistics via Peircian semiotics is visible here (Phillips, 1990).[9]

Intertextuality signifies the process of structural-semiotic transposition of one *textual system* (understood as sign or system of signs) by one or more systems. Following the lead of the linguists Benveniste and Jakobson, and heavily dependent on Bahktin's dialogic model, Kristeva argues

---

from the outset under the jurisdiction of other discourses which impose a universe on it" (1974:188–89); "the transposition of one sign system into another, such that the new signifying sustem may be produced with different 'signifying material' and thus does not have to occur entirely within language" (1974:59); the "literary word is an *intersection of textual surfaces* rather than a point (a fixed meaning), as a dialogue among several writings" (1980:65).

[7] Kristeva's development of the term is itself a complex "intertextual" event. On the psychodynamics of its background see Friedman: 157–58. Kristeva developed the term out of a dialogue with Bakhtin, Derrida, and Lacan as a way of shifting semiotics toward a more open and aggressive ideological criticism. The concept of intertextuality emerges from her paraphrase of Bakhtin: "Every word (text) is an intersection of words (texts—where at least one other word (text) can be read" (1980:66). Derrida's critique of voice is present here as an intertext as well. Derrida is in fact the intersecting point of most theories of intertextuality on account of his subordination of difference between signifier and signified. "Under the name of 'grafts,' he pursues an active intertextual practice, in which intertextuality becomes the critic's method of probing, fissuring, disorienting, and dangerously supplementing the text at hand so as to exhibit its implications and implicatedness" (Clay and Rothstein: 19). Also see Culler (136–54). For a traditional semiotic description of intertextualty see A.J Greimas and J. Courtès, s.v. "Intertextuality."

[8] Cited in Barzilai: 297.

[9] An important critical response to Saussurian structural linguistics was the lifting up of the *pragmatics* of semiosis. Peirce's conception of the triadic sign, therefore, proved especially valuable to Kristeva in her situating semioisis within a lived, historical context. Her Marxian materialist and psychoanalytic critique are evident here. See Phillips, 1986, 1991.

that transposition is key for producing new enunciative and denotative positions. Instead of discrete voices or textual "roles," Kristeva prefers instead to speak of subject and object *positions* ("positionalities") that are always in the process of coalescing in discourse and being reconstituted in this process of structural change as systems interact. The linguistic markers within discourse that refer to these subject and real-world referents (deictics, for example) are in a sense "empty signs" of these positions whose meaning/content is always use- or context-specific. For Kristeva, textual production and subject production go hand-in-hand: the text is a space of shifting subject positions and intersecting sign systems. Critical reading of a text, from her point of view, is a "signifying practice" (following Barthes), a "writing" (following Derrida) in which the text (be it linguistic, somatic, visual, etc.) can be reenvisioned spatially as a field traversed by lines of force in which the various signifying systems (including their subject positions) undergo transposition of varying sorts and in varying degrees of magnitude.[10] Within Kristeva's scheme, the reader or "lector" position of a text is continuously subject to revision as systems (read texts) intersect and reshape the positions that real readers come to occupy. From this perspective, the Fish-sponsored debate about a reader "in the text" or "outside the text" is misleading; we can only speak of a continuing transformation of the potential for becoming a "lector" as it is constrained by conflicting systems of meaning.[11]

In her early theoretical works, Kristeva grounded this transformation process explicitly in psychoanalytic theory. Alongside Freud's two fundamental processes of displacement and condensation stands a third, namely that of transposition ("transposition").[12] Transposition is the possibility inherent within the signifying process itself of passing from one system of signs to another, i.e. to exchange or to alter them. Transposition, in other words, is key to the figurability of language—what Freud speaks of as *die Rucksicht auf Darstellbarkeit*—namely, the specific articulation of a system of signs that takes place between the semiotic and the thetic.

---

[10] "Bakhtin considers writing as a reading of the anterior literary corpus and the text as an absorption of and a reply to another text" (1980:69); and see Leon Roudiez's helpful discussion in his "Introduction" (in Kristeva, 1980:15).

[11] For a clear contrast in the way that "reader" is conceived in two very recent critical readings of gospel texts, see Fowler and Moore, 1989. In Fowler's more "traditional" reader-response approach he can speak of the "reader" of Mark as a person, whereas in Moore's poststructuralist perspective he prefers to speak of the activity of reading. A sense of the contrasting conceptual attitudes toward the category of "reader" can be gathered by reviewing the indexical headings for the subject in both volumes: by and large Fowler's are nominal and Moore's verbal.

[12] Within structural linguistics, Jakobson and Kruszewski have translated the psychological processes of displacement and condensation into the linguistic forms of metonymy and metaphor, respectively.

Transposition points to a fundamental semiotic process that enables translation out of a previous system of signs, by way of an intermediary drive ("pulsionnel") common to both systems, and into a new system with its figurability. This new system may be made up of the same signifying material (e.g. in Luke's passage the relation of narration to text through an overlay of different dialogue and reading subject positions), or it may be made up of new material altogether (e.g. as in the juxtaposition of previously unrelated texts or textual systems—such as the parable and Torah citations in relation to each other, the Septuagint in relation to the narrative context).[13]

For Kristeva the novel best illustrates the semiotic process of transposition essential to intertextuality (1974:59), although her recent foray into biblical texts points to their usefulness in this regard (1995; see The Bible and Culture Collective, 213–17). The novel represents the formation of the romance signifying system as a consequence of the redistribution of several other signifying systems: the carnivalesque, the court poet, scholastic discourse, etc. Because a new thetic articulation results in the passage from one signifying system to another, different enunciative and denotative positions open up for the reader to "occupy." The novel thus opens up the possibility of redefined discursive positions and worlds of reference for the reader. From this we can see, following Benveniste, that the "places" of enunciation in the text (marked by the discursive roles of speaking subjects) and its denotated objects (the textual world of reference) are by definition not self-sustaining, self-identical, and full, but are always constructed, differential, and structurally empty positions within a discursive matrix that is always already a transposition out of other signifying systems, a composite of an ongoing semiotic process along a trajectory that does not end (see Phillips, 1991:91).[14] Like the rapid transmutation of viruses, intertextual systems can be readily transposed into another, and along with those systems their different discursive positions; the dialogical positions of "speaker" and "hearer," "writer" and "reader" are always in a fluid relationship to one another and thus "incomplete."[15]

---

[13] Levi-Strauss identifies this very process in formation of myths as the work of "bricolage."

[14] Kristeva, 1974:59. For a look at how Kristeva applies the notion practically, see 1969:191, 195, 255.

[15] In Kristeva's view, transposition as a process brings about a new articulation of enunciative and denotative positionality. That the subject of the discourse (or *énonciation*)and meaning of text are positionalities means that the position taken by writer and content of text are "effects of its language rather than autonomous entities" (Rajan: 65). These positionalities are not "stable" because text is ever in process of being transformed to something else. What is carried over in the transposition is itself a *product* of transposition, of intersection of ideological surfaces; there is a nonidentity between the two.

The semiotic difference between *text* and *subject* thus fades. By extension, the lines distinguishing reader, writer, and text cannot be semiotically maintained:

> The writer's interlocutor, then, is the writer himself, but as reader of another text. The one who writes is the same as the one who reads. Since his interlocutor *is* a text, he himself is no more than a *text rereading itself as it rewrites itself*. The dialogical structure, therefore, appears only in light of the text elaborating itself as ambivalent in relation to another text (Kristeva, 1980:86–7; my emphasis).

Intertextuality is always socially located. Kristeva situates the production of the subject and the text, then, within a wide socio-semiotic framework informed by Marxian thought. For her, reader/writer positionalities have socio-political context and are never empty discursive positions removed from cultural (read political) significance.[16] Consequently the "lector" position constituted as a result of the intertextual process is always already coded for determinants such as gender, class, race, and ethnicity.[17] Set within the context of a Marxian model of value production, intertextuality so envisioned takes its place then as one of several forms of socio-semiotic productivity.[18] One of the contentious critical debates today is over the extent to which Barthes's and Foucault's "death of the Author"—with which concept Kristeva closely identifies—has actually worked ironically to remove the subject from history.[19]

---

[16] In contrast to certain forms of reader response and aesthetic criticism grounded in the phenomenological tradition. Cf. Iser.

[17] The notion of intertextual reading with which Raja works is essentially one that retains an existentially situated subject who is intergenerated with language, and this as "socially dialogized and not simply as self-reflexive" (72). This view of the reader parallels the renunciation of the author in which the reader is little more than a receptacle; there is a kind of transcendentalism of the reader as figure of totality. To avoid evaporation of history, deconstruction needs an historical subject whose intention can be described. But this notion of intention is not of an author transcendent to writing or to the text, but rather as an intent of consciousness refracted by difference between language and its object; subject is both an interiority and a "subject to law." See her discussion of Lacan and Foucault (73).

[18] See Raja: 64. This notion of intertextuality is very different from the "intratextuality" associated with the Yale School, which "creates an intersection of textual surfaces that blurs the boundary between outside and inside, or between reference and figure, largely to absorb the outside into the inside. It is wrong to say this is a politically "empty" appropriation of literary critical theory. Rather, it is an illustration of a certain aesthetic ideology that can imagine itself romantically set apart from history. For critique of the Yale School on this point see Hirsch.

[19] Friedman (145ff.) is very helpful in charting the ways in which feminists on either side of the Atlantic have reacted to the "erasure" of the author/subject. On the one hand Peggy Kamuf and Alice Jardine embrace the "antihumanist" project of French poststructuralism and contend feminists take advantage of the radical possibilities that the "death of cartesian subject/author" offers; Barbara Christian, Elizabeth

We can perhaps begin to see why intertextuality understood as the semiotic process of transposition is useful for thinking about Luke's text and the reader's "role" that the text inscribes. Gospel-writing and rewriting is a transposition of different *textual systems* of inner and outer webs of relations. First, at the macro level, the Gospel can be viewed as a rewriting of multiple oral and written texts and traditions—discourse traditions (including Q), example stories, aphorisms, parables, narrative traditions (including Mark), infancy stories, miracle catena, passion narrative, and the like—which form and source criticisms of the Bible seek to identify in diachronic terms. But the Lukan narrative also stands at the intersection of complex "cultural" systems (along with the literary[20] we could mention linguistic, religious, political, and socio-economic) which are reductively labeled "Gentile" and "Jewish," cf. Ac 28:28) and in a complicated relationship with diverse commentary and theological traditions as well. Mapping these complex systemic relationships is tricky. To be included as well are those "critical" discourses, such as feminism, psychoanalysis, and deconstruction, which position the reader in a quite different way in relation to the text and its history of readings.[21]

Second, at the micro level, the Gospel is a transposition of the relationships between *particular* narratives and discourses, characters, citations, actions, and the like within texts. The reading subject of Luke's text, by this logic, is constituted within a matrix of inner and outer discursive relations. Determining the "complete" intertextual context for the reading and writing of Luke's text is hardly possible: what would it mean historically to know all ($\pi\hat{\alpha}\sigma\iota\nu$, Lk 1:3) of the systems and transpositions that intersect and give us "Luke," or virtually any other text for that matter? Likewise, it is impossible to reduce the subjective possibilities that a text offers to one reader role, since such a role is a function of the relation of "texts," including the ones generated by the critical approach itself.[22] The

---

Fox-Genovese, and Nin Baym reflect resistance to the French influence altogether in favor of indigenous criticism rooted in women's selves and experiences; and then there are others like Nancy Miller who combine french poststructuralist theory self-consciously with American Feminism. The debate over the collaboration of feminism in general with deconstruction is part of this larger debate. See Miller, Friedman, Rajan.

[20] The debate over Lukan "septuagentalisms" is a case in point. Is this to be regarded as rhetorical "weakness" of Luke's Greek style or a an intrinsic feature of the way Luke employs text (eg. the LXX) to construct his readership?

[21] For example, consider the granular relationship of *The Women's Bible Commentary* to both Lukan text and the male-dominated commentary tradition that applauds Luke's "liberal" attitudes toward women while at the same time ignoring the silencing and submissive gestures of the text.

[22] This is one the most obvious blind spots of much biblical reader-response criticism (see The Bible and Culture Collective, 38–67).

important point is that reduction to one—be it of text, context, reader, meaning, reading—is impossible; it is a gesture that masks desire and power.

Self-consciousness about the intertextual process highlights the self-involvement of the reader in the reading/writing process, an echo of Bultmann's truism about exegesis. Going further, there can be no reader who does not rewrite the text in some fashion in his or her image as a reader of the text, for there is no way to divorce who and what "I" am in some essential way from the texts "I" read. Poststructuralist concepts like intertextuality can in fact be used in an uncritical way to support an ideology by making a work's meaning, context, intertext appear unquestionable or by reaffirming a certain reader's reading.[23] Reading for system and process in and of itself does not assure responsible reading, for any "critical" reading strategy can occlude its interests. Some other kind of intervention is necessary that works with this critical notion of intertextuality as systemic process and transformation of the subject to move us toward critical accountability. It is this role, I argue, that feminism (of a certain sort) and deconstruction (also of a certain sort) play (see Jobling; Miller). Just posing the intertextual question, however, is no guarantee that a liberatory ideological self-reflection and self-critique will follow, as should be clear from the ways many biblical critics have used the concept of intertextuality to advance conservative theological agendas.[24]

Boyarin's (12) recent work on reading midrash illustrates how a critical understanding of intertextuality and a healthy dose of deconstructive sensibility work together effectively in reading ancient religious texts. Reading midrash "intertextually" helps us to see the text (1) as a *mosaic* of conscious and unconscious citations drawn from earlier and other discourses (cf. Kristeva, 1969; 1974 and Barthes, 1981); (2) as essentially *dialogical* in nature—contesting their own assertions is an essential part of the structure of texts (Bakhtin, 1984; Todorov, 1984:41–74); and (3) the material expression of *cultural codes* (both conscious and unconscious) that constrain and enable production of new texts within culture (Bal, 1987; Barthes, 1981). Boyarin says of these codes that they "may be identified with the ideology of the culture, which is made up of the assumptions that people in the culture automatically make about what may or may not

---

[23] See Rajan's critique of Yale School "intratextuality" (64).

[24] On intertextuality I have in mind Hays, Buchanon, and Van Iersel. But the example could be multiplied to include "Implied Reader," "reader response," and more (see Burnett, 1990). Rajan's comments are important here: "For the reflexiveness of intertextuality requires a process in which not simply is textuality reappropriated to material use through its transposition into the life of someone outside the text, but also the realities in which we as readers participate are resituated as ideologies by their transposition into the text" (70).

be true and possible, about what is natural in nature and in history" (12).²⁵ This is true both with respect to the ancient texts that have already been read and the critical writings about them. I read Luke's text, then, intertextually situated within a messy literary critical tradition and cultural setting that strives to makes sense of the complexities of Luke's text as a reading about writing and a writing about reading,²⁶ a reading/writing in which the two activities are conceived together as a semiotic act in which I am implicated. Reading intertextually means, by this definition, focusing upon the writing of Luke as a web of discourses and upon my reading likewise as an intersection of critical pressures.²⁷

What does this brief foray into poststructuralist intertextuality suggest for our reading of Luke? Two things, at least. First, there is no neutral or degree zero reader of texts, no degree zero context for reading. Both reader and text find their provenance in culture and the shifting, conflicting, complicated, interposing systems of meaning that intersect, cancel, and transpose. Reading and writing Luke as a religious text means entering then into an ongoing process that necessarily brings interests and ideology into the analysis, no matter whether the critical point of view is redactional, historical, literary, feminist, or some combination of the above. To read Luke even in a self-consciously intertextual way is to join in with the author/s of the Gospel in a larger social constructive process that seemingly can't be halted or contained semiotically from "the out-

---

²⁵ Boyarin (39) views midrash as a trope for a certain kind of reading that explores the interstices and indeterminacies of Scripture. Midrashic intertextuality, following Gerald Bruns, has a second important feature. It is concerned with the self-glossing character of the Bible (in Alter and Kermode: 626–27).

²⁶ From Derrida's point of view the deconstructive project has always had a pedagogical and institutional transformative aim that has not been appreciated. Leitch quotes from Derrida's "Ou commence et comment finit un corps enseignant" (in *Politiques de la philosophie*, ed. Dominique Grisconi [Paris: Bernard Grasset, 1976]) "deconstruction...has always had a bearing in principle on the apparatus and the function of teaching in general." Derrida's effort to recast the teaching of philosophy in the Group for Research on Philosophic Teaching (GREPH) is illustrative. For more on the pedagogical import of deconstruction, see the collected essays in Atkins and Johnson and Ulmer, 1985b.

²⁷ Central to the notion of intertextuality is the recognition that intertextuality is not a feature of a particular genre or text-type but is characteristic of all texts (Boyarin: 14); intertextuality is constituitive of the structure of literary texts *per se*. What this means from a semiotic perspective is that texts (including Luke's are not: "organic, self-contained unities, created out of the spontaneous, freely willed act of a self-identical subject. What this means is that every text is constrained by the literary system of which it is a part and that every text is ultimately dialogical in that it cannot but record the traces of its contention and doubling of earlier discourses" (Boyarin: 14).

side," even if the original author of the text might desire it for narrative, theological, or other reasons.[28]

Second, apart from its importance for texts, reading in a self-critical, intertextual fashion is a responsible and appropriate response to the Bible and other religious texts. Critical reading requires that we pay close attention to the construction of subjectivity and meaning specific to the biblical text. There is something "more" or "other" about this text that commands our attention here. It is more than the "otherness" that we glimpse when talking about the many absent systems that shape and have shaped the many lector positions of text. The superfluity of texts in general takes on a special form in the Bible and the attention it regularly draws to its own status as Book. This means that we are challenged to read attentively for the self-reflexiveness and "emptiness" of the biblical text (Kristeva, 1995:120) in a way that certain types of "scientific" readings that are highly mathematized and unfettered by the text cannot. This "absence of meaning" Kristeva associates directly with the Bible's aniconic strategies for representing God, the "zero-degree of symbol formation," as she puts it (122). Because it is sacred text, the Bible invites a critical reading and rewriting that "is notable for the attention it gives to emptiness" (125). The ethical force for reading the Bible, she argues, derives from the complicated position occupied by the critical reader; it is a position shaped not only by the interests brought to bear upon the text but also forcefully by the text as a preserve of the Other, as a "more than," an excessiveness at work shaping the reader herself. As Luke warns, it is possible to read and hear the text otherwise ($\mu\acute{\eta}\pi o\tau\epsilon$; Ac 28:27). The Bible preserves its own capacity to read and rewrite its readers otherwise, whether for good or ill.

Shaping the Reader for Luke's Text

Let us return to Luke's text and read this pair of dialogs now as an intertextual process. Because subjectivity and textuality are mutually determining, a close look at discursive roles can shed some light on the complicated relationship of Lukan reading and writing to its readers. Following the linguist Benveniste, we might think of the text as a dialog, as the effect of an enunciation that involves a speaker ("I") and hearer ("you"). These dialogic positions are indicated linguistically by a certain category of indexical signs (for example, in the Greek pronominal structure $\sigma o\hat{v}$, $\sigma o\hat{\iota}$, $\mu o\hat{v}$; in verbal structures inflected for person and number; and in deictics of place such as $\tau o\hat{v}\tau o$ and $\grave{\epsilon}\kappa\epsilon\acute{\iota}\nu\eta$; see Jakobson). Subjectivity is textualized and reinforced in the discourses that are to be found

---

[28] Derrida's reflection on the "absence" of an outside (of the text) are extemely pertinent here (1988b).

throughout the narrative at all kinds of levels: in the overarching narration; in the voices of different characters, such as the lawyer, Martha, and Jesus; even in Jesus' internal narration of the story about the Samaritan and the innkeeper. Positioned variously in the narrative and dialogues as the "you" and speaking "I," the reader circulates through the multiple speaking positions and relationships: from lawyer to Jesus to lawyer to Samaritan to innkeeper to Jesus to Martha. Following the narrator's lead, the reader moves vertically and horizontally, in narrational and narrative time and space, even outside of textual time and space. How the text configures these roles determines in part the kind of reader for which it argues; it is also a replication, as Boyarin suggests, of cultural codes before and on the horizon of the text. The positioning can be overt—for instance when the narrator directly addresses the reader as "you" (as in Lk 1:4 "in order to give *you* authentic knowledge"); oblique—as in the third person imperative in Mk 13:14: "Let the reader understand," (contrast Lk 21:21); or covert—for instance when the narrator strictly adopts a third-person speaking strategy (cf. Lk 1:1–4 with 15ff.) and the reader effectively disappears.

Luke's silent lector position in chap. 10 is repeatedly reinforced by the third-person narrational voice that stitches together the interrogatories and the re-cited texts: "and behold, a lawyer..." (v.25); "he said to them" (v.26); "and he answered" (v.27); "and he said to him" (v.28); "But he, desiring to justify himself,..." (v.29); "Jesus said," (v.30); "He said," and "And Jesus said to him" (v.37). Presupposed as "you" to the third person narrator in this discourse, the reader occupies a subordinate discursive position as listener to the narrator who adeptly directs the narrative flow. In Benveniste's discursive terms, the reader occupies a subordinate position vis-à-vis the narrator (Benveniste: 12–14 especially). Reminiscent of the innkeeper whose under-appreciated service enables the Samaritan's deed to look good and thus the narrative economy of the parable to function, the reader sits silently, like Mary, subordinated in this discourse to a kind of dominant subject and voice whose presence is felt in the interstices of virtually every question, answer and citation.

If the author's self is strongly implied in the discursive third person at every turn and transition, the reader is correspondingly felt to be reduced or erased as a presence in the text. Moreover, discursive positions are figured in the actions and characters of the text itself. Unnamed by the narrator, the reader's position is not unlike that unnamed man who fell among robbers. Almost a tag-along, but not exactly an after-thought, the reader is "naturally" relegated to the discursive subordinate position, somewhat like the servile innkeeper. And like the silent sister Mary who listens to Jesus, the reader is set up narratively and discursively to occupy the passive role of "you" to narrator, of the wounded man to the Samaritan, Mary to Jesus. Implied, silent, subordinate, and pliable, the reader is invited to identify figuratively with the narrative portrayal of the silent woman (and the wounded man) in a position constructed especially for her. The narrator praises the reader's role as silent Mary ($ἀγαθήν$, v.42) in contrast to her doubly questioning lawyer-like sister Martha. But what is best ($ἀγαθήν$) for Jesus may not be what is best for the reader.

The Martha-Mary pronouncement text builds upon the subject construction in the Jesus-lawyer dialogue. The reader function[29] is a structural site for the narrator to work his recitational prowess as he confidently defines the law, repeats the Jesus parable, and now gives Martha proper advice all for his reader's benefit. Also like Martha, who finds her servile role subordinated in its own way to her silent sister, the reader is rendered invisible—discursively, figuratively, and soon narratively (in contrast, for example, to Theophilus, the named reader in 1:3, or to the reader identified only by the proper name "reader" in Mark's Gospel, 13:14). Nor does Luke have any larger plan to memorialize her as Mark does the anointing woman in Mk 14:8, who serves Jesus and Mark's narrative purpose. Positioned as observer to a very crafted, balanced dialogue between Jesus and the lawyer, the reader serves like Martha—it is readerly service that enables the narrator's explanation of Torah, the parable, the narrative re-citation and re-reading of Jesus to succeed. After all, if there are no ears to hear (cf. 10:24), no readers to re-read and re-cite as Luke desires, his elaborately doubled and doubling patterned recitation would be neither heard nor seen.

Although the rhetoric doesn't immediately suggest it, the passive reader is complicitous in her passivity and the narrator's besting of the reader. To read Luke lukewise the reader must be silent and submissive. If the reader didn't read, it would be the same as if Martha stopped serving and Mary started speaking, the innkeeper asked for his funds in advance, the priest's and Levite's service preempted the Samaritan's neighborly action, the Lawyer didn't ask his question, and Jesus didn't set up the Lawyer with a cleverly re-written question to make his point. It just wouldn't be the same text or reading or reader. Just as Mary makes Martha's lines work, like the sit-down, straight woman to the stand-up comic sister, the reader is inscribed in the text in a specific way to make the narrator's discourse work, to make the re-citations go, to make the

---

[29] Kristeva (1986) follows Foucault (1977) in constructing the reader function as a positionality of the subject within a discourse. In contrast to the implied reader of narratological theory, the reader function (also the "lector") is a semiotic and discursive structure inscribed within a social space that is made up of overlapping discourses. See also Miller for discussion of the political/ideological implications of asserting the "death of the Author" function.

narrator look good. In other words, the reader exercises *her role* by remaining the passive reader.

This happens because the narrator does everything rhetorically possible to insure the creation of a passive reader. As Tannehill notes (4), the Lukan narrator has a persuasive voice, "always seeking to weave a spell over us [the readers];" this narrator is not unreliable, just very skilled at inscribing an appropriate role for the reader and rereading many other attempted writings so as to produce orderly narrative (καθεξῆς σοι γράψαι, 1:3)—Luke dominates reader and writings. Leaving nothing to chance, Luke positions a strong narrator within a tightly woven dialogue that leaves little room or doubt as to what the reader can do and what the answer to the double question "What is written? How are you reading?" might be. There are no surprises or stumbling blocks here. No question goes unanswered, no answer lacks its question. All ties together. The many-as-one. The reader witnesses to and participates in an orchestrated display of rereading and rewriting: Torah responds to one question, Jesus' parable the other. All the reader-as-lawyer, reader-as-Martha has to do is respond and read, following Jesus' lead; it's a perfect set-up. In the face of such discursive order (καθεξῆς) there is little room or reason for resistance or disagreement, it seems, on the part of the reader. The reader can't go wrong—only go right; the reader is destined to "go read and write" as Luke will direct, and to see the Lawyer as an exemplar. With the right reading and the right reader assured (ἀσφάλειαν, 1:4), the reader finds herself effectively doubled up (but not out of laughter) just as Jesus doubles up the lawyer and Martha (Μάρθα, Μάρθα) in order to illustrate how silent sister Mary makes his point in 10:42. If within the narrated discourse the lawyer is enjoined to "Go, and do likewise," the reader who reads Luke's textual responses to the question intertextually is likewise enjoined to go read (ἀναγινώσκεις) and write (γράψαι) likewise—to read and write "Lukewise."

Luke's narrative control is strong and evident across the surface of the entire Gospel and Acts. It emerges in Luke's own hendiadic gesture that links texts, utterances, episodes, and writings. Doublets, doublings, and pairings enable the narrator to trope the reader syntactically, semantically, and pragmatically by means of repetitive patterns in this passage. For example, in 10:25 the narrator starts off with a double question that brings the reader to take the two questions syntactically and semantically as one. They form a linked, complex construction in which the semantic content of the second element doubles up the first: the two questions form a sentential or discursive *hendiadys*. Far from being merely repetitive, the pairings produce something new: the many-become-one. Luke's preference for double texts and pairings has long been recognized,[30] although here in Luke 10 the reader is presented with an intensification of the doubling and pairing that suggests something more than a benign duplication of episodes (Fitzmyer: 81–82)[31] or just a correspondence with Acts. It is tied specifically to the self-reflexive question that both signals this one-by-two movement and ruptures it.

The narrator links the questions hendiadically (a one-by-two question) in service of his larger discursive purpose. Hendiadic question is paired with a double hendiadic ethical exhortation [(cf. v. 27 ("love the Lord . . . and your neighbor as yourself")[32] and the double injunction of v. 37 ("Go, and do likewise")]. Luke frames the reading of the Torah and parable intertexts both separately in their respective halves of the dialogue and together with hendiadic question and injunction.[33] The hendiadic structure of question-and-exhortation[34] frames and subordinates both the Torah citation and the parabolic story, which are now interpretively linked together in a one-by-two textual relationship—law-by-story, Deuteronomic citation-by-Samaritan parable that is read ambiguously. Like Martha-by-Mary, these links frame also the reader's subordination and complementarity, dependence, and difference.

---

[30] Fitzmyer reads the doubling in chronological terms as evidence of the Gospel writer's deep dependency upon the Q source to complete the narrative. Perhaps this is one of those sources mentioned in 1:1 that Luke is rewriting. Tannehill reads the text differently. He notes the fact of the doubling not as a redactional issue but as one of characterization, specifically the double characterization of men and women. I give this doubling yet a different reading below.

[31] Fitzmyer identifies in excess of a dozen "doublets" in Luke's text. The explanation of the phenomenon is "somewhat complicated." There are apparent instances where Luke has inherited passages from Mark, Q, and Luke's special source; others in which Luke seems actively to avoid doublets, revealing what Bussman calls a "fear of doublets." How one accounts for their presence in the text (tradition, literary dependence, rhetorical purpose) is a function of the reading framework with which one operates.

[32] "Hendiadys" is defined as "the use of two words connected by a copulative conjunction to express a single complex idea" (Smyth, par. 3025). Strictly speaking, we do not have a paratactic construction here, as is the case in 2:47 and 21:15 (also cf. Acts 1:25, 14:17, 23:6); however to specify parataxis limits the notion to a syntactic use. We intend it here semantically as a rhetorical trope for the organization of a portion of Luke's text. See Moulton (335) for limited discussion.

[33] Even in English translation the double verbal structure using verbs related to motion (come, go, stay) has a clear hendiadic flavor if not function.

[34] There is evidence that Luke's text could be framed in a midrashic reading context: his language is replete with septuagintisms (Fitzmyer); the controversy setting of the text is traditionally Jewish (Bultmann); Luke's way of posing the question "How are you reading this?" reflects Jewish methods of argumentation (Jeremias cited in Marshall 1978:433) in the form "How do you *recite*?" The intertextual structure and use of the citations is suggestive of a midrashic interpretive style (cf. Boyarin). The point here is that it is read in other scholarly ways.

This is a small example of a larger pattern of hendiadic writing and reading that is visible throughout Luke's writing. Doubling,[35] doublets, pairings, and hendiadic textual patterns can be traced across the gospel-and-history textual surface as part of a writer's view of a unified one-by-two volume corpus (Luke-Acts).[36] The parallel openings of the Gospel and Acts further serve to strengthen this rhetorical linkage and the complementarity of texts: Luke-Acts is to be read together—intertextually—one in relation to the other, like Deuteronomy and the Samaritan parable. If hendiadys is a Lukan intertextual reading and writing strategy that serves to unify and structure question, exhortation, gospel text, and history,[37] then what purpose is served with this new unity? As the narrator sets up the lawyer to read and write, Luke sets up the reader to read this one narrative (διήγησιν) in relation to the many (πολλοί) previous efforts to compile a narrative.[38] Luke must have in mind a substantial written/oral corpus, including what has been drawn up in-house before (1:1, ἀνατάξασθαι διήγησιν), what is being written now (1:3, γράψαι), and what will come later (Ac 1:1, the second book, the implied contrast to τὸν μὲν πρῶτον λόγον ἐποιησάμην). In addition, the corpus includes unnamed Hellenistic texts which the prologue's form and content bring to mind. Just as the writer must write against the background of this literary system, so too the reader must read against an intertextual horizon.[39] Luke instructs his reader to read/write via a hendiadic intertextual strategy that relates question to injunction, Torah to Jesus story, gospel to history, lawyer to Martha, first book (πρῶτον λόγον) to second book.[40]

To summarize, Luke positions the reader in a third-person posture, silent and listening within a text rhetorically structured and figured by a

---

[35] Tannehill (132–39) notes this doubling tendency and points to Luke's numerous male/female pairings. He interprets this to be a sign of the author's desire to enhance the position of women. For a more detailed description of such pairings, see Cadbury (233–35). But contrast Schaberg: 275.

[36] The initial hendiadys of the Gospel occurs in 1:2 (αὐτόπται καὶ ὑπηρέται); so Marshall, 1970:41.

[37] See White on rhetorical troping of the historian; Burnett, 1990.

[38] On the significance of ἐπειδήπερ, Marshall (1978:41) argues that Luke's motive in using the work of previous writers "positively" is to justify his own further efforts, rather than to supercede their work with his own. Why must it be one position or another, unless a defensive binary reading logic prevails? Harold Bloom argues that strong readings need a predecessor against which to write.

[39] For both Jauss and Iser "interpretive horizon" or "horizon of expectations" serves as a conceptual equivalent for "intertextuality." See Clayton and Rothstein (26).

[40] The extent to which a hendiadic strategy functions macrotextually is open to further question. I propose this as a suggestive reading strategy for all of Luke-Acts.

one-by-two logic;⁴¹ subjectivity and narrative structure go hand-in-hand. From the narrator's side, the squaring off of lawyer-and-Jesus/Jesus-and-Martha unfolds dramatically in a narrative weave in which Deuteronomic citation and Samaritan parable are stitched together with the Martha discourse to form a single, dialogic unity, a piece of textual whole cloth within which the transposed subject positions of the lawyer and reader overlap and intersect. The narrator's confident story-telling technique (1:3 πᾶσιν ἀκριβῶς καθεξῆς σοι γράψαι), forcefully announced at the start, subsumes by this gesture *all* (πᾶσιν) textual differences in a totalizing way within a single orderly account which reads question in relation to answer, Deuteronomic text in relation to Jesus story, narrative character in relation to the reader, reading in relation to parenesis. Character, discourse, subject, and reading are written for Luke's reader in such a way as to produce a reading διά the text ("through", "by way of") with the goal of establishing a reader to read and write likewise, to read and write Lukewise.⁴²

DECONSTRUCTIVE READING AND THE READER

It all seems so orderly (καθεξῆς) for the reader, almost too good to be true. It seems good for Luke (ἔδοξε κἀμοί, 1:3), too, who writes with confidence having followed everything (παρηκολουθηκότι . . . πᾶσιν) so attentively (ἀκριβῶς). Luke's text presents from start to finish a reading and a writing that gives every appearance of sewing it all up. A narrative so orderly (καθεξῆς) and arranged for the reader that there are no rips, tears, or snags in the textual fabric to catch her eye. From the narrator's point of view the citational folds blend seamlessly into the overall narrative fabric. The reader is appropriately mystified and spell-bound by the implied author's weave (Tannehill: 4). But is every reader bewitched? Is every question answered? Apparently not. Are there any textual remainders not yet put in proper order? There remains Luke's open question, which is Jesus' question, that continues to lie before the eye and in the ear of any reader who has eyes and ears to hear it (cf. 10:24); it is a question the text blurts out long after Martha has been quieted and in spite of Luke's best efforts to answer it.

Luke's strongly valued narrative unity demands a third-person narrational style appropriate for producing the effect of a textual wholecloth and a subservient reader. In contrast to the smooth, accomplished Helle-

---

⁴¹ Fitzmyer (82) refers to H. Schurmann who suggests that the doublet construction is a sign of Luke's "forgetfulness." Hence there is no narrative "logic" that can explain its presence.

⁴² Of course contrast Mark's opacity and textual irresolution.

nistic rhetoric of the prologue (echoes of Josephus and Philo), the fabric of the one discourse with the Lawyer shows traces of having been reworked by some bricoleur from the many (πολλοί) materials (the parable, the Torah) and in translation (the Septuagint). On close scrutiny the composite character of the text and its seams are not so transparent;[43] the numerous seams in the text belie his effort to achieve the desired "connected narrative' (1:3). Notwithstanding his rhetorical strategy, is Luke in complete control? Of his material? His reader?

Reading with a deconstructive strategy, what are we to do with Luke's hendiadic writing strategy? The reader's discursive role as established by Luke's persuasive narrator seems formalized and finalized, but the one servile reader is not the only discursive position possible in relation to this text. For one thing, *other voices* are preserved in this text, which is itself the intersecting space of many texts and discourses (both implicit and explicit) drawn from a variety of sources and traditions, including contemporary critical strategies: Deuteronomy, Leviticus, Q and Luke's special source, Augustine, Calvin, Fitzmyer, Conzelmann, Fiorenza, Schaberg. To the extent that Luke is an already-read-text transposed by systems of meaning (literary, theological, feminist, etc.), these voices are "there." They inhabit Luke's narrative and leave behind barely discernible traces of the voices and discourses drawn from other writings and readings (1:1) that have been latently inscribed within "the text" awaiting some critical needlework to unravel and resew the fabric into a different text for different readers. This is Lukan "henoglassia" overwritten and silenced by a powerful narrator and a powerful reading strategy in search not only for one narrative but one voice, a "lukoglassia." As long as these many different vestigial discursive positions and discourses have already been written/read into the text, *it is possible*—indeed *inevitable*—that Luke's texts are to be read otherwise. For these discourses are a sedimented history of readings and writings that have already taken place and point ahead to others yet to unfold. Reading otherwise is already an inherent possibility of Luke's text (cf. Ac 28:27).

Certain critical interventions facilitate reading otherwise. Schaberg's feminist critique for one; Derrida's deconstruction for another. The seams among cited texts and narrative levels and the subject positions are made to stand out, however, when the reading perspective becomes suspicious (goes deconstructive); that is, once I as reader take responsibility for intervening for the Other by looking for the intertextual matrices, different voices, conflicting logics and discourses and subject positions, conflicting cultural codes, and the like. I saw difference, not sameness, read plurality

---

[43] See Fitzmyer on Luke's Septuagintisms and suspected Aramaisms, Hebraisms, and Semitisms (114–27).

not unity, heard many voices not just one. My deconstructive reading didn't just happen in a capricious way; I first had to read Luke's text in the setting of traditional literary and historical criticism, the discourse that Derrida calls the "guard rail" that protects the text. Next I had to look carefully at eye-level across the textual surface for what was below and above. My attention was snagged initially by a text which addressed *me* directly as a reading subject to respond to the double question "What is written? How are you reading?" Then by an awareness that this text was laced with doublets and hendiadic and double gestures that encouraged me to look for the seams, for the many and for what was other than it seemed. The Lukan seams/seems (ἔδοξε, 1:3 and δοκεῖ, 10:36) stood out. In spite of itself the Lukan text as writing invited this *other* way to unravel this text not only because it too is a reading of many texts but also because it addressed me directly as reading subject with the very question that Luke has Jesus enunciate to the Lawyer in order to best him. The semblance of whole cloth gives way under the force of a deconstructive gaze to reveal a patch-work of texts, lector positions, and interests stitched and sutured together in an way that sought to hide all the signs of earlier sewings. But Luke's strategy didn't completely pay off because I paid attention to the text, not only to what he said and how he said it, but also to what was not said. The one thing needed (ἑνὸς δέ ἐστιν χρεία, v.42) to read otherwise turned out to be Luke's own text.

The writer of the Gospel acknowledges situating the reading-writing of the Gospel-Acts in the context of the Hellenistic literary system and the Greco-Roman world and privileging his own reading.44 The many (πολλοί) accounts that have been attempted (1:1) yield in Luke's rewriting but *one* narrative (διήγησιν) about the things accomplished among them (περὶ τῶν πεπληροφορημένων ἐν ἡμῖν πραγμάτων). But as reader/writer I also do what Luke does; I too situate Luke's text in the context of a different textual, linguistic, ideological, and gender system, one that is composed not merely of ancient Greco-Roman texts but of the feminist texts of Schaberg and Miller, the deconstructive writings of Derrida and Barthes, the semiotic readings of Kristeva and Peirce, and the traditional redactional exegeses of Tannehill and Fitzmyer. "What is written in the law? How are you reading it?" beckons me to a self-reflexive, intertextual reflection about *my* literary system, *my* context for reading, *my* interests, and their relationship to Luke. It invites me narratively and discursively to raise questions about my role as a suspicious reader in the text: "What does it mean for Luke to *rewrite* the Deuteronomic text by way of Torah and parable within this

---

44 So Streeter (548), cited in Fitzmyer (92): Luke's narrative is the work of a "conscious litterateur of the Greco-Roman period." Compare Marshall (1970:40) who draws the opposite conclusion. Also Fitzmyer: 287.

literary system, and how are we readers *re*reading this intertextual production?" In this way the ethical question of the good (ἀγαθήν) and the right (ὀρθῶς) confront me in the text.

The appearance of an orderly or complete writing with its corollary Lukan passive reader on the one hand and the irrepressible invitation to multiple writings and resistant readers of Luke's text on the other proves to be a source of productive tension in Luke's text. Even though Luke has done a persuasive job of mastering his many sources and reading them using hendiadic and doubling tropes across the text,[45] the fact remains that that is not enough to keep me from reading otherwise; in spite of what Luke may desire or try to do to direct the reader and the writing, both escape Luke's rhetorical control (cf. Schaberg: 275), if they have good eyes and ears (10:23–24). Try as he might, Luke can't fully contain the range of meanings or reading responses readers give to the question "What texts are written here, Luke? How are you reading them?" with the same exactitude as he cleverly manipulates the lawyer and Martha.

The nature of the literary structure of 10:25–42 and its formal relationship to vv. 38–42 is a case in point. Where does the reader find the beginning and end of the textual boundaries? Does the text end with the double injunction to the Lawyer, with the Mary and Martha pronouncement story, after the lesson on prayer, or elsewhere?[46] In spite of Luke's confessed καθεξῆς, as he writes he leaves linguistic, textual, and rhetorical gaps[47] that serve as trace markers or snags where other readings and writers catch, take hold and begin to unravel and restitch. For example, the undecidability of the structural organization of the Gospel-Acts text itself is a matter with which the author wrestles but cannot resolve. At the

---

[45] Fitzmyer represents the consensus view that the writing represented in 10:25–37 is to be attributed to the writer Luke, even if the writer made use of existing special source materials.

[46] Marshall (1978:439) makes an interesting case for seeing a three-part structure: the Jesus/Lawyer exchange (10:25–37); the Mary/Martha pronouncement story (10:38–42) and the teaching on prayer (11:1–13). What makes his reading interesting is that he attempts to recuperate the Martha/Mary pronouncement story in relation to what precedes and to relate it to what follows based in part on thematic linkages with being friend (φίλον, 11:5) and the parallelism between the question posed in 11:5—"Which of you who has a friend..."") and the question put to the lawyer about the neighbor (πλησίον, 10:26)—"Which of these three..." (cf. Talbert: 125–56).

[47] See Fitzmyer (299) for a discussion of the question whether Luke makes use of all the source material available to him and duly constructs a narrative in which nothing (available) is left out. He refers to F. Mussner (253–55), who says that Luke "writes without a gap." From an intertextual perspective the dialogical structure and recitations suggest just the opposite: since *other texts* and *other speakers* could be written in the text not all (πασίν) that is possible to write or to read has been. To say there is no gap is to say there is no Otherness that could make its appearance in the text.

macro level Luke cannot write the text *one* way without it also being written *many* ways.

Deconstructive reading exposes a tension in the Lukan writing, a desire at one level rhetorically to be resolved but one that cannot finally be limited or erased textually. As a writing Luke's text cannot escape the fact that even if it desires to be the *one* accurate narrative, it is a diachronic rereading/rewriting of many texts and it stands always already synchronically *in relation to other* texts within a literary system, within a complex cultural production past and present. Its difference from its source texts and traditions, as well as from competing narratives, underscores Derrida's semiotic point that when viewed as a signifier the text presupposes other signifiers as part of a system. Difference is a productive force issuing into new readings and texts, and is at the same time a material reminder that there is no escaping the textual system as both history and structure, only a spilling or slippage over into another one (cf. Derrida's often misread, "There is nothing outside of text"). Difference from other texts and readings is the ground for the possibility of a meaningful writing and a brake upon any claim to stand on high textual ground outside of history or independent of structure.

Luke's effort to resolve the problem of the *one* (narrative) versus the *many* is part of a broader gesture of control that figures expressly in the episode of Martha and Mary.[48] It is not a complete surprise that Luke's rhetorical concern with the one and the many should lead to a writing in which that very figure is inscribed figuratively in the narrative itself. The "one/many" figure encodes the value of "inclusion/exclusion." It is useful to think about this figure as the return of that which Luke may have sought to repress (the many). The "one and the many" resurfaces in the Martha and Mary story both in the narrative exchange between Jesus and Martha and in the disputed textual tradition that deepens the importance of the episode—not only for Luke's overall writing logic but for Luke's narrative argument.[49] The focus of attention here on the phrase "one

---

[48] Of the more than fifty occurrences of πολύς or its variants in the Gospel alone, nearly half address either explicitly or implicitly a contrast between many and one. For example, the many/one figure is explicit in 4:25, 27; 8:30; 9:37; 10:41, 42; 12:19; 14:16; 21:7; also the constrasts between a lot and a little and something and nothing are used in 7:46, 10:2, 40; 13:29 and 16:10. Clearly πολύς in this context has a very wide contrastive use.

[49] Fitzmyer characterizes 10:42 as "complicated" because the readings are conflictual. There is manuscript support for the reading "one thing that is needed;" some support also for "many things that are needed;" and some significant attestation of what he ends up calling the most "reliable" reading that combines both, "many and one thing are needed" (P^{75}) (Fitzmyer: 894) Fitzmyer mentions Dibelius in support of this more difficult reading. Cf. 18:22, a doubling of the exchange in 10:25–37 with respect to the dialogic format and the one/many contrast. Contrast Talbert, however, on

thing is needful" (ἑνὸς δέ ἐστιν χρεία) is Luke's figure for control, while it is my figure for the impossibility of control.

The question of reliability or certainty in reading and writing (ἀσφάλεια; cf. Acts 5:23) one text versus many is then at the heart of an unresolvable tension—the *pharmakon*—that is present not only in the issue of textual and readerly production in the time of the original writers and readers of Luke's text, but also in the history of the commentary and critical tradition upon Luke's text. Part of what is at stake in determining the text is ascertaining *how* it can be read, by whom, and in what context. The uncertainties of reading on the points of overall literary structure and the use of both Greco-Roman and Septuagint rhetorical elements clash with the certainty (ἀσφάλεια) Luke was announcing. Ironically, as text and intertext Luke's narrative illustrates the undecidability of either prescribing or proscribing with certainty the way a reader can read a text, notwithstanding the fact that the narrator might wish it otherwise.

Reread and rewritten in this way, Luke's double question, "What is written in the Law and how are you reading it" cannot possibly be restricted to the narrator's world, or indeed to any intertextual setting; it too becomes a question that escapes the confines of the Lukan matrix. It becomes an undecidable question addressed to *me*, indeed to each and every reader about the process of reading, writing, and subjectivity in the biblical text's construction and deconstruction, about gaps, doubling back, contradictions, undecidable nodes in the semiotic processes not before considered. We encounter these "disorderly moments," these ruptures in Luke's sutured text (moments that Luke seeks to write over or erase) when we read and write it especially in relation, as Derrida says, to "philosophy and literature, science and literature, politics and literature, theology and literature, psychoanalysis and literature." And, I would add feminism and literature. Luke's overwritten text and double questions find themselves necessarily in a different discursive position at the intersection of semiotics, deconstruction, ideology, psychoanalysis, and feminism and also of new reader subject positions that, like Martha, will not take the author's speaking sitting down.[50] Resistant and aggressive, more really like Martha than Mary, we read here a meta-question about Luke's manner of reading and writing as a fundamental statement about Writing in general and a question about our responsibility as readers (Derrida, 1976:6).

---

this more difficult reading (125–26) who prefers to speak of this episode as a "thought unit." See Schaberg: 288.

[50] The multiplicity of different critical reading strategies that enables us to think about a deconstructive or intertextual reading approach is itself an instance of intertextuality.

Conclusion: Reading Otherwise

Daniel Boyarin begins his *Intertextuality and the Reading of Midrash* by acknowledging the cultural and ideological site from which he reads and writes. His is an example other exegetes (especially male readers) ought to take to heart. Situating himself as a western-educated, Jewish intellectual, Boyarin singles out Derrida's deconstructive project and contemporary literary theory as his key conversational partners.[51] Literary theory functions for him as the site where "fundamental issues" can be addressed today, wide-ranging issues that include the nature of language, the subject, ethical accountability, the meaning of Scripture, the task of interpretation, and more. Literary theory provides a bridge once reserved for theology and certain branches of philosophy into difficult questions about life, the role played by Scripture as a literary text. To use Giles Gunn's chiastic expression, literary theory cultivates both a culture of criticism and a criticism of late twentieth western culture.

Following Boyarin's lead, deconstruction and feminism serve that end for me. I have tried in this essay to take seriously Luke's invitation to read both the text and me as its reader. The textual invitation to read Luke's rewriting intertextually and deconstructively is then an*other* kind of rewriting that is responsive to Luke's textual question, although it does not duplicate the narrator's desire for a Mary-like subordinate partner. Luke's hendiadic strategy is a strong reading response to the textual differences here (reading and doing). As such it is a challenge for me to read Luke's text otherwise (as reading and writing in an intertextual mode); to think of reading and writing as a coming face-to-face with Luke's *otherness*—the otherness of the Samaritan, the wounded man, the displaced sisters, the Torah, Jesus parable, those other silenced voices that have read Luke's text over time—an otherness which finally leaves no reader or reading safe from the text's interrogation or in control of its meanings.[52] It is this otherness that Schaberg also wants me to hear.

---

[51] Derrida's project remains the broad theoretical background against which Boyarin's investigation of Midrash as an intertextual phenomenon takes place. Deconstruction, from Boyarin's perspective, is important because of its capacity to put in question all interpretive acts (xii). Deconstruction is, to cite Derrida, ". . . a coming-to-terms with literature" (1985:13).

[52] Derrida and Barthes approach the issue of controlling the reading of a text from different angles. For Derrida, the capacity to generate different readings underscores the very *undecidablity* of a text, that is the excessive nature of meaning itself exemplified by a writing that discloses under close examination strategies of meaning production preferred as well as those suppressed. Deconstruction's is that way of reading that looks for the excess built into the very strategy of limitation itself. For Barthes' position, see 1981:31–48.

The invitation to read intertextually, deconstructively, semiotically, with feminist consciousness is plain. That is one way to read the otherness of this text. But there are others. For example, what about the relationships between the Deuteronomic citation and the parable, which we have not explored? Following Boyarin, might we be tempted to reverse the order of "influence" and chronological intertextual connection and explore to what extent Torah translates the parable rather than the other way around? Is the Septuagint text of Deut 6:5 with its dialogic structure "reading" the entire dialogic context of the Lawyer and Jesus in a rabbinic-style midrash of the Samaritan parable so that the interpretive energy flows from past to present? What would it mean to think of reading and writing as moving interpretively forward and backward in time and across time?[53] If we read aggressively and in such a writerly fashion, then in what way might the Martha and Mary discourse function as midrash upon the parable *and* the dialogic narrative context as a way of speaking directly of the *woman as Other* according to the religious code (figured in the parable as the Samaritan), and the Other according to the gender code (figured as the Unnamed reader of Luke's text)? An intertextual "intergesis" may in fact encourage a hypertextual reading that can go in any number of directions in an effort to query the intertext, the literary system, and the historical context of Luke's as well as our writing and reading. If Luke's Martha and Mary function as his transposed and figured readers—Luke's reader and other writerly readers invited into the conversation—then it may be that the author's divided representation and his doubling and pairings reflect a portrait of women that may be thicker and more complicated (he "supports" women versus he "controls" women) than initially appears and deserving of a closer look. In short, reading intertextually and deconstructively can serve in a multitude of ways as a response to Luke's question, one that generates a multitude of readings and writings that preserve, pass on, and transpose Luke's text for other readers to come but in different, more responsible ways than traditional narrative or commentary strategies can imagine. These are issues yet to be explored in light of an intertextual and deconstructive approach to reading the Gospel (see Moore, 1992).

Why should we *not* be satisfied with reading this text Lukewise, as a neat persuasive one-by-two? On what grounds would we choose to read this way as opposed to that? This is the question of responsibility as reader. As a reader, Luke the writer wants to write an orderly account of "the things which have been accomplished" (1:1) as a corrective and indeed a supplement (a rewriting of previous accounts that displaces other

---

[53] Compare Calloud (65) in this volume on the "forwards and backwards" role of figures and the figurative trajectory in reading the Scriptures.

writings) and overwrites them into a single text in order to fix with certainty the meaning of what has been and will be written. For us, however, while invited to read and do Lukewise, we are also deliberately invited by the text to reread and rewrite the text intertextually and deconstructively, expressly in relation to Luke's reading. Call it, if you please, an invitation to a writerly response, not a *one-by-two* but a *two-by-one* reading, a *dys*-reading[54] that stresses the difference between Luke's reading and ours, a reading that looks for ways to loosen, not fix; multiply, not reduce reading possibilities, a reading for the many not the one.

Finally, in reading Luke's text deconstructively it is good (ἔδοξε, 1:3) to read for the other: for the parts rather than the whole, between the written lines, in the seams between its elements (textual, discursive), in the junctures between the distinct textual citations and allusions, in the gaps that exist between question and answer, enunciation and utterance, against the overarching and overwritten narrative grain of Luke's hendiadic interpretive strategy. By situating myself as a "resistant" reader who refuses to be constrained by the discursive positions of either the lawyer or Luke's imagined reader, I take responsibility for repositioning myself as a critically constituted *historical* reader for a reading in the gaps and fissures of the workings of the Luke's text, in the spaces of its semiotic, intertextual, institutional production, with its ever-present patriarchical and conflictual view of women.

Attending to Luke's question quite explicitly, I have worked at reducing the distance between reading and writing, a distance interposed as a result of certain hermeneutical strategies—ancient and modern—for reading texts. As a writerly reader I have rewritten Luke's text by stressing its discontinuities, ignoring the boundaries of formal limits (generic, narrative, discursive, textual, logical, and performative), searching for an*other* logic and the logic of the *Other*) than the one that Luke offers. I know that in this process I partially write myself as a subject and as a subject matter into the text. Practically speaking, this amounts to wedging apart a text whose rhetorical energy is focused upon unifying differences and reducing reading options by troping the reader hendiadically through question, injunction, text, corpus, and subject in order to reign in the otherness that comes to expression syntactically in the double question put to the lawyer/reader in v.26, semantically in the figure of caring for the other, and pragmatically in the double injunction, "Go, and do likewise." Reading in a writerly fashion means showing how Luke's text finds itself

---

[54] This can be called a "disorderly" reading only given a context and set of reading rules that presuppose a determinative meaning and reading of the text. In another sense, however, it is a *dys*-orderly reading, affirming multiple rather than singular interpretive possibilities.

in tension with its own explicit purposes and finally proves incapable of constraining the otherness of the intertextual dynamics at work within its network as an instance of a broader understanding of textuality, intertextuality, and subjectivity. Viewed this way, the Gospel text warns us off as it attracts us to the control that Luke seeks to exercise, saying, Reader beware.

WORKS CITED

Alter, Robert
    1990   *The Pleasures of Reading in an Ideological Age*. New York: Simon and Schuster.

Alter, Robert and Frank Kermode, eds.
    1987   *The Literary Guide to the Bible*. Cambridge: Harvard University Press.

Attridge, Derek, ed.
    1992   *Acts of Literature*. New York; London: Routledge.

Bakhtin, Mikhail
    1981   *The Dialogic Imagination*. Ed. Michael Holquist. Trans. Caryl Emerson and Michael Holquist. Austin: University of Texas Press.
    1984   *Problems of Dostoevsky's Poetics*. Trans. and Ed. Caryl Emerson. Minneapolis: University of Minnesota Press.

Bal, Mieke
    1987   *Lethal Love. Feminist Literary Readings of Biblical Love Stories*. Bloomington: Indiana University Press.
    1988   *Murder and Difference. Gender, Genre, and Scholarship on Sisera's Death*. Bloomington: Indiana University Press.

Barthes, Roland
    1977a   "From Work to Text". Pp. 55–164 in *Image Music Text*. Trans. and Ed. Stephen Heath. New York: Hill and Wang.
    1977b   "The Struggle with the Angel." Pp. 125–41 in *Image Music Text*. Trans. and Ed. Stephen Heath. New York: Hill and Wang.
    1981   "Theory of the Text." Pp. 31–47 in *Untying the Text. A Post-Structuralist Reader*. Ed. Robert Young. Boston: Routledge & Kegan Paul.

Barzilai, Shuli
    1991   "Borders of Language: Kristeva's Critique of Lacan." PMLA 106:294–305.

Benveniste, Emile
    1970   "L'Appareil formel de l'énonciation." *Langages* 17:12–18.

Bible and Culture Collective
    1995   *The Postmodern Bible*. New Haven: Yale University Press.

Brawley, Robert
    1991   "Intertextuality in John 19:28–29." Paper presented to the Society of Biblical Literature Literary Aspects of the Gospels and Acts Group.

Brodie, Thomas Louis
    1984   "Greco-Roman Imitations of Texts as a Partial Guide to Luke's Use of Sources." Pp. in *Luke-Acts. New Perspectives from the Society of Biblical Literature Seminar*. Ed. Charles Talbert. New York: Crossroad.

Boyarin, Daniel
    1990   *Intertextuality and the Reading of Midrash*. Indiana Studies in Biblical Literature. Bloomington: Indiana University Press.

Burnett, Fred W.
    1988   "Exposing the Implied Author in Matthew: The Characterization of God as Father." Paper presented to the Literary Aspects of the Gospels and Acts Group, The Society of Biblical Literature Annual Meeting. Chicago, IL.
    1990   "Postmodern Biblical Criticism: The Eve of Historical Criticism." *Semeia* 51:51–80.

Cadbury, Henry J.
    1968   *The Making of Luke-Acts*. London: SPCK.

Clayton, Jay and Eric Rothstein, eds.
    1992   "Figures in the Corpus: Theories of Influence and Intertextuality." Pp. 3–36 in *Influence and Intertextuality in Literary History*. Madison: University of Wisconsin Press.

Culler, Jonathan.
    1982   *On Deconstruction: Theory and Criticism after Structuralism*. Ithaca: Cornell University Press.

Derrida, Jacques
    1972a   "Structure, Sign, and Play in the Discourses of the Human Sciences." Pp. 247–65 in *The Structuralist Controversy. The Languages of Criticism and the Sciences of Man*. Ed. Richard Macksey and Eugenio Donato. Baltimore: Johns Hopkins University Press.
    1972b   *Dissemination*. Trans. Barbara Johnson. Chicago: University of Chicago Press.
    1972b   *Positions*. Trans. Alan Bass. Chicago: University of Chicago Press.
    1976   *Of Grammatology*. Trans. Gayatri Chakravorty Spivak. Baltimore: Johns Hopkins University Press.
    1977   "Signature Event Context." *Glyph* 1:172–97
    1979   "Living On. Border Lines." Pp. 75–176 in *Deconstruction and Criticism*. Ed. Geoffrey Hartman. New York: Seabury.
    1982   "The Time of a Thesis. Punctuations." Pp. 34–50 in *Philosophy in France Today*. Ed. Alan Montefiore. Cambridge: Cambridge University Press.
    1985a   "Deconstruction in America: An Interview." *Critical Exchange* 17:1–33.
    1985b   *The Ear of the Other: Otobiography, Transference, Translation*. Ed. Christie McDonald. Trans. Peggy Kamuf. Lincoln: University of Nebraska Press.

1988b   *Limited Inc.* Ed. Gerald Graff. Trans. Samuel Weber and Jeffrey Mehlman. Evanston, IL: Northwestern University Press.

Detweiler, Robert
1989   *Breaking the Fall. Religious Readings of Contemporary Fiction.* Studies in Literature and Religion. London: Macmillan.

Dibelius, Martin
1956   *Studies in the Acts of the Apostles.* Ed. H. Greeven. London: SCM.

Drasima, Sipke, ed.
1989   *Intertextuality in Biblical Writings. Essays in Honour of Bas van Iersel.* Kampden, Netherlands: J.H. Kok.

Eagleton, Terry
1983   *Literary Theory. An Introduction.* Minneapolis: University of Minnesota Press.
1986   *Against the Grain: Selected Essays.* London: Verso.

Fisch, Harold
1985   "The Hermeneutic Quest In *Robinson Crusoe.*" Pp. 213–35 in *Midrash and Literature.* Ed. Geoffrey H. Hartman and Sanford Budick. New Haven: Yale University Press.

Fitzmyer, Joseph
1981   *The Gospel According to Luke (I-IX). Introduction, Translation, and Notes.* The Anchor Bible. Vol 28. Garden City: Doubleday.

Foucault, Michel
1972   *Archaeology of Knowledge and the Discourse on Language.* Trans. M. Meridan Smith. New York: Pantheon.
1977   "What is an Author?" Pp. 113-38 in *Language, Counter-Memory, Practice.* Ed. D. Bouchard. Ithaca: Cornell University Press.

Fowler, Robert M.
1992   *Let the Reader Understand. Reader-Response Criticism and the Gospel of Mark.* Minneapolis: Fortress.

Genette, Gérard
1991   *Palimpsestes: La Littérature au second degré.* Paris: Seuil.

Greimas, A.J. and J. Courtès
1982   *Semiotics and Language: An Analytical Dictionary.* Trans. Larry Crist, Daniel Patte, et al. Bloomington: Indiana University Press.

Gunn, Giles
1987   *The Culture of Criticism and the Criticism of Culture.* Oxford: Oxford University Press.

Handelman, Susan
1982   *The Slayers of Moses: The Emergence of Rabbinic Interpretation in Modern Literary Theory.* Albany: State University of New York Press.

Hart, Kevin
    1989   *The Trespass of the Sign: Deconstruction, Theology and Philosophy*. New York/Cambridge: Cambridge University Press.

Hartman, Geoffrey
    1984   "The Culture of Criticism." *PMLA* 99:386-97.

Hays, Richard
    1989   *Echoes of Scripture in the Letters of Paul*. New Haven: Yale University Press.

Hirsch, David
    1991   *The Deconstruction of Literature: Criticism after Auschwitz*. Providence: Brown University Press.

Jakobson, Roman
    1971   "Shifters, Verbal Categories and the Russian Verb." Pp. 130–47 in *Selected Writings*. Vol. 2. Word and Language. Mouton: The Hague.

Jardine, Alice
    1985   *Gynesis: Configurations of Women and Modernity*. Ithaca: Cornell University Press.

Jobling, David
    1990   "Writing the Wrongs of the World: The Deconstruction of the Biblical Text in the Context of Liberation Theologies." *Semeia* 51:81–118.

Johnson, Barbara
    1987   *A World of Difference*. Baltimore: Johns Hopkins University Press.

Kaufer, David and Gary Waller
    1985   "To Write Is to Read Is to Write, Right?" Pp. 66–92 in *Writing and Reading Differently. Deconstruction and the Teaching of Composition and Literature*. Ed. C. Douglas Atkins and Michael Johnson. Lawrence: University of Kansas Press.

Kermode, Frank
    1985   "The Plain Sense of Things." Pp. 179–94 in *Midrash and Literature*. Ed. Geoffrey H. Hartman and Sanford Budick. New Haven: Yale University Press.

Kristeva, Julia
    1968   "Problèmes de la structuration du texte." Pp. 297–316 in *Théorie d'ensemble*. Ed. Philippe Sollers. Collection Tel Quel. Paris: Editions du Seuil.
    1969   *Semeiotikē. Recherches pour une sémanalyse*. Collections Tel Quel. Paris: Editions du Seuil.
    1974   *La révolution du langage poétique*. Collections Tel Quel. Paris: Editions du Seuil.
    1980   *Desire in Language. A Semiotic Approach to Literature and Art*. Ed. Leon S. Roudiez. Trans. Thomas Gora, Alice Jardine, and Leon S. Roudiez. New York: Columbia University Press.

1983 "Within the Microcosm of 'The Talking Cure.'" Pp. 33–48 in *Interpreting Lacan*. Ed. Joseph H. Smith and William Kerrigan. Trans. Thomas Gora and Margaret Waller. Psychiatry and the Humanities 6. New Haven: Yale University Press.

1986 "The System and the Speaking Subject." Pp. 24–33 in *The Kristeva Reader*. Ed. Toril Moi. New York: Columbia University Press.

1995 *New Maladies of the Soul*. Trans. Ross Guberman. European Perspectives. New York: Columbia University Press.

LaCapra, Dominick
1983 *Rethinking Intellectual History. Texts, Contexts, Language*. Ithaca: Cornell University Press.

Lategan, Bernard and Willem Vorster, eds.
1985 *Text and Reality: Aspects of Reference in Biblical Texts*. Semeia Studies. Philadelphia: Fortress.

Leitch, Vincent
1983 *Deconstructive Criticism: An Advanced Introduction*. New York: Columbia University Press.

1985 "Deconstruction and Pedagogy." Pp. 16–26 in *Writing and Reading Differently: Deconstruction and the Teaching of Composition and Literature*. Ed. C. Douglas Atkins and Michael Johnson. Lawrence: University of Kansas Press.

Levinas, Emmanuel
1969 *Totality and Infinity. An Essay on Exteriority*. Trans. Alphonso Lingis. Duquesne Studies. Philosophical Series 24. Pittsburgh: Duquesnes University Press.

Lyotard, Jean-François
1984 *The Postmodern Condition: A Report on Knowledge*. Trans. Geoff Benington and Brian Massumi. Theory and History of Literature 10. Minneapolis: University of Minnesota Press.

Mai, Hans-Peter
1991 "Bypassing Intertextuality. Hermeneutics, Textual Practice, Hypertext." Pp. 30-59 in *Intertextuality*. Ed. Henrich Plett. Research in Text Theory 15. Berlin: Walter de Gruyter.

Marshall, I. Howard
1970 *Luke: Historian and Theologian*. Grand Rapids: Zondervan.
1978 *The Gospel of Luke. A Commentary on the Greek Text*. Grand Rapids: Eerdmans.

Miller, Nancy
1986 "Arachnologies: The Woman, the Text, and the Critic." Pp. 270–95 in *The Poetics of Gender*. Ed. Nancy Miller. New York: Columbia University Press.

Moore, Stephen D.
　1989　　*Literary Criticism and the Gospels: The Theoretical Challenge*. New Haven: Yale University Press.
　1992　　*Mark and Luke in Poststructuralist Perspectives. Jesus Begins to Write*. New Haven: Yale University Press.

Peirce, Charles Sanders
　1931–1958　*Collected Papers*. Ed. Charles Hartshorne and Paul Weiss. 5 Vols. Cambridge: Harvard University Press.

Phillips, Gary
　1985　　"History and Text: The Reader in Context in Matthew's Parables Discourse." *Semeia* 32:111–38.
　1986　　"Text and Enunciation as Interpretant: A Peircian Contribution to Textual Semiotics." Pp. 1031-1040 in *Exigences et Perspectives de la Sémiotique/Semiotics—Critical Process and New Perspectives. Récueil d'hommage pour Algiridas Julien Greimas*. Ed. H. Parret and H.-G. Ruprecht. Brussels: Benjamin.
　1988　　"The Authority of Exegesis and the Responsibility of the Critic: The Ethic and Ethos of Criticism." Paper delivered to the Structuralism and Exegesis Section of the Society of Biblical Literature. Chicago, IL.
　1990　　"Exegesis as Critical Praxis: Reclaiming History and Text from a Postmodern Perspective." *Semeia* 51:7–49.
　1991　　"Sign/Text/Difference: The Contribution of Intertextual Theory for Biblical Criticism." Pp. 78-101 in *Intertextuality*. Ed. Heinrich Plett. Research in Text Theory 15. Berlin: Walter de Gruyter.

Plet, Henrich
　1991　　"Intertextualities." Pp. 3-29 in *Intertextuality*. Ed. Heinrich Plett. Research in Text Theory 15. Berlin: Walter de Gruyter.

Pratt, Mary Louise
　1992　　"Humanities for the Future. Reflections on the Western Culture Debate at Stanford." Pp. 13–32 in *The Politics of Liberal Education*. Ed. Darryl Gless and Barbara Herrnstein Smith. Durham: Duke University Press.

Rajan, Tilottama
　1992　　"Intertextuality and the Subject of Reading/Writing." Pp. 61–74 in *Influence and Intertextuality in Literary History*. Ed. Jay Clayton and Eric Rothstein. Madison: University of Wisconsin Press.

Riddell, Joseph
　1979　　"From Heidegger to Derrida to Chance: Doubling and (Poetic) Language." Pp. 231–52 in *Martin Heidegger and the Question of Literature*. Ed. William Spanos. Baltimore: Johns Hopkins University Press.

Riffaterre, Michael
　1979　　"Sémiotique intertextuelle. l'interpretant." *Revue d'Esthétiques*. 1/2:116–128.

Ringgren, Helmer
  1966   "Literarkritik, Formgeschichte, Überlieferungsgeschichte: Erwagungen zur Methodenfragen der altestamentliche Exegese." *Theologische Literarzeitung* 91:41–64.

Schaberg, Jane.
  1992   "Luke." Pp. 275–92 in *The Women's Bible Commentary*. Ed. Carol A. Newsome and Sharon Ringe. Louisville: Westminster/John Knox.

Schaub, Thomas
  1992   "Allusion and Intertext." Pp. 181–203 in *Influence and Intertext. Influence and Intertextuality in Literary History*. Ed. Jay Clayton and Eric Rothstein. Madison: University of Wisconsin Press.

Schnider, Franz
  1977   "Das Gleichnis vom Vorloren Schaf unde seine Redaktoren: Ein Intertextueller Vergleich (Lk 15:4–7, Mt 18:12–14)." *Kairos* 19:146–54.

Schürmann, H.
  1954   "Die Dublettenvermeidungen im Lukasevangelium." *Zeitschrift für katholische Theologie* 76:83–93.

Schüssler Fiorenza, Elisabeth
  1986   "A Feminist Critical Interpretation for Liberation: Martha and Mary: Luke 10:38–42." *Religion and Intellectual Life* 3:21–35.

Smyth, Herbert Weir
  1956   *Greek Grammar*. Rev. Gordon Messing. Cambridge: Harvard University Press.

Sternberg, Meir
  1983   "The Bible's Art of Persuasion: Ideology, Rhetoric, and Poetics in Saul's Fall (1 Sam 15)." *Hebrew Union College Annual* 54:45–82.

Streeter, B.H.
  1924   *The Four Gospels: A Study of Origins. Treating of the Manuscript Tradition, Sources, Authority, & Dates*. London: Macmillan.

Talbert, Charles H.
  1982   *Reading Luke. A Literary and Theological Commentary on the Third Gospel*. New York: Crossroad.

Tannehill, Robert
  1986   *The Narrative Unity of Luke-Acts. A Literary Interpretation. The Gospel According to Luke*. Vol 1. Foundations and Facets. Philadelphia: Fortress.

Todorov, Tzvetan
  1984   *Mikhail Bakhtin. The Dialogical Principle*. Trans. Wlad Godzich. Theory and History of Literature Series 13. Minneapolis: University of Minnesota Press.

Turner, Nigel
  1963   "Syntax." *A Grammar of New Testament Greek*. Vol III. Edinburgh: T. & T. Clark.

Ulmer, Gregory L.
    1985a   "Textshop for Post(e)pedagogy." Pp. 38–64 in *Writing and Reading Differently. Deconstruction and the Teaching of Composition and Literature.* Ed. C. Douglas Atkins and Michael Johnson. Lawrence: University of Kansas Press.
    1985b   *Applied Grammatology. Post(e)-Pedagogy from Jacques Derrida to Joseph Beuys.* Baltimore: Johns Hopkins University Press.

Voelz, James W.
    1989   "Multiple Signs and Double Texts. Elements of Intertextuality." Pp. 27–34 in *Intertextuality in Biblical Writings: Essays in Honour of Bas van Iersel.* Ed. Sipke Draisma. Kampden, Netherlands: J.H. Kok.

Vorster, Willem
    1988   "The Protevangelium of James and Intertextuality." Pp. 262–75 in *Text and Testimony. Essays on New Testament and Apocryphal Literature in Honor of A.F.G. Klijn.* Ed. Tjitze Baarda. Kampen: J.H. Kok.

White, Stephen
    1991   *Political Theory and Postmodernism.* Modern European Philosophy. Cambridge: Cambridge University.

MULTIPLE SIGNS, LEVELS OF MEANING AND SELF AS TEXT: ELEMENTS OF INTERTEXTUALITY

James W. Voelz
Corncordia Seminary

ABSTRACT

Intertextuality is normally understood as involving written texts, especially a given text's use of previous written texts. Barthes reminds us, however, that a text is a "tissue of quotations drawn from innumerable centers of culture" (1977:146), quotations which may be both written and non-written. Furthermore and concomitantly, intertextuality is not a phenomenon of given texts as static objects, as much as it is a phenomenon of readers making meaning of a (perceived) complex of textual signs and their meanings. Again in the words of Barthes: "...there is one space where this multiplicity is focused and that place is the reader, not, as was hitherto said, the author. The reader is the space on which all the quotations that make up a writing are inscribed..." (148).

This essay explores what sorts of complexes of signs and meanings impinge upon a reader/receptor intertextually. It will be contended that these include:

1) the various complexes which exist at several "levels" in a given text,

2) the experiential text of self (one's own life experience as a complex of signs and meanings), and

3) the complex of signs and meanings which constitute the experiential text of interpretive communities.

The essay will consider the relationship between these three major "text types" and will contend that a "confessional" understanding of the interpretive task is not only desirable but inevitable and necessary, and that not only in a Christian context.

I. INTRODUCTION

A text seen intertextually may be understood as a product of "various cultural discourses" (Culler, 1982:32). In the words of Roland Barthes, "The text is a tissue of quotations drawn from innumerable centers of culture" (146). Such a description embraces all factors which relate to the production of meaning in and by a text, from the side of both the author and the reader alike. Indeed, from an intertextual perspective, the reader or receiver of a given text is quite key. Meaning is produced by readers, who produce such meaning "intertextually" on the basis of a multiplicity of signs, both written and non-written, which impinge upon them in their world. Again, in the words of Barthes, "... there is one space where this multiplicity is focused and that place is the reader, not, as was hitherto said, the author. The reader is the space on which all the quotations that make up a writing are inscribed ..." (148). Perhaps best put, we may say from an intertextual perspective, that, through the presence of a multiplicity of texts, both written and non-written, the meaning of a text *arises* in the presence of an interpreter. In this essay, I consider several basic theoretical matters relating to an intertextual approach to textual interpretation, matters which are concerned both with signs and meaning, and with the number and types of texts involved.

II. Elements of Intertextuality

A. Preliminary Considerations

An intertextual approach to textual interpretation sees texts, as we have noted above, as products of "various cultural discourses." This means that intertextuality concerns itself, not only with the relationship between a text of verbal signs and other texts of verbal signs (or, more specifically, between a text of written verbal signs and other texts of written verbal signs), but it also and especially concerns itself with the relationship between a text of signs *of any sort* and other sets of signs as text, whether verbal or non-verbal in nature. Thus, Jacques Derrida calls history *"le texte général,"*[1] an unbounded, general text. If this is so, then semiotics—the theory of signs—is critical for its insights tell us, not only that signs and meaning must be distinguished one from another, but also, and for our purposes especially, that signs may be both verbal and non-verbal; that meaning is signed not only by words but also by things (e.g. fashions, food), relationships (e.g. temporal sequence, possession of a make of car), actions (e.g. shaking the fist, kissing), etc.[2]

Now, this means that it is best to understand "text" as a set or complex of signs, which is to be interpreted against the background of other signs or sets/complexes of signs. At which point two questions arise: "What signs or sets of signs constitute a text?" and "Against which other signs/sets of signs are these signs to be interpreted?" I would like to suggest that it is best to understand and to answer these questions in the following way:

---

[1] Jacques Derrida, "Avoir l'oreille de la philosophie." P. 310 in *Ecarts: Quatre essais à propos de Jacques Derrida*. Ed. Lucette Finas et al. Paris: Fayard, 1973, cited in Culler, 1982: 130.

[2] See, e.g. Blonsky.

B. Step I: Focus on the Text to be Interpreted

1. Which signs or sets of signs constitue a text?

A text is a complex of signs which themselves exist on several levels (cf. structuralism). Therefore, texts may be read on several levels, according to what constitutes the sign set.³

a. The most basic reading of a text, what I shall call a "Level 1" reading, considers the markings on the pages of a written text (or the sounds of an oral text) as sign, and the denotative meaning of this sign or complex of signs may be designated *"sense"*. Thus, Luke 7:14b-15a: . . . καὶ (ὁ) Ἰησοῦν εἶπεν· νεανίσκε, σοὶ λέγω, ἐγέρθητι. καὶ ἀνεκάθισεν ὁ νεκρὸς καὶ ἤρξατο λαλεῖν, means: "And he (Jesus) said, 'Young man I say to you, "Arise."' And the dead man sat up and began to speak;" not: "The disciples went to buy bread and ate it."

b. A reading of a text on the second level considers as sign the meaning of the acts depicted by the words as sign(s) (in the case of narrative) and/or the ideas asserted by the words as sign(s) (in the case of treatises, letters, etc.), and the meaning of these signs may be designated *"significance."* In the text from Luke we have just considered, the activity depicted, i.e., the resurrection of the young boy, has significance, and that significance may be that the Kingdom of God and the powers of ὁ μέλλων αἰών have come among the people of Nain.⁴ Other examples: the act of the Jewish leaders trying to stone Jesus (John 8:59) may well signify that he had blasphemed; the truth, according to St. Paul, that the spirit and the flesh are at odds with one another (Gal 5:17) may be said to signify that in this age, ὁ μελλων αἰων is never fully present.⁵

---

³ For a fuller explication of (and a slightly different approach to) the concept of the three levels of meaning which now follows, see J. W. Voelz,"The Problem of 'Meaning' in Texts," *Neotestamentica* 23:33–43. The explanation which I offer is *not* dependent upon the now classic analysis of E. D. Hirsch, though the reader will notice similarities, especially in vocabulary. Hirsch's approach is, I believe, incomplete, for he seems not to distinguish, among other things, between "significance" and "application" (see below).

⁴ Two caveats must be entered here. First, the question of *validity*, relating, as it does, to this or any other suggested interpretation, is a separate matter and will be treated in some detail below. Second, the relationship between what is portrayed by the signs of a text and the reality outside that text is also a separate matter. For a basic consideration of this latter issue, see Lategan and Vorster.

⁵ Note that meaning is involved even as it is with Level 1 signs. The different terminology suggested serves to alert the reader that a different type or level of sign is being read. Thus, one may talk about the sense of a text and know one is referring to the meaning of the marks on the page as "signs", or one may talk about the "significance" of a text and know that one is referring to the meaning of what is depicted or conveyed by those marks on the page.

c. A reading of a text on the third level considers as sign "the fact of writing" a given sign set, in the manner in which it is written, and with its sense or significance. That is to say, *the fact that something is included in a given text at all*, or that it is said the way it is said—that fact *implies* something about the author and his or her *Sitz im Leben*. Questions of *Einleitung* are concerned with this level, as are historical-critical[6] and structuralist approaches to interpretation.[7]

To continue the example from Luke above, Luke includes the story of the resurrection at Nain in his Gospel (indeed, he is the only Gospel writer to do so). Does that fact tell us something about Luke or about his audience? In other words, the fact that Luke deals with this matter may reveal something about him and his time: perhaps the problem of the death of believers was acute, or, perhaps there was a question concerning who Jesus was and the nature of his power (cf. "Level 2"). Other examples: the fact that John the Baptist appears throughout the book of Acts may indicate that his place was still problematic for early Christians; ungrammatical speech may reveal a lack of formal training for the writer of the Apocalypse.

These, then, are the kinds of signs which may be said to comprise a text. And it is these kinds of signs, or, rather, texts on these "levels", which, it would seem, are interpreted by receptors of a text intertextually.[8] Or, perhaps better put, it is these signs, as we have described them, which are interpreted by a textual receptor by "matrixing", i.e., by being connected with other signs or sets of signs for interpretation. This leads us directly to our second point.

2. Against which other signs or sets of signs are the signs of a given text to be interpreted?

a. Our first set of answers to this question is given if we consider several examples on so-called "Level 2" (the level of "significance," reading the activities depicted or ideas presented as signs), to see how intertextuality is displayed, that is, to see how "matrixing" of signs is actually done. Several points may be made.

---

[6] In much historical-critical interpretation, the text is primary evidence, not for the events or circumstances allegedly portrayed or discussed. Rather, it is primary evidence for the circumstances of the life and times of its author and community.

[7] Structuralism sees signs and their meaning as revealing important information about the maker of the signs. See, e.g. Claude Lévi-Strauss' statement (341): "Myths signify the mind that evolves them by making use of the world of which it is itself a part. Thus there is simultaneous production of myths themselves, by the mind that generates them and, by the myths, of an image of the world which is already inherent in the structure of the mind."

[8] And note that they *are* interpreted intertextually—a point not to be glossed over or missed. It is standard to say that signs are interpreted according to a "code." But a code (cf. a dictionary) is based on, and is itself nothing other than, another text!

i. Often signs on Level 2 (events/ideas) are matrixed with other events or ideas as signs in *some sort of context*. Thus, the story of Mary and Martha in Luke 10 may be connected to the immediately preceding story of the Good Samaritan, which matrix may signify that, while the Lord "desires mercy and not sacrifice," deeds of kindness do not earn divine approval. The context for interpreting events or ideas, however, may be very large. In the letters of the Pauline corpus, often the first portion is "promise" (i.e. statements about what God has done [cf. Eph 1–3]), while the latter portion is "parenesis" (commands to the recipients [cf. Eph 4–6]). These sections, each of which encompasses many verses, may be connected, which matrix may show that, in Paul's/"Pauline" theology, God's saving activity is not dependent upon the obedience of his people.

ii. Often signs (events/ideas) are matrixed with other events/ideas of *similar content*. Thus, all of the healing stories in the Gospel of Matthew may be connected (cf. Jesus' own reply to John the Baptist's disciples in Matt 11:2–5), which matrix may signify that Jesus is divine, or that in his ministry ὁ μέλλων αἰων was present. Several unusual events of Jesus' ministry recorded in Mark may be connected: e.g. his taking two tries to heal a blind man (8:23, 24), getting angry (3:5), and being unable to do miracles (6:15), which matrix may signify that Jesus was totally human. Contrasting connections are also possible. Thus, Jesus tells his disciples in Matthew (10:6) to go only to the lost sheep of the house of Israel, but then he goes to the region of Tyre and Sidon (15:21), which matrix may be challenging for the reader to interpret.

iii. Often events or ideas may be matrixed with events depicted or ideas expressed by *the same denotative signs* on Level 1. Thus, the meal shared by Jesus after his resurrection with the two men from Emmaus in Luke 24 may be connected to the meal of the Last Supper, on the basis of the similarity of the denotative signs in 24:30 and 22:19: λαβὼν τὸν ἄρτον εὐλόγησεν καὶ κλάσας ἐπιδίδου αὐτοῖς, καὶ λαβὼν ἄρτον εὐχαριστήσας ἔκλασεν καὶ ἔδωκεν αὐτοῖς (cf. also 9:16), which matrix may signify that the meal in Emmaus had eucharistic benefits for its participants.

We may say, therefore, that *textual events or ideas are matrixed with other textual events or ideas which are in proximity, alike or contrasting in content, or portrayed by the same denotative signs*.[9]

b. But in the actual act of interpretation, we must not and do not limit ourselves as strictly as we have just done. Considering once again, for the sake of manageability, only examples on so-called Level 2 (i.e. interpreting events depicted or ideas for what I have termed "significance"), we can see and say the following:

---

[9] We may add that textual events or ideas which are repeated, related in time, or related by cause and effect are also subject to matrixing.

i. Matrixing for interpretation often is *not restricted to signs on the same level of the text*. Let us return to the example from Luke 7 considered above. The act depicted by the words as sign in verses 14–15 (the resurrection of the lad) may easily be matrixed with the statement of the crowd in verse 16: ἐπεσκέψατο ὁ θεὸς τὸν λαὸν αὐτοῦ. In this way, the meaning of an activity depicted (Level 2) is given explicitly by the meaning of the words as sign (Level 1). It may be observed, however, that in such cases the appropriateness of the matrix must still be judged, though it may seem quite obvious at first, for one would not readily use the meaning of Βεελζεβοὺλ ἔχει in Mark 3:22 to help determine the significance of the activity described in verse 11 of chapter 3: καὶ τὰ πνεύματα τὰ ἀκάθαρτα, ὅταν αὐτὸν ἐθεώρουν, προσέπιπτον αὐτῷ καὶ ἔκραζον λέγοντα ὅτι σὺ εἶ υἱὸς τοῦ θεοῦ.

ii. Matrixing for interpretation often is *not restricted to the same text*. Thus, the significance of the Christ-event as portrayed in the Gospel of Mark may be revealed in 2 Corinthians 5:19: θεὸς ἦν ἐν χριστῷ κόσμον καταλάσσων ἑαυτῷ (cf. also Gal 4:4–5). Indeed, the significance of events or ideas may be most clear when matrixed with other texts which contain different versions of the same story or thought. Matthew's genealogy would be much less meaningful if Luke's were not available. Luke's mention of Naaman in describing Jesus' return to his home town (4:27) would be much more difficult to interpret, if we did not see the other synoptic writers omitting it.

iii. Matrixing for interpretation often is *not restricted to the same type of text*. By this is meant that the signs in written texts need not be matrixed with the signs of other written texts. Not only oral texts are in view here. One must also consider what might be called "experiential texts" (cf. Derrida's view of history as *le texte général*). *A reader must be seen as a text*. Or, perhaps more accurately, the states, actions, hopes, fears, and knowledge of a reader's life-experience comprise a "text." Thus, the significance that Jesus is divine, perceived in the matrix of Jesus' miracles in Matthew (cf. 2.a.ii. above) may well be the result of a *further* matrix between these activities portrayed and the interpreter's own experiences in life. But my experiences in life could lead to another conclusion, e.g. that Jesus was in league with Satan (cf. Mark 3:22 and 3:11 [2.b.1. above]). The same is true for the perceived "significance" that Jesus was totally human, derived from a matrix of several passages in Mark (cf. 2.a.ii. above). My experiences in life could lead me to conclude that, as fully human, he was not also fully divine (*contra* classical Christology) but simply possessed by God. It may be noted that life-experience as text enables one to read a text on Level 3, i.e. with reference to the life and times of the author and/or of the author's audience.[10]

c. What, then, may be concluded?

i. We may say, on the basis of our study of interpretive strategies on Level 2, that the signs of a text, no matter on what level they may be, are interpreted against other signs in the same text, against signs in other texts of the same kind (e.g. written), against signs in other texts of different kinds (e.g. written vs. life-experience), and against signs on different levels. And all of this takes place easily and simultaneously.

ii. It seems that it is also true to conclude that several types of sign sets or texts are particularly important in and for the interpretive task. That is to say, when a given matrix of signs is interpreted, certain types of (component) signs/sign sets/texts provide anchors, as it were, for the interpretation of all other signs within that given matrix; they constitute, so to speak, "the final court of appeal." These are (A) explicit explanation (explanation on the level of sense [Level 1]) by an authority (cf. 2.b.i. above), (B) the interpreter's own life-experience (cf. 2.b.iii. above), and, perhaps, (C) the interpreter's own system of beliefs (which factor may be seen as closely allied to the other two and generally dependent upon them). To put it another way: We asked at the beginning of this discussion, "Against what other signs and sets of signs are given signs to be interpreted?" In actual fact it is necessary to divide the question and to distinguish between the signs *with which* a given sign set it to be understood, and the signs *by which* a given sign set is to be understood. To ask about the former (signs "with which") reminds us that signs are never interpreted in a vacuum but always as a complex or matrix, and it directs our attention to *what complex of signs is actually to be interpreted*. To ask about the latter (signs "by which") is to remind ourselves that all signs are "not created equal," that some seem to be more important and more dominating than others—they are interpretive "keys," as it were—and it directs our attention to which signs/sign sets of a given matrix serve as judge, so that *their meaning*—determined, it would seem, apart from and prior to the meaning of the given matrix as a whole—is determinative for the meaning of the complex of signs under consideration. The three factors which we mentioned above are sometimes found simply in the first category here delineated—they may simply be components in a matrix to be interpreted. But more often than not they also comprise the second category; frequently, they provide, as we have styled it, the "final court of appeal." Against them and against their meaning—in the light of them and

---

[10] Indeed, it may be observed that, if a story is not congruent with our life experience, we begin to interpret it on Level 3 (even though we may intend not to), with observations about the author's system of beliefs, community standards, etc.

in the light of their meaning[11]—a complex of signs is interpreted and understood.

C. Step II: Focus on the Receptor as Text

When a given text is read, simultaneously another text is also read, namely, the reader, or, perhaps better put, the life-experience of the reader of the text. In the preceding section, we indicated the importance of this factor, viz., life-experience of the reader as text, in that part of the interpretive process which focuses upon the text to be interpreted. But here we seek to view the reader as text from a different point of view. In this section we seek to see him or her, not as a factor in the interpretation of the signs of a given outside text. Now we seek to see him or her as a separate text read in concert with the text to be interpreted, or, perhaps better put, in relation to a given text which is being read. In traditional terms, it would be put thus: interpreters make "application" of a given text to themselves. But it is, we contend, much more accurate to say that, as readers read, they read not only the signs of a given text in intertextual relationship, also with their own life-experiences as sign, to obtain a meaning for that text—but they read also and simultaneously their own life-experiences as textual sign and relate them and their potential meanings to the signs and to the meanings of those signs on the various levels which comprise the given text, to make sense of their own life-experiences as textual sign, i.e. to "apply" the text to themselves. We may see this by turning, once again, to the story of the lad from Nain (Luke 7). Considering what we have said above regarding signs and meanings on Levels 1, 2, and 3 of this text, the following applications of these meanings may be seen:

> From Level 1: Jesus will raise me on the Last Day;
>
> From Level 2: Jesus was God come to visit his people and brought the blessings of ὁ μέλλων αἰών (cf. Isaiah 26:19); therefore, there is no other God for me;
>
> From Level 3: If we fear death, it is not unusual or sinful, for the people of Luke's time did as well.

It is, then, the text of the life-experience of the interpreter which is being interpreted in each application, and this is done by establishing an intertextual relationship between this (life-experience) text and the given text which is, overtly, being interpreted. Such a procedure provides, again

---

[11] How is the meaning of the key or anchor signs of—the judges within—the matrix determined? As noted above, that seems to be done apart from and prior to the given matrix. Which means that they are part of another prior matrix, which is itself interpreted. But that prior matrix will also have key or anchor signs whose meaning is determined apart from and prior to that matrix... (and so on *ad infinitum*).

in traditional terms, the meaning of a given text for the interpreter and/or for that interpreter's community. Indeed, it is this sort of intertextuality, proceeding *from* the life-experience text of the interpreter *to* the text in question, which has taken on overarching importance in a so-called "postmodern" approach to literary texts.

III. Meaning and Intentionality

A. The Question

We have spoken of a reader providing a meaning for a perceived sign-set of a text, or of meaning arising in the presence of a reader. But is any meaning actually *there* within a text? Does a text actually have meaning, in and of itself? Is reading in any sense interpretation, or is it essentially meaning manufacture and production?[12] From what I have said above, my emphasis has been on meaning production/manufacture, and I do not want to vitiate these points. The following, however, must be observed:

B. Basic Considerations

1. Texts are not arbitrary collocations of signs, with no pre-conceived intentionality (such as a pattern made by ink dripping from an uncapped pen), neither are they chance collocations of such signs (such as abstract art produced by paint thrown upon a canvas). Texts have meaning which is intended. We know this, not from being receptors of various texts. *We know this from being producers of various kinds of texts.* Text production—our text production—is not aimless. Intended meaning is a goal. What that intended meaning is, however, is often elusive or obscure, and one can never appeal to it (i.e. to the intentionality of the author) as a hermeneutical key to the interpretation of a given text. Furthermore, it is doubtful whether the intended meaning of a given text exhausts the meaning of that text.

2. The concepts of levels of signs and a second experiential text help to clarify the matter of intentional meaning and its problems.

    a. The meaning of Level 1 signs is normally intended, is often clear (provided one knows the language code),[13] and usually exhausts the meaning of those signs.

---

[12] Thiselton (499, 501–502) distinguishes between "understanding" and "reading" as two different models of approaches to texts and, therefore, two different views of the nature of texts themselves. The first is characteristic of a traditional posture, the second of postmodernism.

[13] Codes are actually other instances of (similar) texts (cf. note 8 above).

b. The meaning of Level 2 signs (deeds/ideas) is also normally intended, but it is much more difficult to discover, because on this level matrixing is increasingly obscure. Furthermore, it would seem that such intended meaning is not so fully or completely exhaustive of the potentialities of the signs as is the meaning on Level 1; authors of stories, for example, do not think about and consider every conceivable matrix of deeds and words, even within the confines of their own tale.

c. The meaning of signs on Level 3 is often not intended—indeed, an author may not even be conscious of a text's signing at this level. Therefore, intention never is exhaustive, and, since interpretation at this level is dependent upon a matrix to an interpreter's experiential text, intended meaning is even more elusive and obscure.

d. Finally, application—the reading of one's experiential text as sign against the target text—may be intended, though normally in a very general way; it is normally not exhaustive, and again, dependent as it is on one's experiential text, it is the most elusive and obscure.

3. Genre is a key. Not all texts are constructed in the same way. Some texts are highly intentional, normally focusing on the signs of Level 1 (cf. a railway time-table), while others trade upon ambiguity (cf. metaphysical poetry or science fiction), with a heavy emphasis on interpreting the signs on Level 2.

4. The time of composition is a key. Older texts of a literary nature are, in general, less open-ended than are recent texts,[14] which makes the problem of reading ancient texts with modern eyes a problem, which is much more fundamental and thoroughgoing than the problem of the meaning of rituals of the past.

C. *Position Summary and Final Considerations*

We may summarize what we have said relative to the intentional meaning of a text in the following way:

Does a text "have" a meaning which reflects the intention of its author? Yes.

Does the intentional meaning of the author exhaust the meaning of the text? No.

Can the intentional meaning of the author be determined? Perhaps, but it is increasingly elusive as one moves:

—From signs on Level 1 to those on Level 2 to those on Level 3,

---

[14] This is, of course, a broad generalization and may well be disputed. In any case, it does not relieve us of the problem of the nature of the Gospel of Mark or other pieces of ancient literature, and it certainly does not solve all problems of interpretation.

—From meaning of the target text to its application, i.e. to a focus upon the meaning of the experiential self as text,

—From genres which intend to convey information (e.g. a travel brochure) to those which have a more existential goal (e.g. love poetry), and

—From older literature to more recent literature, especially to those which trade upon ambiguity of signs.

It is for this reason that those who argue for intentionality, for a text containing a meaning, and against the open-endedness of postmodern approaches to a text, on the one hand, and those who argue the opposite, on the other, find evidence for their positions within the total spectrum of the literary production which we possess.[15] It should be noted that pragmatics[16] and an understanding of meaning as the experience one has while reading[17] do not provide a contradiction to what has been said.

---

[15] This is similar to the point made by Thiselton (473), following Patrick Grant:

> ... for those theorists who are accustomed to handle poetic, imaginative, fictional, and metaphorical texts, the notion of self-referring textuality can readily assume the status of an axiom, while for those who have been schooled in a discipline in which history, incarnation, situations, and evidence are fundamental, such an approach, far from being axiomatic, is problematic.

[16] Pragmatics considers what a use of language signs (*parole*) is intended to accomplish. I would strongly contend that, with one exception, all uses of language are at their root *semantic*, i.e. intended to convey or to produce meaning, speech-act theory notwithstanding. Even a command may be analyzed as linguistic shorthand for: "I want you to do this, *and I really mean it*. If you don't do it, there will be consequences." An utterance or communication would not be semantic at its root, only if it in no way depended upon interpretation of signs, the production of meaning, and concomitant understanding, but such interpretation, production, and understanding is precisely the foundation for all action based upon any utterance or communication. (Thus, many utterances/texts which are not overtly informative have as their basic function to inform the recipient of the speaker/writer's attitudes, values, and intentions.) The only exceptions, it would seem, are performative utterances, which actually change situations, such as a declaration of marriage by a judge to a man and woman which establishes their marriage bond. What a speaker/author intends to accomplish with a text concerns something other than the meaning of a text and is outside the scope of this presentation.

[17] I am not contending that a text may be seen simply as a container, so that meaning is simply the content of a text (cf. Moore: 64) I fully recognize that the meaning of a text may well be the experience one has while reading (Moore: 159), and, further, that this experience may be what the author does, in fact, intend. But in such cases, the experience one has while reading is a reaction to meaning perceived and that experience is itself a sign, a sign (which itself) is intended to be read. An excellent example is given by Robert Fowler (131):

> The experience of reading Mark 4:11–13 can be summarized briefly. The temptation here is to say that the text tells us that those who "see" often are in fact "blind," and those who "hear" often are in fact "deaf." The text, espe-

IV. Validity of Interpretation and the Community

Finally, we may ask, "Is there any control in all of this? Is everyone's interpretation equal—or, more technically expressed, equally valid—in the end?"[18] The answer is a definite "sort of." The key is the *community*. The interpretive community brings a sort of objectivity and a stamp of approval/disapproval to all interpretations. It is a simple fact that no one reads in a vacuum. Everyone learns to read in a community.[19] It is, therefore, the community which sets the standards for and gives approval to the matrixing of signs and their meaning, the interpretation of matrices of signs, and all of the operations which go into textual interpretation and application. Therefore, the question really is, "Are all *community* interpretations equal?" There is probably no agreement on this answer,[20] and a fully reader-oriented answer would be "Probably" or "Definitely, Yes".

---

cially the parenthetical comment in 4:12, does say something like that, but far more important than what the text *says* is what it *does*. We are not merely *told* about those who "see and yet do not see," *we are given the opportunity to experience this for ourselves*. The reader lives through the experience of being shut out of insight and understanding by an opaque veil, followed by the gift of sight and understanding, in a surprising reversal of position with those who had started out on the favored side of the veil.

The experience of reading Mark 4:11–13 is illustrative of the experience of reading Mark's Gospel as a whole in several respects. For one thing, reading Mark is less a matter of being informed of certain facts and ideas and more a matter of being given the opportunity to live through certain kinds of experiences.

Here, the experience of reading is part of the reader's life-experience, and this experience is a set of signs—a text—which the reader seeks to interpret and to understand. It is for this reason that the well-known "compass for critics" laid out by Paul Hernadi (369–86) is either deceiving or quite wrong. There is no "axis of appeal" that is not fundamentally dependent upon—not only linked with—the "axis of representation." Otherwise put, a rhetorical effect can take place only after signs are first interpreted semantically. Indeed, before a rhetorical appeal can take place, decisions concerning the relationship between what is depicted/asserted by the sign set and reality outside the text—itself a separate step (cf. note 4 above) but collapsed by Hernadi's compass—must *first* be made, because, e.g. a text determined to be fiction has a different rhetorical appeal than one determined to be an attempt at history.

[18] Patte (2) has proposed the intriguing distinction between "validity" and "legitimacy." A "legitimate" interpretation, he asserts, is one which is congruent with the data—the "meaning producing dimensions" of the text. A "valid" interpretation is one which is "moral" and benefits the human community at large. (Note that he is not distinguishing between interpretation and what we have called "application" with these two terms.) This distinction is helpful to a certain degree, but it presupposes—improperly, I believe—an objectivity for the so-called "meaning-producing dimensions" he detects.

[19] Community instruction encompasses such basic things as grammar. For example, does a ἵνα clause ever convey result in the NT? The answer is disputed.

[20] See especially Culler, 1975:113–30, and Fish: 465–85. See also Chapter 7: "Stories of Reading That Have No Ending: An Introduction to the Post-Modern Bible" (Moore: 108–130), for an excellent overview of the problem.

But I would propose the following: that community which has produced, received, and preserved a given set of documents—or, better put, that community whose experiences as text include the production, reception, and preservation of a given set of documents—is likely to teach its members to read those documents in a way "congenial" to them—that is, in such a way as to find in them what reasonably may be found (= what intended meaning there may be), and, to allow further meanings to arise, meanings which are congruent with what intended meanings there might be. In such a community there will be, to use reader-response terminology, people who can assume the role of the implied reader of the documents which are part of the life-experience as text of that community. That is to say, that community's members possess the competencies (cf. Culler) for interpretation called for by its documents, for they operate by a set of beliefs, standards, and knowledge (= life experience as text) congruent with the beliefs, standards, and knowledge of those who produced those documents and, therefore, congruent with the beliefs, standards, and knowledge assumed by the texts themselves. Therefore, to be able to assume the role of the "implied reader" for a given set of documents, one must be a member of the community of those documents and be taught to read by it.[21]

What does this mean for a reading of, the books of the NT? It means, I believe, the following: The books of the NT are books produced, received, and preserved by the Christian community.[22] Therefore, that community is likely to teach its members to read these documents in a way congenial to them, to assume, as we have said, the role of the implied reader as they read. And, therefore, to be able to assume the role of the "implied reader" of the documents of the NT, one must be within the Christian community and be taught to read by it. Put into my own terms: as one is in the church and adopts what is confessed (its beliefs, standards, etc.), one's experiential text becomes congruent with the experiential text of those who produced, received, and preserved those NT texts.[23] And such a congruent

---

[21] Note that this analysis does not mean that a text is a "waxen nose", as many who evaluate positions such as this seem to fear (cf. Thiselton: 538–39, 546–50), though it is far more waxen than many do believe. A text, because it is an item of intention, because it is not an arbitrary pattern with no pre-conceived intentionality, does have the ability to judge the community of which it is a part. In other words, a text can "rise up on its hind legs" and say to the very people whom it serves: "You are wrong! You must rethink!" And this dialectical relationship between text and community, between the produced and those who produce and who preserve, is seen repeatedly within the history of the church.

[22] Note that the question of canon comes immediately to the fore.

[23] Much more traditionally expressed, to be in that Christian community is to adhere to and confess its *creeds*. Such creeds are not something foreign to the books of the NT. On the contrary, they are—and from the first were seen as—"of a piece" with

experiential text is necessary, for it is an important factor in every facet of dealing with any text.[24]

V. CONCLUSION

Intertextuality is a concept which is broad in scope. It may properly be applied to the idea that a given text is composed of prior texts, both written and non-written alike[25] (cf. I. Introduction, above). If it understood that such a textual composition is within the ken of the author, then an intertextual investigation is source-oriented. If it is understood that such a textual composition is outside the author's ken, yet detectable apart from that author and that author's consciousness, then the investigation is text-oriented (cf. structuralism). I have preferred, on the whole, to be receptor-oriented in this contribution, investigating how a reader makes meaning of a text—by relating its signs on every level to signs (both written and

---

these very books. (The creeds were either materially identical with the *regula fidei* or a minimal summary of it [Hanson: 64–68], and the NT Scriptures were seen to be materially identical with this same *regula* [Hanson: 110], a "crystallization" of it in a given setting [108]). Therefore, to adhere to the creeds gives one an orientation to the books of the NT, an orientation which is congenial to them. (It was for this reason that many of the early church fathers contended that the heretics had no right to use the Scriptures against the church in their argumentation [cf. Irenaeus, *Adversus Haereses* 1. 1. 20, and Tertullian, *De Praescriptione Haereticorum*, 15–18]).

To focus on one portion of this in my own terminology, I would say that adherence to the creeds enables one to matrix the signs of a text for interpretation and then to interpret that matrix of signs in a way which is congenial to the text, for the creeds are of one piece with that text and provide, as it were, the interpretive key or the anchor sign set, whose meaning is, practically speaking, determinative for the meaning of the complex of signs under consideration. (By contrast, Irenaeus says that the heretics "override the order and structure of the Scriptures," acting as someone would do if he were to break into pieces a mosaic portrait of the Emperor and reassemble it to make a picture of a dog or a fox. *Adv. Haer.* 1.1.15. [cited in Hanson: 105].) It must be noted, however, that the NT Scriptures retain their authority as sign set on their own, and that creedal interpretations must always be able to appeal to matrices of signs— independently determined and interpreted—within these Scriptures which support assertions in the creeds.

Please note that I am perfectly aware of the ambiguities and difficulties which remain in this position. Who is a Christian, which texts are canonical, which creeds are normative, etc.—all such questions must be explored and are impossible to answer cleanly.

[24] It may be noted that it is in this context that the role of personal faith must be placed and understood. Faith is not some sort of "trump card" which gives instant knowledge of history (eliminating need for study) or which gives total linguistic competence (enabling the interpreter, e.g. to fill in all ambiguities of meaning and referent, or to matrix signs and interpret them without difficulty). Rather, it gives ultimate congeniality with the text, so that the interpreter may truly be a reader and not a critic, may be moved to listen rather than to judge.

[25] See also the concept of "grafts" in texts. Texts may be seen as grafts of ideas from other texts (Level 2 intertextuality). Cf. Culler, 1982:134–41.

non-written) elsewhere in the text, in other texts of like character, and in other texts of diverse character.

We have seen that, in macro-structural terms, *two texts* are involved when any text is interpreted, both the given text and the life-experience of the interpreter as text. It is for this reason that interpretation has both a static/objective and a dynamic/subjective element as it proceeds. Because we interpret intertextually according to rules, many involving matrixing—and such rules are largely subject to the viewpoints of interpretive communities which exist outside ourselves—there is a static/objective character to interpretation. But because the semantic components to be matrixed and the matrices themselves must be perceived, because such perception is done by an interpreter, who is always different and ever changing, and because the second text, the life-experience, of each interpreter must be different, interpretation is dynamic and subjective, ever in a state of flux.

Works Cited

Barthes, Roland
 1977 *Image, Music, Text.* New York: Hill & Wang.

Blonsky, Marshall, ed.
 1985 *On Signs.* Baltimore: Johns Hopkins University Press.

Culler, Jonathan
 1975 *Structuralist Poetics: Structuralism, Linguistics, and the Study of Literature.* Ithaca: Cornell University Press.
 1982 *On Deconstruction: Theory and Criticism after Structuralism.* Ithaca: Cornell University Press.

Fish, Stanley
 1976 "Interpreting the *Variorum.*" *Critical Inquiry* 2:465-85.

Fowler, Robert
 1989 "The Rhetoric of Direction and Indirection in the Gospel of Mark." *Semeia* 48:115-34.

Hanson, R.P.C.
 1962 *Tradition in the Early Church.* Philadelphia: Westminster.

Hernadi, Paul
 1976 "Literary Theory: A Compass for Critics." *Critical Inquiry* 3:369-86.

Hirsch, E. D.
 1967 *Validity in Interpretation.* New Haven: Yale University Press.

Lategan, Bernard C. and Willem S. Vorster
   1985   *Text and Reality: Aspects of Reference in Biblical Texts.* Philadelphia: Fortress.

Lévi-Strauss, Claude
   1963   *Structural Anthropology.* Trans. Claire Jacobson and Brooke Grundfest Schoepf. New York: Basic.

Moore, Stephen D.
   1989   *Literary Criticism and the Gospels: The Theoretical Challenge.* New Haven: Yale University Press.

Patte, Daniel
   1991   "The Polysemy of a Quotation: Four Legitimate Critical Exegetical Readings of Matthew 8:17 and the Questions They Raise About the Vocation of Male European Exegetes." Paper presented to the seminar on "The Rôle of the Reader in the Interpretation of the New Testament" of the SNTS meeting. Bethel, Germany.

Thiselton, Anthony
   1992   *New Horizons in Hermeneutics: The Theory and Practice of Transforming Biblical Reading.* Grand Rapids: Zondervan.

CHRISTOLOGICAL SLIPPAGE AND IDEOLOGICAL STRUCTURES IN SCHWARZENEGGER'S *TERMINATOR*

Roland Boer
United Theological College

ABSTRACT

This paper invokes some of the categories of analysis suggested by Fredric Jameson: transcoding, figuration, utopian analysis, and a dialectical foldback which includes the critic in interpretation. Thus, it traces the intertextual relationship between some biblical texts and the two *Terminator* films, the significance of the slippage of savior figures between the two films, the factors which may account for their popularity, and the ideological structures which make the writer an avid consumer of Schwarzenegger's films. A recurring theme is the need to relate the films to a series of theological, ideological, social, political and economic "texts" or contexts. The paper also suggests a socio-economic connection for intertextuality itself and closes with a call to "inter-methodology."

INTRODUCTION

For the biblical scholar one of the more interesting areas opened up by the theory and practice of intertextuality is the relationship between the biblical text and contemporary popular culture. Of course, the relation between Bible and culture is in itself not new, but has generally been restricted in the past to questions of how the Bible has influenced culture (normally understood as "high" or "serious" culture). Intertextual theory, however, enables a more sophisticated and complex analysis of such a relationship by recognizing the presence of other "texts" in that relationship, including those of a methodological, ideological, political and personal nature. Thus, in what follows I will explore the intertextual interface between the Bible, James Cameron's Christologically orthodox (so Jameson, 1991:384) *Terminator* (hereafter T1) and the less orthodox *Terminator II: Judgment Day* (hereafter T2), starring Arnold Schwarzenegger, the cultural theories of Fredric Jameson, and my own situation as critic and consumer of these various "texts." Of Jameson's approaches four will be used, three of which are highly productive in interpreting these filmic texts but one of which is somewhat neglected in Jameson's recent work:

the reading strategies are transcoding, figuration, utopian analysis, and the dialectical incorporation of the critic in the interpretive process.

Briefly, transcoding is the ability to use the many methods or codes of the contemporary scene in such a manner that there is movement from one code to the other in the same way that a translator moves from one language to the other in the process of translation. Figuration searches for mostly peripheral formal or structural elements which function as "figures" or traces of social and economic features. Utopian analysis—that most fascinating of Jameson's textual strategies—seeks out the utopian dimensions of literary and cultural products. Dialectical criticism, as "thought to the second power," factors into the interpretive process the self-consciousness of the critic as one who operates in a particular social and historical context. In the following analysis I will make use of each of these strategies as follows: after outlining the contribution of the notion of transcoding to the discussion of intertextuality, the specific intertextual relationship between the *Terminator* films and the biblical text will be developed. The idea of figuration then comes into play to determine the function of the Christological motifs in the films. Utopian analysis will attempt to locate the popularity of the films, and finally what I will term dialectical foldback will seek out both my own ambiguous place in the interpretation and a weakness in Jameson.

As far as the films themselves are concerned, in its broad strokes the plot of the second film reduplicates that of the first: an assassin is sent back from the future to eliminate the one who is to save the human race. A bodyguard also arrives from the future who predictably saves the one who will be leader (the bodyguard is in fact sent by the leader of the future to save himself). The major difference between the two films lies in the transformation of Arnold Schwarzenegger, a transformation which is central to this discussion. First, however, we turn to consider Jameson's strategy of transcoding.

Transcoding

Transcoding is a response to the proliferation of methods or theories in the contemporary (poststructural) situation: it is the ability to use those methods or codes, moving experimentally from one code to the other in an effort to test their various strengths and weaknesses. The ability to translate from one method or code to the other is more important than testing them all against an ultimate method. Transcoding requires the ability to speak those various codes or ideolects, a skill comparable to speaking and translating a foreign language:

(I have to learn to speak it, for example; I can say some things more strongly in one foreign language than in another, and vice versa; there is no Ur- or ideal language of which the imperfect earthly ones, in their multiplicity, are so many refractions; syntax is more important than vocabulary, but most people think it is the other way round; my awareness of linguistic dynamics is the result of a new global system or a certain demographic "pluralism"). (Jameson, 1991:394)

In his earlier days, when he was more of a literary critic than a cultural critic, Jameson used to call this activity metacommentary. The difference between transcoding and metacommentary is small, metacommentary tending to be limited to a specific cultural product: it is then an accounting for the existing (and possible) interpretations of the text or cultural product. Often Jameson will begin analyzing a text by noting the major types of interpretation that have been offered; this phase then provides the basis for further discussion.

Transcoding has been introduced into the discussion for a reason. The codes or methods which the transcoder uses may be described as semi-autonomous: each has distinguishing features that set it apart from others, but this autonomy is only partial, since the ability to move from one code to the other suggests a certain inter-relationship or fundamental unity between the codes. I am moving into Althusserian terms here, for the whole notion of semi-autonomy was developed by Althusser as part of his discussion of structural causality, a notion which was intended to solve some central problems in Marxism. Althusser's extremely influential move was to argue that for Marx "mode of production" designates not the economic realm alone but the structure as a whole; each of the sectors—economic, political, judicial, ideological and cultural (the latter four belonging to the more traditional "superstructure")—is now understood to be semi-autonomous and potentially able to be dominant at any particular time rather than the previous understanding of a preset program which always ran in favor of the economic. My argument in this paper is that the notion of semi-autonomy may be fruitfully connected with that of transcoding: the possibility of transcoding is permitted by the partial autonomy of the codes, for they are related but distinct.

While transcoding will be used in the analysis to follow, the term—along with semi-autonomy—also makes some contribution to the question of intertextuality. It would seem that some of the now old-fashioned ideas of structuralism (Althusser developed a structuralist Marxism) find their proper use in the poststructural arena of intertextuality. Therefore it would be useful to speak of texts as being semi-autonomous: both interrelated in a host of complex patterns and autonomous to some degree in that they inversely affect one another. This is the sort of thing that is happening with the *Terminator* films in their relationship to the biblical texts and other contemporary "texts."

Semi-autonomy, transcoding, and intertextuality must, however, be situated socially and economically. Transcoding, in which any workable code will do, and the existence of intertextuality, in which a free-play of texts continually threatens to break out, are possible in a situation in which no code or text can any longer be assured the status of being the protector of the social system or the status quo. In other words, neither a unifying ideology of society nor a collection of authoritative texts (the canon) remains to bolster and protect the system. A major reason for this ideological and canonical collapse is itself suggested by the nature of transcoding and intertextuality: both bear all the marks of cultural and literary versions of commodity exchange, each item—text or code—with some local variation in taste, appearance, and texture being interchangeable with the other. Such a situation of virtually infinite exchange leads to a celebration of the practice of consumption, a pleasurable release in each act of consumption which has little or no bearing on the nature of the product itself. In other words, the commodity form—in its own right the reification of social relations—has been reified. Transcoding and intertextuality become therefore the methodological and textual projections, respectively, of the activity of commodity consumption. All of this suggests that the possibility of transcoding and the existence of intertextuality indicate a more fundamental unity of the historical situation, namely late capitalism.

By means of this detour, transcoding and intertextuality have been grounded, although briefly, in their social and economic basis. As far as the *Terminator* films themselves are concerned, transcoding or metacommentary takes the form of searching for possible interpretations, achieved or potential. A number of readings have already been offered for these films: the theological, or more specifically Christological, in which the major themes of the story of Christ may be located (Large; suggested by Jameson, 1991:384); the psychological as mediated through Lacan, where the relations of the family loom large in analysis (Pfeil; Penley[1]); a generic reading in which the films are understood as contemporary contributions to the genre of film-noir (Pfeil); and the political which attempts to uncover the film's reactionary status (Pfeil). It might be possible to suggest others such as the Freudian, with an emphasis on the child's killing of the father; or the ethical, in the way the film raises issues such the nature of good and evil in terms of the use and abuse of technology; the ideological, where one notes the typical liberal solutions, such as calm and rational

---

[1] David Seljak, of McGill University, has also found this to be a pervasive element of the films.

discussion (the talking cure), to problems of human survival or destruction; and so on. Each approach would seem to have something to offer and would seem to be based upon signals in the films themselves. The analysis which follows will draw on most of these in some way or another; suffice to say at this point that the following discussion relies most heavily upon the theological and the psychological readings, with the addition of a third approach, namely, utopian analysis.

Within the theological interpretation, there is also a different sort of transcoding taking place in these films: the use and transformation of biblical passages and contemporary "texts" (this is more properly an intertextual question). First, the contemporary references. The debt to Philip K. Dick comes through at many points: the near future (Los Angeles in 2029) apocalyptic scenes, the evocation of the nuclear holocaust and life before and after, the ambiguous relationship between humans and machines, particularly in their conflict with one another and in the whole question of the nature of androids or cyborgs.[2] The first words of T1 might have come straight from Dick himself:

> The machines rose from the ashes of the nuclear fire. The war to exterminate mankind had raged for decades, but the final battle would not be fought in the future. It would be fought here, in our present: tonight.

Further debts to Dick may be located in specific scenes or episodes: the leader teaching human beings how to break out of the camps set up by the machines, the cyborg infiltrators into the human underground hideouts, and so on. On a different intertextual plane Fred Pfeil (21, 27) notes two unconscious and unintentional connections with events contemporary to T2. First, the combination, in the figure of the second Terminator in T2, of a white male Los Angeles police officer with terrifying and formless evil came a few months after the racist brutality of Police Chief Gates of LAPD had gained wide media attention and (a point which Pfeil does not note) a little before the videotaped bashing of Rodney King by four LAPD officers. A second contemporary echo comes with T2's opening post-nuclear scene of the techno-war between machines and humans, in which Pfeil finds an echo of the wildly popular Gulf War where com-

---

[2] P. K. Dick's *Do Androids Dream Electric Dreams* became the basis of the film *Blade Runner*. The question of the relationship between humans and machines is fascinating: it would seem to date in its contemporary form from the advent of industrialization. It is common practice to lament the impositions of machines upon humans, comparable to the Romantic laments over technology today. However, there is an ambiguity reflected in these films: machines threaten humans (thus the war between machines and humans) but human beings are in many respects very machine-like (the cyborg is a human-machine).

puterized killing machines operating in virtual reality or cyberspace hunted down and destroyed the humans.

Comparable perhaps to the Dick literate, the average biblical literate should have no difficulty picking up the biblical stories and texts that are referred to, borrowed, quoted, commented upon, and remolded. Indeed, in proper intertextual fashion, the *Terminator* films "must be seen in a relationship of tension and superposition to some older text [the Bible] without which the first cannot be properly understood" (adapted from Jameson, 1988:20).

Three closely related types of texts make their conscious and unconscious appearance: texts of messianic expectation, apocalyptic texts, and those which might be described as Christological, i.e. those which deal with the story of the birth, life, and death of Jesus Christ. In the first category we find the texts from the Hebrew Bible traditionally understood by Christians as foreshadowing the arrival of Jesus Christ.

Even though Isaiah 7:10–25 would seem to refer to the birth of a child in the near future to the royal house of Ahab, it has also been understood to look forward to the birth of Christ. In some respects it seems to function as a preliminary suggestion for the basic story line and context of T1: the name of Sarah J. Connor comfortably fills the slot of the "young woman" who will bear a son at some time in the near future (in T1 the child is not born until some time after the film closes). Even the ominous threat of vengeance upon the enemies of Ahaz, King of Judah, and the desolate scorched-earth scene of the land of those enemies suggests the "storm" (see the closing scene in which Sarah drives off into the storm clouds and wilderness) or war between humans and machines which lies just over the horizon of T1 and in which the child to be born will take part.

Other texts of promise with a more general relevance include Isaiah 9:2–7, which echoes in some ways the words of Kyle Reese—the protector sent back from the future by Sarah's son in T1—who speaks of John Connor as the one who turned around the war between humans and machines, breaking the dominance of the oppressors and bringing about their downfall. Similarly, Isaiah 9:2–7 speaks of the great turn in fortunes produced by the Messiah: light comes to those who have walked in darkness, the rod of the oppressor has been broken, since a child with authority has been born, the "wonderful counselor" and "prince of peace." Isaiah 11:1–10 (especially v. 2, which speaks of the wisdom, understanding, counsel, and might of the Messiah) should also be added to this list of messianic texts.

After the messianic texts come the more strictly Christological ones. Firstly, there are those associated with the birth of a savior. The annunciation story in Luke 1:26–38, with its bewildered and innocent Mary and the heavy promises for her child, is echoed in T1 in the message Sergeant Kyle Reese, #DN38416, brings back with him from the future: "there was one man who taught us to fight, to smash the metal; he turned it around. His name was John Connor. Your son, Sarah, your unborn son." The remainder of this dialogue—between Reese and Sarah Connor under a deserted country road bridge as they take a rest from the relentless pursuit of the Terminator—fills out the detail, much of it concerned with Sarah Connor and her nature. As Mary in Luke's narrative, Sarah is an ambiguous figure. Mary is the perplexed and coerced mother of the savior to be, yet she is also the one who speaks the powerful and subversive words of the Magnificat (Luke 1:46–55). Similarly, Sarah Connor exudes the happy-go-lucky innocence of the struggling American girl who works in a fast-food outlet and cannot even balance her check-book; yet she is, in the words of Kyle Reese, "the legend," "the Mother of the future." The message from the future John, relayed by Reese, to Sarah reads: "Thank you, Sarah, for your courage during the dark years. I can't help you with what you must soon face, except to say that the future is not set. You must be stronger than you imagine you can be. You must survive or I will never exist." This powerful and strong Sarah Connor is the one who begins to emerge at the end of T1 and comes out fully in T2.

Closely following the annunciation story is that of the conception of the child. T1 in fact pushes the implications of the Gabriel visit in Luke to its logical conclusion: the bearer of the message (Gabriel/Reese) becomes the father of the child. However, here we find some of the alterations to the biblical texts which become crucial at a later point in this discussion. Reese makes the transition here from Gabriel to Joseph in a number of ways: he becomes the father of the child; his mission is to protect Sarah in the same way that Joseph in Matthew 1:18–25 and 2:13–15 follows divine instruction and protects Mary; with their tasks complete, Joseph and Reese fade from the narrative. A few touches complete the feeling that there is some remixing taking place: the motel appears in T1 at the beginning of the child-producing process, while in Luke the inn appears at the other end; in T1 it is the father, Reese, who is the virgin and not the mother.

The transition to the Matthew (1:18–2:15) narrative has already been made. Two features stand out from this text. The flight to Egypt (Matthew 2:13–15) is located at the end of T1 when Sarah flees into the desert mountains to shelter from the difficult time to come (she is, however, alone and the child is yet to be born). More important perhaps is the connection to be made between King Herod and the Terminator: the effort to eliminate the child to be born or recently born requires a surplus of violence, the Terminator through its relentless pursuit and Herod through the massacre of the children.

The burden of this comparison between film and biblical texts is to establish the Christological nature of at least the first *Terminator* film. If this remains in doubt then the crude but nonetheless effective device of names should set those doubts to rest. Sarah Connor of course bears the name of Abraham's wife in the Hebrew Bible; the woman who was to bear Isaac from whom, according to the narrative, the Israelite people were to come. John Connor, the child who will save the world, bears the initials J.C., initials shared with none other than Jesus Christ. If this is not enough, Sarah Connor's middle initial is also J., which gives us S.J.C..

Before moving onto T2, it is important for our discussion to characterize a little more closely the target and the pursuer of T1. Firstly, the target, John Connor, will be (or is, depending on the time perspective) the savior of humanity. In the words of Reese, who followed the John Connor of the future and is also his father, the son is strong, generating a level of trust in people so that they would die for him. It was this savior who taught the few surviving humans how to fight back, how to break out of the camps and attack the machines, to the extent that victory was in their hands as the humans smashed the central computer system—this is why the Terminator was sent back to eliminate the mother and thus rid the future of the son.

And then there is Arnold Schwarzenegger: literally all brawn and no brain, for he is a cyborg, an android, a human machine with living skin, hair, flesh, muscle, blood, even bad breath, all of which encases an alloy frame operated by a sophisticated computer mechanism (Schwarzenegger, with such limited acting ability and an already mechanical gait, seems eminently suited to the role of cyborg). Extremely difficult to distinguish from human beings (like the famous replicants in *Blade Runner*), this cybernetic organism is one of the latest: systems model 101, which superseded the old 600 model with its rubber skin. Like the devil him- or herself, the Terminator has no feelings, but is programmed to kill, and indeed at the end of the film, when all the flesh has been burned off in the gas tanker explosion, the cover has gone and we come face to face with the black, gleaming satanic metal of the Terminator with its glowing red eyes and in all its robotic originality. In the tradition of stark apocalyptic dualism, Schwarzenegger represents all that is evil (note the gratuitous violence: he rips people from phones and runs over toy trucks) and the savior to be born all that is good.

The second film will experience some massive shifts in these characterizations; but firstly, the intertextual situation. While we are not privileged with the birth itself, in T2 the story picks up with John Connor in his early teens, much like the precocious twelve year old divine child at the temple of Luke 2:41–52, except that now the temple has become the shopping mall, video arcade and storm-water culvert. Perhaps the most powerful text with which T2 connects is that of Revelation 12 (here we move into the third category of biblical texts: the apocalyptic). The text of Revelation 12 is indeed important for both films with its depiction of the pursuit of the woman by the red serpent before she has given birth and then her escape after the birth to the wilderness (Rev 12:1–6; T1), the apocalyptic heavenly battle between the forces of the serpent (= the computers and machines) and of Michael and the angels (= the humans) (Rev 12:7–12; in the future of both films), the defeat of the dragon's forces and its subsequent pursuit of the woman with the child (Rev 12:13–17; T2). A significant feature of this text is the repeated escape/rescue sequence: the serpent pursues the woman who is saved by God (Rev 12:5–6), by eagle's wings (Rev 12:14), and by the earth itself (Rev 12:16). In both T1 and T2 the relentless pulse and intensification of the chase, progressively more desperate as the final confrontation draws near, holds the plots of the films together. Finally, the words describing the child might equally apply to John Connor: "And she gave birth to a son, a male child, who is to rule all the nations with a rod of iron" (Rev 12:5).

It is with the mention of birth pangs in Rev 12:1 that this passage connects with another, namely the protoeuangelion in Gen 3:8–21. There are four points of connection. Firstly, there is the pain: in both the Revelation and Genesis passages the mother cries out in her birth pangs. Similarly, Sarah Connor also suffers much pain; in her confinement in the psychiatric prison, but more importantly in what she knows about the future, graphically depicted in her dreams about witnessing the nuclear explosion in the children's playground. Pain and suffering have made her tough, and in T2 Sarah Connor has realized the potential of the first film, a tough Mary more of the Magnificat than of traditional feminine qualities: she works out day by day in her cell in the psychiatric prison, preparing for the first of many escapes from the clutches of the second Terminator sent to destroy her son; wearing a gunbelt, intent in her mission, she is more at home in the company of Latin American revolutionaries than among young suburban women.

Secondly, there is in the Genesis passage the hard labor for the father figure (Adam), which echoes dimly Schwarzenegger's hard work in disposing of the second Terminator, the sweaty labor of the foundry workers at the close of the film and even the image of the hard-working dad off to work at the foundry himself (Schwarzenegger descending into the molten metal). Thirdly, there is the relationship between mother, son, and serpent: the Genesis passage speaks of the perpetual conflict between the serpent on the one hand, and the mother and son on the other. So also both Terminators are programmed to destroy: first Sarah Connor in T1, and then John Connor in T2, not ceasing in their missions until the objective is achieved. Finally, cross-referencing takes place between serpent and second Terminator: the serpent is to spend its life sliding along on the ground, indistinct from it (even eating dust). In a similar fashion the second Terminator is made of liquid metal, taking on the form, for a brief period of time, of all that it touches, and also slithering along the ground on more than one occasion. In one brilliant sequence the human form transforms itself into a checked linoleum floor covering, subsequently oozing back into shape to attack yet another victim (the mental institution guard). In both texts—Genesis and Revelation—nearly all the characters are there: the mother (Sarah Connor), the child (John Connor), and the serpent (both Terminators). The only missing parallel is the figure of the protector.

The lake of fire constitutes the central item of the last of the apocalyptic passages to be considered: the beast and the false prophet who descend into the lake of fire in Rev 19:20 and 20:10 find their echo in the destruction of both Terminators in the pool of molten metal at the steel foundry. But it is the existence of two Terminators in T2 that signals a tension and slippage within and between the films, a slippage which now becomes our concern.

Thus far our focus has been on the first of the possible codes by which the films may be read; namely, the Christological reading which takes its basic argument from the level of intertextuality between the Hebrew and Christian Bibles and the *Terminator* films. It is a familiar and therefore extremely predictable story: the only interest lies in the means the narrative uses to achieve its predictable closure. While other interpretations or codes will be appropriated in due course, the Christological reading itself requires the use of the second of Jameson's methods to be used in this analysis: figuration.

Figural Slippage

Figuration is essentially a formalist enterprise* in which mostly peripheral formal or structural features and elements are identified as indicators that things apart from the overt plot and character systems are happening in cultural products, that there are more substantial and deeper patterns and contradictions at work. In Jameson's work, figuration assumes an explicitly Marxist platform in which the "figures" are traces of social, political and economic features. The key which needs to be empha-

---

* *Note of the Editors*: For a different view of "Figuration" see the article by Jean Calloud, "Figure, Knowledge, and Truth."

sized, however, is that figuration operates with the form and structure of the text first and foremost, rather than with the content, which is of secondary importance. This enables the critic to delve into all this reactionary material (since most contemporary cultural production is of an overtly and ominously reactionary nature) and come up with some surprises. The search is for those tell-tale but often inexplicable pieces that unsettle, disrupt, or are unnecessary embellishments. Figuration is indeed Jameson's own way of connecting the debate over "representation" with the Marxist interest in "mediation."

Apart from the clear Marxist dimensions of this way of reading cultural products, two of the terms used here rely upon Freudian thought. Firstly, figuration is very much indebted to Freud's use of the term "displacement" to describe how sometimes unimportant details (slips, peripheral parapraxes, etc.) are the key to an interpretation (for example, a peripheral dream image with a low emotional content may hold the key to the meaning of a dream filled with powerful images and activity). Secondly, the notion of a significant slippage (significant in that it hides something), which is used here as a basis for figuration, is itself quite Freudian. In the same way that figuration moves through elements such as slippage to seek more significant references, so also the Freudian agenda moves through the slips, the parapraxes of everyday life, and so on, to the truth.[3]

The significant slippage in the two *Terminator* films involves the wholesale readjustment of Schwarzenegger's roles from T1 to T2. Two phases establish the grounds for the slippage: the change in his status from bad guy to good guy; and the close relationship between the new good guy and the official savior, John Connor. We will discuss these two phases in turn.

The two films begin in virtually identical fashion: two figures arrive, heralded by electrical disturbance and the winds of some future time, naked and open to investment with the messages supplied after their arrival in the present. In both cases the gleaming bulk of Schwarzenegger arrives first, followed by a figure much slighter in physical build. It is here that the similarity in character systems breaks down, for T2 delights in inverting all the viewer expectations: in T1 Schwarzenegger appears as the relentless killing machine while the second figure who appears, Kyle Reese, comes as the resourceful protector. In T2 the roles are reversed: Schwarzenegger has become a slightly gentler cyborg whose task it is to protect John Connor, while the second figure is now the deadly

---

[3] I owe these observations on the Freudian nature of the notions of figuration and slippage to David Seljak, who teaches on Freud and the Psychology of Religion at McGill University.

Terminator, at whose hands death is infinitely more intimate and insidious (this Terminator delivers death by means of knife-like formations at the ends of its fingers and arms; the first *Terminator*, Schwarzenegger, relied upon superior firepower). In order to assist those viewers whose credulity has been strained with this reversal the characters themselves come to the rescue: both Sarah and John Connor must go through the massive reassessment process of having the terror from the past become the protector of the present. For closer watchers, however, something is different from the moment Schwarzenegger meets his first humans on the second trip back: none of the bikers in the bar are killed, and the crowning touch comes when Schwarzenegger, fully clothed in the trademark leathers obtained from one denuded biker, turns to another loud-mouthed, gun-toting biker and—contrary to expectations of another blasted corpse—removes and dons the biker's shades before riding off to the sounds of George Thorogood and the Destroyers.[4]

It is surprising how easily we as viewers accept the explanation for Schwarzenegger's transformation: this simulacrum of the first Terminator in T1 has been reprogrammed by none other than the future John Connor. The savior from T1 has been able to work the greatest of miracles and bring about the conversion of Schwarzenegger from the embodiment of evil to whatever this new film has in store for him. This change in Schwarzenegger is enabled both by his concurrent venture in *Kindergarten Cop* and by a sleight of hand or blurring of identities; for strictly speaking this cyborg is a different figure from the one that was comprehensively destroyed in T1. Indeed, the parts of the first Terminator remain in T2, although official reports state that there were no remains. However, it is the same star playing the different roles and the viewer soon finds that the centripetal force of Arnold Schwarzenegger merges the two separate figures of T1 and T2 into one.

The nature of the reprogrammed cyborg is of central interest. Like the promised "kinder and gentler America" of George Bush, for whom Schwarzenegger used to campaign, this android fills a different role from T1. While we have already invoked the Christological interpretation or code, we will now add to that the psychological reading with its emphasis on the family. As far as character slots are concerned, Schwarzenegger takes up the place vacated by Kyle Reese in T1, namely, as the father. T2 works away at the mother, son, and Schwarzenegger relationship in order to generate a strange new, but still familiar, form of the nuclear family. Fred Pfeil argues that by means of the "play of opposition and symbiosis

---

[4] Pfeil is mistaken when he identifies the particular song as "Born to be Bad"; it is in fact "Bad to the Bone," but anyone may be forgiven for confusing Thorogood's songs.

essential to T2" the film is able to play with more off-beat variations of the family while coming down hard on the essential social and libidinal necessity of the family as such. Thus Linda Hamilton's Sarah Connor is a "fully operational warrior-woman," a "phallic mother with a complete set of soldier-of-fortune contacts, cache of weapons and survivalist skills" (Pfeil: 29). Yet for all her toughness, Sarah Connor is unable to save the world: the real star must do that while Sarah's motherly anguish over the nuked playground of her dreams reveals her softer, more genuine, self. Arnold himself arrives "available for refunctioning from killing machine to nurturant proto-father" (Pfeil: 29); yet despite efforts to "humanize" him he remains sufficiently aloof from emotions, in order to fill the more traditional role of the detached but hard-working father. Even John Connor, the rebel leader and savior of the world who in both T1 and T2 sends figures back to protect himself, slips gradually into place as the dependent, dependable, and obedient child. At the same time this new family is removed from the traditional domestic space of suburbia—the foster parents—and relocated in the dead zones of freeway, institution, research center, mall, plant, and guerrilla encampment in the California desert. Even the feminist and racial critiques are permitted to say their (misdirected) pieces—Sarah Connor's rage is directed at the black middle class Dyson family—as part of this total affirmation.

All this would seem to be the case for this "earthly family," but it only goes part of the way toward the more important "holy family." Schwarzenegger's filling of the father slot brings about some important modifications of that slot: Kyle Reese, despite his arrival from the future, was a total flesh and blood human being. The reprogrammed cyborg is not completely human, adding to this family a dimension concerned with the traditional science-fiction motif of the relationship between humans and machines. This alteration in the family make-up provides a great deal of room for developing the question of the nature of human existence and its limits, and that development takes the form of the growing relationship between the android and the savior-to-be, John Connor, a relationship which enables the "new person" in the cyborg to develop. It is John who develops this new person in Arnold, teaching him—in a manner reminiscent of a child learning to speak—how to speak (slang) as a human, to behave as a human, and indicating in some way what it means to feel pain as a human being (focused on the external sign of tears).

Yet the relationship between savior and cyborg is permitted to flower through a crucial change in the role of the mother. At a certain point Sarah Connor abdicates her role as androgynous parent. Watching Schwarzenegger and John striking up their relationship, Sarah's voice-over reflects: "of all the would-be fathers, this machine was the only one that measured up." It wouldn't drink or come home late; it wouldn't neglect the child or run off and leave him; it would be there to protect him. From this point on the basic familial relationship is that between father and son, while the mother falls into the background (a little like the Holy Spirit in Christian doctrine). In the most traditional of patterns her nurturing of the child is over; his approaching adulthood requires a masculine touch. Sarah's peripheral status vents itself immediately in the futile commando attack on the Dyson family.

There are, then, two phases in the realignment of Arnold Schwarzenegger in T2: the switch (in a more than figural sense) from evil to good and the growing relationship with John Connor. Both phases of Schwarzenegger's rehabilitation enable the crucial slippage of the films to take place: the transfer of savior roles between T1 and T2. The reprogrammed cyborg is ready for perhaps the most important reinvestment of the whole film, for the conventional identification of John Connor as the savior of the human race is now gradually eroded and displaced onto Schwarzenegger. This transfer takes place in almost direct proportion to the increasing intimacy of father and son. When the climax of the film appears on the screen it is not John Connor who makes the final sacrifice, but Arnold Schwarzenegger who sacrifices his life so that humanity might be saved.

The story that brings the slippage in savior figures to the fore turns on one of the many temporal twists characteristic of both films. In order to avoid the nuclear war—"Judgment Day"—our heroes—mom, dad, son, and coopted middle class black scientist Dyson—realize they must obliterate the remains of the destroyed cyborg from T1, since it is the parts from that cyborg that provide the stimulus for the construction of the new supercomputer system (Skynet); the system that eventually takes control and tries to eliminate humans. The vital pieces are obtained from the fortress of the corporate research center and destroyed in the lake of fire in the steel works. Yet one revolutionary computer chip remains: that which is located in Schwarzenegger's own alloy head. At Schwarzenegger's command, John Connor (since Terminators cannot self-destruct) must then pull the lever which allows Arnold to descend into the lake of fire.

Arnold Schwarzenegger has become the savior of the world. The word for this used to be "patripassianism," the suffering of the father instead of, along with, or as the son: once branded as a heresy, its modern recovery owes a great deal to Jürgen Moltmann's *The Crucified God*. Indeed, in a further twist to this Christological slippage, the sacrifice is preceded by a resurrection scene.[5] Impaled (the suggestion of a cross can hardly be avoided) with a crowbar by the second Terminator, Schwarzenegger lies beaten and "dead," until—and this is almost as difficult to believe as his initial conversion—the power backup kicks in and the red glow returns deep in his eyes. He literally rises from the dead, coming over the turning pulley-wheel (grave-stone?) to finish off the second Terminator. Lazarus has nothing on this scene.

The transfer of savior roles is complete, for in the act of destroying the source of information for the new Skynet system the future nuclear war is averted, along with the battle between machines and humans, and therefore the need for John Connor to lead humans to victory over the machines. John Connor has been comprehensively outplayed as a savior.

In order to excavate the significance of this slippage recourse must be had to the notion of figuration, or Freudian displacement. The first figurative leap connects the Christological slippage, which passes us by with little notice, with an even more peripheral feature of the film: obsolescence. In all his sophisticated newness, Schwarzenegger-as-Terminator in T_1 comes with the mind-blowing terror and fascination of the marketable technological "breakthrough," enhanced all the more by his trip back from the future. By the time we get to T_2, the old model Terminator has been superseded by the latest product in the Terminator assembly line. It is the new product which enthralls and threatens with its as yet unfathomed technological wizardry. Schwarzenegger on the other hand now enters that realm of domesticated obsolescence which characterizes the familiar appliances and furniture—including the essential nuclear family structure—of a middle-class household. Apart from the well-worn dad, he resembles in some respects an overgrown action figure for the bored John to play with. The technological sophistication with which he has been assembled is no longer a mystery, but is now explained by Arnold, exploited by the corporate research laboratory, and reprogrammed in some near future time.

It is in the process of obsolescence that the films inscribe their own gap in time (1984 and 1991), for the computer graphics, the virtual reality, required to produce the figure of the second Terminator was simply not available in 1984. The "special effects" of T_1 were spectacular, but they date in comparison to the $90 million extravaganza of T_2.

Yet the process is not restricted to these two figures alone. In T_1 Kyle Reese provides Sarah Connor, and therefore us, with enough information to situate the android out to eliminate her: Schwarzenegger in the first

---

[5] In this continual rearrangement and overplay of images, the descent into the lake of molten metal is also a descent/ascent into clouds of smoke, evoking the ascension of Christ into the clouds.

film was a new model cyborg, systems model 101 with living tissue over a computerized metal skeleton, who replaced the older 600 model with its rubber skin. By the second film the T101 has been superseded by the advanced prototype T1000, a radically new development constructed out of liquid metal alloy. There are therefore three cyborg models—T600, T101, and T1000 (presumably the "T" designates "Terminator" but Toshiba made a laptop known as the T1000, and the "T" also conjures up Toyota)—that present us with a sequence of models and their subsequent obsolescence. Perhaps the only hint that the T1000 may be flawed lies in its early prototype status.

This regular rhythm of continual product upgrade suggests a very different time scale than the stark apocalyptic one of the overt story line. While the first figural leap led from the Christological slippage to the process of obsolescence, the second figural move is from this rhythm of continual product upgrade to that which it indicates quite clearly: the patterns of the market. Rapid obsolescence—indeed a technological know-how which is able to depict its own obsolescence—is a feature of the late capitalist mode of production in which we now live. The Christological or Trinitarian slippage, therefore, functions as a figure for the contradictions of the market, which must continually trip over itself to produce ever newer items in a futile effort to overcome those contradictions. The terror depicted in these films, then, is located not so much in the Terminator figures themselves as in the all-consuming frenzy of the market; or rather, the terror of the market, of capitalism, is displaced onto the Terminators.

The suggestion that the market is the ultimate signified is reinforced by the play in time and tense in both films: the future, past, and present are blurred into one another through a variety of techniques. Some scenes operate with the temporal distinction clearly in place: the dream or nightmare sequences of Sarah Connor, particularly those which depict the nuclear holocaust (the other time shifts toggle back and forth over this divide but Sarah focuses on it); the storytelling in T1 of Kyle Reese in which the visual depiction of the rat-infested and smoke-filled underground reinforces the words which try to describe that future to Sarah; the beginning of T2 with its battle scene of humans versus machines over the same children's playground which features in Sarah's nightmares; and even the basic story line in which a Terminator and a Protector are sent back from the future either to eliminate or protect John in his fetal or pubescent state. By means of these sequences, and by Kyle Reese's awareness in T1 that he was in legendary times, the present is elevated to the status of some mythical time in which all that is significant for the future takes place.

The time difference would seem to be clear: Los Angeles in the "present" (1984 and 1991) and Los Angeles in 2029, a mere forty five or thirty eight years away (in good P.K. Dick fashion) yet separated by the nuclear war that opens on August 29, 1997. Beginning with the statement at the opening of T1 that the final battle "would be fought here, in our present," a number of sequences break down the time difference which appeared to be so clear. In T1 the time avenues through which Schwarzenegger and Reese came have been destroyed (they seem to have been restored for T2): there is no escape from the battle of the present. The father of the child, Reese, is the one sent back by the son to protect his mother so that he himself could be safely born. As Pfeil notes (25) the apocalypse is in many respects already upon us in the present, with official power running amok (the sadistic mental hospital, the security systems of the slick corporation, and the heavily armed and violent police) and a group of guerrillas opposing the power network all the while surrounded by fireballs and piles of bodies.

However, the main mechanism of temporal distortion and the breakdown of historical depth comes with a fundamentally materialist move: the contrast between the physical temporal progression of the films as they turn on their spools and that of the "real" time depicted in the films. Thus we have the photograph of Sarah taken by the Mexican boy at the end of T1, which is the photo treasured by Reese in the future of "real" time (as in an earlier flash forward) but which has already appeared in the past of "filmic" time (the photo in fact gains its significance for us from this earlier appearance). Further, the death of Kyle Reese in the "present" should cancel his future existence and thereby invalidate the earlier depictions of him in that future, but for the physical temporal progression of the film, Reese's life, whether in the future or in the present, does in fact come to an end; there is no more of Reese in any temporal mode after his death. While this conflict in temporal sequences may be accounted for by the point that Reese was sent back from the future, the major breakdown of the "real" temporal sequence takes place in T2 with the saving activity of Schwarzenegger: his self-sacrifice removes the last trace of the technological know-how which could provide the base for the Skynet computer systems, thus averting the nuclear war, the battle between humans and machines, and the soteriological role of John Connor himself. The circumstances which set up the stories of both films have now been removed. One final twist completes the collapse of temporal separation: in both films we are told that the events depicted in the film were the result of the near victory of the humans, led by John Connor, over the machines. In two final and desperate bids, the Power Network attempts to save itself from imminent defeat. Yet the depictions of the future give little impression that the humans are in control: they appear hounded, weary, and virtually beyond hope. It would seem that the victory which is referred to is in fact the one that takes place in the present. The John Connor of the future has set in motion a series of events which result in his own birth and then final victory over the machines. The future/past/present conflict is resolved at the close of filmic time, thus collapsing all temporal difference.

This play with time bristles with interpretive possibilities, but the main point is that there is a chronic loss of historical depth. It all gets thrown together in an undifferentiated conglomeration or historical pastiche. It is this approach—or rather lack thereof—to history which has been identified and traced by Fredric Jameson on many occasions as the loss of history which is so characteristic of postmodernism. Such a loss is ultimately the result of a commodity culture in which items from very different times and places may appear side by side on the shelves in their identical plastic wrappers or in the catalogues in identical glossy photographs. Not only are people, as consumers, brought to the same level by capitalism, but historical periods and moments are also leveled into one flat expanse. In this way, the play of time and tense reinforces the figuration of the market located in the Christological slippage.

The intertextually-based Christological reading of the *Terminator* films has now been carried a stage further with the identification of the figuration of the market in the Christological slippage between Schwarzenegger and John Connor, and in the understanding of history as such. But how is the terror of the market to be faced and overcome? The answer is found in the next interpretive code to be used, which is that of utopian analysis.

Utopia and Popularity

Both T1 and T2 were huge successes at the box office, a phenomenon which makes them all the more intriguing. The search for a major reason for such vast popular appeal has recourse to Jameson's strategy of utopian analysis, which seeks out the utopian dimensions of even the most reactionary and resistant material. Utopian analysis always appears with its partner, ideological analysis, the negative moment of any reading. This relationship between ideology and utopia in Jameson's work owes a considerable debt to Paul Ricoeur's negative and positive interpretation, or the hermeneutics of suspicion and recovery, as well as to the utopian drive of Ernst Bloch (Jameson, 1976). In this appropriation of Ricoeur and Bloch, ideological analysis absorbs into itself the hermeneutics of suspicion (understanding ideology for the moment in the traditional sense as false consciousness); utopian analysis, on the other hand, carries on the task of the hermeneutics of recovery, searching for the point where, especially in the very act of avoidance and concealment, the wish and hope for something vastly new and better shows through in a cultural product.

Jameson pushes the relationship, or the dialectic, of ideology and utopia to its logical conclusion. With the reminder of the importance of class in all this, specifically a conflictual or Hegelian (master-slave) notion of class consciousness, Jameson argues that "all class consciousness—or in other words, all ideology in the strongest sense, including the most exclusive forms of ruling-class consciousness just as much as that of oppositional or oppressed classes—is in its very nature Utopian" (1981:289; see 1976:57–58). Along with the specific notion of class consciousness that operates here, two further limiting factors close down the more dangerous implications that Jameson wishes to avoid: the first—following logically from the notion of class consciousness—designates "Utopian" as that which "expresses the unity of a collectivity" (1981:291); while the second turns the whole discussion on its head by specifying the proposition just quoted as allegorical or figurative; i.e. that collectivities of whatever kind imperfectly foreshadow the collective life of a future classless society. In this sense, then, Jameson argues that ideology is utopian, and vice versa; and thus that Marxian negative and positive hermeneutics can be separated only at the peril of their analytic power.

It is Jameson's identification of ideology and utopia that forms the basis of the argument for the popularity of the *Terminator* films. For few would doubt that these films constitute some of the most ideologically repulsive material in mass culture today; yet at the same time they are powerful and attractive because they tap into the utopian urge and drive, which is normally deflected in so many ways. Identifying the negative moments of the film from its structural connections to big business down to Schwarzenegger himself is a reasonably straightforward task. There is the Romantic notion that humans are somehow more than and better than machines and yet threatened by them. The taboo "i" word of contemporary market theory looms large in both films, namely, the various institutions which attempt to crush the individual spirits of the characters: John as subject to the welfare system of foster care; Sarah in the psychiatric prison; the police force that tries to wipe them all out; even the overgrown corporation that uses whatever means to get ahead of its competitors. The connection between the Right's claim to the family and the valorization of the family in this film needs no special elaboration. Schwarzenegger even does his bit for the National Rifle Association with the by now traditional trip to the gun store or weapons arsenal to stock up before piling the screen full of bodies (thus in *Raw Deal, Commando, Total Recall*, as well as *Terminator* 1 and 2). Schwarzenegger's intrusion as a star into the film has already been noted, but here it is his own political activity which comes to the fore. Known as "Conan the Republican" he has campaigned for Reagan and Bush, despite being married into the Kennedy clan. More recently, Schwarzenegger appeared in Barcelona at the 1992 Olympic Games leading the official White House delegation to the Games on behalf of George Bush. Business connections are not far behind, for he was also in Barcelona to open yet another nightclub (known as Club Hollywood) as part of the combined business operations of himself, Sylvester Stallone (whose film-based political messages—e.g. *Cobra*—are much more blunt) and Bruce Willis. Such is the savior figure of T2.

However, what is most fascinating are the modes of utopian gratification in the midst of this reactionary turf. Apart from the collective utopian wish-fulfillment offered by the depiction of the disintegrated and reconstituted family, the fundamental utopian appeal of these films is based upon tapping into the political unconscious of people by means of the Christian savior story (a story with which most people who view the films will have some vague and nodding acquaintance). The films enthrall people by means of the self-sacrifice of Arnold for the human race; but Arnold's sacrifice is specifically designed to neutralize the development of Skynet (Internet? Bitnet?), the global computer network which is supposed to take over and then attack human beings. Indeed, Skynet is the real enemy in T2, and thus the T1000 disappears from view while the Skynet laboratory is being destroyed. (On a material level the T1000 and Skynet coalesce, since, as noted above, the physical production of the T1000 in the film was achieved by sophisticated computer graphics.)

This is perhaps the place to deal with the problem of "technolust," since the whole question is important to this stage of the argument. A major feature of the utopian gratification of films such as these lies in the consumption and thrill of the technological expertise which has gone into their production (consumption itself being an expression of utopian desire). Indeed the "special effects"—alternating with timed packages of violence—of T1 and T2 repeatedly topped the list as one of the most appealing aspects of these films. While the satisfaction of technolust is important for these films, arguments that focus on technology as such remain suspicious and unimpressive. I follow Jameson's suggestion that our awe and fear of communication and information networks, whose symbol is the ubiquitous computer terminal, are merely the displaced awe and fear of the global but unseen networks of the market, i.e. late capitalism. In a material sense these electronic networks are in fact primarily military and business tools. They therefore indicate in quite concrete terms the other reality of capitalism.

With this point in place it is possible to complete the argument. Skynet functions as a second major form of figuration in these films, in this case figuring the military and economic grid of late capitalism. The code of utopian analysis thus connects at this point with that of figuration: the real and final terror and enemy is nothing other than the relentless and comprehensive market. This is where the utopian power of the films finally lies, since in depicting the destruction of Skynet they pick up and assuage the basic but hidden fear that people have of the market, displaced as it is onto technology. However, people are assured that what will overcome the market is not some state of brutal anarchy, but a cooperative utopia in which humans dominate technology and the market. In other words, the market's contradictions and threats are overcome and Judgment Day is averted.[6]

Although the family offers the picture of a utopian collectivity, and although the consumption of technology offers libidinal satisfaction, they remain important but secondary features of the utopian dimension of the *Terminator* films. The primary utopian factor is the hope and wish for a process of revolution, for the violent destruction—in response to the institutionalized and covert violence embedded within competition—of capitalism. Here I disagree with Jameson when he emphasizes the collectivity as the focus of utopian wishes; in these films the revolution takes equal if not prior position in the utopian schema.

Indeed the revolutionary process is central to a number of other films in which Schwarzenegger features. In the more superficial and crude *Commando*, revolution is given a negative assessment: Schwarzenegger deals with third world guerrillas and mercenaries in a style that would make Stallone's *Rambo* sit up and take notice. Although the physique of the former Mr. Universe plays a role in nearly all his films, it has become gradually less obvious as a theme. In *Commando* the theme is still quite strong (although it is by no means the dominant factor of the film as, for example, in *Pumping Iron* or *Hercules in New York*) although it must make room for other dimensions. A similar situation applies to *Conan the Barbarian*, but in this case the revolutionary theme becomes a little more in-

---

[6] Judgment Day is of course the nuclear holocaust, brought about by the computer networks to rid the world of humans. There is another referent here, however, for T1 and T2 straddle the collapse of the Soviet Union and the communist governments of Eastern Europe. As these were rolled back, the threat, in the popular psyche at least, of nuclear confrontation seemed to disappear overnight. Its removal in T2 would seem to reflect this change in some way. The nature of the Terminators becomes interesting in this respect: the heavily armed Terminator of the first film is a confrontational figure while the Terminator of the second film is much more sinister and unpredictable, changing shape and form and taking on the appearance of familiar people. The enemy has become much more difficult to locate: it used to be over there in a clearly definable form and place, but now it may be amongst us.

teresting,[7] for here Schwarzenegger struggles out of a youth spent in slavery to overthrow the oppressive regime under which people must live. Indeed *Conan the Barbarian* first gives us the classic features of the Schwarzenegger revolution: a small band of revolutionaries overthrows the tyrannical regime and gives everyone their freedom. Thus in *Running Man* Schwarzenegger becomes the last fugitive hope against an oppressive system which gives its "criminals" (political prisoners) the chance to be released should they be successful in the wildly popular television game show "Running Man," based on the traditional generic item of the human hunt. In this case Schwarzenegger succeeds in outsmarting the game and overturning the system itself.

Along with the *Terminator* films, however, the most sophisticated treatment of the revolution comes with *Total Recall*. Not content with worthwhile but disinherited citizens, in this film the revolutionaries signify their status as social outcasts by carrying in their bodies the grotesque deformities induced by radiation (the contrast with Schwarzenegger's physique is quite deliberate). This fringe status is enhanced by the situation of the struggle on Mars, where these outcasts carry on a subversive operation against the oppressive control of the protective canopy by those in power. In the battle for the supply of oxygen, which would then give people freedom, Schwarzenegger assists the freedom fighters in their revolution, the result being the release of a vast amount of moisture into the atmosphere of Mars which gives everyone the freedom to breathe their own air.

The question as to why such reactionary films should be so concerned with the problem of the revolution brings us to the final and unresolved contradiction of the *Terminator* films and those films like it. In each case—*Conan the Barbarian, Running Man, Total Recall, Terminator* 1 and 2—the pattern of a small band of freedom fighters destroying the oppressive system is based not so much upon any notion of a revolutionary destruction of capitalism, but rather upon the revolution at the beginning of capitalism. For the freedom fighters evoke the small but dedicated bands of merchants who through their labors against great odds brought about the collapse of the feudal order and the advent of capitalism. The model for these films then is the bourgeois revolution of an earlier time, which was in no sense a gentle process, but one which involved invasion, exploitation and violence.

The eternal return of the bourgeois revolution in these films indicates that the wished for utopia on the other side is none other than a classical liberal one, for liberalism itself remains a utopian quest—if only we could

---

[7] The libidinal cross-investment between sexual body and revolution is a further element worth pursuing at another time.

get rid of state interference, if only we would let the market rule, then we could get about our wealth creation without hindrance and all would be golden. Even the iron foundry at the close of T2 expresses this nostalgic wish for a more classical stage of liberalism with its economic base in the heavy industry of a bygone era. The contradiction of course for the *Terminator* films is that they present the revolution as one directed against capitalism, but a liberal utopia beyond capitalism is a contradiction in terms.

Dialectical Foldback

I did, however, promise a complication of all this, which involves broadening the horizon beyond the cultural products themselves to include the interpreter or critic. This is a dimension all too readily forgotten in the work of Fredric Jameson, which has served as the model of interpretation thus far. In earlier works, particularly *Marxism and Form*, Jameson argues that "dialectical thought is in its very structure self-consciousness and may be described as the attempt to think about a given object on one level, and at the same time to observe our own thought processes as we do so" (1971:340). For Marxism "the self-consciousness aimed at is the awareness of the thinker's position in society and in history itself, and of the limits imposed on this awareness by class position—in short of the ideological and situational nature of all thought..." (1971:340). Yet if we view the whole of Jameson's corpus, this concern for the inclusion of the interpreter too often translates into the study of other critics and other interpretations. There is, in other words, a gradually diminishing effort to bear out in practice this axiom from *Marxism and Form*.

One of the consequences of the absence, or rather concealment, of the interpreter is that the selfsame interpreter is thereby enabled to attain some form of omniscience. Concealment and control tie in together here: not only am I able as critic to efface my presence through the interpretive tools I am using but by means of this self-effacement I am also able to achieve some interpretive omniscience. I suspect that the threat of the omniscient critic is not restricted to Jameson and that much criticism, biblical or otherwise, operates with a similar covert critic who in the final copy conveys little if any of the uncertainty and tentativeness of all interpretation.[8]

In order, then, to activate the mechanisms of deconcealment and factor myself into the interpretive process, as well as to widen the intertextual nature of my reading by including the "texts" of my own situation, I

---

[8] A fascinating study would be to investigate the various ways such critical concealment is achieved.

will have recourse to three items, one methodological and two from the *Terminator* films: the Althusserian understanding of ideology, the function of Schwarzenegger himself in the films, and the generic item of hand-to-hand or warrior combat.

In a major contribution to the reassessment of ideology which lies behind the earlier discussion of ideology and utopia—"Ideology and Ideological State Apparatuses (Notes Towards an Investigation)" (Althusser, 1971:121–73/1984:1–60)—Louis Althusser suggests that ideology "represents the Imaginary relationship of individuals to their Real conditions of existence" (1971:153). That is to say, ideology gains a more neutral and permanent function over against the traditional Marxist notion of false consciousness. Apart from the Lacanian sense of terms such as "Imaginary" and "Real" (it was Althusser's feat to incorporate Lacan into a structural Marxism), there are two dimensions of this definition which are important for this discussion. First, ideology is by this definition a form of mediation or mapping between individual and totality, rendering the relationship imaginable and possible, yet including at the same time signals of the difficulty of doing so. Second, one of the significant means of mediation between the individual and the conditions of existence is that of narrative. Ideologies are, in a sense, buried narratives or stories. I would suggest, therefore, that the *Terminator* films are ideological in Althusser's sense of the term: these stories assist me in mapping myself onto the context of late capitalism, as I suspect they do for a good many other people as well.

However, in elaborating on precisely how this might be so, we need to move on to the next item, which is the role of Schwarzenegger himself. In the preceding discussion I have designated the various characters of the films by their character names—John and Sarah Connor, Kyle Reese and so on—yet in the case of Arnold Schwarzenegger I used the actor's name rather than his movie persona as the Terminator.[9] The fact that this feature of the discussion was initially unconscious is perhaps even more significant: it signals to me a substantial libidinal investment in the glossy carapace which constitutes the public person of Arnold Schwarzenegger, which is much greater than the two *Terminator* films. There is, in other words, a half-conscious investment on my part in Schwarzenegger—once described as a condom with muscles—which has the sexual as its primary driving force. As a male in the dying years of the second millennium Schwarzenegger provides a sinister and reactionary point of identification in the context of the fundamental challenges of feminism. Yet my own identification or investment is not in the Terminator character alone; it is

---

[9] I owe this observation to Gary Phillips, who read an earlier version of this paper.

in the much larger projection or public persona which we know as Arnold Schwarzenegger, a projection which is enabled by and indeed fundamental to the star system as that has been developed by Hollywood. Schwarzenegger fills what is by now the familiar category of the Hollywood superstar with its complex and constructed collection of images and representations which constitute the "star" in question. Schwarzenegger then is much more Arnold Schwarzenegger in his films rather than any specific character or role, and I would suggest that my unintentional designation of Schwarzenegger by his superstar title rather than by the specific character of the films both reflects the Hollywood star system and its success in selling its various superstar commodities to consumers such as myself. Yet it is the star system, in producing the superstar Schwarzenegger, which also provides the ground upon which my own process of investment may operate.

There is, however, a curious twist to the star system as it applies to Schwarzenegger. A useful distinction here is that between the Hollywood star or superstar and the character actor who often plays a supporting role in Hollywood films but is more commonly found as a basic element of the television series.[10] It would seem that Schwarzenegger is the first to successfully bridge this gap; he is, therefore, a superstar character actor, or the first "McDonald's superstar," predictable and somewhat bland but immensely popular and successful. In an adaptation of the barb directed at Katherine Hepburn, Schwarzenegger has been described as having the ability to act out the emotional range from A almost to B. I would suggest that it is because of his inability to act that he has been able to combine superstar and character actor (it is not a coincidence that his greatest films—*Terminator* 1 and 2—are precisely those in which he plays the role of a cyborg, a character for which his inability to act is a virtue, for machines do not behave like humans). This combination of superstar and character actor has indeed made of Schwarzenegger an even more highly consumable item than is usual for the star system. It is at this point that the economic links up with the sexual: libidinal investment takes place all the more readily with this product's easy accessibility.

Let me sum up the argument thus far: the *Terminator* films serve the crucial ideological function of enabling me to map myself onto late capitalism and they do so by means of the star system in which Schwarzenegger has become the superstar character actor, both highly sexual and consumable. How might I then map my own situation as interpreter of these

---

[10] John Candy may of course be cited as an example of a Hollywood character actor, but then his comedy films occupy a second or third level behind the blockbusters in which superstars are traditionally found. Candy has in fact shown glimpses, such as the appearance in *J.F.K.*, of ability beyond his usual character.

films? There would seem to be two processes going in my assessment of these films. The first offers a conscious criticism and attempts to account for their popularity. While this is going on the second, largely unconscious, is also taking place in which I identify with and appropriate these films as my own stories. On this level I might identify the following. From a gender perspective they allow me to glory in machismo and male dominance while professing to have disposed of these things. From a religious, or more specifically biblical perspective, they offer a way to relate my particular belief system, generated out of a European Calvinist perspective, to contemporary society. It is deeply gratifying to find the biblical texts forming part of the intertextual context of these films. Racially, as an Austrian by birth Schwarzenegger permits me—born in a colonial country from Teutonic (Dutch) parents—a fleeting if very submerged satisfaction in Aryan superiority. Physically and sexually, Schwarzenegger reinforces my associations between virility and the abnormal muscles produced by steroids and pumping iron. From a political perspective, a virulent opposition on my part to capitalism and the forces of the market is gratified by the figuration in the films of the destruction of precisely those forces (see above). And from the class dimension, I remain a member of that fraction of the middle class constituted by the intelligentsia, attempting eternally to flee that class but equally eternally caught up in its class consciousness. It is to the essentially monotonous and humdrum situation of the middle class that the video-store genre of "action" supplies a ready response. Here is all the excitement and stimulation the middle class seeks in order to escape its deadpan everyday existence, comparable in fact to the overpriced thrill-seeking activities such as white-water rafting or skydiving whose primary customers are white-collar employees of the large corporations. These films indeed provide an articulation of middle-class consciousness. My appropriation of all these dimensions of the *Terminator* films, while offering a rational critique of them, is signalled most clearly by that fact that I remain an avid consumer of Schwarzenegger's films.

However, such an effort at mapping briefly undertaken above can never be complete, and this incompleteness is itself suggested by precisely that element in the films which may be said to provide primary ignition for such existential identification in the first place. This element both opens up and problematizes my investment in the films. It is of course the generic item familiar from folklore—and this includes the Bible—of hand-to-hand or warrior combat.[11] Essentially a pre-capitalist folk motif, rang-

---

[11] That many generic conventions carry through from folklore to popular culture needs further exploration, but the possibility opens up a potential crossfertilization of methods from one to the other. This is the way, it seems to me, that biblical studies may make greater use of cultural critical theories.

ing from David and Goliath to medieval jousting, it closes out three of Schwarzenegger's films—*Commando, Terminator* 1 and 2—and constitutes a major plot item in *Predator*. In each case it is a duel to the death, or at least destruction. That my investment is in some trouble, however, is signalled by the fact that Schwarzenegger is not always the victor. In *Commando* all is well: the old antagonist of special agent Matrix (Schwarzenegger), now working as a mercenary for a tinpot third world island despot, meets his well deserved end. The problems begin with T1, for here it is Schwarzenegger himself who comes to an extraordinarily violent end as the Terminator at the hands of Reese and Sarah Connor, only to be restored as temporary victor in T2 before he goes to a second death. This ambiguity of victor/victim is best played out in *Predator* in which there is a fine interplay of hunter/hunted, between the human commando (Schwarzenegger) and the highly sophisticated and superior yet also barbaric and revolting alien. This film indeed leaves itself all too obviously open to psychoanalytic interpretations focused on questions of internal conflicts between good and evil, barbarism and civilization, same and other, and so on. Thus, in the alien creature the human predator meets himself face to face and sees prefigured in the self-destruction of the alien his own destruction, for the alien, as Schwarzenegger in T2, is not destroyed by another but commits suicide. Warrior combat, then, constitutes a point of ideological entry into these films for the viewer and critic: this is where individuals may begin the process of locating themselves in the larger totality, yet this same feature indicates the complexity, incompleteness, and ultimate uncertainty of precisely that effort of mapping.

Summary and Conclusion

I have argued that the *Terminator* films have rich intertextual connections with the biblical text, particularly those sections which are messianic, Christological, and apocalyptic. Yet the films make their own unorthodox contribution to the intertextual situation through what I have termed Christological slippage, a feature which has a logic of its own: the significant slippage of the function of savior from John Connor to Schwarzenegger sets off a series of connections which locate the ultimate figuration or referent as the market itself. The displaced savior story does service in the attempt to eliminate the terror of the market, but in the attempted process of elimination it plays upon and redirects the utopian theme of the revolution. At the same time the films and the superstar Schwarzenegger provide an opportunity for my own libidinal investment as well as an incomplete articulation of how I imagine myself as a refugee middle class consumer within the context of late capitalism. It would seem then that the *Terminator* films touch on fundamental questions of human existence under capitalism. They serve both an ideological function in providing narratives which assist individuals in locating themselves within the totality and, unconsciously aware that capitalism is not much of a life, they seek a futile escape by a revolutionary, but regressive, transformation to an impossible utopia.

In the process of this argument a number of codes or methods of reading were used in order to explicate the intertextual situation of the *Terminator* films: theology (with biblical and Christological emphases), psychology, figuration, utopia, and ideology. The codes were also grouped under the various reading strategies of Fredric Jameson—transcoding, figuration, utopia and dialectical foldback—with a note that Jameson himself makes inadequate use of the latter. His own analyses would benefit from a greater consideration of this item. The use of the various semi-autonomous codes, however, would seem to constitute an effort in transcoding, or "inter-methodology" (metacommentary is a better term), where the strengths of the various possibilities were strung together into the one argument. This is to my mind a useful and versatile mode of interpretation, although its contribution to the notion of intertextuality remains to be explored.

WORKS CONSULTED

Althusser, Louis
    1971   *Lenin and Philosophy and Other Essays*. Trans. Ben Brewster. London: New Left Books.
    1984   *Essays on Ideology*. London: Verso.

Jameson, Fredric
    1971   *Marxism and Form: Twentieth-Century Dialectical Theories of Literature*. Princeton: Princeton University Press.
    1976   "Introduction/Prospectus: To Reconsider the Relationship of Marxism to Utopian Thought." *Minnesota Review* 6 Special Supplement: Marxism and Utopia:53–58.
    1981   *The Political Unconscious: Narrative as a Socially Symbolic Act*. Ithaca: Cornell University Press.
    1988   *The Ideologies of Theory*. Volume 2, *The Syntax of History*. Minneapolis: University of Minnesota Press.
    1991   *Postmodernism, or the Cultural Logic of Late Capitalism*. Durham: Duke University Press.

Large, Ron
    1991   "American Apocalyptic." *The Fourth R* 4/5:1–8, 16.

Moltmann, Jürgen
    1974   *The Crucified God*. London: SCM.

Penley, Constance
    1990   "Time Travel, Primal Scene and the Critical Dystopia." In *Alien Zone: Cultural Theory and Contemporary Science Fiction Cinema*. Ed. Annette Kuhn. London and New York: Verso.

Pfeil, Fred
    1992   "Revolting Yet Conserved: Family Noir in *Blue Velvet* and *Terminator 2*." *Postmodern Culture* 2/3 (E-Journal: pmc-list@unity.ncsu.edu).

INTERTEXTUAL TREKKING:
VISITING THE INIQUITY OF THE FATHERS
UPON "THE NEXT GENERATION"

Susan Lochrie Graham
Toronto School of Theology

ABSTRACT

Although Gene Roddenberry, the creator and producer of "Star Trek" and "Star Trek: The Next Generation", rejected Christian belief, biblical narratives and images are part of the cultural intertext which helps to shape the series. Intertextual theory provides a critical means of exploring the ways in which ideas and images are incorporated into a narrative, even in contradiction to the stated intention of an author. Influence studies, using the categories of narratology, provide a unified reading "with the grain" of the text. Using Rabinowitz's taxonomy, this analysis shows that the series incorporates biblical stories and icons primarily by means of adaptation and parody. But intertextuality calls this kind of reading into question, and suggests that from other reading positions, the text subverts itself. Using the phrase from the opening credits, "where no one has gone before," as a starting point, the analysis explores readings that the text has both suppressed and invited. Reading intertextually, through a psychoanalytical intertext, shows that the text is profoundly split. A reading "against the grain" of the text enables the reader to explore the text's unconscious and bring to audition a voice that had been silenced.

1.

In Jean Shepherd's short story, "The Lost Civilization of Deli," a group of anthropologists studying the ruins of what was once New York City come across a videotape of the Charmin television commercial. They conclude that the meaning of the civilization they are studying is contained in the riddle of the cult objects displayed in the film, those little white rolls of paper, apparently scrolls of text, which people are exhorted not to squeeze. And while the example is amusing to readers who know the cultural intertext, the story highlights the idea that narrative, in this case the narrative of the television commercial, shapes our experience and gives meaning to life, and that television is the major storyteller of our time.

In "Television Drama as a Sacred Text," Quentin J. Schultze calls for critics to interpret television "exegetically, as the theologian interprets sacred text" (4). Biblical scholarship typically directs its gaze "behind" the text to its origins, searching for the author and his context, arguing that meaning must bear some recognizable relation to authorial intent, and inferring that intent from the meaning produced by interpretation. The anxiety to discover paternal origins pervades the field, although success is limited. While the techniques of exegesis employed by biblical scholars to determine legitimacy are not designed to solve the same kind of problems faced by culture critics, critics in both cases share an interest in the interpretation of text, in discovering what a text might mean and how it might function in the culture which has produced or which uses it.

Religious communities tell their stories to reinforce their identity; and if what is posited for a religious community also proves true for any cultural group, then in North American society television would serve not only to reinforce community identity, but as Gregor Goethals points out, to reinforce existing institutions, whether political, social, or economic (64). Moreover, apart from this stabilizing function of the narrative, the television medium itself is a conservative form, which reinforces the "intuitive sense that there is order and meaning in the universe, a reinforcement, therefore, of the religious instinct" (Murray-Brown: 30). It may be helpful to examine one of television's most "sacred" texts, the current series "Star Trek: The Next Generation" (ST:TNG), in terms of certain of its intertexts, in an effort to clarify ways in which religious ideas and images are mediated in the new medium of television.

But because nothing can be said if everything can be said, some limitations are necessary. Texts suggest their own fault lines, and the codes that form their intertexts signal "ways in," places where interpretation may begin. These markers connect to other texts, including the multiple intertexts that come together to form "the reader." Our understanding, the product of the interaction of these various texts, is contingent on them; that is, what a text may mean depends on the intertextual grid through which we read. Consequently, our interpretation is necessarily provisional. I want to begin reading the text of the series through the intertext of an interview with Gene Roddenberry, the creator of "Star Trek" (ST), and until recently, the producer of ST:TNG, moving from the series to the interview, back and forth through the cultural and symbolic codes that form both texts, and finally questioning, even more provisionally and anxiously, my own role as a reader and the intertexts that allow me to interpret in this way. I am aware that the narrative of ST:TNG that I have chosen to "read" and interpret is a visual and aural "text." Fred Burnett notes that "it is debatable that image has priority for the reader/viewer" (4), at least in the case of a sustained narrative typical of a television series. I have occasionally touched on the function of images, a complex issue, but I have chosen here to focus on the soundtrack.

2.

Shortly before his death, Gene Roddenberry gave a rare series of interviews to David Alexander, the editor of the journal *The Humanist*. In the published text of these interviews, "Roddenberry," Alexander's distillation, whose name I have designated with quotation marks to indicate the gap between the person and his textual representation, is portrayed in terms that encourage the reader to pay attention to the relationship between his biography and the narrative, that is, the text of ST:TNG. That voice from the grave, indeed we might say, the voice of the Father, serves as an intertext which focuses on certain areas of concern, controlling and limiting the ways in which the reader-viewer approaches the text.

Much of the interview concerns "Roddenberry's" religious journey from a Southern Baptist boyhood to his rejection of religion so defined and its replacement with "philosophy," specifically with "humanistic" ideas. His discussion of religion, along with his description of his family, suggest that religious and psychological intertexts might be useful grids through which to read. In this context, certain details stand out that might not otherwise seem important (Rabinowitz, 1987:186). Murray Krieger has helpfully provided the metaphors of "window" and "mirror" to bring two aspects of texts into focus (28). Intertextuality, too, opens up windows on other texts and provides mirrors to reflect textual structures. But the view from the intertextual window is not a fixed textual reality; and the mirror's reflection catches the reader too. To extend the metaphor, intertextual meanings are like the patterns of colored glass mirrored in a kaleidoscope, an ephemeral illusion of unity which is somehow "there," and which changes with each new position of the viewer. Readers would like more certainty, although chaos theory tells us that in an open universe knowledge is limited to local sites (Cf. Hayles: 209–35). We wish to "think globally," to borrow the ecological slogan, to find unifying and totalizing structures, but we are forced to "interpret locally." Our anxiety and our desire is translated into the quest for the methodological grail, a model that will ensure certitude by fixing interpretations (Cf. Raval: 234). But like the images in the kaleidoscope, our meanings are unstable. This does not mean that there is no meaning, no point in attempting to interpret texts, but rather that all interpretation is necessarily provisional. "Roddenberry" is open to a variety of interpretations, and the text of the interview, in Derridean terms, is a supplement whose language both suggests and conceals the fissures or grafts in the narrative of ST:TNG.

As a child, "Roddenberry" perceived the world as "supernatural," a place where unexplained events were always attributed to supernatural causes, generally the will of God (Alexander: 8). Reacting to his experience of "complete astonishment" at a communion liturgy during his adolescence, Roddenberry comments that from that time on religion seemed to him "largely nonsense—largely magical, superstitious things" (6). Classifying Jesus and the church along with Santa Claus, as things that do not exist, he decided that "the church, and probably largely the Bible, was not for me" (6). When he became aware of the problem of evil, he was told that "God was on high and he controlled the world and therefore we must pray against Satan. Well, if God controls the world, he controls Satan" (7), and therefore God must control evil. Between his inability to understand the communion liturgy on any other than the literal level, and his fruitless wrestling with the question of theodicy, Roddenberry felt that religion, by which he meant the Christian teaching and practice to which he had been exposed, was "full of inconsistencies" and "pretty foolish" (7).

"Roddenberry's" religious attitudes, then, include his personal rejection of "religion" because of its "superstition" and "foolishness," and his belief both in the possibility of individual human growth and in the ongoing evolution of humanity (30). Agnostic rather than atheistic, he valued decency and honesty, hard work, strong family ties, and individual human freedom—which generally takes the practical form of minding one's own business, reflected in the series in the "Prime Directive" of noninterference. These attitudes and values are the basis for his "humanist philosophy," dramatized in ST and ST:TNG, which he intentionally used as a vehicle for teaching his "overview on life and the human condition" (14). He worked closely with the associate producers and writers who create the scripts, claiming that it is not possible to "separate the working producer from writer or writers and the other creative elements, which ... may be producers who guide writers into writing those kinds of scripts" (16). Since his death, the rest of the staff has had the responsibility for seeing that his vision continues (15), a vision that in the more than twenty-five years of ST and ST:TNG has developed into a powerful intertext to guide their choices and provide direction. What interests me for the moment is not the workings of this intertext, the traditions generated by the television program and films, but instead the ways in which the biblical and, broadly speaking, Christian intertexts function in the texts of ST:TNG, in spite of "Roddenberry's" explicit disavowal. It is this disavowal which suggests one way into the narrative.

3.

The term intertextuality may be understood as a substitution for the earlier concept of influence; the difference between the two, as Jay Clayton and Eric Rothstein make clear, is that "influence has to do with agency, whereas intertextuality has to do with a much more impersonal field of crossing texts" (4). The word "intertextuality" was coined by Julia Kristeva, although it is itself an intertextual product in the very sense that Kristeva rejects: the sources for the word include Bakhtin, Derrida, and Lacan (cf. Phillips: 119). Strictly speaking, Kristeva rejects the "banal" misreading of her term "intertextuality" as "the study of sources," now preferring the term "transposition" and restricting intentional literary references to what she calls influence (1976:59–60). In this paper, I am attempting to use the term in a way more typical of North American critics, as a general term which includes influence, and thus does not entirely exclude issues of authorial intention or insist on the wholly nonreferential character of the literary text (Clayton and Rothstein: 3–4).

The difficulty which arises in trying to have it both ways, so to speak, is that the critical methods that enable us to analyze influences require a fixed position from which to read, often designated in narrative theory as "implied reader," or "ideal reader." In a response to this problem, Tilottama Rajan argues that the intertextual reading function is not to be identified with the "implied reader," the subject fixed by the text, but rather can be seen as a "site of dialogization" (70), a voluntary state a reader enters rather than a coercive position. As Gary Phillips has pointed out, since every reader, and indeed each reader who re-reads a text, comes to it and reads it through slightly different experiences, what "the reader" knows can never be fixed (121). If a reader accepts the role inscribed in the text and at least provisionally aligns his or her understanding with those expectations, the resulting interpretation is at least partially a product of the intersection of that methodological intertext and all the others. It may be possible in this way to include influence in intertextual interpretation, with the realization that the inclusion of the narratological intertext is a choice responding to a reader's desire for origins, unity, and clarity. The drive to produce unifying and clarifying explanations, particularly within academic interpretive practice, responds to a desire to repress a frightening sense of fragmentation. Fred Burnett comments that one of the constraints placed on professional interpreters is "to efface any discussion of what sacred texts and meanings are reinforced by the narratives we produce" (1992b:9). Unifying and totalizing interpretations serve theological purposes, reinforcing, for example, the notion of the human subject created in the image of God.

One of the effects, then, of reading through a narratological intertext is to fix the reader's position, at least provisionally, as "authorial audience." The cultural code, what the "author" assumes the reader will know, is inscribed in the text, and the reader is invited to read from this perspective. In this way, an effect of verisimilitude is created: the fiction is "true to life," and therefore believable (Culler: 142–3). Since the genre of science fiction by definition requires fantastic elements, its "truth" is necessarily the product of some code which enables the reader to accept impossibilities as "real." Critics may write about the author's ideas and beliefs, but as Michael Moriarty points out, to use this sort of psychologizing language is misleading (3). Whether the "author" agrees with or believes in the truth of certain elements of the cultural code is irrelevant: the code functions independently. According to Alexander's interview, "Roddenberry" rejects the Bible and Christian ideas. Nonetheless, they form part of the symbolic and cultural codes of the text with which both "Roddenberry" and his readers are familiar. As such, they provide one way into the text, a perspective for understanding and creating meaning.

Since in the case of ST:TNG, "Roddenberry" has explicitly stated his intentions, it may be illuminating to examine the relationship between authorial intention and intertextual effects. Does a writer actively search out and raid his or her predecessors, creating a new possibility of meaning by putting earlier material into a different context? In this case, we might say that the author "intends" that meaning and puts it "in" the text. Interpretation would then be a matter of simply getting the meaning "out" again. This process is more difficult when "figurative" language is used; the meaning of a poem is supposed to be more difficult to decide than the meaning of more "literal" uses of language, a supposition which is called immediately into question by anyone who has tried, for example, to put together a swing set following the directions in the box or run a computer by using the manual.

But the process of writing may be a more passive activity in which prior works form an intertext which imposes itself, enabling the author to intuit connections which are then, consciously or not, incorporated. When, as Moriarty says, an interpretation contradicts explicit statements by the author, either disavowal or suppression may be at work (3). In any case, whether we view the process as mostly active or mostly passive, the question of intentionality implies that the hermeneutical event occurs in the mind of the author, either consciously or unconsciously; that is to say, the author creates the meaning.

The post-structuralist critique of subjectivity which challenges the concept of the reader has also called the idea of the author into question. Roland Barthes prefers to call the producer of a text the "scriptor," a role that exists only in the time of the text and its reading (1977:170). Kristeva too attacks the concept of the author as "founding subject," preferring to think of author and reader as positions in the play of intertexts that produce the effect of meaning, dissolving the autonomous text with immanent meaning into an intertextual web (1986:32). The notion of the author as a semiotic position is more easily seen in the case of ST:TNG, where in spite of "Roddenberry's" attempt to name himself as "writer" (16), the scripts are produced by a team. The "writer" is as much a fiction as "Roddenberry" himself is.

But even if we retain the notion of the author as a source of meaning, it is of course not the only possibility: the hermeneutical event may also occur in the mind of the reader, a position most aptly described by Northrup Frye as a picnic to which the author brings the words and the reader brings the meaning. In the world of academic interpretation, this is not a popular position, of course, since chaos would result in our orderly halls of interpretation if all meaning were thought to be radically subjective. Various attempts to circumscribe interpretation have been made. Among reader-response critics, "interpretive communities" provide security by limiting the meanings that are acceptable, thus keeping chaos at bay (cf. Fish).

What seems more likely is that meaning happens in the intertextual convergence of "author" and "text" and "reader," where the interpretation, what Harold Bloom calls a "misreading," is the result of intertextual mediation. We read through texts to experience effects of meaning, one of which is the illusion that the meaning we experience is our own.

Narrative purports to designate reality, to denote. But the text remains open and is multiplied by what Barthes calls "connotation," the intertextual interplay of the text with itself and with other texts, including those of the "reader" (1970:14–16). George Aichele has identified connotation as the feature of a text that signals intertextual possibilities, in Barthian terms, the "way into the polysemy of the classic text." The references to various cultural codes which produce these effects may indicate a conscious intention on the part of the author who cites the code to establish the verisimilitude of the text, its "guarantee of intelligibility," as Culler says (142). Less explicit allusions, on the other hand, what Richard B. Hays calls "echoes," and even whispers, cannot easily be attributed to intentionality. Hays finishes his survey of the problem with the comment that "typologies," the cultural and symbolic codes which link texts, "come to us unbidden, impose themselves upon us in ways that we understand through a glass darkly" (33). It may be helpful to read these allusions through the symbolic and cultural codes of the text, exploring ways in which influence functions, and then to turn to the more difficult problem of references to codes which both the "author" and the "text" have suppressed, but which nevertheless come to us "unbidden."

4.

The direct borrowing from or reference to the Bible and other religious texts, either in the form of quotation or paraphrase or explicit allusion, is limited in ST:TNG, probably because the author can intentionally exercise more control over explicit reference to prior works than over other sorts of intertextual effects. Thus if "Roddenberry" wishes to exclude the biblical text, it is easily done in the case of explicit reference.

Peter Rabinowitz (1980:246–9) suggests a helpful taxonomy of literary borrowing which is based on the distinction in narratology between authorial and narrative audiences. For our purposes, the authorial audience is the reader in the text, the reader, that is, who is postulated by the implied author, and who understands what the author means. The narrative audience is usually comprised of the actual characters to whom the narrator tells the story. Rabinowitz's model is designed for narrative in which the reader-critic can discern a difference between authorial and narrative audiences, and hence between implied author and narrator.

Rabinowitz begins with the question of whether or not the authorial audience knows that borrowing has occurred, and what effect that knowledge has. If, for example, the audience does not know, and if knowing would diminish the effect, Rabinowitz classifies the borrowing as plagiarism. If the effect remains the same whether or not the authorial audience recognizes that the borrowing has occurred, Rabinowitz call the procedure "adaptation" (1980:246). Adaptations may take the form of allusions in which the terms have been generalized through use, losing their specialized connotations in the process. The allusion to "lost sheep" in the episode "Up the Long Ladder" is an example. The term is used to refer to a group of people who find themselves outside the mainstream of Federation contact, signaling for help. It is not necessary to hear an echo of the Lukan parable of finding the lost in order to understand Picard's comment. Similarly, the primary female member of the group protests that she does not want to be "Eve," an allusion to Genesis which is adapted in this context to mean any female founder of a community, without the theological implications that the biblical reference might suggest.

It is not, of course, "Roddenberry's" intention to provide a contemporary context in which the biblical text can be heard in a fresh new way. Thus when borrowing does occur, its effect generally does not depend on the authorial audience's recognition of the source. The effect would be the same as any reference to the general literary intertext that ST:TNG draws on. The title of the episode "Sins of the Father" is a quotation from the Decalogue, which the authorial audience might recognize as biblical, although perhaps without knowing where it comes from; it is an adaptation, as is Guinan's comment to Q when he appears as a human being, "How the mighty are fallen" ("Deja Q"). In this case, the quotation's ironic effect does not depend on the contrast between its original context and the adaptation here.

ST:TNG does not retell the biblical story as it does other literary texts, probably because Roddenberry has specifically rejected it. Quotations from the Bible are ordinarily adaptations; explicit allusions to the biblical text and echoes of it tend to be what Rabinowitz calls "parody" (1980:247). In this case, the authorial audience is familiar with the original, while the narrative audience is not. This sort of borrowing relies for its effect on the authorial audience's recognition of the original and its enjoyment of the changes, which are not necessarily humorous, made in the new version. In parody, the audience's ability to distinguish between the original and the version presented make the effect of irony possible: it is in this sense that Linda Hutcheon speaks of the "inner difference at the heart of similarity" (x).

The structure of the entire series, a "record of the voyages of the starship *Enterprise*," suggests the archetypal myth (in Northrup Frye's sense) of the quest. This myth is part of a larger intertext that functioned as an intertext for the biblical writers and continues to function as such in contemporary times. Its modern American form is the myth of the frontier, which is one of the dominant themes of American television, as is the theme of separation from one's family of origin, and the encounter with strangers and enemies who can become friends and who can then be assimilated into one's society (Kottak: 101). The myth of the frontier, for example, finds its biblical counterpart in the voyages of biblical characters from patriarchal times until the early Christian era. On the other hand, more specific points of connection in plot are one indication that the biblical intertext has found expression. The voluntary separation from the family and the difficult reunion with an elder brother, aspects of the parable of the Prodigal Son, form an intertext for the episode, "Family," where Picard returns to France. The echo suggests an implicit criticism of Picard, who like the Prodigal Son rejected the responsibilities of home and family in order to live a life of adventure, and indeed, the episode touches on the elder brother's resentment of him.

In another parodic echo of a biblical image, Picard explains theories of life after death, commenting that some people believe that they will change into an indestructible form maintained forever in a garden

("Where Silence Has Lease"). The garden image suggests prelapsarian times rather than the world to come, although in this context the authorial audience will also recognize an allusion to the idea of "Heaven."

Plot structure may echo aspects of the Gospel stories of Jesus in ways that are clearly parodic. "Transfigurations," for example, an episode whose title suggests a biblical intertext, presents a character who is in the process of evolving to a super-humanoid. He has the gift of healing by touch, and he is able to raise the dead Worf to life. John, as he is called, is presented as a man of strength and serenity who relates to others in an "almost spiritual" way. He sees himself as on a journey that he must complete, although he does not understand it until the end. Others of his society try to kill him because he is "evil," which is to say, he threatens the existing social order. Dressed in a white jumpsuit, a visual parody, he ultimately experiences transmutation into a creature of light, prophesying that others "who are willing will follow me." Here the biblical story is represented in a way that enables viewers to see the Christ story in terms of human development and perfection. "Transfigurations" presents a Christ figure without a cross, as if the experience on the mountaintop were the end of the gospel. The elimination of the need for suffering, providing triumph over evil in a humanistic context where the good need not suffer, is of course a change from the biblical text. By parody, Roddenberry is able to transform the biblical story, reinscribing it in a humanistic context; but the effect of the borrowing of the plot structure is to represent the Christian theology it has transformed as biblical. Thus by the intertextual effect, the biblical text is changed for the viewers.

There are also striking Christological echoes in "The Child," an episode which parodies the Incarnation. In this case, Deanna Troi, the ship's counselor, becomes pregnant by a light, suggesting a spiritual rather than carnal conception, and her son Ian is born and grows miraculously, becoming a young adolescent in days. When he learns that his existence threatens the health of the people on the *Enterprise*, he allows himself to die for their well-being. What is missing in this case is the victimization of the innocent that is a part of the Christian understanding of Jesus' self-offering, and in both this episode and "Transfigurations," any reference to the divine as it is understood in the Judeo-Christian tradition.

The narrative audience in ST:TNG does not recognize biblical allusions, so the borrowing techniques are limited primarily to adaptation, in which the biblical referent is irrelevant, and parody, in which it is transformed. In handling religious aspects of the general cultural intertext, on the other hand, a greater variety of techniques is possible. The categories that Rabinowitz has developed for literary borrowing are equally helpful in understanding how the cultural intertext works in the production of the meaning.

5.

Following Rabinowitz's nomenclature (1980:246), I have called borrowing adaptation when audience recognition that borrowing has occurred is irrelevant to the effect produced. In making reference to the religious aspects of the general cultural intertext, adaptation is more frequent than other sorts of borrowing. Like specifically biblical vocabulary, when religious vocabulary is used, it is often adapted, with the result that it loses its religious connotations: Data is told that it isn't "a sin" to be different ("Tin Man"), for example; or two renegade Klingons tell Worf that he is "lost among infidels" ("Fugitives of Glory"). Adaptation may be visual as well: in an example which the authorial audience is likely to recognize, Q appears dressed in a monk's habit ("Hide and Q"), waving his cross at Picard, whom he accuses of "blasphemy," also an adaptation. Because in the case of adaptation the audience's knowledge of the original is irrelevant, an identification of an instance of this kind of borrowing is difficult to test. In the visual adaptations, it may be difficult to say with any degree of certainty that there is indeed a reference being made to a religious context, and that the recognition of that context is irrelevant to the effect. In the verbal examples, vocabulary with specific religious connotations which the audience may or may not hear is used in a broader sense; Picard's reference to a newborn baby as a "small miracle," or "purgatory" as the description of the life of an ill and elderly man, are cases of generalization in the development of the terms, which have now lost their specifically religious connotations.

A retelling, which assumes that neither the authorial audience nor the narrative audience is familiar with the details of the original, is used to clarify historical references in ST:TNG, where Picard can explain events in human history with which both audiences are unfamiliar. Cultural references specifically religious are less common; Professor Moriarty, a holodeck recreation of Sherlock Holmes's adversary ("Extraordinary, My Dear Data"), comments that the computer, a cultural reference which he does not know, is "wiser than the oracle at Delphi," which he does. The audience is told that the oracle at Delphi, a name which it may recognize but know little about, is a source of knowledge, like the computer. Moreover since the oracle functioned in Hellenistic culture as a source of divine revelation, the allusion suggests that the computer has similar divine characteristics; if the audience is unfamiliar with the Hellenistic referent, this effect is lost.

When the effect depends on the authorial audience's familiarity with the original, the borrowing is a case of parody (Rabinowitz, 1980:247). Most of the ceremonial events in ST:TNG take the form of parody, used in this sense. In "Data's Day," Picard presides over O'Brien's wedding to Keiko, a Japanese woman. The ceremony is a parody of a contemporary wedding. The authorial audience is expected to recognize certain elements as allusions to the event: Data acts as "father" to the bride, escorting her to O'Brien, who stands before the Captain. The bride wears an elaborate dress, in this case, a kimono. Picard, as Captain, explains his role by recounting the history of weddings performed by ships' captains "throughout history," which is to say, Western history since the Renaissance. The bride and groom share a chalice, Picard says a few words, and the couple kiss. The authorial audience is familiar with a variety of religious and secular wedding ceremonies, and will recognize both the explicit allusions and the metalepses, which will vary according to the tradition of weddings the audience knows. The ceremony is secular, so no references to God are expected, nor prayers of any sort. The statement of intention is also missing, as are the vows and the signing of any documents. These legal requirements of the wedding service are not recognized, either by the authorial or by the narrative audience, as necessary. The allusions to the giving of the bride, the authority of the captain to do the ceremony, a ceremonial sharing and a kiss, suggest a legitimate wedding to the audience without the risk of offending certain viewers by associating the ceremony too closely with one religious tradition or another. Furthermore, the audience's familiarity with the details of the ceremony need not be great; the audience will not reject the realism of the ceremony so long as enough elements are provided.

Other ceremonies which are parodies include funeral or memorial services ("The Schizoid Man" and "Skin of Evil"), an allusion at a formal dinner to "breaking bread" ("Time Squared"), which is characterized by Picard as "the symbol of friendship and community," and "a practice we have gotten away from," and a naming ceremony in which Picard and his wife name their son and offer a buffet meal to their friends ("The Inner Light"). In all of these cases, the narrative audience need not make the connection with Jewish or Christian culture, although the authorial audience can. Ceremonies which are closely associated by the viewing audience with the Jewish or Christian traditions are secularized, while at the same time retaining their social functions: the baby is named, the couple is wed, friends share a community meal, the dead are mourned. The elements which are retained in each case provide the minimum necessary to ensure that the authorial audience recognizes the ceremony and accepts its verisimilitude; and those who are very familiar with the religious ceremonies may fill in gaps by metalepsis and find that the effect is heightened by those associations.

Explicit references to supernatural figures include the holodeck presentation of Troi as a Greek "Goddess of Empathy" ("Hollow Pursuits"), who encourages Barclay to cast off his inhibitions and embrace love, truth, and joy. Both the narrative audience and the authorial audience recognize the figure as fictional, a borrowing from Greek mythology. Rabinowitz calls this category of borrowing "criticism, not only because it frequently involves an interpretation of the original work, but also because, by paying attention to how the characters approach the original, we can often discover how we in turn should approach the work in front of us" (1980:247–8). The "real" Troi meets her holodeck goddess version and is offended. But the exaggeration of the characterization is recognized by both the narrative and the authorial audiences, and the narrative audience's amusement and scorn for the goddess image reinforces the attitude that such supernatural figures are to be taken as false and ridiculous. At the same time, the fantasy of the holodeck world is underlined, and in contrast, the "reality" of the ship is reinforced. Indeed, commenting upon the conventions of a genre in a work which is of that genre is a way of establishing the "reality" of a text. In ST:TNG this effect is often accomplished by establishing the world of the holodeck as a "non-reality" within the "reality" of the *Enterprise*, thereby reinforcing the verisimilitude of the rest of the narrative. But the holodeck also functions as a space where the unconscious is allowed expression, so the attitude of the characters toward it bears further exploration.

The holodeck projection of the figure of evil is given several forms in "Devil's Due," a retelling of the Faust myth. The personification of evil takes the form of the female figure "Ardra," who returns after a thousand years to enslave the planet Ventax 2. Ardra is one form of many; the Devil, complete with red tights, horns and pitchfork, is another. Ardra herself is a "fraud," in Picard's words, not a supernatural creature, and the Devil is merely a magician's illusion. The development in the society of Ventax 2 is due to changes made by people, not to supernatural agency. Society was transformed by the creation of a "fundamental theology," the legend of Ardra; but that legend was created to serve a social function, and the "theology" has no basis in truth. Picard's attitude indicates that evil is an illusion and that theology is a fictional human creation which fills psychological and social needs. The effect of the critical borrowing is to ridicule one concept of evil, denying the existence of systemic evil and attributing evil to the wickedness of a bad people. The view of ST:TNG, as of television in general, is that evil can be checked by action against individuals who are evil, and it can be kept under human control (Schultze: 25).

Occasionally the presentation of Q in the series operates as a critical borrowing. Q, an immortal character who has supernatural powers, is a god-figure in several episodes. Q has the power to arouse a response of fascination and fear which are characteristic of the holy (Otto: 31, *passim.*), as is clearest in the pilot to the series, "Encounter at Far Point, Part 1," in which he is perceived as threatening, and as something "beyond" what is usually considered a life form. Primarily because of his trickster qualities, Q's character suggests the world of Greek and Roman mythology, of which this is a parody, rather than the God of the Judeo-Christian tradition, and yet his difference from biblical images of the divine suggests a suppressed comparison. Q once takes human form ("Deja Q"), in an incarnation that may be read as a metaleptic allusion to Christian theology; indeed, he is redeemed and allowed to rejoin the Continuum with his powers restored because he is willing to sacrifice himself for the good of others. Since the characters in the series recognize something of the holy in Q, their response to him is illuminating: he is scorned, mocked, and ignored whenever possible. While the series inscribes the holy, then, its response is ridicule.

When the narrative audience considers the borrowing to be nonfiction, that is, a reference to a historical phenomenon, they may consider the reference either to be true or false. If they consider it to be false, then the borrowing is a revision; if true, it is expansion (Rabinowitz 1980:248). In ST:TNG, historical references are usually taken by the narrative audience to be true, that is, as expansions. Allusions to history, such as Picard's mention of "the Dark Ages," and the "Inquisition" ("Who Watches the Watchers"), are examples: no one hearing Picard questions whether the events truly happened. Other references to religious historical phenomena include a mention of the torture of heretics and witch hunts ("The Drumhead"), which in context is also a reference to McCarthyism. A final example, one which poses a more interesting problem, is the case of the table blessing, giving thanks for the meal, which is a Betazoid custom. The authorial audience recognizes the reference to the custom of "saying grace" in Western culture, a custom with which they are familiar. The narrative audience, watching the transposed blessing, does not interpret it as an earth custom, so they are mistaken about the source of the reference. It is then a kind of parody, but one which is also an expansion, because although the narrative audience is mistaken about the origin of the original, they still consider the custom to be historically true. This allusion, along with Troi's mother's exclamation "Thank the four deities," and her exalted titles sketch a religious system in place for the Betazoids which is a parody of the Greek pantheon.

The Betazoids are not the only culture to have religious ideas: the Klingons believe in an afterlife, as the "roar" which warns the spirits of the dead that "a Klingon warrior is about to arrive" shows ("Fugitive of Glory"). In what we might call Klingon religious thought, the body is "an empty shell" to be disposed of after the death of the person, whose spirit lives on. The Klingons, while technologically as advanced as the humans, are in other ways less "evolved." They are less rational, more savage, and they have superstitions about death that are no longer accepted on Earth. Their afterlife is a parody of the Western idea, and the effect is to ridicule that idea, even though Worf and his culture are treated with respect.

The biblical and religious intertexts of ST:TNG are incorporated and impose themselves in a variety of ways. The types of borrowing which Rabinowitz has developed for explicit literary references are helpful in classifying the effects of other sorts of intertexts, particularly what I have called the religious intertext, limited to some aspects of Christian thought and iconography. Adaptation, where the religious content has been gutted, and parody, in which the effect both supports and undercuts the religious content of the reference, are the most common categories in the series, and retelling, when it is used, avoids the biblical text. Thus, in spite of "Roddenberry's" explicit disavowal of the Bible and a form of contemporary Christianity, biblical and religious intertexts function to shape the narrative world of ST:TNG.

ST:TNG may provide viewers with the only version they know of the religious narratives that have helped to form human beings in Western culture. This was made very apparent to me in a computer conversation with a "Trekker," who in answer to my query about examples of intertextuality, suggested that Picard's experience of a second life in "The Inner Light" reminded her of the biblical story in which Jesus, hanging on the cross, imagined himself living a normal life, married to Mary Magdalene, with a family (Hendrix). Clearly intertextuality, in this case the literary intertext which includes Katzanzakis's *The Last Temptation of Christ,* or at any rate the film version, worked to transform the biblical story for this reader, who then also watched the episode through the transformed biblical intertext.

This anecdote raises a serious question for professional readers, and for students of the Bible particularly: must intertextual readings, particularly those exploring issues of influence, be linear? Can it ever be legitimate within the constraints of academic interpretation to read backwards through history? Fred Burnett has raised the question whether "even a very broadly conceived influence study" might be combined with a Kristevan approach to intertextuality (4). Kristeva understands intertextuality as a process, as the signs from one discursive system are transposed into another. The reader positions, which she calls "positionalities," produced by this transposition are not stable, but are constantly in flux (1976:59–60). When we limit intertextuality to effects of influence, what Kristeva would call "source" criticism, two conditions appear. Influence studies limit the direction of borrowing and work under the assumption of fixed reading positions. Historically speaking, ST:TNG cannot be a source for the Bible, which antedates the series. Hendrix's reading is illegitimate by academic standards which require us to read with certain historical constraints firmly in place, through a very specific and usually unacknowledged intertext. Narratological studies are thought to be a revolutionary way to break the hegemony of historical readings in academic discourse. But this exploration of ST:TNG, using narratological categories, has produced an interpretation that goes with the grain of the text, along the lines of the cultural code which is inscribed. The power structure implied in that cultural code, its patriarchal hierarchy, its capitalist economics, remain firmly in place and indeed unquestioned. To read with the text, to desire to "consume" the cultural and literary intertext by putting the Bible and Christian theology to the service of humanism and capitalism, substitutes for other less acceptable desires which cause anxiety and must be suppressed, displaced, covered up. So while it is possible, and even useful, to look at intertextual influences from a narratological viewpoint, this is one reading position, produced by one methodological intertext, among many. It enables a reader to interpret with the text, aligning his or her understanding with the expectations inscribed in the text. But a reader may resist this role, bringing other intertexts to a text, desiring to make other connections in the process of interpretation. Reading against the grain of the text gives voice to strands of narrative meaning that are often silenced when the reader plays the role of authorial audience. Intertextual studies, at least of the sort which are concerned with influence, do not seem necessarily to produce the ethical readings that Gary Phillips calls for, readings against the grain of the text which give voice to those who voices are silenced. Where might such a reading begin? How do readers recognize seams and fissures in the text which are both offered up for interpretation and covered over at the same time?

6.

Subjected to the questioning that David Alexander puts to him, "Roddenberry" generates a discourse which points to fissures, which when pressed open up in the texts of ST:TNG as well. Alexander, in creating this character, represents a split subject who attempts to control the split by inventing a public persona who masks the private person's unacceptable ideas. These ideas, "personal desires, personal needs," must be dealt with by conversion, changed into "decent things" (19). Whatever cannot be converted is silenced: there are "powerful things you don't talk about" (11), which must be covered up. "Roddenberry" pretends these "powerful things" are conscious and subject to his control, although he indicates some anxiety about the difficulty of keeping them under wraps: there is "a limit to how much of a smoke-screen you can throw up" (12) "Roddenberry's" "secret" thoughts are dangerous, threatening to "turn people against me" (12). The public persona is a conscious creation, an acceptable personality which can be exposed "in a carefully regulated way" (18), with "a certain amount of dishonesty" (7) to cover up what is unacceptable on the one hand and impossible to acknowledge on the other.

The overdetermination of cover-up language, its reiteration throughout the interview, suggests that "secret" things may have been suppressed in the narrative of ST:TNG as well. Indeed the text itself points in this direction. The opening credits claim that the series explores previously unknown places "where no one has gone before." In the original ST series, before public pressure for inclusive language and political correctness encouraged the change, "no man" had gone there before. What is hidden and inaccessible is brought to light, mapped out, explained, logged and left open for others to develop. The desire to explore what is at the edges of human knowledge and consciousness is part of the frame of the show, but at the same time, the phrase invites us as readers to explore the edges of our reading practices, to pay attention to what has been relegated to the margin. Where, then, has "no man" ever gone before?

In the episode entitled "Where No One Has Gone Before," the Traveler explains that "space and time and thought aren't the separate things they appear to be." The Traveler's mental powers make it possible for the *Enterprise* to travel over a billion light years from this galaxy. When the boundaries between the mind and the external universe, between subject and object, are blurred, images from the unconscious minds of the crew members are suddenly and disturbingly projected into their conscious experience. This is dangerous, as Picard explains, because they lose the ability to distinguish between the conscious and the unconscious, something that is necessary for human sanity. The anxiety produced by these irruptions from the unconscious is greater than the desire to explore further, and so the ship returns to this galaxy, to what is relatively better known, where the uncontrollable images of the unconscious are once again suppressed. But the text itself, at this point, suggests that to read along the sightlines of a psychoanalytic code might be a fruitful way to proceed. With this in mind, a re-reading of Alexander's interview of "Roddenberry" suggests where the fissures might be. This is a reading against that text, forcing it to yield to pressure, perhaps even an abuse of power.

The world of "Roddenberry's" childhood was peopled by his mother, "the angel in my life" (9), and his father, a "difficult" man (10) with "an ugly side" (9). "Roddenberry" recalls some "bad things" about his father (9), although he is at great pains to justify him, claiming his behavior was "legitimate for him at that time"(9). He fears his powerful father, and his discourse displays great anxiety, reiterating the fear of discovery, exposure. "The world was a cruel and difficult place," he says, "so I learned to cover myself" (7). But this was a lesson learned far earlier and reiterated here. Barthes comments that every narrative narrates the Father (absent, hidden, or hypostasized) (1973:20), and Elizabeth Wright notes that "though the Father says 'no' to desire, the unconscious can get by" (149), even if the object of desire must change. In the play of substitution, "Roddenberry" submits to the power of the Father and finds a new object, the promises of liberal humanism: "autonomy, transcendence, certainty, authority, unity, totalization, system, universalization, center, continuity, teleology, closure, hierarchy, homogeneity, uniqueness, origin" (Hutcheon: 57). His desire finds expression in writing, which gives him a sense of omnipotence: "You do become God" (19). In the reiteration of themes of sexuality and death, the Father returns. Perhaps the anxiety that Picard expresses when faced with images of the unconscious is engendered by this paternal return in the text. In "Roddenberry's" position as writer-God, where the Father's power can be challenged and usurped, everything that was forbidden is permitted; the narrative uncovers the desires that he had so compulsively hidden.

7.

In exploring familial relationships portrayed in ST:TNG, the near absence of intact nuclear families is striking. Other than the family formed by O'Brien, Keiko, and their baby, no regular character is part of a family group of mother, father, and children. Adult characters regularly lack one or both parents, which is perhaps not surprising taking into consideration the age of the characters and the dangerous life styles characteristic of the science-fiction adventure genre. But the pattern is worth considering. Of the adult male characters whose parents play a role in the series, Picard's parents are both deceased, as are Worf's; Riker lost his mother when he was a child. Spock, who bridges both series, has a step-mother.

In the two cases where the fathers play a role in the series, the episodes portray difficult father-son relationships. Riker's father arrives on board unexpectedly in "The Icarus Factor," and in the guise of an attempted reconciliation, he repeats the competitive drive for superiority that has apparently always been characteristic of their relationship. He challenges Will, who attempts to avoid the confrontation; ultimately they engage in a sports contest, a final battle, in which Will discovers that his father had always won by cheating. Will's triumph includes the realization that even as a youngster he had had the strength to win in a fair competition, but that the competition had not been fair. In this episode, the balance of power is redressed in Will's favor, and having shown that he has successfully negotiated the Oedipal conflict, he takes his position as a powerful male, reinforcing his right to the sexually dominant role he plays in the series. In this he is like Captain Kirk of the original ST series, who is also portrayed as an aggressive and sexually dominant male. The characterization of both is highly conventional, requiring them to intervene against individuals and societies, deviant elements who are outside the Federation's umbrella and therefore "other." As is typical for the genre, what is "other" in fantasy, "the shadow on the edge of bourgeois culture," takes various forms, including "black, mad, primitive, criminal, socially deprived, deviant, crippled, or (when sexually assertive) female" (Jackson: 121). Like Kirk before him, Riker interacts with female characters who are his "other," in some way or another inferior, weak and submissive, or if actively and successfully resistant, in some way evil. Yet the characterization of Riker is appealing to female viewers, not only because he meets societal standards of male attractiveness, but also because of the power he displays. Lacking his power, female characters are allowed to participate in it by becoming objects of his desire, thus being placed in a traditional submissive feminine role, a stereotype which the series reinforces (Cranny-Francis: 275–76).

Riker's principal female partner in the series is Counselor Deanna Troi, who is half-Betazoid, and has remarkable powers of intuition which enable her to do her work. In the episodes which touch on her professional functions, she works primarily with women and children in grief counseling, using popularized psychological techniques rather than psychoanalysis. "The Loss" shows Troi as a victim of the loss of her powers, which she experiences as a loss of identity. Riker comments with some satisfaction that her loss makes her "normal," that is, inferior to him. Stripped for the space of an episode of her identity and power, she grieves; Riker's acid response is to mock her and to call into question the appropriateness of her use of her gifts. Indeed the very existence of female power outside of male control is called into question: Troi is told that her technical training will enable her to do her work adequately, that her intuitive powers are not necessary. At the end of the episode when she regains her powers, Riker offers her an apology, which she graciously accepts. For women, the lesson of the episode is clear: any real female power is exceptional and can be lost, and it should never be used to make males feel anxious.

The other adult male character who is involved in conflict with his father is Spock, whose character was developed in the original ST. Spock, who is half-human and half-Vulcan, is logical and unemotional in contrast to human characters like Kirk. But Spock's father Sarek, a full-blooded Vulcan, is until his last illness always in complete control of his emotions. Spock's lack of emotional control, attributed to his human mother, is the source of his sense of inferiority to his father. After his father's death, Spock is able to resolve the conflict by means of a "mind-meld" with Picard. Having shared Sarek's mind, Picard can act as a surrogate to provide the space where Spock can experience his father's thoughts and feelings, and receive his blessing ("Sarek").

As with Kirk-Riker, Spock is an enormously popular character, particularly with female viewers. Anne Cranny-Francis comments that women identify with Spock because of his "otherness." Unlike the desire to be an object of male desire aroused by Kirk-Riker, Spock provides a different experience of the other, one "analogous to women's experience of the world." Spock's conflict with his father revolves around his desire to be integrated into Vulcan society, from which he is partially excluded because of his human heritage. Spock thus "articulates the dilemma of women ... who are, by reason of their gender, consistently excluded from the active, decision-making processes of society" (Cranny-Francis: 277). Because of his alienness, then, Spock is attractive. But while he is an object of female desire, he characteristically refuses sexual relationships. Cranny-Francis sees this absence or lack as a "locus of desire for female viewers. Simultaneously, the absence signified, which the woman desires, is the symbol of Spock's maleness, the phallus. Spock is thus defined as the site of a desire which is preeminently phallocentric" (277).

Male children play out another aspect of this psychological drama. With the exception of Lal, Data's "daughter," all the children of the regular characters are male. Wesley Crusher's father Jack is dead, having lost his life on a mission under Picard's orders. Picard plays the role of the surrogate father, and a closeness between Picard and the boy's mother is developed in the series. Wesley expresses anger at Picard for the death of his father ("The Bending"), but the absence of the father enables the boy precociously to take on adult male roles as the series defines them. In "Pen Pal," for example, he is put in command of a team of adult scientists, to learn to exercise "authority." He plays a protective role toward his mother, even to the point of saving her life ("Wesley's Experiment"). The series toys with the dangerous fantasy of the seduction of a boy by his mother in "The Game," in which an apparatus which sends light stimuli to the eyes causes intense and addictive physical pleasure. Dr. Crusher attempts to force Wesley to use the device, but he successfully resists, with the help of a girlfriend, thus demonstrating his substitution of a more appropriate object of desire. When he reaches late adolescence, he follows in his father's footsteps by entering the Academy for training as a Star Fleet officer.

In another episode, an adolescent boy is picked up after an accident. The boy, Jono, is human, although Endar, the man whom he considers his father, is not. Endar, who had lost his wife and family in a battle, by the rules of his culture had the right to take the child of a dead enemy. He picked Jono, his "chosen son," and raised him. The female crew of the *Enterprise*, both Troi and Dr. Crusher, attempt to prevent Jono from rejoining his father, fearing that the boy had been abused by Endar. Ultimately Jono rejects the human role forced on him by the women and takes on his identity as "son of Endar." After attacking and nearly killing Picard with a knife, Jono is allowed to return to his own society. Picard explains that to deny him the right to return to the society he is now prepared to enter fully as an adult would be to commit a "crime" against him.

When the text plays out the competition between fathers and sons, the sons usually triumph. But the triumph does not result in the possession of a female character, either a mother or a mother surrogate. Rather, a new object of desire is substituted, and the boys are welcomed into the privileged world of the adult males with whom they identify. The mothers of male characters, with the exception of Dr. Crusher and Troi, do not usually survive and often die unpleasantly. In spite of the idea often reiterated in the series that twentieth-century feminist issues have been long since resolved, female characters are portrayed as passive, weak, and victims. Strong females, like Kaylar and Tasha Yar, meet violent deaths. Other female characters are sexual objects for males.

It is worth pondering why there are so few girl children in the series. Indeed, when Data manufactures the android Lal, it has neither sex nor gender. Data allows Lal to choose, explaining mildly that the choice is superficial: it will affect her personal appearance. As machines, presumably neither Data nor Lal has an unconscious, although the series introduces desire, an element that would create the split in a human subject. Indeed, Data's "full functions" include sexual attraction to human female characters, apparently consummated in the case of Tasha Yar ("The Naked Now"), and Lal "loves" Data, her "father." In this way, Lal is an "improvement" on Data's design: she feels emotions. But her emotions result in her "death," a massive short circuiting that no one can repair. At the end, Data reactivates her for a moment, long enough for her to express gratitude to him for her life. Data then deactivates her and she "dies."

Thus the series reiterates the primal Oedipal scene from a male point of view, often resolving it in the successful substitution of male power and privilege as the object of desire. Female characters are sexual objects, often giving birth to male offspring and then dying. The series suggests that men and women have achieved equality, but the roles indicate that ST:TNG reinscribes patriarchal values of male domination of all others, physical prowess and rationalism. Mothers, who can be dangerously seductive and thereby threaten the necessary repression and substitution of desire, often die in the series; if like Dr. Crusher and Troi they have ongoing roles in the narrative, their power and their sexuality are controlled and defined by males.

This brief excursus into the text's unconscious has produced a reading against the grain, exposing the Oedipal conflicts that the narrative would cover over and deny. "Roddenberry's" intent was certainly not to narrate this story, which has surfaced in spite of his desire to repress it. He claimed to want to "set the record straight," but the interview and the series, like all narratives, slide off plumb. But then, too, so has mine.

8.

What can be said in conclusion? I am acutely aware that this study reinscribes the split that it describes, and that the assumptions that inform my analysis are marked by the same fissures and slides that I have found in "Roddenberry" and the text of ST:TNG. My text can be read as a Barthian text of pleasure, reading with the grain, exploring its sources and the movement of those intertexts, with the resultant sense of fullness of meaning and unity. But it can also be read as a text of bliss, re-read and written from its own fissures, exploring its own anxieties. I have attempted to chart two contradictory aspects of intertextuality, to find points of intersection, however provisional, and to suggest where the details of these readings might connect with the social matrix, that is, with real people. While my study no doubt reenacts what I have analyzed, and while all texts and interpretations can be seen to slide in a joyful Derridean play of signification, the texts of ST and ST:TNG form a powerful intertext in modern culture. The series is shown daily on hundreds of stations to millions of viewers, who are passively entertained with these narrative events and images that undergird the most conservative aspects of contemporary culture in ways that are detrimental to those the culture defines by exclusion as "other." ST:TNG may claim to "go where no one has gone before," but Einstein warned us that the universe is circular: the last stop on the *Enterprise* is right back where we started.

WORKS CONSULTED

Aichele, George
    1995   "Jesus' Frankness." *Semeia* 69/70:261-80.

Alexander, David
    1991   "Gene Roddenberry: Writer, Producer, Philosopher, Humanist." *The Humanist* 51:5–30, 38.

Barthes, Roland
    1970   *S/Z*. Paris: Editions du Seuil.
    1973   *Le Plaisir du Texte*. Paris: Editions du Seuil.
    1988   "The Death of the Author." Pp. 167–72 in *Modern Criticism and Theory: A Reader*. Ed. David Lodge. London and New York: Longman. Orig. Pub. in *Image, Music, and Text*. Trans. Stephen Heath. New York: Hill and Wang, 1977.

Bloom, Harold
    1975   *A Map of Misreading*. New York: Oxford University Press.

Burnett, Fred
    1992a   "Response to George Aichele." Unpublished paper presented to the SBL Semiotics and Exegesis Section, San Francisco.
    1992b   "Response to Susan Graham and Christopher R. Douglas." Unpublished paper presented to the SBL Semiotics and Exegesis Section, San Francisco.

Clayton, Jay, and Eric Rothstein
    1991   "Figures in the Corpus: Theories of Influence and Intertextuality." Pp. 3–36 in *Influence and Intertextuality in Literary History*. Ed. Jay Clayton and Eric Rothstein. Madison: University of Wisconsin Press.

Cranny-Francis, Anne
    1985   "Sexuality and Sex-Role Stereotyping in *Star Trek*." *Science Fiction Studies* 12:274–83.

Culler, Jonathan
    1975   *Structuralist Poetics: Structuralism, Linguistics, and the Study of Literature*. Ithaca: Cornell University Press.

Fish, Stanley
    1980   *Is There a Text in This Class?* Cambridge: Harvard University Press.

Goethals, Gregor
    1991   "The Electronic Golden Calf." Pp. 63–79 in *Video Icons and Values*. Ed. Alan M. Olson, Christopher Parr, and Debra Parr. Albany: State University of New York Press.

Hayles, N. Katherine
    1990   *Chaos Bound: Orderly Disorder in Contemporary Literature and Science*. Ithaca: Cornell University Press.

Hays, Richard B.
    1989   *Echoes of Scripture in the Letters of Paul*. New Haven: Yale University Press.

Hendrix, J.
    1992   Response. Compuserve Science Fiction Forum.

Hutcheon, Linda
    1988   *A Poetics of Postmodernism: History, Theory, Fiction*. New York: Routledge.

Jackson, Rosemary
    1981   *Fantasy: the Literature of Subversion*. London: Methuen.

Kottak, Conrad Phillip
    1990   *Prime-Time Society: An Anthropological Analysis of Television and Culture*. Belmont, CA: Wadsworth.

Kristeva, Julia
    1976   *La Révolution du langage poétique*. Paris: Editions du Seuil.
    1980   *Desire in Language: A Semiotic Approach to Literature and Art*. Ed. Thomas Gora, Alice Jardine, and Leon S. Roudiez. Trans. Leon S. Roudiez. New York: Columbia University Press.
    1986   "The System and the Speaking Subject." Pp. 24–33 in *The Kristeva Reader*. Ed. Toril Moi. New York: Columbia University Press.

Moriarty, Michael
    1991   *Roland Barthes*. Stanford: Stanford University Press.

Murray-Brown, Jeremy
    1991   "Video Ergo Sum." In *Video Icons and Values*. Ed. Alan M. Olson, Christopher Parr, and Debra Parr. Albany: State University of New York Press.

Otto, Rudolf
    1976   *The Idea of the Holy*. London: Oxford University Press (1923).

Phillips, Gary A.
    1995   "'What Is Written? How Are You Reading?' Gospel, Intertextuality, and Doing Lukewise: Reading Lk 10:25–42 Otherwise." Semeia 69/70:111-47.

Rabinowitz, Peter J.
    1980   "'What's Hecuba to Us?' The Audience's Experience of Literary Borrowing." Pp. 241–63 in *The Reader in the Text: Essays on Audience and Interpretation*. Ed. Susan R. Suleiman and Inge Crosman. Princeton: Princeton University Press.

1987 *Before Reading: Narrative Conventions and the Politics of Interpretation.* Ithaca: Cornell University Press.

Rajan, Tilottama
1991 "Intertextuality and the Subject of Reading/Writing." Pp. 61–74 in *Influence and Intertextuality in Literary History.* Ed. Jay Clayton and Eric Rothstein. Madison: University of Wisconsin Press.

Raval, Suresh
1981 *Metacriticism.* Athens: University of Georgia Press.

Schultze, Quentin J.
1990 "Television Drama as Sacred Text." Pp. 3–27 in *Channels of Belief: Religion and American Commercial Television.* Ed. John P. Ferre. Ames: Iowa State University Press.

Shepherd, Jean.
1981 "The Lost Civilization of Deli." In *A Fistful of Fig Newtons.* New York: Doubleday.

Wright, Elizabeth
1984 *Psychoanalytic Criticism: Theory in Practice.* London and New York: Methuen.

JEZEBEL RE-VAMPED[1]

Tina Pippin
Agnes Scott College

ABSTRACT

The body of the dead and defeated Jezebel in 2 Kings 9 and Apocalypse of John 2 returns in multiple texts as the classic *femme fatale*. Jezebel is the vamp/ire who roams the texts of culture and gender relations. The point in this article is not to re-construct or re-form the biblical image of Jezebel, but to trace the trace of "jezebel" through various texts from the biblical period to the present, using theories of intertextuality and the social construction of the body of the dead woman.

INTRODUCTION

Southern women in the United States define Jezebel:[2] wicked; scheming; cheap harlot; either promiscuous or a complete whore; female form of gigolo; biblical queen; wife of Ahab; gave her husband bad advice; evil and treacherous; two-faced; one who seduces men and leads them to destruction; a woman who gets around; not ashamed; bimbo; I didn't know what it meant until my roommate called me this; someone who is wild, free, and comfortable with her sexuality; uninhibited, some might say slutty; a beautiful name; a Southern Belle with a mind and will and sex drive who is damned for not fitting the stereotype of a helpless, frigid woman; Scarlett O'Hara; Bette Davis in the red hoop dress in the 1938 film; condescending term used for African American women in the time of slavery; "Gene loves Jezebel;" flirty girl, light, flighty, aloof, or dirty slut; free spirit, happy, cute, very feminine; always a lady (but not always nice); slinky; powerful; ambitious; calculating; ruthless; eaten by dogs; taking pleasure from material things; self-centered; decorated woman; painted face; Cosmo clothes; sensual; she has been given a "bad rep" by many scholars and people; she is famous for her badness; vamp,

---

[1] A different version of this article appears in *A Feminist Companion to Samuel and Kings*. Ed. Athalya Brenner (Sheffield: Sheffield Academic Press, 1994).

[2] I conducted an informal survey of college students (ages 18 to 50), Atlanta area artists, and members from both Episcopal and Southern Baptist congregations.

vampire, temptress, femme fatale, siren, witch—a woman who takes or ruins the life of another.

The complex and ambiguous character of Jezebel in the Bible serves as the archetypal bitch-witch-queen in misogynist representations of women. Beginning in 1 Kings 16 through 2 Kings 9 and reappearing again in Apocalypse 2:20, Jezebel is the contradictory, controlling, carnal foreign woman. The common pronouncement (still widely used in the contemporary Southern United States), "She is a regular Jezebel," underlies the imagining of Jezebel that begins with the Apocalypse 2:20 passage and has referred to countless women from political queens—including, Mary Tudor, Mary Stuart, and Isabella I—to movie queens, such as Bette Davis, Vivian Leigh, and Elizabeth Taylor.

A sampling from different older and more recent biblical commentaries corroborates this view of Jezebel as sexually evil and a demon woman: Ahab's "evils . . . are laid at her door. . . . she came near to bringing the house of David to extinction" (Culver: 589–90). She is seen as having totally disregarded Israelite law and custom. To these more common reactions add: "She was a *woman of masculine temperament* and swayed her husband at will" (Gehman: 492).[3] *Jezebel is the foreign influence*

---

[3] Emphasis added. On the masculinity of the Jezebel figure, see Patricia Morton (153): Black women's history "has been shaped in the image of Jezebel who deserved what she got because she was other than womanly. And the image of black womanhood as other than womanly has served to confirm black manhood as other than manly, and thus to confirm that the Negro was other and less than fully deserving of racial equality."

In an early twentieth century drama (McDowell, 1924), Jezebel speaks twice her desire to be male: "Oh, would I were a man that I might go myself with them and face Elijah too" (12) and "Oh! God! If only I had been a man!" (21). In film representations the jezebel is termed a "superfemale" as opposed to the more masculine "superwoman." The superfemale is "a woman who, while exceedingly 'feminine' and flirtatious, is too ambitious and intelligent for the docile role society has decreed she play. She is uncomfortable, but not uncomfortable enough to rebel completely; her circumstances are too pleasurable" (Haskell: 214). The film image that comes to mind is Bette Davis in her Academy Award-winning role in the 1932 *Jezebel*, in which she plays a Southern woman who schemes and destroys those around her and eventually almost destroys herself. In the final scene she rides off toward possible vindication. *Publishers Weekly* describes this jezebel image of Bette Davis from a recent book on the actress: "Fuller tells us little more about Jezebel herself than that she eats Carnation Instant Breakfast, reads the *Daily News* and smokes Vantage cigarettes by the carton. Davis's fans won't be surprised by her abrasive and distant manner. But they may tire of hearing the star shrieking, 'Kee-ryst!' while smashing out cigarettes wherever she pleases, over and over again" (1992:101).

Teresa de Lauretis expresses a parallel notion in her feminist critique of Derrida: "Were I to do so, however, I would earn Derrida's contempt for 'those women feminists so derided by Nietzsche,' I would put myself in the position of one 'who aspires to be like a man,' who 'seeks to castrate' and 'wants a castrated woman'. . . . I shall not do so, therefore. Decency and shame prevent me, though nothing more" (47).

that is dangerous and brings destruction. In considering Jezebel, her reputation precedes her, regardless of how narrow or misogynist the reputation is presented.

The Woman's Bible of 1895 turns to another dimension of Jezebel: "Jezebel was a brave, fearless, generous woman, so wholly devoted to her own husband that even wrong seemed justifiable to her, if she could thereby make him happy. (In that respect she seems to have entirely fulfilled the Southern Methodist's ideal of the pattern wife entirely fulfilled in her husband.)" (75)! Jezebel is the equal and rival of Elijah; the deeds of genocide both perform are seen as "savage" (75).4 The newer women's bible states that Jezebel "met her death with characteristic audacity: she painted her eyes, adorned her head, and greeted Jehu from her window with a caustic insult" (Exum: 489).

I am "re-vamping" the generally accepted view of Jezebel as an evil woman from the biblical to the modern representations of her. Using theories on intertextuality from Bakhtin to Thibault and contemporary film theory, I trace the relations between the biblical text and other texts (drama, poetry, film, and art). The codes and signifying practices governing Jezebel's presence in a variety of texts have implications for the hermeneutics of gender and sexuality. In other words, the "trace" of Jezebel is in her adorned face peering through the lattice (representing the face of the goddess Asherah), with the image of her corpse as a vivid reminder of the defeat of the goddess-centered cultures—"they found no more of her than the skull and the feet and the palms of her hands" (2 Kgs

---

4 Elijah is "that much-overestimated 'man of God'" (75). Ellen Battelle Dietrick adds a contemporary note, calling on the reader "to imagine why Jezebel is now [1895] dragged forth to 'shake her gory locks' as a frightful example to the American women who ask for recognized right to self-government" (75). Are these "gory locks" also an allusion to Medusa—dread/dreaded/dreadful/dreadlocks?

9:35). The text of the goddess is distorted and placed in only negative terms. I do not intend to un/recover a heroic woman figure from the biblical narrative or to redeem a "bad" woman of the Bible. I want to deal with the cultural representations and the interactions of readers with the image of Jezebel. A rereading of different texts of Jezebel reveals the complexities of "that cursed woman" who fought to retain her indigenous culture, as it underlines the continuation of the "curse" for all women who claim autonomy—sexual, religious, or political.

JEZEBEL

The Hebrew name, "Jezebel" has been defined variously: from "unexalted, unhusbanded; or the brother is prince" (Gehman: 492) or "where is the prince?" (Exum: 489)[5] to *chaste* quite inappropriate" (Culver: 589). "Jezebel" means the monstrous female—loose and let loose, woman.[6] Why is the monster, here the jezebel, so fascinating? What is the seduction, the draw into the dangerous darkness where the "monster" lurks?

Like the use of the curse on Ham as a justification for slavery of Africans, jezebel was the designation of the sexually dangerous African American slave woman. The juxtaposition of the images of the mammy and the jezebel served as an apologetic for the exploitation of the female slave. Deborah White[7] describes these divisions in terms of the madonna-

---

[5] E.B. Johnston (1057) finds a wordplay in Jezebel's name: *zebel* in Jezebel's name is made a pun in 2 Kings 9:37 with the word "dung" (*domen*).

[6] On the double monster in the mother and daughter relationship see Gallop. She finds the mother-daughter relationship reflected in groups of women: "One monster cannot be separated from the other." I think this idea has interesting implications for the Jezebel-Athaliah connection; is the narrator of 1–2 Kings presenting us with a pair of monsters?

[7] See Chapter One, "Jezebel and Mammy: The Mythology of Female Slavery." White states (46): "Southerners, therefore, were hardly of one mind concerning African-American women. Jezebel was an image as troubling as it was convenient and utilitarian . . . . On the one hand there was the woman obsessed with matters of the flesh, on the other was the asexual woman. One was carnal, the other maternal. One was at heart a slut, the other was deeply religious." Patricia Morton (10) follows White's argument: "By labeling the female slave as a Jezebel, the master's sexual abuse was justified by presenting her as a woman who deserved what she got . . . . by labeling the slave woman as a sexual animal—not a real woman at all." Morton adds (33) that the jezebel was scapegoated: "Still cast as Jezebel, the black woman was assigned responsibility for the supposed sins of black as well as white men" (33). See also Victoria Bynum (35ff). In discussing the Jezebel in Apocalypse 2, Elisabeth Schüssler Fiorenza rightly draws on the southern tradition: "Like the historical queen Jezebel, she has served in Western thought as the archetype of the sexually dangerous woman. During the time of slavery, for instance, the image of Jezebel, the whore, became the controlling image of black womanhood in white, elite, male propaganda" (135).

whore: the mammy is a-sexual; loving; warm; maternal; dark-skinned; big; older; wears formless clothes; covers her hair with a kerchief; is loyal, religious, and pious. The women slotted as jezebels are sexual; provocative; young; with changing skin color; comely; promiscuous; provocatively dressed; a breeder; rebellious; a whore.

The white masters created these images to control and dominate the female slave. The mammy represents the desire for a positive image for African Americans. The jezebel was an excuse—of masters to justify their own adolescent and later adulterous behavior. White women blamed the jezebels in order to deny the rape and oppression of slave women. The jezebel acted out of the constraints of race and gender. The cultural "Africanisms"—of women having children before marriage and of exposing more of their bodies in the field as they worked—were misunderstood by whites. The whole system was constructed by and for the white male, which left white women finding ways to discredit the slave women.

So jezebel is not an abstract sign but a real physical presence—for antebellum culture and also in popular culture in the United States. Can one get outside the popular culture meaning of Jezebel?

Re-Vamped

Recent biblical scholarship reveals the ambiguity of the character Jezebel and the religious/political rather than the sexual intention of her painted face in the murder scene. But the term "jezebel" has distinct social meaning that is biblical (in Hosea; Ezekiel 16; the "strange woman" of Proverbs; the false prophetess of Apocalypse 2). Whoring and fornication is associated with strange religion and strange culture. Claudia Camp remarks that in the story of Naboth's vineyard, the Deuteronomic Historian may have blamed Jezebel for Ahab's deed: "Shifting of the blame to the foreign woman forms part of that era's polemic on the dangers of intermarriage" (104).[8] The jezebel schemes with both her mind and body. She has "been around"—in/from foreign territory (Tyre; Africa), and she brings danger with her. Therefore, her body must be destroyed. Look closely at the remains: skull; feet; palms of her hands (2 Kgs 9:35).

---

[8] Camp is following Alexander Rofe on this point. Peter Ackroyd states that "Jezebel becomes a type; into her figure is projected in detail the hostility to what is believed to be alien practice" (256). Elise Boulding (209) adds: "Foreign women were dangerous role models for Israelite women, with their political ways and priestess notions. We shall see the same scenario played out again 1,000 years later, in the Christian church fathers' distrust of pagan women and their priestess tradition. The sexual seduction aspect of this struggle is, I suspect, a male rationalization."

Viewing the Dead Body

The image of Jezebel is difficult to identify iconographically; her portrait and scenes from her life are rare.[9] Still, she is portrayed as the temptress. Both men and women are drawn to her. Even though 2 Kings 9:37 pronounces that "no one can say, This is Jezebel," the irony is that "This is Jezebel" is exactly what people said ever since this Deuteronomic proverb. The death scene most tellingly drawn is in Gustav Doré's *La Sancta Bible* in the print, "Les Compagnons de Jéhu Retrouvent la Tête et les Extremités de Jézabel." The eye of the viewer is drawn to the central image of Jezebel's severed head, peacefully beautiful in its silence and separation from her body. The severed head is veiled here; in the picture of the previous scene of Jezebel being thrown out of the window by the eunuchs, "Jéhu Fait Préipiter Jézabel," her hair is loose. The viewer is face-to-face with Jezebel. Does death bring her back to a virginal state? Is this face the death mask of the ideal woman? Is the ideal woman a dead woman—silent, fragmented, and powerless? Is the viewer responsible for her death? Is this the severed head of Medusa, a warning, a marker to other women who seek power?

In Doré's vision, Jezebel's two hands and one foot remain. Whereas her head is covered, the hands and feet are exposed and thereby eroticized.[10] There is no blood and no corpus; only the extremities remain. The hands and foot seem to gesture. In her reading of "Rembrandt's" drawing of the Levite's wife on the threshold in Judges 19, Mieke Bal states, "The hand of this woman is crucial: It tells about death and about representation. It does not 'see,' but it speaks about mis-seeing. . . . It demonstrates that her gesture is phatic, enforcing semiosis" (370–71). So Jezebel's hands in the Doré drawing are poised and regal, even inviting. This Jezebel has been dis-abled, immobilized; her life (and evil doings) interrupted. In the sexual politics of this death scene the soldiers dominate; they stand over her transfixed, while one of them lifts her severed head for viewing. All that is left are the outermost parts. Why these body parts? These remains seem excessive, some textual excess—the excess of horror?—the excess of desire?

Jezebel's dead body parts are the signs of the liminal body, made even more liminal by their being dung on the fields. No one owns this body; she is denied the appropriate burial as a King's Daughter by the dogs who eat her. Jezebel the Queen is now Jezebel the dog food. Her flesh is de-

---

[9] The Index of Christian Art at Princeton University lists about twenty representations of Jezebel up to 1400 C.E. Of these there are approximately 10 portraits; the rest are from three scenes of her life.

[10] Bram Dijkstra refers to "the dead woman as object of desire" in his work on 19th-20th century iconography of evil women (51).

voured. Jezebaal/Asherah is eaten. "The corpse of Jezebel shall be like dung" (2 Kgs 9:37) shows the shaming and utter destruction of the Canaanite/Phoenician religion. The focus on scatology appears again in Jehu's destruction of a temple of Baal in 2 Kgs 10:27: "Then they demolished the pillar of Baal, and destroyed the temple of Baal, and made it a latrine to this day." A similar scatological joke is made at the Mt. Carmel contest (1 Kgs 18:17). The reference to dung, outhouses, and a Canaanite god's indisposal point to a way to dismiss and shame the enemy by referring to them by particular body parts (the Philistines as the uncircumcised ones) or by/as their body functions. Jezebel as dung represents the ultimate impurity. Thus, Jezebel and her religion are excrement to be excreted.

What is left of Jezebel is more than the sum of the dead body parts. In the horror of the death scene and the gaze of the viewer on the public execution—the fall, splattering blood, trampling horses, eating dogs, leftover flesh—the death of the female is forcefully presented. According to Virginia Allen in her study of the femme fatale, "Dead women, exotic women, embody a fierce and total rejection of living women" (186). Of course, Ahab also died a miserable, public death with the dogs drinking his blood. Ahab followed the evil ways of many kings before and after him, but he was "urged on by his wife Jezebel" (1 Kgs 22:25). The representation of Jezebel's death is different. She represents the power behind the throne, both political and spiritual. Her scattered body parts are a gendered focal point for the viewer, and their seductive power in Doré is intact. The power and seduction of Jezebel linger. Even after the destruction of the house of Ahab (especially Jezebel's daughter Athaliah, 2 Kgs 11), Asherah returns, and Jezebel returns. So again, are the body parts markers, signs of warning: beware of foreign women and queen mothers; beware of all living women?

Despite warning, Jezebel returns eternally as vamp/ire, the phantom-ghost who roams time haunting both men and women. Jezebel is the vamp/ire that cannot be killed, who roams through other texts and times and women. She has a future in a different form; she is constantly reformed in the image of male desire and fear. The "original" Jezebel is tangled up in its cultural texts, including the biblical story, that is its own invention of Jezebel. All texts of Jezebel are copies (Baudrillard's *simulacra*). Who's telling the truth? Everyone is. And no one is. Even the severed head speaks in tongues: tongues that are political, queenly, indigenous, elite, evil, religious, female, sexualized, monogamous, mothering, and murdered. The head speaks in the tongues of all the "texts" of Jezebel. The biblical text presents both the limits of Jezebel and her limitlessness. From the confines of her house she is the anti-prophet to Elijah the prophet (cf. Apoc 2:20). Jezebel talks to Jehu from her high window within female space. When she enters the male world, she is thrown to her death. Crossing that boundary is her last act—in the Deuteronomic text.

The Intertext of Desire

Jezebel is a fantasy space. She is an effect, a personality, a lifestyle, an ethical way of being female in the world, and an intertextual turn for the worst. Her multiple stories are parodies, including the biblical story. As parody the Jezebel "texts" are ironic, contradictory, ambiguous, and paradoxical. Postmodern theorist Linda Hutcheon equates parody with intertextuality. Hutcheon relates:

> It [parody] is also not ahistorical or de-historicizing . . . . Instead, through a double process of installing and ironizing, parody signals how present representations come from past ones and what ideological consequences derive from both continuity and difference. (1988:93)

The biblical Queen Jezebel is reconsidered with each subsequent "text." There is no closure to the story of Jezebel's death in 2 Kings; as parody, Jezebel engages the reader in a montage of images.

Tom Robbins recreates a parody of a modern Jezebel/Salome in his book, *Skinny Legs and All*, by questioning the tradition handed down in Western culture. The main character, Ellen Cherry, thinks to herself:

> What had Queen Jezebel done to earn the distinction as our all-time treacherous slut: In the Bitch Hall of Fame, Jezebel had a room of her own; nay, an entire wing. For fixing her hair and applying makeup? Was it implied that she went to the window to *flirt* with the rebel warrior? And if so, was that so wicked that it should wreck her reputation for three thousand years? The trimillennial lash bat?
>
> As Ellen Cherry walked the rain-rippled pavement of Seattle, bumpershooting from restaurant to restaurant in search of a job, she bore upon her back the weight of a skull, a pair of feet, and the palms of two hands. The nails of the feet were lacquered vermilion, a pretty ribbon fluttered from a lacuna in the skull. And she would wonder as she walked, 'What is the Bible trying to tell us?'
>
> That Satan is a hairdresser?
>
> That Elizabeth Arden ought to be fed to the poodles?
>
> (33)[11]

---

[11] Robbins' protagonist Ellen Cherry considers Jezebel "her doppelgaenger." He describes her search for the biblical Jezebel: "She had procured a Bible and gone searching for the lurid details of Jezebel's debauchery. From Sunday school, she had a hazy picture of a thoroughly immoral harlot who costumed herself like a rock 'n' roll vamp, but she couldn't recall a single biographical fact. Imagine her surprise when the

Robbins is a lover of Jezebel, and his book is a *jouissance*. He plugs into the tradition of Jezebel as the ultimate femme fatal and creates a parody out of this web of desire. Jezebel's grave is empty; she stalks new victims in creative ways, forever crossing boundaries and challenging convention.

Mieke Bal points to the Jezebel narrative as an "ideo-story;" that is, a story taken out of context. Bal gives the example of a tabloid story, "Devilish Ladies Who Everybody Loves to Hate," which includes "Lilith, Jezebel, Delilah, and ... Sappho. ... The Combination of the four figures is a function of the principle of coherent reading. ... Both within and between the four stories, contradictions and problems are repressed" (1988:11). That Delilah is not a liar or that Jezebel is not an adulteress gets lost in the ideo-story. The reproduction of popular mythology is a priority in the reading process.

This reading of Jezebel in predominantly sexual terms is socially grounded. A social semiotics which draws from Bakhtin's heteroglossia is useful in reading for Jezebel. The textual voices on Jezebel are many; they overlap, origins unknown (except the general patriarchal culture which is women's context). Paul Thibault promotes a "neomaterialist social semiotic," uniting theory and practice into the study of semiotics.[12] Thibault is involved in asking ethical questions of theory—that intertextual theorizing challenges existing hegemonic relations. In other words, intertextuality is grounded in a social context/community with certain dominant assumptions about how the world operates. The sign "jezebel" is imbedded in social relationships and in a range of "texts." As John Frow states, "Texts are therefore not structures of presence by traces and tracings of otherness. They are shaped by the repetition and the transformation of other textual structures" (45). Jezebel is not an image but *images*, a plural form.

The whoring Jezebel is of course the most seductive image. In discussing seduction and prostitution in Flaubert, Ross Chambers writes: "In the homosocial world, literature must pose, in order to gain acceptance, as a figure of powerlessness, helpless or charming: a child or a woman . . . .

Old Testament Book of Kings informed her that Jezebel was a royal—and faithful— wife" (32).

[12] Thibault defines social semiotics as a theory that moves semiotics "beyond its self-identification with many of the foundational ideological assumptions of Western culture" (3). Social semiotics is connected with social heteroglossia as follows: "The systems of voices in the social semiotic, including potentially unvoiced meanings and practices, comprise the relations of social heteroglossia through which relations of alliance, consensus, opposition, conflict, and co-optation among voices are positioned and articulated in specific texts and intertextual formations" (25). Morgan (8) relates this point: "Indeed, *culture* itself, or the collection of signifying practices in a society, *is radically intertextual.*" On the materiality of language see Kristeva.

Literature, in short, must camp it up" (155). Thus, the passage in Apocalypse 2 stands out: Jezebel refuses to repent and continues to beguile and fornicate. "Beware, I am throwing her on a bed, and those who commit adultery with her I am throwing into great distress, unless they repent of her doings; and I will strike her children dead" (Apoc 2:22–23). And the Jezebel in 2 Kings 9 paints her face and fixes her hair boldly to face death and the fulfillment of the prophecy of the enemy. What would the apocalyptic Jezebel say to the narrator John in reply? What would Queen Jezebel say to the narrator of her life story? Are their only traces skull and feet and palms of the hands and dead children?

An outside Jezebel has invaded the text, a Jezebel who would proclaim (as did Ellen Cherry's cynical mother Patsy in *Skinny Legs and All*), "Of the Seven Deadly Sins, lust is definitely the pick of the litter" (106). But the biblical Jezebel does not seek or find sexual pleasure. Looking out the lattice, Jezebel is framed. She is also imprisoned. In the biblical text, as well as in early twentieth century "devotional fiction," Jezebel is a prisoner in her own palace; she never leaves or confronts men (like Elijah) on the outside. Jezebel remains inside; acting behind the lattice. All attempts to colonize her fail.

The colonial nature of the jezebel text and the oppression of the jezebel voice is apparent in the sadistic retelling of her death. In her book on the effects of imperialism on the reading process, Laura Donaldson calls for a "materialist-feminist semiotics" that "requires that we not only recognize how micrologies of power keep certain information systems in place while simultaneously suppressing others but also resist the temptation of an unmediated politics of meaning" (120–21). The discourse on Jezebel is guided through the colonial mind. The image of the Other, the foreign, the dangerous and thereby seductive woman is used against medieval women and slave women and Southern women who break with tradition. Tom Robbins attempts to decolonize Jezebel:

> Jezebel. Jezebel. Painted Queen of Israel. I am praising thee, O Queen of Israel. Whore of the Golden Calf. Strumpet of Baal. Jezebel. Slut of Samaria. Our queen whom the dogs are eating. The watercourse of the Jews is flowing through thee. Jezebel. My Queen. Whose daughter is ruling in Jerusalem. From whose womb is pouring the House of David. Mmm. Jezebel. Priestess of Fornication. Mmm. Queen of Spades. Queen of Tarts. O Jezebel, you are my queen, I exalt thee and praise thy sandals. (348)

Even though in popular western culture to be called a jezebel is not a compliment, there is a strange connection/ disconnection to Jezebel.

Women read themselves as Jezebel, as having the "jezebel spirit."[13] Are we happy/satisfied when Jezebel is splattered and trampled by horses and eaten by dogs? What have we done with the story of Jezebel? Is her story continually recolonized, reopened, the brief scenes of her life reenacted and reinscribed?

WORKS CONSULTED

Ackroyd, Peter R.
    1985   "Goddesses, Women and Jezebel." Pp. 245–59 in *Images of Women in Antiquity*. Ed. Averil Cameron and Amélie Kuhrt. Detroit: Wayne State University Press.

Allen, Virginia
    1983   *The Femme Fatale Erotic Icon*. Troy, N.Y.: Whitson.

Bal, Mieke
    1987   *Lethal Love: Feminist Literary Readings of Biblical Love Stories*. Bloomington: Indiana University Press.
    1988   *Death & Dissymmetry: The Politics of Coherence in the Book of Judges*. Chicago: The University of Chicago Press.
    1991   *Reading "Rembrandt": Beyond the Word-Image Opposition*. New York: Cambridge University Press.

Barbor, H.R.
    n.d.   *Jezebel: A Tragedy in Three Acts*. London: Arthur Brenton.

Barnard, P. Mordaunt
    1904   *Jezebel: A Drama*. London: Francis Griffiths.

Boulding, Elise
    1992   *The Underside of History: A View of Women through Time*. Vol. 1. Revised Edition. Newbury Park: SAGE Publications.

Bronfen, Elisabeth
    1992   *Over Her Dead Body: Death, Femininity and the Aesthetic*. New York: Routledge.

Bynum, Victoria E.
    1992   *Unruly Women: The Politics of Social & Sexual Control in the Old South*. Chapel Hill: The University of North Carolina Press.

---

[13] An older woman student of mine recently commented that Jezebel is that (or any!) evil woman who steals husbands. Then she added with a wink, "There's a part of Jezebel in me."

Camp, Claudia V.
　1992.　"1 and 2 Kings." Pp. 96–109 in *The Women's Bible Commentary*. Ed. Carol A. Newsom and Sharon H. Ringe. Louisville: Westminster/John Knox.

Chambers, Ross
　1990　"Alter Ego: Intertextuality, Irony and the Politics of Reading." Pp. 143–58 in *Intertextuality: Theories and Practices*. Ed. Michael Worton and Judith Still. Manchester: Manchester University Press.

Culver, R.D.
　1975　"Jezebel." Pp. 589–90 in *The Zondervan Pictoral Encyclopedia*. Vol. 3. Merrill C. Tenney.

de Lauretis, Teresa
　1987　*Technologies of Gender: Essays on Theory, Film and Fiction*. Bloomington: Indiana University Press.

Dijkstra, Bram
　1986　*Idols of Perversity: Fantasies of Feminine Evil in Fin-de-Siècle Culture*. New York: Oxford University Press.

Donaldson, Laura E.
　1992　*Decolonizing Feminisms: Race, Gender, & Empire Building*. Chapel Hill: The University of North Carolina Press.

Exum, Cheryl
　1985　"Jezebel." P. 489 in *Harper's Bible Dictionary*. Ed. Paul J. Achtemeier. San Francisco: Harper & Row.

Frow, John
　1990　"Intertextuality and Ontology." Pp. 45–55 in *Intertextuality: Theories and Practices*. Eds. Michael Worton and Judith Still. Manchester: Manchester University Press.

Gallop, Jane
　1989　"The Monster in the Mirror: The Feminist Critic's Psychoanalysis." Pp. 13–24 in *Feminism and Psychoanalysis*. Ed. Richard Feldstein and Judith Roof. Ithaca: Cornell University Press.

Gehman, Henry Snyder, ed.
　1970　*The New Westminster Dictionary of the Bible*. Philadelphia: The Westminster Press.

Haskell, Molly
　1987　*From Reverence to Rape: The Treatment of Women in the Movies*. Chicago: The University of Chicago Press.

Hemer, Colin J.
　1986　*The Letters to the Seven Churches of Asia in their Local Setting*. Sheffield: JSNT.

Hutcheon, Linda
　1988　*A Poetics of Postmodernism: History, Theory, Fiction*. New York: Routledge.

Johnston, E.B.
   1982   "Jezebel." Pp. 1057–1059 in *The International Standard Bible Encyclopedia*. Ed. Geoffrey W. Bromiley. Grand Rapids: Wm. B. Eerdmans.

Kristeva, Julia
   1975   *Revolution in Poetic Language*. Trans. Margaret Waller. New York: Columbia University Press.

McDowall, H.M.
   1924   *Jezebel: A Tragedy*. Oxford: Basil Blackwell.

Morgan, Thais E.
   1985   "Is There an Intertext in this Text?: Literary and Interdisciplinary Approaches to Intertextuality." *American Journal of Semiotics* 3/4:1–40.

Morton, Patricia
   1991   *Disfigured Images: The Historical Assault on Afro-American Women*. New York: Greenwood.

Riffaterre, Michael
   1990   "Compulsory Reader Response: The Intertextual Drive." Pp. 56–78 in *Intertextuality: Theories and Practices*. Ed. Michael Worton and Judith Still. Manchester: Manchester University Press.

Robbins, Tom
   1990   *Skinny Legs and All*. New York: Bantam Books.

Schüssler Fiorenza, Elisabeth
   1991   *Revelation: Vision of a Just World*. Proclamation Commentaries. Minneapolis: Fortress.

Stanton, Elizabeth Cady, ed.
   1974   *The Woman's Bible*. Seattle: Coalition Task Force on Women and Religion.

Sternberg, Meir
   1985   *The Poetics of Biblical Narrative: Ideological Literature and the Drama of Reading*. Bloomington: Indiana University Press.

Thibault, Paul
   1991   *Social Semiotics as Praxis*. Minneapolis: University of Minnesota Press.

Walker, Dorothy Clarke
   1955   *Jezebel*. New York: McGraw-Hill.

White, Deborah Gray
   1985   *Ar'n't I a Woman? Female Slaves in the Plantation South*. New York: W.W. Norton.

"THE GETTING OF NAMES":
ANTI-INTERTEXUALITY AND THE UNREAD BIBLE
IN TONI MORRISON'S *SONG OF SOLOMON* AND *BELOVED*

Nicole Wilkinson
Vanderbilt University

ABSTRACT

Intexuality may be, as Robert Alter maintains, a necessary element of all literature, since literature incorporates and recapitulates its own past. Not all literature celebrates its literary past, however—at least not without ambivalence. In these two novels, Toni Morrison refers to the Bible repeatedly, but the Bible that her characters carry they do not read. For Morrison—a renowned reader and writer herself—reading and writing are suspect; alien to African American culture and tainted by their use in the hands of the white oppressor. Though present in these stories, the biblical text is silent, at times unresponsive and at other times notably irrelevant. This tension between the presence of the Bible and the absence of the Bible's written content, expressed most clearly in the processes of naming that occur in these novels, epitomizes Morrison's fierce ambivalence toward the written word, and possibly toward language itself.

In Toni Morrison's novel *Song of Solomon,* the third generation of men named Macon Dead discovers that his grandfather accepted this unfortunate name upon being freed from slavery, as a way of breaking with the miseries of the past. The fact that the name of the new, free present was conferred accidentally by a drunken white soldier, thus replacing the name purposely, if carelessly, given by the former slave owner, indicates something of the struggles in Morrison's novels between past and present. In *Song of Solomon* and *Beloved* particularly, Morrison shows us people whose efforts to be free of an afflicted past only enmesh them deeper in that past, like victims of the tar baby after whom another of her novels is named.

In these struggles the Bible is neither innocent nor transcendent. It is a part of the oppression of the past, a text by definition carrying with it a value of literacy foreign to African culture. Texts of any kind are themselves a way of mediating between past and present. Writing is, among other things, a way of preserving the present, making time into space—the space of a piece of paper, which can be given to the future. But for Morrison this means of negotiating between past and present is profoundly foreign to and destructive of African Americans. Rather than being simply a way of connecting past to present, it is in effect a way of connecting to and reproducing a particular past of pain.

Writing is one of the weapons belonging to whites, and to read is to invite white voices into the reader's head. Intertextuality, in the sense of an echoing between written texts, is in these novels not perceived as a strengthening resource, but as the inextricable relationship with the tangles of the self-perpetuating past. Representing not only the white man's religion, but in its cold writtenness his very thought processes, and the forcible imposition of both, the Bible in these novels is handed on unread. What is lamentable for Morrison is not that the recipients are unable (she hardly mentions that they were in fact forbidden) to read; what is lamentable and thorny and ultimately interesting for Morrison is that the Bible is handed on at all. Inextricably related to the past, the Bible appears in and shapes the present; read or unread, it is there.

"The fathers may soar/And the children may know their names," reads the epigraph of *Song of Solomon*, and we quickly see that on the road toward this desire the Bible has been a faulty vehicle. In both *Song of Solomon* and *Beloved* names are a central symbol of the juncture of past and present. Emerging from the identity and experience of the parent to become the shape of the child's identity and the frame of the child's experience, names metonymically represent everything that one generation hands on to the next. Within the first twenty pages of *Song of Solomon*, there are three stories of the tangled process of naming, the third of which begins this novel's references to the Bible.

The first is the name of the street, which the authorities named "Mains Avenue," but which people called "Doctor Street" after "the only colored doctor in the city," until the city felt it necessary to post signs declaring that the street was and would be "Mains Avenue and not Doctor Street" (4). The street thence becomes known as "Not Doctor Street." The city authorities are deeply, irrationally concerned that the residents of Mains Avenue refer to it as such (post office officials are barraged with mail for a street with no official existence). In the end they neither win nor lose this fight, but are frustrated by an obfuscation, a joke. Who has the power to name and who does not is the issue. This first story of naming is emblematic of the novel's conclusions: white people will name you what they wish and try to make you call yourself by that name; black people in struggling against the blitz on their identity will end up with names which are neither free nor slave—neither "Doctor," to show a pride in a black man's achievement, nor "Mains" to ignore his existence, but "Not Doctor," which is to say, "He is here, but we may not say so." The major characters in these novels continually must break up the language handed down to them by whites, in order to make from the pieces a language of their own.

The second story about names is the novel's first reference to the naming of Macon Dead. Here the second Macon Dead remembers his father's name, in the midst of a general contemplation of names:

> Surely, he thought, he and his sister had some ancestor, some lithe young man with onyx skin and legs as straight as cane stalks, who had a name that was real. A name given to him at birth with love and seriousness. A name that was not a joke, nor a disguise, nor a brand name. But who this lithe young man was, and where his cane-stalk legs carried him from or to, could never be known. No. Nor his name. (17–18)

There follows a recitation of the names that Macon does know, of his own family, beginning with his parents, who "in some mood of perverseness or resignation, had agreed to abide by a naming done to them by somebody who couldn't have cared less" (18) and turning to himself. Macon bears his father's name, and this name he has handed down in turn to his son, who for reasons still more sordid is called "Milkman." Macon Dead the second has named his two daughters as his sister was named—by opening the Bible at random and pointing to a word. Why he abides by this practice—the tool of an illiteracy he does not share—is never explained, except to say that the naming of his younger sister made a deep impression upon him. The daughters themselves and their names—Magdalene and First Corinthians—are less important to the story than is this Macon Dead's sister, whose name is Pilate.

His wife having died in childbirth, the first Macon Dead broods alone over the Bible he cannot read, in search of a word that looks suitable for his daughter's name. Laboriously, he copies this word onto a slip of paper, "as illiterate people do, every curlicue, arch, and bend in the letters," (18) and hands it over to the midwife to read. When she protests that the name is first of all a man's name, and secondly the name of the man who killed Jesus, he replies,

> "I asked Jesus to save me my wife."
> "Careful, Macon."
> "I asked him all night long."
> "He give you your baby."
> "Yes. He did. Baby name Pilate." (19)

"Pilate," then, is the name of unanswered prayer and the inability to read. The lack of conversation between this man and Jesus, this man and the Bible, or rather the lack of response to him from either the Bible or Jesus, brings him to name his daughter after the man who killed Jesus, the name of the Christian Bible's anti-hero. The midwife wants to burn the slip of paper bearing the tormented name, but Macon Dead insists, "It come from the Bible, it stays in the Bible," (19) an apt description of the Bible's autistic silence directed toward him—whatever comes from the Bible never gets to him, even when it passes through his hands.

Pilate's name would seem to imply that her appointed task is in some sense to kill Jesus, to lose the faith that let her parents down. But in fact she engages in no such struggle. Pilate's father prayed to Jesus and his prayer went unanswered; in the naming of his daughter, Macon Dead seems ready to kill Jesus himself. But for Pilate, Jesus has no real existence from the start. He is never real or present enough to cause her to struggle with him or with the faith he is supposed to engender.

Having squirmed out of her dead mother's womb largely without the midwife's assistance, Pilate loses in the days of her infancy any trace of ever having been attached to an umbilical cord. Like Eve in the riddle, Pilate has no navel. She is a woman without physical connection to the past, cut loose from her mother without a scar or a trace. In the later novel, *Tar Baby*, Son is irked at the well-to-do white family's not knowing the real names of their hired help: "It bothered him that everybody called Gideon Yardman, as though he had not been mothered" (138). Pilate comes as close as anyone can to being genuinely unmothered, but she is thus freed from a past not authentically her own, while Gideon seems unmothered because he is being robbed of his authentic past. A name is an ancestry for Morrison.

The death of Pilate's father completes her orphaned—and freed—status and cancels any remaining debt she bears to the past that created her. Yet before she leaves the farm for which her father has been killed, Pilate takes the only word he ever wrote out of the Bible from where it has been kept, puts it into a small brass box, and insists on having it made into an earring, with which she pierces her own ear, and which she proceeds to wear until the day she dies. Why? Pilate is the one character in this novel who is wise; she knows what she wants and whom she loves; and she is troubled neither by regrets nor embittered dreams. She is a woman without a navel, as innocent as Eve (for all that her brother accuses her of being a serpent [54]). Why then does she pierce her own ear with the name produced by her father's troubled past? Her brother says it is because she is "fluky" (19), and her nephew, Milkman, in a moment of drunken bewilderment, speculates that Pilate keeps not only her own name, but his own and everyone else's in that brass box (89). In the end it is part of the troubling mystery of Milkman's own past—this unconventional woman wearing her name in an earring—and it remains in a sense a mystery to the reader, a part of Pilate's insoluble, attractive quirkiness.

But it is a mystery that illumines: the earring-name is physically painful to Pilate—her earlobe becomes infected from the piercing. It is unread and unreadable—although written it is preserved not in order to be read but in order to be worn. Neither she nor her father who wrote it ever read this biblical word which is her name. It is a part of Pilate, constituting, together with her father's bones, the sum total of her inheritance. But unlike the bones, the name is an inheritance composed in a language that neither person speaks. This is exactly what the Bible is here: an inherited language alien to both ancestor and heir.

This is not to say that the Bible cannot be used for survival in the white world, since it is a language in some way meaningful to whites. The Bible is quoted only once in this book, and then it is an act of deception and survival, completely and expressly insincere. In an effort to get Milkman and his friend Guitar out of jail, after they are arrested in possession of her father's bones, Pilate swears that the bones are those of her dead husband, who was lynched in Mississippi fifteen years earlier, bones she kept out of fidelity: "Bible say what so e'er the Lord hath brought together let no man put asunder—Matthew Twenty-one: Two. We was bony fide and legal wed, suh" (208). Milkman is impressed, both by her ability to change her way of speaking and even her appearance so as to become what the white policeman wants to believe she is, and by her quotation of the Bible: "He thought Pilate's only acquaintance with the Bible was the getting of names out of it, but she quoted it, apparently, chapter and verse" (208). "Apparently," is the operative word here. Chapter and verse she indeed quotes, but they are not the chapter and verse of the quote she recites. Milkman does not notice, and moreover the policeman with whom she is speaking is apparently as impressed as Milkman. They remain absolutely unaware that Matthew 21:2 is Jesus' instruction to his disciples to find the Palm Sunday colt; it has nothing whatsoever to do with marriage, any more than Pilate herself has had anything to do with marriage. This false allusion is never exposed in the story. Even among the readers, it is only those obsessed with textual details—the fundamentalist or the critic—who will ever take notice.

Here is the disturbing and interesting thing about Morrison's use of the Bible. It is not difficult to grasp the significance of Pilate's citation of the Bible in this context. She is attempting to project the image of a good slave which will render her harmless in the eyes of the police and enable her to get her nephew out of jail. But as a reader I found myself expecting that even in a misquotation, even in the context of duplicity, the biblical reference would have meaning for the story. I expected to find some connection between the real Matthew 21:2 and the situation in which it emerges. The citation, however duplicitous, has the air of an allusion. But it is not one. It is safe to say that Jesus' instructions on untying and bringing the colt have absolutely nothing to do with this novel. The only relevance of this passage lies in what it is not—it is not "Whatsoe'er the Lord hath brought together, let no man put asunder."

In fact, there are no biblical allusions as such in this novel. The Bible is emphatically unread, and while it pops up continually, the sound of its contents never resounds in the story. Biblical references are dropped into this book, but there is no answering echo from its depths.

The only possible exception is the novel's title. Surely the use of the name of a biblical book can be assumed to be an allusion to the contents of that book. Indeed there are some intertextual possibilities here. Like the novel, the biblical book has something to do with race, or at least with skin color. Both the verses "I am black, but comely," (1:5, KJV) and "Look not upon me, for I am black" (1:6) could easily connect to the murderous and ultimately forlorn love of Milkman's cousin and lover, Hagar, whom Milkman abandons for lighter-skinned women with "silky hair the color of a penny" (319). And the verses lamenting the singer's treatment at the hands of "my mother's children" also carry some relevance. "They made me keeper of the vineyard," says the poet, "but my own vineyard have I not kept." Pilate is a winemaker, and her father owned a farm, which he was not allowed to keep, which he was killed for operating too successfully. The narrator of the novel *Song of Solomon* emphasizes that to own the land one works is the great dream of Macon Dead's friends and neighbors, that he is the one who realizes this dream, and that it is that ownership and the message it sends which get Macon Dead murdered (237).

But we can go no further with the allusion of the title. Morrison provides us with no indication whatsoever that we are to look to the Bible for clues to the novel. Even so much as the above is more than the novel itself urges us to do. In fact, the name Solomon, when it comes up in the novel, is a distortion of Milkman's only ancestor with a real name, Shalimar. In fact in her conversation with the police, Pilate calls her non-existent husband Mr. Solomon, a name she says she used "cause he was such a dignified colored man" (208). Like the Matthew reference, the name Solomon is a red herring. It is the "flying African" Shalimar (325), disguised and dressed up in the clothes of a American black man trying his best to be "dignified," exactly what whites at once insist that he be and prevent him from being. Meanwhile the real Shalimar quite literally flies away. The title "Song of Solomon" is itself a disguise, only an apparent reference to the biblical book of the same name, in fact a reference to an entirely different story, unwritten; indeed, a song.

Robert Alter claims that allusion is a necessary component of all literature since "each stage of literature incorporates the previous stages, the impulse of literary creation being constantly self-recapitulative" (140). But Morrison has a grudge against literature, not against the process of creation but against the activity of reading and writing. Allusion to such texts as the Bible is exactly what this novel seeks to avoid. The entire story searches for some past which is authentic and powerful, to get out of the squelched almost-pride expressed in the name of Not Doctor Street—pride in a black man's ability to *almost* make it in the white world—and looks for an ancestor with a real name, a man with an amazing and African talent—namely, the ability to fly. The most admirable living character in the book has no navel, and she too is said to have the ability to fly, to break loose of the white world as it is and go where she will. This is what the novel seeks—a present freed of the white past, a present built on its own, African past. To this past, reading and writing are alien, and the process of literary allusion to which Alter refers is antithetical, for it connects the work to the wrong past. Allusion maintains continuity within the cultural heritage of texts. But these novels share with Larry Neal the sense that written literature is strictly a western enterprise, alien and irrelevant to African American culture in the sense that: "The text could be destroyed and no one would be hurt in the least by it" (Leitch: 337). This story does not want to build on the literary past of the West, but upon its own oral and musical African past, which, like Milkman, it first must find.

Many scholars and biblical critics have emphasized the role orality and illiteracy have played in the shaping of African American biblical interpretation. Renita Weems emphasizes that any effort to teach or to learn reading among blacks was forbidden by law. It is a consequence of that prohibition, says Weems, that African Americans have only recently acquired access to "many of the accoutrements of culture that cultivate and support reading," and that "many still view reading as an activity that is at once commendable and ominous" (60).

For Morrison, however, this is not the point. In *Beloved*, the slaves on the benevolent Garner plantation are invited to learn to read, "but they didn't want to, because nothing important to them could ever be put down on paper" (125). Baby Suggs, in other respects the same emblem of wisdom for *Beloved* that Pilate is for *Song of Solomon*, wishes that she could read the Bible "like real preachers." But when we hear about her sermons, it is clear that they are better off for their lack of biblical reference.

> She did not tell them to clean up their lives or to go and sin no more. She did not tell them they were the blessed of the earth, its inheriting meek or its glorybound pure. She told them the only grace they could have was the grace they could imagine. (88)

Baby Suggs wants to read the Bible, but her sermons speak to her community because she is free from the constraints of the text.

In the end, this is not so far from what Weems is saying. She points out that it was precisely because the Bible was an aural experience for most African Americans that the community felt free to interpret it for themselves, "without allegiance to any official text, translation, or interpretation" (61). Thus the way in which the Bible is interpreted depends for Weems on "one's overall disposition to the act of reading itself" (62). Morrison may be seen as taking this viewpoint to the extreme. The culture is so aural/oral in her novels that the Bible's text per se does not exist, interpretation is so free that it is not interpretation at all, and the central act of interpretation, the sermon, when authentic, bears no relationship whatsoever to any text.

For all this break with literary and biblical tradition, however, the novel *Beloved* cites the Bible in what is perhaps the plainest possible form of allusion, the epigraph.

> I will call them my people
> which were not my people;
> and her beloved,
> who was not beloved.
> Romans 9:25

Beloved, the ghost of a girl killed in infancy by her mother, goes by the name inscribed on her tombstone. Mistaken for a natural person for much of the book, she is called "Beloved" and appears never to have had any other name; the question this book asks is whether she was in fact beloved, by her mother and murderer.

In this novel, Morrison provides a metaphor for the African American woman's struggles with the past: the ghost of a child, killed as a sort of violent euthanasia, comes back to haunt its mother. "When the four horsemen came—one schoolteacher, one nephew, one slavecatcher, and a sheriff" (148), Sethe was forced to choose between allowing her children to return to a life of slavery or ending their lives in freedom. Her experience of the cruelties of slavery makes her wild enough to attempt to slit all of her children's throats before the apocalyptic horsemen can stop her.

The allusion to Revelation here is consistent with Morrison's anti-intertextuality: the men on horses notably do not stand on the side of ultimate justice. Rather, with the sheriff among them, they symbolize of the justice of the white legal system; the horsemen of a white apocalypse. More than that: the text, the myth of the apocalypse, becomes in this reference the property and the weapon of white authority.

Only one child, a daughter, dies by Sethe's hand; the rest survive and endure through their mother's jail sentence to grow up in freedom, having been effectively ruined as slaves by the attempted murder. The murder serves its intended purpose, in other words. Both mother and children remain free, and the baby girl is essentially sacrificed to the survival and freedom of the others. Although Sethe seems to have been correct that this was the only way out, the infant still haunts the survivors. Sethe did what she had to do to live through the past, but until Sethe turns her powers of destruction against the natural enemy, the ghost of what she had to do—her child—will neither leave her alone nor forgive her.

Like Pilate's name, Beloved's name is first of all a written word. When she first appears as an adult in the story, Beloved spells out the letters of her name as she introduces herself, and Paul D. recognizes "the careful enunciation of letters by those, like himself, who could not read, but had memorized the letters of their name" (52). Her name is, like Pilate's, a series of letters, in her case literally carved in stone—her headstone.

Her mother has paid the stonecutter with "ten minutes" in exchange for the writing of these letters, "her knees wide open as any grave" (5). Sethe wanted the stone to say "Dearly Beloved," the two words which together constituted "every word she had heard the preacher say at the funeral (and all there was to say, surely)" (5); but she does not think to offer the stonecutter another ten minutes for the word "dearly." She does this much: she sells herself to get her baby's headstone engraved with the most important word, "Beloved," as a way of proving that the child was in fact beloved.

But later Paul D., who was a slave with Sethe at the supposedly enlightened Garner plantation, wonders whether this kind of naming can create what it describes:

> Garner called and announced them men—but only on Sweet Home, and by his leave. Was he naming what he saw or creating what he did not? . . . Did a whiteman saying it make it so? Suppose Garner woke up one morning and changed his mind? Took the word away. (220)

The reader must wonder, does writing "Beloved" on a pink headstone make the murdered child beloved? More fundamentally, does God's promise, quoted in Romans that those who were neither beloved nor God's people will be called so, make any difference? Is it a promise of future comfort as compensation for the pains of the past? Or is it just a matter of semantics? Do words, even supposedly divine words, have the power to transform what is, or do they only obscure it?

In the end, the reader must conclude that Sethe did love the child she killed, however incompatible love and murder may seem. Yet the baby's name does not suffice to prove what it describes. "She thought it would be enough, rutting among the headstones with the engraver. . .That should certainly be enough" (5); but it is not, and a lengthy and nearly fatal haunting follows. Thus the Romans epigraph is thrown into profound ambiguity. Since Beloved actually is beloved, it makes sense to call her so. From this perspective the Romans passage becomes a sort of peacemaking with the past, a sending back into it of the love and respect it so sorely lacked. But to call her "Beloved" does not make her so, an idea that invades the Romans passage and makes it at least in one sense another meaningless white man's promise. God is heard saying how he will name the woman and the people who were unloved and neglected, but they remain the same people. The names have changed, but the relationship remains the same.

It is clearly dangerous in this novel to depend too much on a word, certainly a white person's word, because words, to the extent that they are self-conscious, written, laid out to be trusted or mistrusted, by definition work in the interests of whites.

For words to work for the enslaved and imprisoned African Americans in these novels, they must be turned on themselves, twisted, broken, and sent underground in codes understandable only to those who have ears to hear. On the chain gang in Alfred, Georgia, Paul D. and the others "sang it out and beat it up, garbling the words so that they could not be understood; tricking the words so their syllables yielded up other meanings" (108). Vincent Wimbush maintains that slavers purposely frustrated communication among the slaves, and that it was in response that some slaves adopted the language of the Bible, an acceptable vocabulary in which unacceptable things could be simultaneously hidden and expressed (82).

A well-known example of this is the double meaning of many spirituals, at once about physical escape to the North and spiritual escape to Jesus. When Sethe's husband first sees the signal for their escape to begin, he lets the others know by singing, "Hush, Hush. Somebody's calling my name. O my Lord, O my Lord, what shall I do?" (224). In subsequent verses of the song, it turns out to be Jesus who is calling; but those verses are never sung in this novel. The spiritual level of the song is here nothing but a ruse for the real meaning of escape. There is no double meaning, in the sense of two active meanings operating simultaneously; there is only a false and a true meaning. White people consistently do not know the real names of blacks, so that if someone is calling Halle's name, it is not likely to be anyone so pale as Jesus is said to be in these novels (Cf. 1977:115, where Guitar speaks of Jesus' "bleeding heart. His cute li'l old bleeding heart," and assures Milkman that Jesus was, if not white, certainly a northerner).

For Morrison, religious language—indeed language itself—is most meaningful when it is used for purposes other than those for which it was apparently intended. Meaningful words are those broken up to form other words: the spirituals used as a signal for escape, or, as in the naming of Pilate, the Bible used to say something bitterly opposed to the faith.

Significantly, from the moment of her father's death Pilate carries with her wherever she goes both his bones and the name which constitutes his one written word. Mistaken for gold by her nephew, the sack of bones is, like the name, not an inheritance of wealth, but simply an inheritance: the physical remains of the trouble and love that her father lived. She carries both all of her life—as one does carry one's own name—and when both the bones and the name are buried, Pilate herself is killed upon their grave by a young man with no patience for the burdens and twisted texts of the past.

There is no owning of this language of the Bible; it can be carried, used, taken apart and made into an earring, but it cannot be accepted as given. Like the sack of bones, the Bible is a sad and burdensome legacy. It is a reminder of past pain with no more life or use than the bones themselves; yet a legacy it is nevertheless. Its words pass through the hands and lips of the characters, but they remain always an alien, white language. In these novels, African Americans use the scripture sometimes for the same reason they use English—because all other language has been stolen from them—and sometimes because it will enable them to get their relatives out of jail. They do not use it because they themselves believe in it, and at no point do they read it.

Here, as it does so often, the Bible acts as a metonym for all texts, and for textuality. Texts in their own right, these novels strain against what is forced upon them by that identity, as their African American characters struggle against the givens of being African American. In both cases, the struggle is against the literary and experiential fact of what has been and its presence in what is, or in what is written. Intertextuality has to do not only with literary heritage or relationship; it also involves, as is clear in *Beloved*, issues of power and culture. Texts and readers have real and not only literary pasts; both bear scars from the conflicted history of their relatedness.

When Milkman sums up his troubles by admitting that he does not like his name, Guitar informs him, "Niggers get their names the same way they get everything else—the best way they can. The best way they can." Milkman asks, "Why can't we get our stuff the right way?" But Guitar assures him, "The best way is the right way" (88). The Bible, however mute and alien, is, according to these novels, part of the way black people have gotten their names—it is part of how these characters came to be who they are. As such, it has been a means to the end of survival, not an ideal or desirable means, but a means that came to hand. It is only to the extent that "the best way is the right way," that the Bible earns a place in these stories at all.

WORKS CONSULTED

Alter, Robert
    1989   *The Pleasures of Reading in an Ideological Age*. New York: Simon and Schuster.

Leitch, Vincent B.
    1988   *American Literary Criticism from the 1930s to the 1980s*. New York: Columbia University Press.

Morrison, Toni.
    1988   *Beloved*. New York: Plume.
    1981   *Tar Baby*. New York: Signet.
    1977   *Song of Solomon*. New York: Signet.

Weems, Renita.
    1991   "Reading *Her Way* through the Struggle: African American Women and the Bible." Pp. 57–77 in *Stony the Road We Trod*. Ed. Cain Hope Felder. Minneapolis: Fortress.

Wimbush, Vincent.
    1991   "The Bible and African-Americans: An Outline of an Interpretative History." Pp. 81–97 in *Stony the Road We Trod*. Ed. Cain Hope Felder. Minneapolis: Fortress.

TEXTS, MORE TEXTS,
A TEXTUAL READER AND A TEXTUAL WRITER

Peter D. Miscall
Iliff School of Theology

ABSTRACT

I reread my first works that deal with parallels between stories within Genesis-Kings. I was more interested in proving that the parallels were "really there" than with the phenomenon of intertextuality. At one level, intertextuality is reading two or more texts together and in light of each other; the bases for the reading and the effects on understanding the texts develop mutually. Intertextuality is not a staged process in which one first proves the parallels and then assesses their impact. To assess the phenomenon of intertextuality, I revisit the tale of David in 2 Sam 23:13–17 and enter the realm of intertexts. The realm includes both biblical texts and other critical texts and I find no clear distinction between primary and secondary texts. I as reader am part of the web; the "I" who reads the text is already a plurality of other texts. Finally, I as writer am part of the intertextual world as I write yet another text to take its place in and over against other texts.

---

1. INTRODUCTION: RETROSPECTIVE

In my first published works on biblical narrative (1978, 1979, 1983), I was concerned with tracing and evaluating parallels and analogies between separate stories within the larger corpus of Genesis-Kings; I spoke of a series or group of parallels as a web or a network (1983:14). I was influenced by Robert Alter's notion of "narrative analogy," the literary aspect of biblical narrative "through which one part of the text provides oblique commentary on another" (1981:21; cited in Miscall, 1978:28–29). I was also inspired by Robert Polzin's structuralist analyses, particularly that of the three wife-sister stories in Genesis 12, 20, and 26 (Miscall, 1979).[1]

My focus was mainly on material in Genesis and 1–2 Samuel with secondary attention given to stories in Judges and 1 Kings. These are all

---

[1] Anticipating my discussion, I note the complexity of the fact that I was citing Alter from separate articles in *Commentary* and *Critical Inquiry* that were subsequently included as chapters in *The Art of Biblical Narrative* (see Alter's Preface: xi). Further, in "Literary Unity" I was discussing Polzin's study of the wife-sister stories; Polzin, in turn, responds to my article in that issue of *Semeia*.

part of the one corpus, Genesis-Kings, which I considered and still consider to be the post-exilic work of "one author." (The last phrase is in quotation marks because I am no longer so sure of what authorship meant or entailed in ancient Judah.) Therefore, I was comparing and contrasting parts of the same text to arrive at better and more comprehensive readings of that text.

I viewed this analytic tool as a two-staged process. First, I had to demonstrate or prove a basis for comparing the texts at hand through noting similar words, themes, structures, or such. Then I would move to showing the significance of the parallels for understanding one or more of the individual stories in question. Although I became a little more complex in my analyses in *Workings of Old Testament Narrative*, I was still quite limited in my approach. A network of parallels would be established between particular narrative texts and its significance was then assessed mainly through thematic impact and relevance. The parallels clarified, enriched, or even complicated and confused the reading of the story that served as the study's focal, starting point.

With hindsight I can say that I had some anxiety about what I was doing, that I was anticipating readers of my text who were trained in traditional biblical studies and who would, I thought, demand such a multi-staged process: prove that the analogies are "really there" and then assess their impact. On the other hand, I was deeply involved in intertextuality and intertextual reading and writing without being explicitly aware that I was. At one point in *Workings* I use the term, but only to disclaim any such study.

> My focus has been on the "textuality" of the text . . . Because of the restriction of my reading to selected passages and their parallels . . . I have given little attention to the closely related, if not synonymous, notion of "intertextuality," i.e., a given text exists because of its differences from and relations to the network(s) of other texts. . . . this is a topic for future consideration. (139–40)

That future is now, but a major point of this essay is that I was already giving that notion not a little attention. In this article I want to reflect on a particular set of parallels treated in *Workings*, on how and why that analysis has changed over the intervening years, and on how a certain notion of intertextuality casts this look back on my work in a light very different from that implied in a phrase such as "how my ideas and work have developed."

2. David and the Well: Sacramental Solidarity or Brutality?

The story I focus on is related in 2 Sam 23:13–17.[2] David is in his stronghold at Adullam and the Philistines are garrisoned at Bethlehem. David thirsts and desires.

> "I wish someone would get me water to drink from the well of Bethlehem that is by the gate." Three warriors broke through the Philistine camp; they drew water from the well of Bethlehem that is by the gate and brought it to David. But he was not willing to drink it and poured it out to the Lord, and said. "Far be it from me, O Lord, that I should do this. Can I drink the blood of the men who went at the risk of their lives?" Therefore he was not willing to drink it.

I was drawn to the story because it contains elements of Alter's betrothal type scene, the "encounter with the future betrothed at a well." He analyzes the meetings between Abraham's servant and Rebekah (Gen 24:10–61), Jacob and Rachel (29:1–20), Moses and Zipporah (Exod 2:15–21) and Ruth and Boaz (Ruth 2). The main elements of the type-scene include the encounter with the woman or women at a well, the drawing of water, the woman's (women's) rushing home with the news of the meeting and, finally, the conclusion of the betrothal usually after an invitation to a meal (52). He notes that David's betrothals

> all involve bloodshed, . . . : the 200 Philistines he slaughters in battle as the bride-price for Michal; his threat to kill Nabal, Abigail's husband, . . . ; and his murder of the innocent Uriah . . . Are these betrothals by violence a deliberate counterpoint to the pastoral motif of betrothal after the drawing of water? (61; cited in Miscall, 1978:89)

I related the 2 Samuel tale to the type-scene on the basis of the two elements of drawing water from a well and giving water to drink. But this water is not drunk; at the time I did not notice the inversion of the motif, "the invitation to a meal."

David pours out the water while proclaiming his oath and I commented:

> The event is usually interpreted as an indication of the fierce loyalty of David's men to him, and of David's appreciation of such loyalty and daring (1983:90).

This is a possible reading, but it "has to exclude the possibility that the men's daring is in response to a petty desire; it is not daring, but foolhardiness" (90). The pouring out can be of water or of blood; the latter reading is based on a parallel with the wise woman of Tekoa's statement to

---

[2] The discussion of the story and the parallels is in 1983: 88–95.

Joab, "We must all die, we are like water spilt on the ground, which cannot be gathered up again" (2 Sam 14:14).

In *Workings* I develop the themes of blood and betrothal through brief discussions of Shimei's curse on David, the man of blood (2 Sam 16:7-8), David's command to Solomon to kill Shimei (1 Kgs 2:9), David's killing and circumcising of 200 Philistines for Michal's hand (1 Sam 18:20-28) and the Lord's attempt to murder Moses (Exod 4:25-26). Zipporah foils the attempt with a circumcision and calls Moses (?) "a bridegroom of blood"; the phrase is an accurate description of David in 1 Samuel 18. I continue to develop a "complicated web or webs of analogies" (89) by including Genesis 34, the rape of Dinah which is marked by intermarriage, circumcision and violence; this is paralleled by Amnon's rape of Tamar in 2 Samuel 13. These, and other parallel texts, intone themes of family violence, murder and threats to the existence of the family, and I employ the themes as the main point or significance of the parallels.

I could easily expand this analysis by extending and detailing the comparison and contrast of the network of parallels in the manner of most of the articles in *Reading Between Texts*. However, I want to look at an issue that permeates the biblical and the secondary texts, Alter's and mine, but that is not focussed on, if even seen, in the latter. This is the presence (or absence) of women and their roles, often active and positive,[3] in the series of parallel texts that were established beginning with Alter's betrothal scene. Even though a betrothal involves both a man and a woman, Alter and I talk as though the stories were about only the man, the hero.[4] Thanks to the burgeoning number of studies of the last 15 to 20 years that focus on women and gender-related issues and themes, this is no longer the case. The number of women and men raising the issues and the number of articles and books published are far too many for me to list; Trible, Exum, Fewell, Eskenazi, and Bal have had the largest and earliest impact on my writing. Indeed I contributed an article, "Michal and Her Sisters," to the volume on Queen Michal co-edited by Tamara Eskenazi; in that article I attempt to place the women of the David story at the center of the reading.

In my first works, in comparing and contrasting texts within a network of parallels, I frequently used commonalities to highlight differences between the texts. However, in these tales of betrothals and of women

---

[3] Two notable examples are Zipporah and Abigail, both of whom save the "hero," respectively Moses and David. When the Lord seeks to kill Moses, Zipporah acts quickly and decisively. "Zipporah took a flint; she cut her son's foreskin; she touched his feet; she said, 'You are a bridegroom of blood for me'" (Exod 4:25).

[4] Alter (52-53) describes the betrothal type-scene as an encounter with a "girl or girls." I originally cited this without comment; in this article, I refer to the meeting with a "woman" or with "women."

and men, especially those involving Moses, Saul and David, the common features of the subservient role and the harsh treatment of women stand out. From the point of view of the women, there is a terrible sameness to the texts. Women, regardless of their contribution to the life and status of the "heroes," quickly recede into the background and can be readily given to or taken from men by other men.[5]

Brueggemann, in reference to the story in 2 Sam 23:13–17, speaks in glowing terms of David's men who "must have *adored* him all the more [my emphasis]" after David's "magnificent gesture of solidarity," his

> act of sacramental imagination, ... No doubt this story is told to enhance the greatness of David.... He has a longing (a desire, if not a need), and he is intimate with his men ... They are his comrades in arms, not his servants. (391)

This is the most positive reading of the episode that I know of. However, from the point of view of women, or rather from that of the total absence of women from 2 Sam 21:15–24:25, this sounds more like male bonding and the solidarity of an old boys' network.[6] In this context, my negative reading (1983:91), i.e. that David "mindlessly and needlessly spill[s] others' blood for his own purposes," is given an added cutting edge. Essentially we could say that David treats others similarly, whether men or women. Brueggemann, then, has it wrong. For David, as for other ancient kings, "in high royal theology, the others exist for the sake of the king," and David does assume "that he is entitled to the benefit of the service and risk of others" (391) regardless of the outcome for the others.[7]

3. Intertextuality

I want now to look at the above discussion from the explicit point of view of intertextuality rather than from that of an expanded reading. For

---

[5] Both Linafelt and Miscall, 1991, treat the theme of "the taking of women as a sign of male power" (Linafelt: 99). Moses and David, despite all the other differences between them, share this disregard for women, especially wives. Zipporah and her two sons, Gershom and Eliezer, are dealt with in briefest form in Exod 2:15–22, 4:20, and 18:1–6. In the latter passage they are with Jethro when he comes to meet Moses but immediately disappear from the narrative. In 18:6 it is reported to Moses that Jethro is approaching "with your wife and her two sons," but in the next verse only Moses and Jethro greet each other. Wife-daughter and children have exited.

[6] Although it would go beyond Brueggemann's intent, in this mode of reading we could infer more from his phrase "intimate with his men."

[7] I am quoting Brueggemann against himself and out of context; he denies that the cited statements apply to David. I also note that the translation of *yit awweh*, David's initial feeling and motivation—longing, desire or need in Brueggemann, myself, and others—can be given a negative twist as crave or covet (see Num 11:4, 34; Deut 5:18; 12:20; Ps 106:14; Prov 13:4; 21:16).

me, at present, intertextuality and intertextual reading are richer and more complex concepts and praxes than the establishment and thematic assessment of the existence of a few parallel or analogous texts. Gayatri Spivak defines intertextuality as "the interweaving of different texts (literally 'web'-s) in an act of criticism that refuses to think of 'influence' or 'interrelationship' as simple historical phenomena" (Translator's Preface to Derrida: lxxxiv).[8] In her introduction, Danna Nolan Fewell states that

> the basic force of intertextuality is to problematize, even spoil, textual boundaries, those lines of demarcation which allow a reader to talk about *the* meaning, subject, or origin of a writing. Such borders, intertextuality asserts, are never solid or stable. Texts are always spilling over into other texts. Miscall puts it nicely (in this volume): "No text is an island." (1992:22–23; author's emphasis)

Quoting a passage that quotes myself is already an example of intertextuality.

Intertextual reading takes us into the realm of the "general text" in which Derrida's debated maxim finds its home. "There is *nothing* outside of the text [there is no outside-text; *il n'y a pas de hors-texte*]" (158; author's emphasis). On the other hand, as Beal reminds us,

> For the practice of intertextual reading, however, as opposed to theories of intertextuality, one must have such lines of delimitation, no matter how arbitrarily they may be set, and no matter how quickly they may be transgressed. That is, no intertextual reading can choose the "general text" everything, all at once, everywhere—as its object of interpretation. (28)

This returns us to the reader who must decide what limits are to be placed on what is to be read and how it is to be read. The "what" and the "how" can also be called "the text" and "the method," but with the understanding that intertextuality, as theory and as praxis, questions the status of this distinction. In other words, the reader reads texts and pro-

---

[8] Shoshana Felman's "Turning the Screw of Interpretation" is a masterful example of an intertextual reading that reads Henry James's ghostly short story, "The Turn of the Screw," along with texts by Freud, Lacan, and Edmund Wilson, a "Freudian" interpreter of the short story. Her goal is to read the texts together and to let them "read" each other; she is not proposing a new Freudian or Lacanian interpretation that will be better than and will displace those of Wilson and others.

I cite her on page 9 of *Workings* in reference to the establishment of some pattern or meaning, some truth, of a text which is unavoidable if we are to read any text. However, she argues, "Freud has raised, and taught us to articulate [another question]: what does such "truth" (or any truth) leave out? What is it made to miss? . . . What, precisely, is its residue, the remainder it does not account for?" (Felman: 117; author's emphasis). Citing her had an effect in my text that I missed; I did not account for her intertextual reading and its presence in my work.

duces readings that are produced, published, as other texts; these texts and the other texts are, in turn, read by other readers who produce yet other texts.[9]

In both *Workings* and *1 Samuel*, I was uneasy with this role of the reader and tried to locate the undecidability and ambiguity of my readings in the text; it was still greatly a matter of proving that these features are really there and arguing that my deconstructive method permitted me finally to see them. However, intertextual reading works as a "staged process" in only a preliminary and provisional way. As one reads a given text in the light of another or other texts—I deliberately use "in the light of" as inclusive of any type of comparison and contrast—the "reasons" for associating the texts and the "effects" on the reading and understanding of them develop in a reciprocal fashion that leads to a blurring of any hard and fast distinction between "reasons" (bases) and "effects."[10] It also renders provisional attempts to regard one text as *the* text and then to assess the effects of parallels with other texts on this one main text.

4. The Intertextual Reader

Roland Barthes' work can be perceived as an extended and complex meditation on the active role of the reader in reading; he consistently argues against considering interpretation as a passive reception of the objective meanings or truths of a text. For my purposes I focus on *S/Z*, his close reading of Balzac's short story "Sarrasine."[11]

Barthes is concerned with the text as a plurality, both on the level of the signifier (language; the words on the page) and the signified (the meaning[s]; interpretation). He doesn't want reading and interpretation to stop because the analyst, the reader, has established the meaning, the truth, of the text. Nor should it stop at the level of the signifier with the establishment of a "final ensemble, . . . an ultimate structure." Barthes

---

[9] In the contemporary academic world, the latter can exist in oral form as delivered at a scholarly convention, in written form whether published or privately distributed or in some electronic form whether on disk or recorded. CD/ROM and electronic mail are only beginning to make themselves felt; in a few years an article such as this will probably spend half or more of its space discussing these forms of text. For the present I focus on texts published in "hard form."

[10] One can read texts together, e.g. Job and Stephen King as in Schlobin, simply because they seem to have little or nothing in common. Does the reader then discover or create the meanings derived from the association?

[11] Although I don't cite it in the text of the article, I insert Barthes' text, *The Pleasure of the Text*, into my text through this note, through the bibliography and through Jane Gallop's *Thinking Through the Body*, much of which is a reading of Barthes' book. The complexity of (inter)textuality is evident in my fourfold use of the word "text" with four different meanings, in this note.

maintains that classical rhetoric, which includes much contemporary literary criticism, accomplishes this by "structuring this text in large masses" (11–12). Large scale divisions of the text can give the illusion that the text has been deciphered, its hidden meanings finally revealed. Such a classical reader severely limits how the text is read and what other texts may play a role in the interpretation. (Despite and probably because of my obsession with undecidability and ambiguity in *Workings* and *1 Samuel*, I was a classical reader who decidedly found undecidability in the text.)

Barthes, to counter this, opts for a reading that proceeds more slowly, step-by-step, and that

> cut[s] up [the text] into a series of brief, contiguous fragments, which we shall call *lexias*, since they are units of reading. This cutting up, admittedly, will be arbitrary in the extreme; it will imply no methodological responsibility, since it will bear on the signifier. (13; author's emphasis)

The lexias are "artificial articulations" of the text made "without any regard for its natural divisions (syntactical, rhetorical, anecdotic)" (14–15). Within these variable and arbitrary dissections of the text, Barthes locates, at the level of the signified, his five codes.[12]

The codes are not objective listings or paradigms that serve to decode the text and to order its meanings in clear form. A code is intertextual.

> The code is a perspective of quotations, a mirage of structures; . . . they are so many fragments of something that has always been *already* read, seen, done, experienced; the code is the wake of that *already*. (20; author's emphasis)

The fragments can derive from other written texts, and Barthes fills his analysis of Sarrasine with references to literature stretching from the classics to the 20th century. Or they can derive from "the Book (of culture, of life, of life as culture)" (21). This is Barthes' concept that is analogous to that of the "general text," and his analysis constantly refers to all sorts of general and scientific knowledge that is available in a culture both within and beyond books.

He uses different metaphors or images, e.g. music and painting, to refer to the text as this ensemble of codes. I want to focus on one of them. Codes are "voices out of which the text is woven" (21); each code is a thread that is woven, braided, by writer and reader, with the other threads to form the text, the braid, the fabric (160). "The text is a tissue of

---

[12] These are: the hermeneutic code which poses a question and its eventual answer; the semantic code which deals with character and thematics; to some extent it overlaps with the symbolic code which deals with theme and structuring elements; the proairetic code which is action and plot; and finally the cultural code which refers to traditional, gnomic, cultural, and scientific knowledge (17–21).

quotations drawn from the innumerable centres of culture" (1977:146). Etymologically text, texture, and tissue derive from the Latin *texere*, to weave. To weave implies threads, plurality, process, and (in)substantiality (text and tissue). A reader such as Barthes is just as much a weaver of the text as the author; he both traces threads (codes) that are already there and, at the same time, weaves another text with his own threads.

There is a heavy emphasis on the reader and the reader's active contribution to the production of textual meaning in contemporary biblical studies. However,

> this "I" that approaches the text is already itself a plurality of other texts, of codes which are infinite or, more precisely, lost (whose origin is lost). (Barthes, 1974:10)

How one reads depends on what one has read. This would be a different article if I wasn't reading and re-reading Barthes; if, for example, I were using Kristeva or Derrida as my major "intertexts."

These other texts and codes, these other threads, are infinite, their origins lost. That is, "I," as reader, am not in a privileged position of a transcendental perspective or viewpoint from which I can gaze upon and gather up all the threads that go into the weaving of this particular textual carpet or tapestry. As reader I am formed by these threads; I am part of the fabric whether warp or woof. I cannot return to the opening analysis of this article and sort out the varied contributions from what I did and am now doing, and what others, whether Alter, Fewell, or Brueggemann, did; I cannot unravel that fabric. Is that analysis a (re)reading of my earlier work, of 2 Sam 23:13–17 in light of my later work and that of others, of my present work in light of my previous work, or perhaps a (re)reading of Brueggemann in light of Felman? (The latter two possibilities subvert the typically firm chronological and developmental criterion.)

Barthes, all other readers, and I are intertextual readers. We live and work in an intertextual universe in which we weave and are woven from the threads that cross and recross to form particular texts and particular readers. There are no absolute or final beginning or ending points. Readers both discern the figure in the carpet and are discerned as the figure in the carpet.

5. The Critical Text As Intertext

> Any literary work, ... exists in relation to other works.... These "other works" can be expanded to include critical writing about literature. In a standard view, criticism is about literature and is therefore a totally separate genre of writing. Literature is creative and original; criticism is secondary and parasitic. Much biblical commentary is based on this view. In a newer

view, whose proponents would claim reflects much critical practice from the inception of literary criticism, the separation is not so radical or distinct. Criticism has its own creative impulses; it is a conversation partner with literature and not a mere neutral observer. Literary writers are affected by critics just as much as the latter by the former.... I bring this ... discussion to a close with the image of a literary world peopled with writers, both literary and critical, and their works, all existing in a complicated network of relations. This is not a closed or finished network; ... another work, literary or critical, is always to be written and added to that world. (Miscall, 1992a:41)

The present essay is part of the textual and literary world. It is an intertext just as much as any biblical or other literary text. It is not a separate work, a non-textual study of texts that can speak definitively about what is happening in those texts. This textual existence is embodied in this article through its dominant concern with critical texts, with "the secondary literature," including many of my own—"my own" is, of course, a textual concept and not a claim to inalienable possession. "My" texts that "I" now read are just as much a part of the textual realm as any other texts.

My understanding and reading of Genesis–Kings will have changed and will continue to change because I read and reread other texts, whether they are considered primary or secondary, literary or critical, and early or late. Intertextuality and intertextual reading question and blur these usually sharp distinctions based on genre and chronology.[13] We can't regard a text as fixed in its significance, as subsequently built on, gone beyond, and superseded. Second, they will have changed because "I," who approach the text, am already a plurality of other texts, a fabric or tissue woven from the threads drawn from the texture of these texts or from their unravelling.

The above discussion of how my understanding of 2 Samual 23:13–17 has broadened was done in textual terms of written texts, including the present one which presents the expanded reading. At the same time, the textual or textural image, as I've questioned previously, renders it obvious that this description of the first part of this essay, "how my understanding of 2 Samual 23:13–17 has broadened," is at best partial and provisional.[14]

---

[13] Gallop deals with an analogous situation when she proposes a "literary reading" of Freud's psychoanalytic texts that are generally considered scientific and nonliterary. Her discussion makes a distinction similar to that of Barthes' between "large masses" and "step-by-step" reading. Annexing Freud's writing to the realm of the literary transgresses the boundary between literary and nonliterary texts. In place of a difference between genres, we have a difference between two kinds of reading: literary and nonliterary. Literary reading here implies painstaking regard for a plurality of signification; nonliterary reading demands reduction to a manipulable sense in the service of efficient use (22).

[14] The word "discussion" itself is an apt example of what Barthes calls "structuring [the] text in large masses" as a way of limiting and controlling the plural-

> If a literary work can serve to defamiliarize our views and notions of reality and of other literature, then criticism can serve to defamiliarize our views and ways of reading given literary works, especially works that are comfortable because we [think we] know how to read them. (Miscall, 1992a:42)

This can be more complicated and the boundaries between literary and critical texts further destabilized. All texts that a reader reads can defamiliarize each other. My reading critical texts affects my reading of both the biblical texts and the many critical studies of them and of the other critical studies of them. (The indeterminate antecedent[s] of "them" mark the flux of intertextuality.) As one critic put it, "No text is an island."

This view upsets any simple developmental or linear model that sees reading and interpretation as always moving forward, as growing in awareness and precision and as coming ever closer to the essential meaning of a given text or group of texts. (I point out these mixed metaphors that are often used in developmental models.) To use my main image, this model speaks of itself tracing the main thread of a text or of a historical progression of texts; the thread should lead to the center of the text. However, J. Hillis Miller has already shown that the image, usually of Ariadne's thread through the Labyrinth, involves the construction of the Labyrinth just as much as it does tracing an already constructed maze. To put it in my terms, to trace a thread(s) is to weave a new text(ure).[15]

6. The Intertextual Writer

However, I, this reader of so many texts, biblical and critical, am also a writer who is writing yet another text, who is weaving yet another fabric or tissue (the individual readers of this article can decide which) from the threads of so many other texts. (Have the other text(ure)s therefore unravelled?)

> This is an opening for Harold Bloom's theory (and practice) of reading and writing, a theory that speaks ... of the anxiety of influence, of the burdensome feeling of belatedness (of coming too late on the scene) and of the conflict with a precursor.... For Bloom, writing and reading, which are two sides of the same coin, are dominated not by establishing meaning and truth but by confrontation with another.... The writer seeks to establish himself over against and in place of the other text.... The new text can be written only by dispossessing and displacing the former, the precursor. (Miscall, 1992b:45–46)

---

ity of text and reading. "Discussion" reduces a lengthy segment of text to one unit that can then have one purpose, to present my broadened understanding through an expanded reading.

[15] As with Felman (see n. 8), Miller has a presence in *Workings*, pp. 3–4, but I did not develop the intertextual effect.

As noted above, in my earlier work I wrote with some anxiety since my studies were departing from what was usually published in biblical journals and series. I was attempting to displace the former and yet, in anticipation of my readers, was casting much of my argument in the expected form of demonstrating what was really in the text and then assessing the features that I had isolated. Now I write in a radically changed situation. In the last decade, literary critical studies—I use the phrase in a general, inclusive sense—have carved out their own place in biblical studies and are now forming their own textual realm as a distinct part of contemporary biblical studies. (I note the violence of the image of "carving" in contrast to that of "weaving," and also note that although this place is distinct, it is still a part of this larger realm.)

I now write with another set of concerns and anxieties. How do I write, how do I dare write, in this expansive realm in which so much (everything?) has already been said? The concern is first with the bare event of writing, with the production of yet another text, and not with the content of that writing, not with the question, "What can I say?" Nevertheless as I have written this essay, woven this fabric, I have accomplished this event of writing and have, in the process, said something. But what have I said? How do I justify an article to be published in *Semeia: An Experimental Journal in Biblical Criticism* when I speak so little about the biblical text?

How do I write, how do I say something different—and it is different, not new—when so many of the precursor texts are my own? How do I write when to do so is to displace and dispossess myself? I write from a different site in the textual world. I who read and write am now another "I," a new plurality of other texts, a different fabric or tissue woven from threads crossing over and through all these texts. Perhaps I read and write now and include texts and threads from the previous writings and readings of Miscall and many others.

Works Consulted

Alter, Robert
    1981   *The Art of Biblical Narrative*. New York: Basic.

Bal, Mieke
    1987   *Lethal Love: Feminist Literary Readings of Biblical Love Stories*. Bloomington: Indiana University Press.

Barthes, Roland,
- 1974   *S/Z*. Trans. R. Miller. New York: Hill and Wang.
- 1975   *The Pleasure of the Text*. Trans. R. Miller. New York: Hill and Wang.
- 1977   "The Death of the Author." Pp. 142–48 in *Image Music Text*. Trans. S. Heath. New York: Hill and Wang.

Beal, Timothy K.
- 1992   "Ideology and Intertextuality: Surplus of Meaning and Controlling the Means of Production." Pp. 27–39 *Reading Between Texts: Intertextuality and the Hebrew Bible*. LCBI. Ed. Danna Nolan Fewell. Louisville: Westminister/John Knox.

Bloom, Harold
- 1973   *The Anxiety of Influence: A Theory of Poetry*. New York: Oxford University Press.
- 1982   *The Breaking of the Vessels*. The Wellek Library Lectures. Chicago: University of Chicago Press.

Brueggemann, Walter
- 1988   "2 Samuel 21–24: An Appendix of Deconstruction?" *CBQ* 50:383–97.

Clines, D.J.A. and T.C. Eskenazi, eds.
- 1991   *Telling Queen Michal's Story. An Experiment in Comparative Interpretation*. Sheffield: JSOT.

Derrida, Jacques
- 1976   *Of Grammatology*. Trans. Gayatri C. Spivak. Baltimore: Johns Hopkins University Press.

Exum, J. Cheryl and Johanna W.H. Bos, eds.
- 1988   *Reasoning With The Foxes: Female Wit in a World of Male Power. Semeia* 42.

Felman, Shoshana
- 1977   "Turning the Screw of Interpretation." *Yale French Studies* 55/56:94–207.

Fewell, Danna Nolan
- 1987   "Feminist Reading of the Hebrew Bible: Affirmation, Resistance and Transformation." *JSOT* 39:77–87.

Fewell, Danna Nolan, ed.
- 1992   *Reading Between Texts: Intertextuality and the Hebrew Bible*. LCBI. Louisville: Westminster/John Knox.

Gallop, Jane
- 1988   *Thinking Through the Body*. New York: Columbia University Press.

Linafelt, Tod
- 1992   "Taking Women in Samuel: Readers/Responses/Responsibility." Pp. 99–113 in *Reading Between Texts: Intertextuality and the Hebrew Bible*. LCBI. Ed. Danna Nolan Fewell. Louisville: Westminster/John Knox.

Miller, J. Hillis
    1978   "Ariadne's Thread: Repetition and the Narrative Line." Pp. 148–66 in *Interpretations of Narrative*. Ed. M.J. Valdés and O.J. Miller. Toronto: University of Toronto Press.

Miscall, Peter D.
    1978   "The Jacob and Joseph Stories as Analogies." *JSOT* 6:28–40.
    1979   "Literary Unity in Old Testament Narrative." *Semeia* 15:27–44.
    1983   *The Workings of Old Testament Narrative*. Chico, CA/Philadelphia: Scholars and Fortress.
    1986   *1 Samuel: A Literary Reading*. Bloomington: University of Indiana Press.
    1991   "Michal and Her Sisters." Pp. 225–38 in *Telling Queen Michal's Story*. Ed. D.J.A. Clines and T.C. Eskenazi. Sheffield: JSOT.
    1992a   "Biblical Narrative and Categories of the Fantastic." *Semeia* 60:39–51.
    1992b   "Isaiah: New Heavens, New Earth, New Book." Pp. 41–56 in *Reading Between Texts: Intertextuality and the Hebrew Bible*. LCBI. Ed. Danna Nolan Fewell. Louisville: Westminster/John Knox.
    1993   "Moses and David: Myth and Monarchy." Pp. 184–200 in *The New Literary Criticism and the Hebrew Bible*. Ed. J.C. Exum and D.J.A. Clines. Sheffield: JSOT.

Polzin, Robert
    1975   "'The Ancestress of Israel in Danger' in Danger." *Semeia* 3:81–98.
    1979   "Literary Unity in Old Testament Narrative: A Response." *Semeia* 15:45–50.

Schlobin, Roger C.
    1992   "Prototypic Horror: The Genre of the Book of Job." *Semeia* 60:23–38.

Tolbert, Mary Ann, ed.
    1983   *The Bible and Feminist Hermeneutics*. *Semeia* 28.

Trible, Phyllis
    1978   *God and The Rhetoric of Sexuality*. Philadelphia: Fortress.
    1984   *Texts of Terror: Literary-Feminist Readings of Biblical Narratives*. Philadelphia: Fortress.

JESUS' FRANKNESS[1]

George Aichele
Adrian College

ABSTRACT

I begin with a consideration of the use of the word παρρησία ("frankly") in Mark 8:32, in what is often regarded as a crucial episode in that Gospel. This word seems out of place in the Markan narration of Jesus' discourse—indeed it appears only here in Mark, and not at all in the synoptic parallels. Furthermore, Jesus speaks "frankly" in this text about the "son of man," a phrase which is troublesome and ambiguous in Mark, and this in turn reinforces the strangeness of his "frank" speech. I argue that Barthes's analysis of connotation, when applied to the Markan text, shows that Jesus' frankness disguises an almost complete lack of denotation—to the theologically naive reader (Barthes's "Martian"), Jesus' indirect speech about the son of man is meaningless. Only the reader who is experienced in the theological conventions of Christianity can understand the saying as "natural." This has considerable implications for a theology of the text and of reading.

THE DISCOURSE OF JESUS

> ... he began to explain to them that the son of man must suffer much and be rejected by the elders and the high priests and the scribes, and be killed, and rise up after three days. He was telling them frankly. (Mark 8:31–32a)

The first of Jesus' three passion predictions in the Gospel of Mark comes immediately after Peter identifies Jesus as "the Christ" and immediately before the exchange of rebukes which ends when Jesus identifies Peter as "Satan." The larger unit which contains this passage, the dialogue of Jesus and the disciples at Caesarea Philippi, has often been regarded as a hinge joining together the two halves of Mark. In the first half of this Gospel, Jesus reveals himself to both demons and disciples as the miraculously powerful son of God, in Galilee and its vicinity. However, in the second half of Mark, Jesus moves with increasing weakness and frustration toward apparent defeat and death in Jerusalem.

---

[1] An earlier version of this essay appeared in the 1992 *SBL Seminar Papers* (Atlanta: Scholars). A version of this essay will appear as a chapter in my forthcoming *Jesus Framed*. Biblical Limits. New York: Routledge.

This brief passage would thus appear to be a crucial one, a turning point both in the identification of Jesus and in the plot of Mark's story. Its significance is both theological and narratological. This makes particularly troublesome the ambiguities which pervade the passage, two of which are of interest here: first, that Jesus was speaking the saying (τον λογὸν ἐλάλει) "frankly" to the disciples, and second, that anyone could speak frankly of "the son of man."

Why is it strange and confusing that Jesus should speak "frankly" (παρρησία) to his disciples? The translation in which this word appears is that of Richmond Lattimore. Both the Revised Standard Version and the New English Bible translate παρρησία as "plainly"; others use "openly" (Jerusalem Bible, Scholars Version) or "very clear" (Today's English Version). "Frankly" as used in this text is unusual in American English as I know it; thus I think that it is appropriate that Lattimore used "frankly" in Mark 8:32, for only in Mark is Jesus' frankness unusual, and therefore remarkable. In his translation of the Gospel of John, Lattimore never once translates παρρησία as "frankly;" he prefers instead what seem to me to be words that are more common in such contexts, such as "openly," "plainly," or "in public."

This is the only time that the word παρρησία appears in Mark. It stands in opposition to the parabolic speech which Jesus reserves for "those who are outside" in order to keep them from understanding (Mark 4:11–12). Several times in Mark Jesus draws the disciples away from the crowd, in order to explain to them (frankly?) what he has been talking about. In similar fashion, at various points in the text the narrator interrupts the story to explain to the reader what Jesus' words mean.

Yet if Mark is frank with the reader at these points, it is no more so than Jesus is with the disciples. In Mark, the disciples are stupid and resistant to whatever Jesus says, for his statements to them as well as to the crowd are ambiguous and paradoxical throughout Mark. Like the disciples, the implied reader of Mark is an insider, privy to explanation of the sayings, but also requiring the explanations. Does the reader understand the sayings any better than the disciples do? Is the reader the true insider of Mark's text? Or is the reader finally just as stupid, confused, and fearful as the disciples are? In Mark it is outsiders such as the Syrophoenician woman (7:24–30) and the scribe (12:28–34) who appear to understand Jesus best.

The very notion that Jesus says anything frankly runs up against one of the more important dimensions of Mark's narrative—what biblical scholarship has long described as the "messianic secret." It's not entirely clear in what sense there is a "secret" in the Gospel of Mark, or what the secret is, but Mark's Jesus is an enigmatic character, the meaning of whose words and the nature of whose deeds are often indeterminable. Thus it is odd that Mark would have Jesus speak frankly (or "plainly" or "openly").

In Matthew and Luke the disciples are much more likely to understand and to approve of Jesus' words than in Mark. However, neither Matthew nor Luke ever uses παρρησία. The fact that both Matthew and Luke have parallels to the Caesarea Philippi episode, and yet both omit παρρησία, is significant. The relation between Jesus and his disciples is from the beginning of these Gospels depicted as a frank one, and the use of this term would therefore be redundant.

There may also be in Mark's use of παρρησία an echo of the speech of the post-resurrection, "living" Christ—a discourse which, however, never appears in Mark's story.[2] Such speech is more typical of discourse gospels such as John,[3] and it stands in striking contrast to the ambiguous, parabolic language of the pre-Easter, earthly Jesus, as that is represented in the synoptic gospels. We might then expect to find the word παρρησία also in the transfiguration episode in Mark, which follows shortly after the encounter at Caesarea Philippi, and which appears to be a post-resurrection story which Mark and other synoptic gospels have "transplanted" to a pre-crucifixion setting. John Dominic Crossan argues that Mark, which presents no post-resurrection appearances of Jesus, has transposed elements of a resurrection tradition from the non-canonical Gospel of Peter "back" to an earlier point in the narrative (1985:172; 1988:*passim*.). Crossan's argument is supported by the explicit juxtaposition of transfiguration and resurrection in *Pistis Sophia*. However, in Mark's transfiguration story, παρρησία does not appear. The disciples are terrified and do not understand what Jesus says. What has happened is not clear to them, although Jesus again speaks of the son of man (9:9, 12).

The Gospel of John in fact uses παρρησία nine times,[4] often in reference to Jesus' words. John's usage is not without its own ambiguity, however, for Jesus' withholding and giving of plain teaching plays an important part in John's Gospel. John is quite ambiguous about Jesus' "openness" and explicitly contrasts it to his speaking in figures (παροιμίαι, John 16:25–29). This play between openness and secrecy may be found in several of the passages where παρρησία appears. John has no direct parallel to the Caesarea Philippi encounter, but a similar episode appears at 6:67–71; παρρησία does not appear in those verses, but it does appear (for the first

---

[2] I assume that Mark ends at 16:8.

[3] See Kelber 75–76. In the early post-resurrection discourse *Pistis Sophia*, Jesus speaks to his disciples "openly" and "face to face without parables" (Hennecke/Schneemelcher: 255–256). In the *Apocryphon of James*, Jesus' pre-death parables are contrasted to his post-resurrection open speech with his disciples (7:1–10; see also 8:1–9, 11:15) (Cameron :59ff.).

[4] John 7:4, 13, 26, 10:24, 11:14, 54, 16:25, 29, 18:20.

time) three times in the next chapter, in relation to questions of openness and hiddenness.

In John the word παρρησία is common, and in Matthew and Luke it is unknown; only in Mark is it unusual. It would seem that Mark's use of the word highlights a prevailing *lack* of frankness—that is, this narrative moment is a unique one for Mark, but not for the other canonical gospels. Παρρησία is symptomatic of something in Mark which does not figure in the other gospels.

The term παρρησία is often used in antiquity to characterize the candor and lack of reserve on the part of Cynic philosophers. It refers to harsh and shameless speech which is often conjoined with outrageous behavior (Vaage). According to Heinrich Schlier (Kittel V:871–74), the word refers to freedom from restraint in speech. While παρρησία is sometimes treated as synonymous with or at least closely related to ἐξουσία (which along with κατεξουσιάζουσιν appears 11 times in Mark), ἐξουσία in Mark is usually understood as referring to possession of a power or right to do or say something.

One must be careful not to exaggerate the relation between παρρησία and ἐξουσία in Mark. In Mark's narrative, Jesus' ἐξουσία is uncertain because of the uncertainty of his identity, as in Mark 1:22, 1:27, and 2:10, where those who are with him are astonished/amazed at his words and deeds, and also in Mark 11:28–33, where the word appears four times as Jesus' ἐξουσία is questioned by opponents. In Mark 3:15 and 6:7, Jesus gives ἐξουσία to the disciples; in Mark 10:42, the gentiles exercise power; and in Mark 13:34, the master gives power to his servants.

Although Luke never uses παρρησία, the term does appear twelve times in Acts.[5] Is it significant that the author of Luke-Acts reserves this word for the second book only? Παρρησία appears 18 times in the New Testament epistles, and particularly in Hebrews and 1 John; in these texts, the term generally seems to refer to the ability of an apostle to speak freely because of power given to her by Christ or God; in such cases, its meaning does approach that of ἐξουσία. In Colossians 2:15, ἐξουσίας and παρρησία are set over against one another; here, however, τὰς ἐξουσίας is conjoined with τὰς ἀρχὰς. Παρρησία is relatively rare in the Septuagint, where it is as often as not associated with God. In 3 Maccabees 7:12, παρρησία is apparently set over against the ἐξουσία of the king.

The word ἐξουσία does not appear in Mark's Caesarea Philippi story. Furthermore, any ἐξουσία which is exercised in the Caesarea Philippi episode in Mark is ambiguous, for the word παρρησία is found in the midst of an exchange of rebukes and counter-rebukes between Jesus and Peter.

---

[5] Acts 2:29, 4:13, 4:29, 4:31, 9:27, 9:28, 13:46, 14:3, 18:26, 19:8, 26:26, 28:31. This last is the final sentence in Acts. See Mealand: 596–97.

The disciples' reaction to Jesus' frank words is unusual even for Mark. Peter immediately responds negatively to the saying, and this in turn leads to Jesus' harsh reply (8:33), which equates Peter with Satan and separates the thoughts of God from the thoughts of men.[6] Jesus is "rebuked" (RSV, ἐπιτιμᾶν) by Peter and "rebukes" (ἐπετίμησεν) him in return. The same verb appears at Mark 8:30, immediately after Peter's confession; Jesus "rebukes" them to tell no one. In Mark 4:39, Jesus rebukes the sea, and elsewhere he rebukes unclean spirits (Mark 1:25, 9:25).

Whatever we make of Jesus' ἐξουσία in Mark, it never provokes this sort of response from the disciples. The people are amazed at it and Jesus' opponents contest it, but the disciples receive it. By contrast, in Mark 8:32b Peter rejects Jesus' frank saying. It is a situation of open conflict between Peter's messiah language and Jesus' son of man language. Thus the strangeness of Jesus speaking frankly is directly tied to the perplexing question (in Mark at least) of Jesus' identity and of his relation to the Christ and to the son of man. Is this the only place in Mark where the disciples, or one of them anyway, understand Jesus? Or do they understand him even here? Mark does not tell the reader what words Peter had to say to Jesus, unlike the parallel account in Matthew 16:21-23, which is explicit about Peter's words.

Although παρρησία appears nowhere else in Mark, it is echoed in the second passion prediction, at Mark 9:30-32, in the word ῥῆμα (Lattimore: "what he said"), which apparently refers to the prediction itself (9:31). Matthew's parallel (17:22-23) omits ῥῆμα, but Luke 9:45 keeps it. Schlier derives παρρησία from παν + ῥη-, the root from which ῥῆμα is also derived.[7] This episode also concerns Jesus' request to the disciples "not [to] have any one know it" (RSV), although here "it" apparently refers to the fact that they "passed through Galilee," or perhaps to what Jesus was saying, not to the disciples' understandings of who Jesus is. Liddell and Scott note that ῥωή, which shares the same root with ῥῆμα and παρρησία, also means "to flow" or "gush," as in "gush with blood."

> In *Cratylus* ... Plato characterizes the position of Heraclitus with ῥοή (ῥέω) as "flowing," and hence as "flux." 'Ρέω, then becomes a metaphor for change,

---

[6] Fowler claims that there is no "uptake" by characters in Mark on Jesus' "son of man" statements; this exchange appears to be an exception. The Cynics were also subject to rebuke (Vaage: 33); however, the Cynics' words and behavior are characterized by a sense of humor which seems absent from the episode at Caesarea Philippi.

[7] Kittel V:871, n.1 (citing Plato, *Gorgias*, 461e). 'Ρη/ῥέω apparently serves as root for a number of Greek words, including ῥῆσις, ῥῆμα, ῥητῶς, and ῥήτρα, which have overlapping meanings. Of these words, only ῥῆμα occurs in the New Testament. See also Liddell and Scott, who derive παρρησία from πᾶς + ῥῆσις, and Debrunner et al., in Kittel IV:75, n.19. Note the phrases μετὰ πάσης παρρησίας in Acts 28:31 and ἐν πάσῃ παρρησίᾳ in Philippians 1:20 (compare 2 Corinthians 3:12, 7:4)

particularly the flux that renders absolute knowledge impossible.... as far as knowledge (or *understanding*) is concerned, any form of ῥέω got buried and became the suppressed, negative term in the philosophical traditions.... if by Mark's time ῥῆμα connoted the impossibility of certainty in knowledge, then how could the disciples understand even when Jesus spoke to them "frankly" (entombed ῥέω, or flux, in the bold speech of παρρησία)? What is encrypted in Mark 8:32 in παρρησία (namely ῥήω as "flux") seems to "rear its connotative head" in ῥῆμα in 9:32!... That is, the very word παρρησία carries within it the *impossibility* of understanding (in ῥέω), which then the entire narrative of Mark "works out" in its presentation of an enigmatic Jesus.[8]

Is Jesus gushing about the suffering of the son of man? Unlike the confrontation at Caesarea Philippi, there is no rebuking, but the episode does end in the disciples' failure to understand τό ῥῆμα. 'Ρῆμα appears only once more in Mark at 14:72, where it refers to Jesus' prophetic statement that Peter would betray him; the word does not appear in Mark's wording of the third passion prediction (10:32–34).

It is also strange that Jesus speaks frankly of the "son of man" (τὸν υἱὸν τοῦ ἀνθρώπου). What is the son of man, and how would anyone speak frankly of him? Mark presents the teaching in indirect quotation,[9] leaving it to the reader to imagine the actual words. If Jesus said (as a direct quote), "The son of man must suffer," or words to that effect—as he does in the parallel passages in Matthew and Luke, and also in the remaining two passion predictions in Mark—then would it be clear what he meant? On the other hand, if Jesus said, "*I* must suffer"—which does not appear in any of the texts—then why does Mark say that Jesus talked about the son of man? Jesus never says, "I am the son of man," in Mark, nor exactly that in any other canonical gospel.[10]

Are we entitled to assume, as many scholars do, that the reader knows who the son of man is, and even what the son of man is? Is Jesus in fact the son of man, according to Mark? If so, the equation is established not by Jesus' words but by Mark's narrative in which Jesus' predictions of suffering (for the son of man) come true for Jesus himself (Mark 10:32–33). With this coincides also a (self-referential) theme of fulfillment of the Scriptures. "[T]he son of man goes his way as it has been written concerning him, but woe to that man through whom the son of man is betrayed" (Mark 14:21). Judas betrays Jesus, but *Jesus* betrays the "son of man," at Mark 14:62. Yet Jesus also "fulfills" the son of man prophecies,

---

[8] Fred Burnett, private correspondence, December, 1992.

[9] According to Lattimore's translation and RSV. Lattimore's translation reproduces some of the ambiguity of the Greek text by replacing quotation marks with less decisive punctuation.

[10] However, see John 6:53–56, 8:28, and 9:35–37. Also compare Matthew 16:13,15 to Mark 8:27,29; see also Luke 22:47–48. These tendencies correspond to what I have elsewhere called the de-fantasizing of Mark by other canonical gospels.

not as the son of man but as the Christ/son of God (14:61) and the King of the Jews (15:2). Perhaps the nearest to an explicit identification of Jesus as the son of man is found at Mark 14:41–42: "Behold, the son of man is betrayed ... see, my betrayer is near."

Yet Mark alone cannot establish this equation; a great deal must be supplied by the reader. In the other canonical gospels, the disciples (and the reader) have much less difficulty equating Jesus with the son of man. For Mark the equation is at best a paradoxical one. Of course, if we read Mark in the larger literary context of the New Testament—and nearly 2000 years of Christian theologizing—then the paradox is resolved as a matter of faith, and the fundamental non-identity behind the various appearances of the phrase in Mark can be overlooked. But if Mark is considered solely in terms of its own narrative totality (limited and incomplete as that is) and apart from the larger biblical and theological context, then the difficulty presented by Jesus' frankness becomes evident. This pure or naive (non-ideological) reading is impossible in reality, but if we do not imagine it hypothetically, we risk missing important features of the text.

Previous to Mark 8:31, the phrase "son of man" appears three times, always in direct quotes from Jesus. At Mark 2:10, "The son of man has authority to forgive sins upon earth,"[11] and at 2:28, "The son of man is lord even of the sabbath." The authority of the son of man is equal to that of God in these sayings. However, on the third occasion, at Mark 3:28, Jesus states that "all shall be forgiven the sons of men (τοῖς υἱοῖς τῶν ἀνθρώπων) ...," apparently using the phrase to refer to ordinary human beings.

This "sons of men" statement is sometimes not regarded by scholars as a "son of man" saying. In the synoptic parallels to this saying, Matthew (12:31) has only τοῖς ἀνθρώποις and Luke (12:10) omits the phrase entirely; however, quite similar phrases appear at Luke 16:8 and 20:34 (οἱ υἱοὶ τοῦ αἰῶνος τούτου) and at Gospel of Thomas 28[12] and 106. The "sons of men" who are forgiven in Mark apparently become the "son of man" who is spoken against in Matthew 12:32 and Luke 12:10. When Jesus' family arrives on the scene shortly thereafter in Mark, the question arises as to whose son or brother Jesus is (Mark 3:31–35). His answer to the crowd is, "whoever does the will of God." Furthermore, in Mark 6:3, Jesus is identified as "the son of Mary and the brother of James." Perhaps these also should be read as "son of man" passages.

Does the teaching at Mark 8:31–32, which boldly describes the son of man as suffering, being killed, and rising, invert both the theological and

---

[11] Here we find "son of man" conjoined with ἐξουσία. Fowler argues that this "son of man" saying should be read as the narrator's commentary, not Jesus's words (114, 116n.); Fowler also treats Mark 2:28 as such a commentary (103–107).

[12] Oxyrhynchus Papyrus 1 (= Thomas 28) has τοῖς υἱοῖς τῶν ἀν(θρωπ)ων.

the narrative significance of the first two sayings, or does it (with 3:28) identify Jesus as a human being? Mark is a gospel in which paradox and ambiguity regarding Jesus' identity appear frequently, but how could this ambiguity be presented "frankly"? Jesus tells the story of the son of man just as Mark tells the story of Jesus. Although in some cases (for example, 2:10) Jesus appears to have himself in mind, at other points the reference of the phrase is not so clear.[13] In 2:28, does Jesus declare himself the lord over the sabbath, or is it the disciples eating the grain who are so identified? Are they the sons of men (as in 3:28), or has Jesus (as son of man) given them a special privilege? The question of how much can be presumed concerning the ability of disciples, Pharisees, or readers to identify correctly the meaning of these words is a significant one, as is the question of whether the words can be uttered frankly by anyone.

Furthermore, what is to be made of the next appearance of the phrase, at 8:38: "He who is ashamed of me ... of him will the son of man be ashamed when he comes in the glory of the father with the holy angels." Do we have here another case of paradoxical inversion? If so, what does this do to the significance of 8:31? What does this glorious son of man (or the one at 13:26 or 14:62) have to do with suffering and death?[14] What is the connection of either of these sons of man with the son who "came not to be served but to serve, and to give his own life for the redemption of many" (10:45)? Are these sons of man distinct from each other, or from the human being, Jesus? But if that is the case, then why does Peter react as he does to Jesus's frank words?

Denotation and Connotation

> Whatever the manner in which it 'caps' the denoted message, connotation does not exhaust it: there always remains 'something denoted' (otherwise the discourse would not be possible) and the connotators are always in the last analysis discontinuous and scattered signs, naturalized by the denoted language which carries them. (Barthes, 1967a:91)

The distinction, and the relation, between linguistic denotation and connotation is a theme which occupied Roland Barthes throughout his ca-

---

[13] See Vermes and Black in Black: 310ff. In Mark 9:11–13, a parallelism is established between the son of man and Elijah. If Elijah = John the Baptist, then the son of man = Jesus—this is a common reading of this saying. But what if these verses are read as Elijah = son of man? (Note the similarities between 9:12b and 9:13.) Could Jesus be proclaiming here that John the Baptist is the son of man? A clear distinction between John and the son of man is suggested by Matthew 11:19 (par. Luke 7:34), to which Mark has no parallel.

[14] The suffering son of man appears also at Mark 9:9, 12, 31; 10:33, 14:21 (perhaps), and 41. See also Mark 12:6.

reer. In his earlier, more typically structuralist writings, the issue played an important role, but it is also a point at which indications of his later development of a poststructuralist analysis of literature may be found. This matter continued to figure as a topic of interest to Barthes in several essays which were written shortly before his death.

Barthes draws on a distinction which has been current in the philosophy of language at least since the writings of John Stuart Mill. Denotation is language used "normally," the "ordinary" or "proper" meanings of words in a sentence. It is what is often called the "literal" meaning. Denotation is closely related to what Gottlob Frege called "reference," the ability of a word to pick out an object (whether actual or ideal) and thereby to "saturate" the function of a well-ordered sentence.[15] This in turn gives the sentence a truth-value, determining it as true or false. Along similar lines, Irving Copi and Carl Cohen define denotation as the "extension" of a word—the list of objects to which it may refer (141). Denotation "translates" reality (Barthes, 1988:174).

The sentence is a sign, and as such it unites a signifier (physical marks, sounds, gestures, etc.) to a signified (a mental representation of some object). This union is denotation. Connotation builds on denotation by adding a second level of meaning. The denotative totality of signifier and signified becomes itself the signifier (or "connotator," as Barthes called it) of some further signified (the connotation). Barthes here follows the views of Louis Hjelmslev.

> ... *a connoted system is a system whose plane of expression is itself constituted by a signifying system.* (1967a:89-90, Barthes's emphasis)

Copi and Cohen define connotation as the "intension" of a word—a set of attributes which provides a "criterion for deciding" whether a word denotes a particular object (141). However, whether connotation is the "sense" (Frege) or intension of a word and denotation is its reference or extension is a matter of some debate among philosophers of language. As Umberto Eco notes, there is a danger of confusing semantic and logical categories (86). In connotation, the reference of a signifier swerves from a denotative signified to a sense "beyond" the denotation. By playing on the sense of the word, connotation requires a shift in the context in which the statement is understood, with the result that the denoted meaning is obscured. Connotation is a parasite on meaning (Barthes, 1967a:30); it is the "static" which "releasing the double meaning on principle, corrupts

---

[15] See Frege's essay "On Sense and Meaning." Compare Eco: "A denotation is a cultural unit or semantic property of a given sememe which is at the same time a culturally recognized property of its possible referents" (86).

the purity of communication" (Barthes, 1974:9). If denotation is τὸ ῥῆμα, connotation is [τὸ] παν [τὸ] ῥῆμα, the full word, or whole word: παρρησία.

Connotation occurs only according to conventionally-established codes. If I say that the cream cheese is turning greenish-blue, the sentence denotes a change in the color of the cheese. However, that sentence also connotes that the cheese is becoming moldy. The connotative code in effect in this case, according to Barthes, would be the code of the semes (1974:17–20).

This view of the relation between denotation and connotation is not unlike the conventional view of metaphor, to which it is closely related, as well as to the conventional understanding of fiction as secondary to and meaningless apart from the nonfictional. Metaphor, fiction, and connotation are all cases of what Frege called "quotation." "In direct quotation, a sentence designates another sentence, and in indirect speech a thought" (Frege: 65). Every narrative is a quotation, as Frege uses this term; it is a "telling about" (regardless of the status of its narrator or of its truth-value), and the reference of sentences which constitute the narrative is disrupted by this separation of levels. "The quotations from which a text is constructed are anonymous, irrecoverable, and yet *already read*: they are quotations without quotation marks" (Barthes, 1979:77).

According to this view, every word in a language (at any given time) has one or more primary meanings. When the word is used metaphorically, it becomes the "vehicle" for a secondary meaning (the "tenor") which is substituted for the primary meaning. The tenor is often an imaginative extension of one of the primary meanings, and it sometimes becomes so widely accepted that it becomes in effect another primary meaning of the word. When this happens, the metaphor "dies."

Because of the importance of convention in these theories of connotation and of metaphor, they are fundamentally conservative. They share the idea that language has a primary level of meaning, in which it operates properly and more or less transparently. Everyone who knows the language has access to this level, the denotation or "literal" meaning, and they probably in fact learned it first. However, this level can be added to through misuse or creative distortion to produce further levels of meaning which usually are less accessible or transparent. Any change in the codes which govern these additional levels of language is regarded as improper or at least irregular, as it would contribute to misunderstanding.

Even in his early writings, Barthes was not satisfied with this view of language, and his dissatisfaction becomes apparent in his discussions of connotation and denotation.[16] In a short essay, "The Advertising Mes-

---

[16] In *Criticism & Truth*, originally written in 1965–66, Barthes used "primary language" and "literal reading" instead of "denotation," and "second language" instead

sage," first published in 1963 (1988), he wrestles with this issue. Barthes imagines the case of a Martian[17]—"someone from another world"—who knows the vocabulary and syntax of "our language" quite well but is "utterly ignorant" of human culture. The Martian is "deaf" to metaphor and connotation. Yet she is able to receive "a perfectly constituted message," a denotation with no trace of connotation:

> ... there is indeed, here on this first level, a sufficient set of signifiers and this set refers to a body, no less sufficient, of signifieds. (1988:174)

The Martian is able to understand a sentence only in terms of the accepted denotation of its words. She is "stupid" in regard to any culturally derived information which might be inferred, no matter how easily, from the sentence. This describes the "analytical character" of denotation as distinct from connotation. The Martian is like a reader who reads the Gospel of Mark in absolute isolation from the literary and theological traditions to which it has been bound. Such naivete can only be approximated as an extreme, impossible limit.

Elsewhere Barthes admits that rigorous denotation is "utopian" (1983:30). However, there is a problem with the concept, even at this hypothetical level. The Martian knows a human language but does not know about human culture. Could one learn a language without any understanding of the cultural matrix in which that language is bound? In other words, is denotation conceivable apart from connotation? And if it is not, then how can connotation be built upon denotation? Might it even be that denotation is *derived* from connotation, that it is a degenerate form of connotation? Barthes notes that "denotation is not the truth of discourse: ... [denotation is] a particular, specialized substance used by the other [connotative] codes to smooth their articulation" (Barthes, 1974:128). Denotation is "raw" language, crude and untenable (Barthes, 1977:63).

Connotation defines the semiological system of myth, according to Barthes (1972:114–115).[18] It is connotation which makes possible the fictional worlds of narrative; without connotation the "readerly" text, the text of pleasure, would be impossible. Barthes contrasts the analytical character of denotation to the "total message" ($\pi \hat{\alpha} \nu \ \dot{\rho} \hat{\eta} \mu \alpha$) of connotation,

---

of "connotation" (1987:69). He expressed dissatisfaction with the implications of this terminology.

[17] Or, he says, an "Iroquois." Barthes apparently thinks of Martians and Iroquois as being equally foreign to "our language." Elsewhere he speaks of the "mythology" which associates Mars with impartial judgment. "Mars [is] merely an imagined Earth, endowed with perfect wings, as in all dreams of idealization" (1979a:28).

[18] However, in this passage, Barthes also equates myth with metalanguage. Compare the diagram in 1972:115 to those in 1967a:90. His further discussion of myth in *Mythologies* (114–17) concerns connotation.

which in the case of the advertising message means always only one thing: buy me! The signified of every connotation, Barthes says, "is at once general, global and diffuse; it is . . . a fragment of ideology" (1967a:91). The entirety of the denotative sign (signifier-signified) is itself the connotator of this ideology. The specifics of the denotation no longer matter (for every ad for every product connotes only this one thing), but they are nonetheless indispensable; as Barthes says, there can be no connotation without denotation. The resulting double message "disconnects" the denotative meaning, which supports an illusion or dream (an ideology) of naturalness: the "innocence" of language (see Barthes, 1986:65–66).

> The excellence of the advertising signifier thus depends on the power . . . of *linking* its reader with the greatest quantity of "world" possible: . . . experience of very old images, obscure and profound sensations of the body, poetically named by generations, wisdom of the relations of man and nature, patient accession of humanity to an intelligence of things through the one incontestably human power: language. (1988:177–78, Barthes' emphasis)

Barthes concludes that the advertising message, in its use of connotation, serves as the archetype of all narrative. Meaning—or in Barthes's text, *franchise*, frankness—returns at the secondary level, after having been delivered from the primary one. The message is explicit about its own doubleness: "the second signified (the [advertised] product) is always exposed unprotected by a frank [*franc*] system, i.e., one which reveals its duplicity, for this *obvious* system is not a *simple* system" (1988:178, Barthes's emphases). The "natural" quality of the advertised object arises from the symbol-system of realism, which denotation produces through the "flux" of the sentence,[19] but this realism is impossible apart from the artificial nature of the message. The connotation says one thing and tells another. It says, quite "literally," that "this is a metaphor."

Connotations of the Son of Man

> "He who has ears to hear, let him hear." This formula, placed at the end of a number of parables in the tradition, discloses their open-endedness toward the audience. . . . Parables were not, therefore, composed chiefly to solve the problems of remembering, storage, or retention, but rather to provoke hearers' imagination to complete the process begun in their storied worlds. (Kelber: 72)

---

[19] ". . . Language, in the elementary aspects of sentence, period, paragraph, superimposes upon this semantic discontinuity established on the level of discourse the appearance of continuity; for however discontinuous language itself may be, its structure is so fixed in the experience of each man that he recognizes it as a veritable *nature:* do we not speak of the 'flux of speech'? What is more familiar, more obvious, more natural, than a sentence read?" (Barthes, 1986:94).

What then does Jesus mean when he speaks frankly of the son of man? Is he saying, as readers usually assume, "This is me"? Or is his very frankness a sign that the son of man can never, even or perhaps especially in Jesus' words, be anything but a metaphor, or even a fiction, that Jesus can never be the son of man, except parabolically, that his own relation to the son of man is indirect and artificial—"natural" only in the sense (as Barthes makes clear) that the "natural" is itself always unreality, fiction, ideology?

Jesus speaks "frankly" in Mark 8:32 because his saying about the son of man in Mark 8:31 comes as close as possible to a purely connotative statement. Like the advertising message, his statement cannot be taken at "face value;" its denotative content approaches zero, and it explicitly requires a connotative convention for elucidation. This is why the absolutely naive reader (like the Martian, a limit case) is unable to understand this saying; the frankness of Jesus is a symptom. Although no language can dispense entirely with denotation, as Barthes says, Jesus' statement comes as close to that extreme as possible. Its denotation is nonsensical, and therefore it refers to nothing. Much like the modern advertising message, Mark's comment upon the saying denotes (frankly) that this is the case. Mark is frank about Jesus' frankness.

Of course, the Christian reader has no difficulty understanding the saying as rich with theological and narrative significance, just as the consumer in modern Western civilization has no difficulty understanding advertising messages. We are not Martians in relation to this text! Corresponding to the conventions of realism which lend to the advertising message its quality of naturalness is an elaborate set of metaphysical and theological conventions which enable the reader to encounter this narrative as though it were transparent. The reader is an insider, aware of the saying's connotations.

In fact, non-Christian readers will also encounter this passage as though its meaning were clear, providing they also are not Martians—in other words, providing they have been sufficiently enculturated with the generalized "Christian values" which dominate in the so-called First World and which (via mass media) are readily accessible even to peoples and cultures in other parts of the world.[20] Although these values are increasingly secularized and the Christian element in them is questionable, nevertheless the correspondence highlighted by this frankness suggests that a strong relationship exists between orthodox Christian thought and the conventions of literary realism—the metalinguistic system which enables us to read a great many stories.

---

[20] There are no more Iroquois (see n.17), at least in this sense!

For Barthes's Martian reader, however, the advertising message is simple, innocent, and utterly misleading, for the denotations of advertising messages are always trivial and their connotations are of supreme importance. The Martian reader will always be mystified by the second level of meaning, the level of πᾶν ῥῆμα. For the Martian who reads Mark, there is no messianic secret, no passion prophecy, no christological revelation, for these do not and cannot appear at the level of denotation. This naive reading of Mark cannot understand Jesus' frankness; the Martian is an outsider, for whom the text is parabolically obscure.

It has long been observed that the Gospel of Mark appears to be an incomplete, fragmentary text. However, the arguments have usually centered upon the alleged awkwardness of Mark's style and especially the abrupt ending of the Gospel, an ending which had already from a rather early date been "repaired" with various supplements. The beginning of Mark is also less than satisfactory, especially when compared to the other canonical gospels. However, the incompleteness of Mark is more far-reaching than merely its end or its beginning. The incompleteness is also to be found in this saying which Mark 8:31 marks as "frank," as well as at numerous other points where the narrative in effect confesses its own failure.[21] The saying is a point of impenetrability, where the Martian, no matter how much of the language she knows, can proceed no further. In Jesus' frankness, the parabolic estrangement of the outsider, and indeed of the entire text of Mark, becomes clear.

Intertextuality and Translation

> The Word, here, is encyclopaedic, it contains simultaneously all the acceptations from which a relational discourse might have required it to choose. It therefore ... is reduced to a sort of zero degree, pregnant with all past and future specifications. (Barthes, 1967b:48, his emphasis)

In a reality composed entirely of texts, intertextuality is the name for that which holds the universe together and gives it meaning.[22] "[T]he book creates the meaning, the meaning creates life" (Barthes, 1975:36). Intertextuality refers to an essential characteristic of every reading, namely, that there can be no first reading, no truly naive reading, no

---

[21] "Thus is translated into narrative the schematic opposition of silence and proclamation. We find it in the parables, in the beginning of the Gospel and in its end, as well as in intermediate narratives" (Kermode: 140).

[22] "If one grasps that every signifying practice is a field of transpositions of various signifying systems (an inter-textuality), one then understands that the 'place' of enunciation and its denoted 'object' are never single, complete, and identical to themselves, but always plural, shattered, capable of being tabulated" (Kristeva: 60).

purely denotative reading. "To read in any real way, then, is to enter into connotation" (Barthes, 1977:79).

And yet, paradoxically, intertextuality also entails that the same book can never be read twice. Each reading is overshadowed by other readings; every reading echoes every other reading. The reader is the product of her previous readings, which she brings to every "new" reading. Yet as soon as it enters into the intertextual net, the new reading also transforms all of the preceding readings. Intertextuality is an ultimately uncontrollable gush or flux of meaning (from denotation to connotation and back again), which can never be pinned down.

Intertextuality is driven by connotation. Therefore, it is not an individual matter, for even the most private of readings is, like all language, ultimately a shared experience. The language of the text is always a public language. My reading is formed in tension not only with my own reading history, but with that of many others. Of most of these other readers I have no knowledge.

To seek intertextual self-awareness is to attempt to think the unthinkable, to unravel meaning and separate denotation from connotation, and ultimately, among other things, to become the naive reader. Insofar as the biblical texts are full of passages such as the one considered here, the semiotician who strives for this goal moves in a direction diametrically opposed to that of the theologian: she wants text stripped bare of all meaning, an inert, alien, inscrutable thing, a token without a type. She seeks a sort of "reading degree zero," which of course can never be.

There are different types of intertextuality: for example, that of an author who deliberately and explicitly alludes to another work, as in James Joyce's *Ulysses* or Tom Stoppard's play, *Rosenkrantz and Guildenstern are Dead*. Intertextuality also arises when one text draws upon or plays with a set of codes which were originally developed in the reading of another text, but without necessarily requiring the conscious manipulation of an author. Yet another type of intertextuality is formed by the reverberation between stories that have arisen from a common narrative structure (genre), although the stories may come from different periods of history or even different cultures. The familiar three-fold or four-fold plot structure of fairy tales from all over the world would be an example of this. However, the aleatory type of intertextuality described here is more remote and accidental than any of these.

The terms "frank" and "frankness" which appear in Barthes's essay are Richard Howard's translation of the French words *franc* and *franchise*. Thus the coincidence which forms the crux of this essay is a merely physical resemblance, a crude pun, between Lattimore's use of the word "frankly" and Howard's use of "frank" and "frankness." This resemblance does not explain why Jesus spoke frankly, but it does suggest that Jesus' frankness implies a double message.

The element of chance inherent in this intertextuality requires a playful and perhaps irresponsible reading. It offends against the belief that scholarship must be systematic, rational, or even scientific. Why choose these texts, and not others also linked by some chance word-play? Fantasists such as Italo Calvino, Stanislaw Lem, and Umberto Eco have already imagined for us the possibility of a gigantic supercomputer impersonally scanning every text ever written, in every language, in every translation. The computer "reads" terabytes of text in the blink of an eye, cataloging every coincidence of word or phrase.

Although this cybernetic monster might generate the true name of God, and thus the end of the universe, as an Arthur C. Clarke story once suggested, it is more probable that it would produce a great deal of trivia, and little of interest. Some may wish to argue that this essay is an example of the latter. Yet although the focus here is on the chance intersection of two texts, the operation of the author's interest is hardly by chance. Each reader brings to bear upon the text an intertextual network which both defines and reflects a field of ideologies, beliefs, and interests. The reader *is* this network. Within this network, not every word is of equal value. What causes one word to stand out, to draw one's interest, and another does not? No reading is ever free from the concrete particularities of its context.

Perhaps all that the different types of intertextuality share in common is an "effect of meaning" which one text has on another, although even that effect is probably quite different in different types of intertextuality. In any case the effect only arises through a reading of the texts. Texts cannot produce or affect one another without the human medium of the reader. The coincidence of words between Barthes's essay and the gospel of Mark was there, in the sheer materiality of the texts, before my own interests drew it into the light, but its signifying effect can only come into play when it begins to operate in my reading, or someone else's—indeed, it is the intertext which defines the nature of the reading. Every reading is re-reading, and it is in that "re-" that the intertext appears.

In his famous essay, "The Task of the Translator," Walter Benjamin described what he called "literal translation." Benjamin's theory stands at the opposite extreme from the views of Bible translators such as Eugene Nida and J.P. Louw, whose theories are dominant in the Bible translation societies today. Literal translation values translations that illuminate the text in ways that it could not do for itself. According to Benjamin, in literal translation the original is brought back to life, and "pure language" imprisoned within the original text is "liberated" (71–72, 80). The value of translation lies in interlinear confrontation with the original text, not in infallible transmission of some meaning hidden within the text. Like a tangent to a circle, the translation harmoniously supplements and complements the original; in the space and the silence between parallel lines of text appears pure language, the pre-Babelian language of God.

Benjamin is a mystic, but he is also a materialist. Translation, he says, has nothing to do with meaning. There is no meaning to be transferred from one text to the other, through what Nida and others call "dynamic equivalence." There is only the tension between two texts, which is marked only at the level of the signifier. Barthes's text translates Mark, in the Benjaminian sense; it illuminates the text of Mark as Mark cannot illuminate itself, revealing the frankness of Jesus to be the frankness of Mark itself, and yet a frankness which conceals an enigma, a revelation which disguises a mystery. Can Mark be frank about the frankness of Jesus? It would take yet another frank text to assure the reader of this—and perhaps that is indeed what Matthew and Luke attempt to do, initiating a succession of texts which culminates, but only for the moment, in my own frankness.

At a certain point in two English translations and perhaps only here, two apparently quite different originals touch one another. Richmond Lattimore translated the word παρρησία from the Gospel of Mark as "frankly," and Richard Howard translated Barthes's word *franchise* as "frankness." This is probably only a coincidence; yet it is a suggestive coincidence. It presents an intriguing answer to the questions posed at the start. It is not insignificant. We are here not far from Benjamin's pure or true language which appears through the translation contract between texts. The connotative play between these two texts allows them to illuminate each other in ways untouched by denotation. Each text interrogates and transforms the other; each one becomes an "other" for the other, complementing it even as it reveals its irreducible otherness.

Mark's text and Barthes' text touch each other, but only through the medium of the translations by Lattimore and Howard. The point of contact is a mere accident, a material resemblance. The physical play between the two English translations is insignificant in the Benjaminian sense: there is no transfer of meaning from one text to the other. For this contact between two texts to occur, to become visible, the semiotic codes must be suspended, or at least fade away temporarily, revealing only bare stuff, the physical marks that readers interpret as signifiers. Insofar as these codes are the product of intertextual networks, networks of reading, a paradox results: for intertextuality appears as a moment of incoherence, a failure of the word.

Intertextuality enables reading; without intertextuality there could be no reading. However, intertextuality also refers to physical accidents of the texts which interrupt the smooth flow of reading. The coincidence of signifiers breaks through preconceptions about the gospel; it frustrates theological expectations. Meaning becomes subject to chance, perhaps even the product of chance. The prospects for textual closure become more and more remote. Once again, the desire for frankness has been disappointed.[23]

WORKS CITED

Aichele, George
    1995   "Fantasy and the Gospels: Theological and Ideological Implications." *Journal for the Fantastic in the Arts*, forthcoming.

Barthes, Roland
    1967a   *Elements of Semiology*. Trans. Annette Lavers and Colin Smith. New York: Hill and Wang.
    1967b   *Writing Degree Zero*. Trans. Annette Lavers and Colin Smith. New York: Hill and Wang.
    1972   *Mythologies*. Trans. Annette Lavers. New York: Hill and Wang.
    1974   *S/Z*. Trans. Richard Miller. New York: Hill and Wang.
    1975   *The Pleasure of the Text*. Trans. Richard Miller. New York: Hill and Wang.
    1977   *Roland Barthes*. Trans. Richard Howard. New York: Hill and Wang.
    1979   "From Work to Text." In *Textual Strategies*. Trans. Josué V. Harari. Ithaca: Cornell University Press.
    1983   *The Fashion System*. Trans. Matthew Ward and Richard Howard. Berkeley and Los Angeles: University of California Press.
    1986   *The Rustle of Language*. Trans. Richard Howard. Berkeley and Los Angeles: University of California Press.
    1987   *Criticism & Truth*. Trans. Katrine Pilcher Keuneman. Minneapolis: University of Minnesota Press.
    1988   *The Semiotic Challenge*. Trans. Richard Howard. New York: Hill and Wang. French original: *L'aventure sémiologique*. Paris: Editions du Seuil, 1985.

Benjamin, Walter
    1968   *Illuminations*. Trans. Harry Zohn. New York: Schocken Books.

---

[23] I am indebted to Professors Fred Burnett (Anderson University), Gary Phillips (College of the Holy Cross), and Richard Hutcheson (SUNY/Potsdam) for invaluable assistance in the preparation of this paper.

Black, Matthew
    1967   *An Aramaic Approach to the Gospels and Acts*. 3rd edition. Oxford: Oxford University Press.

Cameron, Ron, ed.
    1982   *The Other Gospels* (ed.). Philadelphia: Westminster Press.

Copi, Irving and Carl Cohen
    1990   *Introduction to Logic*. Eighth edition. New York: Macmillan Publishing Co.

Crossan, John Dominic
    1985   *Four Other Gospels*. Minneapolis: Winston Press.

Eco, Umberto
    1976   *A Theory of Semiotics*. Bloomington: Indiana University Press.

Fowler, Robert
    1991   *Let the Reader Understand*. Philadelphia: Fortress.

Frege, Gottlob
    1952   *Translations from the Philosophical Writings of Gottlob Frege*. Ed. Peter Geach and Max Black. Oxford: Basil Blackwell.

Hennecke, Edgar and Wilhelm Schneemelcher, eds.
    1963   *New Testament Apocrypha*. Vol. I. Trans. R. McL. Wilson. Philadelphia: Westminster.

Kelber, Werner
    1990   "In the Beginning Were the Words." *Journal of the American Academy of Religion* 58:69–98.

Kermode, Frank
    1979   *The Genesis of Secrecy*. Cambridge: Harvard University Press.

Kittel, Gerhard, ed.
    1967   *Theological Dictionary of the New Testament*. Vols. IV & V. Trans. and Ed. Geoffrey Bromiley. Grand Rapids, MI: Wm. B. Eerdmans.

Kristeva, Julia
    1984   *Revolution in Poetic Language*. Trans. Margaret Waller. New York: Columbia University Press.

Lattimore, Richmond, trans.
    1979   *The Four Gospels and the Revelation*. New York: Dorset Press.

Liddell, Henry George and Robert Scott
    1940   *A Greek-English Lexicon*. New edition. Revised by Henry Stuart Jones and Roderick McKenzie. London: Oxford at the Clarendon Press.

Mealand, David L.
    1990   "The Close of Acts and Its Hellenistic Greek Vocabulary." *New Testament Studies* 36:583–97.

Vaage, Leif E.
1992 "Like Dogs Barking: Cynic Parresia and Shameless Asceticism." *Semeia* 57:25–39.

A RESPONSE
WHEN JESUS REWROTE THE CORN MOTHERS:
INTERTEXTUALITY AS TRANSNATIONAL CRITICAL PRACTICE

Laura E. Donaldson
The University of Iowa

> Certain habits of thought and research have formed that are not easy to overcome. A persistent deafness and blindness to concrete ideological reality has become established, involving both the reality of things and social actions and the complex material relations which interpenetrate this reality. We are most inclined to imagine ideological creations as some inner process of understanding, comprehension, and perception, and do not notice that it in fact unfolds externally, for the eye, the ear, the hand. It is not within us but between us.
>
> —M.M. Bakhtin, *The Formal Method in Literary Scholarship*

On a foreboding day in the 1620s, a group of Spanish Franciscans manifested their love for Christianity's God by forcibly entering the kivas of Santo Domingo Pueblo, where they "built crosses on them to delimit a new sacred topography. Indians complained that such defilements put their gods to flight. The friars were delighted to hear this and boasted that they had driven the devil from his house" (Gutiérrez: 72). After this act of epistemic violence, the People observed that "when Padre Jesús came, the Corn Mothers went away" (Gutiérrez: 162). The attempt to expel the Pueblos' most sacred beings by literally and metaphorically overwriting their social text dramatizes how intertextuality, or the absorption and transposition of one signifying system by another, enabled the hegemonic dissemination of culture—here, the narratives of imperial Christianity.

Although this incident originates in the annals of historical imperialism, neo-colonial examples abound, ranging from signs of multinational capitalism (e.g. the Coke bottle taken up by the Bushman in *The Gods Must Be Crazy*), to J.M. Coetzee's rewriting of Daniel Defoe's *Robinson Crusoe* in *Foe* (both functioning as limit texts of Western imperialism) and the biblical story of Jezebel in what Tina Pippin describes as "an intertextual turn for the worst." At the very least this should circumscribe the tendency (initiated by Julia Kristeva herself) to construe intertextuality as always already a "celebration of difference" (Phillips) or, in the guise of the carnivalesque, an absurd replication of norms that actually undermines them (Brawley). Along with the opening scenario, these examples testify to intertextuality's status as much more than "the dialogic space of texts" (Kristeva, in Beal and Linafelt); it also constitutes a material practice of transnational circulation—that is, it transmits, disseminates, regulates, disciplines, and recuperates a plethora of cultural productions which are extraordinarily diverse and unevenly located in political economies of the transnational.

I put intertextuality into the framework of the transnational rather the global in order to make visible the problems that often arise when one crosses cultural borders. Too often, recourse to a monolithic sense of "the global" works to erase not only the concerns of "local" identities, but also the existence of multiple globalities. In this way, according to Inderpal Grewal and Caren Kaplan, "global-local binaries dangerously correspond to the colonialism-nationalism model that often leaves out various subaltern groups as well as the interplay of power in various levels of sociopolitical agendas" (11). The transnational, on the other hand, problematizes a purely locational politics of global-local or center-periphery in favor of the much more complicated lines cutting across such distinctions (Grewal and Kaplan: 13).

I begin with this cautionary note and a brief summary of my own views on intertextuality because I believe that the role of a respondent is not to filter the intellectual work of others through a lens of omniscient critique (a practice that all too many of us have unfortunately experienced); rather, I perceive my project in terms of establishing an oppositional consciousness with the essays included in this volume. Etymologically rooted in the Latin verb meaning "to locate oneself across from," opposition implies that one can only define a position by locating it in relation to others. Because this epistemological process takes seriously the variant logics of different cultures and their placement within asymmetrical power relations (Mohanty: 196), it results in an understanding of culture—including the academic culture that generates such roles as "respondent"—as a terrain of struggle and contradiction rather than a composite of harmoniously discrete entities. In other words, I can only approach these essays by situating them in relation to my own critical concerns (theory in the wake of colonialism), professional identity (a university-based mediator of English, Women's Studies, and American Indian/Native Studies), and life experience (the struggle to understand the often agonistic relationship between my dual Scotch-Irish and Cherokee heritages).

As articulated by Kristeva, intertextuality functions as a virtual slogan for the Tel Quel group's sweeping critique of European structuralism: because of it, they could argue that textual analysis no longer privileged meaning, or the relationship of language to referent, but instead concerned itself with signification, or the interaction of signs and texts in semiosis with other signs and texts (Godard: 569). Kristeva adapts the psychoanalytic term "transposition" to convey not only the infinitely productive network of codes that constitute a text, but also the way this emphasis on interactive semiosis continually brings signification to crisis. In his essay, "'What is Written and How Do You Read?': The Gospel, Intertextuality and Doing Lukewise: Reading Lk 10:25-42 Otherwise," Gary Phillips provides an extremely helpful discussion of Kristevan transposition—and of intertextuality in general (see also Beal and Linafelt). According to Phillips (120), transposition is the key to the figurability of language and represents "the possibility inherent within the signifying process itself of passing from one system of signs to another, i.e., to exchange or to alter them ... Transposition points to a fundamental semiotic process that enables translation out of a previous system of signs ... into a new system with its figurability." Or, in the extended metaphor of Timothy Beal and Tod Linafelt, transposition means that "the rickety old fences that separate one field from another do not prevent seeds from blowing over and being planted—accidentally or intentionally—elsewhere" (21).

However, while the notion of intertextual transposition socially situates the codes, discourses, and voices traversing any particular text, it still, according to Pierre Bourdieu, considers only "the system of works, the network of relationships among texts ... Hence ... they are compelled to find in the system of texts itself the basis of its dynamics" (Bourdieu: 179). Bourdieu suggests that, while we should retain what is useful about the concept—"that at each moment the space of works appears as a field of position-takings which can only be understood relationally" (182)—as intertextual practitioners, we also need to enlarge its referential horizon. Rather than becoming narrowly preoccupied with other texts, we should concern ourselves with reintroducing the agents and producers who act within a specific set of socio-textual relations (Johnson, Editor's Introduction, in Bourdieu: 14). Like the oppositional consciousness of response, then, intertextuality conjures a space of semiotic and political position-takings that accrues meaning only in relation to other possible past and present position-takings and to the field of power, or the operant relations of domination, within society (Johnson: 17). In other words, while Beal and Linafelt's transpositional metaphor emphasizes the seed, Bourdieu would direct them to consider both the nature of the winds blowing the seeds (from which direction do they come? Is it really as random as this image suggests?) and the planters who place the seeds in the ground (what systems of production and circulation allow these particular planters to cultivate the seeds? Why and for whom are they planting the seeds?).

Analyzing the work of transnational intertextuality in "the colonizing process of story changing" (Allen: 240) represents just such an enlargement of referential horizons, since it attends not only to the semiotic transformation itself, but also to the fields of imperialism embedding this transformation. Because of this, I would argue that intertextuality more appropriately belongs within cultural studies rather than in narratology or even sociological poetics: like cultural studies, it reveals narrative and social texts as terrains of conflict and sites of contested positions. The notion of intertextuality as a transnational critical practice refuses to domesticate issues of difference and power, including, for example, its own complicitous history in the attempted annihilation of Native American peoples.

One method of domesticating the contradictions of transnational intertextuality emerges in what William Doty calls "the older cross-cultural comparative-symbolic approach," and what Robert Alter describes as the search for narrative analogy. In his moving autobiographical essay, "Texts, More Texts, a Textual Reader and a Textual Writer," Peter Miscall aptly depicts the characteristic gestures of this approach when he observes: "In my first published work on biblical narrative, I was concerned with tracing and evaluating parallels and analogies between separate (biblical) stories," which were then assessed "mainly through thematic impact and relevance." As a case in point, Miscall reveals that he was originally drawn to the story of David and the Well (2 Sam 23:13–17) because it contained similarities to Robert Alter's construction of the betrothal type scene in *The Art Of Biblical Narrative*. Yet, because the homogenous and unifying gesture of comparison neutralizes the threat of disruption, it prevented Miscall from perceiving how this method of reading marginalized the feminine and enabled him to ignore "the presence (or absence) of women and their roles, often active and positive, in the series of parallel texts that were established beginning with Alter's betrothal scene. Even though a betrothal involves both a man and a woman, Alter and I talk as though the stories were about only the man." Miscall's honest portrayal of his own struggles with the comparative approach and his subsequent move into "the more complex concepts and praxes" of intertextuality should give even the most conservative biblical scholar ethical and critical pause.

Doty's exploration of the comparative method in his essay, "Imaginings at the End of an Era: Letters as Fictions," foregrounds in much more acute form the necessity for a concept of intertextuality as a transnational practice. On the one hand, he offers a welcome analysis of the "self-referencing intertextuality" within Paul's letters and raises many important questions that have been too long neglected by both biblical and literary critics—for example, epistolary Eros, the place of women as epistolary readers and writers and the role of letters in constructing the early Christian community. On the other hand, it is precisely the essay's strengths—its range of theoretical concerns and its engagement with an almost dizzying array of cross-cultural productions—that comprise its most telling vulnerabilities. I found myself growing uneasy at its appeal to "the multiple strands of tradition 'signed' by Jesus, Kafka, Borges, Miller, Fowles and Castenada," and the placement of Paul, Samuel Richardson, Choderlos de Laclos and John Barth in "the same literary frame." My concern here is not the old historicist insistence on the periodized segregation of narrative eras and types; rather, it has to do with how Doty's critical practice perpetuates a too facile globalism that pays virtually no attention to the differential logics and asymmetrical positionings of the sources it appropriates.

Doty draws upon the image of "the cross-referenced matrix," or series of interconnecting symbol systems in his own theories of intertextuality—for him, quite literally, the epistolary exchange—which he then augments with the traditional comparative approach discussed above. I find this paradigm of cross-referencing troubling for several reasons: first, its search for homologies preempts the question of "other," more disruptive patterns of relationship. According to Homi K. Bhabha in *The Location Of Culture*, cross-referencing's "horizon of holism"—the inexorable search for cultural commensurability—ethnocentrically elides the ambivalent, hybrid knowledges that emerge from historically colonized social texts. He also warns against generalizing in this mode at the very moment when a transnational knowledge of the world—and, I would add, intertextuality—is most urgently needed. Bhabha echoes the insights of Grewal and Kaplan when he observes that, "instead of cross-referencing there (should be) an effective, productive cross-cutting across sites of social significance, that erases the dialectical, disciplinary sense of cultural reference and relevance" (128). In the critical practice of transnational intertextuality, a detailed attending to the uneven articulations of power and knowledge within various cultural productions replaces the quest for likeness in the name of a unified globalism.

Intertextuality has redefined the nature of the signifying text as an interactive semiosis rather than a self-contained artifact and several authors in this volume explicitly offer images for such a narrative revisioning. Whereas Doty describes letters as both pieces of textual quilts and the process of quilting itself, George Aichele ("Jesus' Frankness") and Miscall draw upon Roland Barthes' notions of connotation-denotation and the text as an intertextual weave of codes for their own redefinitions. Like Doty's epistolary quilt, Miscall's metaphor of the text as a weaving, or a tissue of quotations drawn from innumerable cultural centers, "implies threads, plurality, process and (in)substantiality (text and tissue)." However, it is precisely around the issue of process that problems of cultural commensurability circumambulate, for both Doty and Miscall beg the question of how, exactly, they assemble their intertextual constructs.

For example, in contrast to Doty, who pieces his (inter)textual quilt together with the act of stitching, I would substitute the act of suture: unlike stitching, which suggests a straightforward discourse of joining, the crosscuts of suture (as in suturing a wound) make visible what skillful sewing attempts to cover over. "Suture" is a term used by film critics to foreground the ideological and technical procedure of splicing one frame to the next and to articulate "one of the most basic processes of that 'compulsory and deliberate guidance of the thoughts and associations of the spectator' known as film editing" (Donaldson: 24–25). The affiliations of suture with the crossings of transnationalism seem clear, since both ask us to consider the larger context of who joins what shots (or cultural productions) to others and for what reasons. Even more importantly, both demand that we ask how this particular pattern of stitching might violently penetrate the individual pieces it connects and what other configurations of joining it excludes.

Similar problems ensue from Miscall's portrayal of the text as a weaving, since one could just as easily interpret the symmetry of a braid in terms of coercive alignment rather than liberatory jouissance, rigidity rather than plurality. The metaphors of both Doty and Miscall paradigmatically expose ideological questions that biblical and literary critics have consistently refused to ask. Further, they nurture a perception of difference as benign variation rather than the threat of conflict, struggle, or disruption. Indeed, I would argue, the intertextual metaphors of the quilt and the braid foster a recuperative pluralism which, in the words of Gayatri Chakravorty Spivak, espouses "the politics of the masculinist establishment. Pluralism is the method used by the central authorities to neutralize opposition by seeming to accept it" (quoted in Meese: 141). To paraphrase Leo Tolstoi's famous query, "What, then, shall we do?" I realize that what I am proposing is a far from easy task and, since I myself am still struggling to realize its theoretical and practical dimensions, I have no ready-made answers. However, several essays in this collection do provide partial hints about things to come in this new transnational (intertextual) world.

The articles by Beal and Linafelt as well as Pippin offer similar critical clues in this regard. While the former offer the exegesis of the cinder, the latter calls for a social semiotic of the trace: both cinders and traces indicate the remains "of the other who has been erased from the text ... but who leaves, if nothing more, erasure marks" (Beal and Linafelt). For Beal and Linafelt, the work of the reader and critic is "to sift through the scattered ashes in search of a still-glowing ember," while for Pippin, she must identify the ways in which intertextual images circulate within and thus reproduce dominant power relations. However, Beal and Linafelt's provocative excavation of Leviticus 10:1–5 actually defuses its radical potential by neglecting the social, while Pippin at least attempts to contextualize the intertextual through "a neo-materialist social semiotic" (Thibault) and "a materialist-feminist semiotics" (Donaldson: 1992).

In "Sifting For Cinders: Strange Fires in Leviticus 10:1–5," Beal and Linafelt frame their discussion by quoting Danna Nolan Fewell's statement that "the force of intertextuality is to problematize, even spoil, textual and interpretive boundaries—those lines of demarcation that allow a reader to talk about the meaning, subject, or origin of a text." This deconstruction of interpretive boundaries is exactly what they proceed to do with the Leviticus story of Nadab and Abihu, one of the most troubling narratives in the entire Hebrew Bible:

> Sifting through the cinders of this story, we alighted on traces suggesting the sacrificial burning of children. Are the children of Nadab and Abihu burned? Or are Nadab and Abihu the children sacrificed for Aaron's sin? Or is it finally our own childlike yearning for the absolute Presence of the Father that is sacrificed? We find ourselves unable to write the ending, for 'the sentence is adorned with all of its dead.' (Derrida, 1991:55; emphasis added)

As one might expect, Beal and Linafelt end their essay with an "Inconclusion," which proclaims the text of Leviticus 10:1–5 "a model of undecidability." Biblical scholars who are more qualified than I will have to evaluate the adequacy of the evidence they bring to this narrative worrying. However, I want to problematize (and perhaps even spoil) the essay's interpretive boundaries precisely because of where they stop—well short, I believe, of that "enlarged horizon" for which this story so desperately calls.

One site of blockage occurs in the essay's investigation of whether the passages in Leviticus contain any connotations of child sacrifice. Indeed, every time Beal and Linafelt's complex discussion—punctuated by its own Derridean intertext—threatens to breach the social, it stubbornly insists upon remaining within the textual. For example, they note that "we find traces that suggest to us the possibility of child sacrifice, an 'almost silent monument' (Derrida, 1991:37) to the children of another Holocaust, buried within the ashes of this text; a sacrificial incineration of Nadab and Abihu's seed." They then link the holocaust of Leviticus 10 and the Jewish Holocaust through the semantic slippage of the phrase *'asher lo'*—"strange fire" and "seed fire." Beal and Linafelt's production of such a rich literary and social nexus might function as an exemplary occasion for traversing both the textual and historical. However, because their referential horizon, in the words of Bourdieu, only considers the network of relationships among other texts, the authors fail to ask such questions as the following: What are the intertextual hierarchies (pure/impure, e.g.) infecting the seemingly neutral choice of who is sacrificed? How does the "seed fire" of Leviticus 10 and Hitler's Germany implicate the story's discourse of chosenness/unchosenness? What are the matrices (pun intended) of the seed fire (or, as Miscall might ask, why can't they see the women/mothers)? And, finally, how can the intertext of Derrida's *Cinders*—written by an Algerian Jew living in the contradictory intersections of French imperialism, German anti-Judaism and Anglo-European patriarchalism—possess only semiotic significance? It is in answer to these interrogations that the essay of Beal and Linafelt, for all its "pyrogenetic" insights and challenging intra-textual conversations, falls ominously silent.

Pippin, in "Jezebel Re-vamped," attempts to address exactly such issues through the biblical figure of Jezebel, whose "adorned face" has imprinted itself upon historically diverse groups of women and who exists as "the archetypal bitch-witch-queen in misogynist representations of women." By exploring the ways in which her image becomes disseminated through the literary texts of Tom Robbins and the social texts of African-American slavery, Pippin shows how "Jezebel" as cultural sign mimics its biblical origins in the ideological processes of demonizing the feminine. It also enables the essay to investigate the close imbrication between race and gender in this demonization. Although one would wish that the essay's arguments were more thoroughly and completely articulated, Pippin's work on Jezebel takes a crucial step in re-situating the critical practice of intertextuality.

Roland Boer, in his essay on "Christological Slippage in Schwarzenegger's *Terminator*," offers some important alternative trajectories in his binding of intertextuality with Fredric Jameson's notion of "transcoding," or the ability to move experimentally between a proliferating number of codes: "The ability to translate from one method or code to the other is more important than testing them all against an ultimate method. Transcoding requires the ability to speak those various codes or ideolects, a skill comparable to speaking and translating a foreign language." While Boer does little more with this point, it yields essential insights for the transnational practice of intertextuality: that is, the placement of transcoding, and by extension intertextuality, in the context of translation—as both the practice of reading and writing and the vehicle through which cultures travel (Homel and Simon: 9)—lays bare the perspectival struggles implicit within any intertextual transformation. It also highlights the role of translators and their often contradictory sociopolitical relationships with the translated—a self-critical terrain virtually suppressed in Susan Lochrie Graham's transparent translation of Gene Roddenberry's religious biography into the ongoing plots of "Star Trek: The Next Generation."

In the abstract for her essay Graham states: "Intertextual theory provides a critical means of exploring the ways in which ideas and images are incorporated into a narrative, even in contradiction to the stated intention of an author"; or again, "a reading 'against the grain' of the text enables the reader to explore the text's unconscious and bring to audition a voice that had been silenced." Through the use of an objectified passive ("are incorporated"), the first passage symptomatically erases all reference to the presence of agents, producers, and translators; the second implies that these silenced voices spring *ex nihilo* from some ahistorical, asocial textual unconscious (I would certainly ask why Graham ignores the much more materialist notion of the textual unconscious articulated by Pierre Macherey in his *Theory Of Literary Production*). Who, in fact, is producing these voices? Graham's essay elides not only her own (inter)textual work as translator of Roddenberry's life, but also ST:TNG's highly mediated modes of literary and cinematic production, including writers, directors, and film editors.

Returning, then, to Roland Boer's discussion, he finds another similarity between transcoding and intertextuality in the way that "both bear all the marks of cultural and literary versions of commodity exchange, each item—text or code—with some local variation in taste, appearance and texture being interchangeable with the other ...Transcoding and intertextuality become therefore the methodological and textual projections, respectively, of the activity of commodity consumption." I want to extend this insight by inserting remarks from a later section of the essay dealing with the figural slippage from the first *Terminator* film to the second rather than with transcoding itself. Although these comments focus on the films' play with time, I believe that they also brilliantly capture the essence of my problem with the practice of a "global" intertextuality:

> ...The main point is that there is a chronic loss of historical depth. It all gets thrown together in an undifferentiated conglomeration or historical pastiche. It is this approach—or rather lack thereof—to history which has been identified and traced by Fredric Jameson on many occasions as the loss of history which is so characteristic of postmodernism. Such a loss is ultimately the result of a commodity culture in which items from very different times and places may appear side by side on the shelves in their identical plastic wrappers or in the catalogues in identical glossy photographs. Not only are peo-

ple, as consumers brought to the same level by capitalism as consumers, but historical periods and moments are also leveled into one flat expanse. (182)

As vehicles of commodity fetishism, both transcoding and intertextuality invite ferocious attention not only to the patterns of exchange they set in motion, but also to the patterns of consumption initiated by readers and writers themselves. Further, by situating transcoding/intertextuality within the historical situation of late (or even post-) capitalism, Boer opens up the possibility of uncovering precisely those transnational asymmetries erased in the monolithic rhetoric of globalism.

It is because I find this part of his essay so productive that I was perplexed about Boer's own very restricted practice of intertextuality in his reading of the *Terminator* I and II (at this point I have to unashamedly admit that I am one of the few potential American viewers who has seen neither of these Schwarzenegger films). In its most conservative sense, intertextuality specifies the relations between one text and those others which are demonstrably present within it (Prince: 46). This description characterizes Boer's intertextuality as well (in this sense, his kindred spirit would seem to be Gerard Genette rather than Fred Jameson), since he confines himself to illuminating correspondences between the sign systems of "T_1" and "T_2" and the biblical messianic texts to which they directly correspond. I cannot explain the gap between theory and practice here, except to speculate that perhaps Boer himself does not always realize the significance of Jameson's framework for intertextual practice. In spite of this, however, his essay contains illuminating and provocative ideas, even if their full import has not yet unfolded.

In retrospect, I believe that this special issue on intertextuality is extremely important for several reasons: it not only identifies the problems emanating from its current critical practice, but also provides a number of perspectives that might be utilized to engage these concerns constructively. As a last (but not final) word, I would like to take up a citation from Homi Bhabha, which I will transpose into a simultaneous benediction and warning about the future of intertextuality: "To that end we should remember that it is the 'inter'—the cutting edge of translation and negotiation, the in-between space—that carries the burden of the meaning of culture ... And by exploring this Third Space, we may elude the politics of polarity and emerge as the others of ourselves" (38–39). Alleluia and Amen.

WORKS CITED

Allen, Paula Gunn
   1986   *The Sacred Hoop: Recovering the Feminine in American Indian Traditions.* Boston: Beacon Press.

Bakhtin, M.M. and P.N. Medvedev
   1978   *The Formal Method in Literary Scholarship: A Critical Introduction to Sociological Poetics.* Trans. Albert J. Wehrle. Baltimore and London: Johns Hopkins University Press.

Bhabha, Homi K.
   1994   *The Location of Culture.* London and New York: Routledge.

Bourdieu, Pierre
   1993   *The Field of Cultural Production: Essays on Art and Literature.* Ed. Randal Johnson. New York: Columbia University Press.

Donaldson, Laura E.
   1992   *Decolonizing Feminisms: Race, Gender, & Empire-building.* Chapel Hill and London: University of North Carolina Press.

Godard, Barbara
   1993   "Intertextuality." Pp. 568–72 in *Encyclopedia of Contemporary Literary Theory: Approaches, Scholars, Terms.* Ed. Irena R. Makaryk. Toronto, Buffalo, and London: University of Toronto Press.

Grewal, Inderpal and Caren Kaplan
   1994   "Introduction: Transnational Feminist Practices and Questions of Postmodernity." Pp. 1–33 in *Scattered Hegemonies: Postmodernity and Transnational Feminist Practices.* Ed. Inderpal Grewal and Caren Kaplan. Minneapolis and London: University of Minnesota Press.

Gutiérrez, Ramón
   1991   *When Jesus Came, the Corn Mothers Went Away: Marriage, Sexuality, and Power in New Mexico, 1500–1846.* Stanford: Stanford University Press.

Homel, David and Sherry Simon
   1988   "Introduction." Pp. 9–11 in *Mapping Literature: The Art and Politics of Translation.* Ed. David Homel and Sherry Simon. Montréal: Véhicule Press.

Kristeva, Julia
   1984   *Revolution in Poetic Language.* Trans. Margaret Waller. New York: Columbia University Press.

Meese, Elizabeth
   1986   *Crossing The Double-Cross: The Practice of Feminist Criticism.* Chapel Hill and London: University of North Carolina Press.

Mohanty, Chandra Talpade
   1989   "On Race and Voice: Challenges for Liberal Education in the 1990s." *Cultural Critique* 14:179–208.

Prince, Gerald
    1987   *A Dictionary of Narratology*. Lincoln and London: University of Nebraska Press.

Spivak, Gayatri Chakravorty
    1993   *Outside in the Teaching Machine*. New York and London: Routledge.

ISSUES FOR FURTHER DISCUSSION:
A RESPONSE

Daniel Boyarin
University of California

RATHER THAN AN ATTEMPT TO PROVIDE some over-all commentary on this collection of interesting but very disparate papers, I am simply going to present some critical and supplemental *Randglossen* in the order of my reading as stimulus and impetus for further discussion of some points in some of the papers.

The most compelling part of "Christological Slippage in Schwarzenegger's *Terminator*" was for me the question "as to why such reactionary films should be so concerned with the problem of the revolution." I shall offer, in the clear hindsight of recent events in the United States, an answer that is related to that of Roland Boer's and that only points up the value of his analysis all the more. Boer argues that these revolutionaries evoke not leftists intent upon the destruction of capitalism but "small but dedicated bands of merchants who through their labors against great odds brought about the collapse of the feudal order and the advent of capitalism." This seems to me an altogether too arcane interpretation, one that hardly speaks to the concern (or the depth of historical knowledge) of those for whom the film is intended. Rather, I suggest, the "revolutionaries" of whom these undoubtedly reactionary films are speaking (and to whom they are addressed) are those of the violent radical right in the United States today. Boer's political analysis of the film forces such a reading and entirely justifies the ideological methods with which his analysis has proceeded. Furthermore, it provides a new (and somewhat frightening) context for the christological intertext as well, given the connections between reactionary violence in America and the so-called Christian right.

I am struck as well by the inscription of political affect in Robert Brawley's paper. By using the terms 'virulent' and 'vicious" with respect to the carnivalesque, he quite pushes the discussion of carnival in a startling new direction. The controversy has not been (as I read it) whether carnival is vicious or not but whether or not it produces effective rebellion against established orders of power and dominance. In other words, 'rebellious' is not encoded (neither by Kristeva nor by Stallybrass) as 'vicious' and negative but as positive resistance to oppression. The reading of the Passion as Carnival that Brawley has hit upon is very promising. I would, however, relocate the carnivalesque, in the light of the above considerations, not in the diegetic world of the mockers of Jesus but in the text itself. The *skandalon* of the Cross is a carnival, a "foolishness' in Paul's terminology! And that is precisely its revolutionary potential with respect to Roman power (and to that of the High Priests as well). Or alternatively, its conservative potential with respect to that same power order if we read Carnival as safety-valve and not as effectively rebellious. In any case, Carnival, according to Bakhtin, for all of its acrid moments, is the cultural structure that has to do with birth, fecundity, life, and reconciliation. It must be remembered that the carnivalesque is strongly associated with dying and resurrected gods as well, supporting Brawley's intuition from another direction (which, to be sure, is mentioned in Brawley's paper, but not, seemingly, connected with Jesus' own death and rebirth). I find that Brawley has missed an opportunity offered by his own insight by locating the carnivalesque in Luke's Passion too narrowly in the mockers of Jesus and not in Jesus himself, too conservatively by locating Jesus as the established order and the mockers as the rebels, when it could (and in my view should) be read in the exact opposite way. Jesus is the carnivalesque figure of rebellion; the mockers are the established order who, nevertheless, within the world of the text indicate just how much of a scandal, a Carnival, a crucified king and savior is. A clue to this alternative interpretation of the relationship of the carnival to the crucifixion should have come with the notice that in Carnival, servants eat with their masters, as explicit a description of the Christian revolution as would be possible to imagine. Much as I sincerely respect Brawley's work in general, I find that this paper participates in an unfortunate tendency (hundreds of years old, if not more) to read Christianity as the defender of established orders and not as their antagonist.

Gary Phillips's paper strikes me as an important contribution in that it clearly delineates the stake in the theory of intertextuality for biblical scholarship. Neither some sort of game of allusion-hunting which some have taken it for, nor a self-indulgent mode of anything-goes exegesis, intertextuality, insofar as it is the condition of all textuality, dictates for exegetical and theological truthfulness other interpretative strategies than have been manifest until now in biblical criticism. Although I find his claims for "deconstructive" reading somewhat overblown, particularly vis-à-vis feminist reading, which seems to *me* to be the most important threat to traditional positivist interpretation, Phillips's paper should help clarify for many readers just why deconstruction is important for them to understand. He argues well for the production of "a writerly reading [that] acknowledges otherness not merely in the form of loving the one foreign to us as the parable recounts, or to embrace that other distant deuteronomic text now brought into relation with Jesus' story, but as other possibilities for reading and writing which Luke's text with its hendiadic prescription covers up as the conscious does the unconscious." Finally, he (at least in part) answers the implicit objection that I have raised above by writing that: "If Luke's text can generate semiotic and deconstructive readings it has the potential as well to produce womanist, ideological or post-modern readings." Deconstruction becomes, as I think Derrida would have it, a potentially political force and not a reactionary recuperation of nihilistic non-politics as the American "boa-deconstructors" of the Yale school (Bloom, Hartman, Miller) have had it.

I would like to remark on a curious misconception in William Doty's paper, one that I think he shares with other scholars of Paul. It seems to me that beyond the sheer fact of being letters, there is almost nothing in common between Paul's Epistles and the responsa literature, neither rhetorically nor politically/socially. For the most part, Paul's letters evoke themselves as the unsought criticisms of untoward behavior on the part of communities for which Paul feels apostolic responsibility—1 Corinthians might be an exception here if we take seriously the suggestions that such language as "It is well not to touch woman'" are the language of interlocutors and not Paul's own. The responsa literature is for the most part a genuine exchange of letters in which one of the participants asks for the view of another, usually on a point of Jewish law but sometimes in matters of doctrine as well, and the latter responds. Indeed, in Hebrew the literature is called to this day: *Questions and Answers*. The rhetoric is entirely different, at least insofar as it is not persuasive in its tone, for the authority of the respondent to determine the law or the doctrine is a given of the situation. Connected to this is Doty's statement that responsa are written to this day by "chief rabbis." Aside from a dearth of such entities in the world—Judaism is not set up as a hierarchy of that sort except where mandated by civil law, as in Israel or Britain—it is simply not the case that responsa are only issued by the titular heads of a hierarchy. Any rabbi writing to any other, asking a question—either as equal or as disciple—and receiving an answer has produced a *responsum*.

I emphasize this point in particular because I have seen this statement, i.e. that Paul's letters are responsa, repeated several times in Pauline scholarship and it makes no sense to me at all. More like Paul's letters are the reports of fragments of Rabban Gamliel's (or his descendants') missives to far-flung Jewish communities enjoining them to practice this way or that, but these are hardly responsa and, moreover, we just don't know much about them. There are also letters from such later authorities as Rav Sherira Gaon and Maimonides which bear more of a phenomenological similarity to Paul's, but these are designed "letters": איגרות; not "responsa": שאלות ותשובות in Hebrew diction. This distinction has its consequences precisely at the point at which Doty intervenes in interpretation of Paul, because the responsa are decidedly not substitutionary for a personal parousia but productive of a body of writing, *ab origine.* The intertextual connections are just not the same. Further, it should really be clear by now that one cannot refer to Paul as responding in any way to "rabbinic Judaism," since that formation was only to come into existence a century or so after his writings. Among its other differences from earlier Jewish formations—Qumran, the Pharisees, Paul!—rabbinic Judaism might be characterized precisely through its particular relation to scripturality and intertextuality. I do not claim that it was produced *de novo* by the Rabbis. Indeed, I and others have already written that Paul provides evidence that it was not, but one can hardly any more read Paul on the background of rabbinic texts, unless in the paradoxical mode by which one reads the Gospel on the background of T. S. Eliot.

Susan Graham's paper is perhaps the best example of intertextual reading in the collection, once it stops being about intertextuality and begins to read passionately. She writes that "public pressure for inclusive language and political correctness encouraged" the shift from: "Where no man has gone before" to "Where no one has gone before" between the first "Star Trek" series and the second generation. She justifies the cynical tone of the comment via a quite brilliant exposure of the thorough conservatism of the gender roles in the second generation series that belies its conscious intentions at a feminist resolution, marked also incidentally by the shift in costume of the female characters from the first to the second series. (Oddly, however, she does not comment on Guinan in this context.) Here we have an instance of intertextual reading at its most powerful, an exposure of codes of (unspecific) reference within which double-meaning is constituted in a text and in which the text subverts its own consciously intended meanings as well as a serious reading of a clearly relevant cotext, the interview with Roddenberry, against and with the grain of "his" fictional text. I would question, however, precisely the dismissiveness of the "political correctness" remark, precisely out of Graham's own description of Roddenberry. Trapped like all of us within the limited universes of our partially raised consciousnesses, isn't it possible that he genuinely thought he was making a feminist intervention—and failed at the same time? I am not sure what motivates my need to "defend" or "apologize" for "Star Trek: the Next Generation" except perhaps for a hovering anxiety that my own intentions in my own texts will be found subverted by unrealized encodings and a desire that I be judged not only on my failures but also on the basis of what I take to be sincere intentions. I call, in other words, for a hermeneutics of critical generosity.

GLOSSARY

The following select list of terms is intended to help situate the arguments of the essays in these two volumes. For excellent additional information see *Encyclopedia of Contemporary Literary Theory: Approaches, Scholars, Terms*. Ed. Irena Makaryk.[1] (Toronto: University of Toronto Press, 1993).

Code—set of rules or conventions enabling the combination and thus communication of signs. Drawn and adapted from Roman Jakobson's six-part communication model, the concept of code is used by Barthes and other structuralists and poststructuralists to explain the extent to which messages are prefigured or already charged with meaning.

Connotation—semantic notion associated with further or "secondary" associations. A central concept in Barthes' semiology derived from the Danish linguist Louis Hjelmslev's structural distinction between the parallel denotative and connotative aspects of the signifier and signified sides of the sign. For Barthes, *denotation* is the presupposed "first order" sign, connotative a "second order" sign built up from denotation. Ideology and myth are "second order" signifying systems. Connotation helps account for the presence of language as a cultural phenomenon within a social field structured by class interests and values.

Denotation—*see connotation*

Echo—metaphor used to describe the intertextual relationship among texts at the level of content. *Echo* can suggest a simple point-to-point or linear connection between texts, in which case it is subject to the criticism directed against influence studies.

Figure—a concept in greimassian semiotics that denotes organizational units of meaning different in structure and function from signs. Figures are complex, "second degree," structures or combinations of elements typically associated with the level of the semantic content of a word, text, sentence, or discourse.

Interpretant—one of the three elements of Charles Sanders Peirce's triadic view of the sign. Peirce's understanding of semeiosis is grounded on a triadic structure of sign (representamen), object, and interpretant, in contrast to the more familiar dyadic structure of signifier and signified associated with Ferdinand de Saussure. The interpretant stands for the "meaning" or "quality of relationship" existing between sign and object.

---

[1] With whose assistance this list was produced.

Comparable to Saussure's signified, Peirce's interpretant, however, is not limited to a mental idea or content; it can also be an action, a practice or habit, physiological as well as mental, thus allowing for an understanding of semeiosis not limited to human use of language.

Intertextuality—term coined by Julia Kristeva to refer to the systemic relationships and processes that govern the dynamic affiliation of texts with one another. Shaped by psychoanalytic and Marxist interests, Kristeva's intertextuality is a cultural phenomenon in which literature and other signifying systems are engaged. Texts within a given culture are (often unconsciously) read in light of one another; they "intersect" to form a "mosaic" in an ongoing process of absorption, transformation, and permutation of one another. Kristeva's social-semiotic orientation (shared by Barthes) contrasts with a restrictive literary view of intertextuality that concentrates on the "influence" of one text or author upon another (cf. Bloom, Hartman).

Indeterminacy—concept associated with Wolfgang Iser, phenomenological criticism, and reader response theory. Refers to that structural character of texts which requires readers to "fill in the blanks" in order to create meaning. In deconstructive theory indeterminacy refers to the principle of uncertainty inherent in all meaning, which makes any final determination of meaning or referent impossible.

Influence studies—an effort to account for "intertextuality" by explaining the relationships of texts to each other primarily in terms of causal factors. Strongly criticized by Kristeva, Barthes, and other poststructuralist theorists for its simplistic, ahistorical, asocial idealization of text, readers, and the reading process.

Intertext—one or more of the "texts" that make up the intertextual mosaic. For Riffaterre, the "intertext" refers to the specific set of texts being viewed as part of a mosaic at a given moment.

Parody—a form of imitation in writing that may include the ridiculing of a style, exaggeration, or mocking of a certain writing habit or practice.

Poststructuralism—umbrella term to denote a stable of critical theories and practices responding in part to 1960s structuralism and modern textual criticism that in various ways dispute notions of objectivity, comprehensiveness, self-evident meaning, and universal validity. Poststructuralist critics such as Barthes, Derrida, Foucault, and Kristeva promoted widespread discussion of the instability of meaning, the effects of texts on culture and the cultural productivity of texts, and the mixing of humanistic and social science approaches.

Readerly/Writerly—two modes of reading and writing made famous by Barthes. The "readerly" (*lisible*) perspective sees writing as "a work," as singular, closed, a finished product, subject to criticism by the reader who is consumer. The "writerly" (*scriptible*) regards writing as "text," as plural, incomplete, in the process of being produced, a bafflement to criticism or commentary, for the reader who is its producer. The readerly/writerly distinction relates to Kristeva's notion of "intertextuality" as process, rather than object.

Reference—action of making sense by drawing attention to a specific state of affairs, object, or context in which language is used. In modern philosophy of language circles, Gottlob Frege distinguishes between "sense" (what propositions state) and "reference" (that about which propositions are stated).

Signifying practice—term referring to the social setting and construction of language as discourse. Kristeva argues that certain types of signifying practice are linked to the production of subjectivity and identity. "Revolutionary" signifying practices destabilize ideology.

Social formation—concept associated with Louis Althusser and social literary theorists used to describe the complex relationship of literature and society and the mutually formative influences between the two. A replacement for an idealist model of social reality (Georg Lukác), "social formation" is a means for speaking about particular ideological, political, economic, and theoretical practices of the social world.

Text—picking up on the word's etymological relationship to weaving (as in *textile*), poststructuralist and intertextual readings often use a concept of "text" to point out the complex intersection of strains of meaning in a given bit of cultural communication. A text in this sense may be any unit of language (written or spoken), or it may be such cultural phenomena as myth, painting, custom, or film.

Textuality—refers generally to the written condition of a literary text as a material object. In structuralist and poststructuralist theory (Kristeva, Barthes, and Derrida, for instance) the term "textuality" denotes a variety of ways of describing texts as they stand in relation to readers and other texts, to the social mode of production, to ideology, and to the semiotic plurality and indeterminacy of meaning.

Trace—a technical term employed by Jacques Derrida and deconstructive critics that invokes the complex metaphysical problem of presence and absence as it relates to meaning. Rooted in Saussure's notion of sign, Derrida's concept of trace points to the fundamental structures of difference that are required for a sign or text to have meaning: a sign is meaningful because of its difference from other signs. A sign's effort to mean in one direction for Derrida gives evidence of what it is trying not to mean; this he and others speak of as a trace, a meaning present by its very exclusion and abscence.

SELECTED BIBLIOGRAPHY

The following list is designed to provide general guided reading on the topic of intertextuality. It is intended to complement the "Works Consulted" lists following the essays in this volume. On the topic of intertextual theory, see the substantial bibliography by Hans-Peter Mai in *Intertextuality*. Ed. Heinrich Plett. Untersuchungen zur Texttheorie 15. (New York: de Gruyter, 1991). For biblical studies with special emphasis on the Hebrew Bible, see the bibliography in *Reading Between Texts. Intertextuality and the Hebrew Bible*. Ed. Danna Nolan Fewell. LCBI Louisville: Westminster/John Knox, 1992).

Bakhtin, M.M. and P.N. Medvedev
    1978   *The Formal Method in Literary Scholarship: A Critical Introduction to Sociological Poetics*. Trans. Albert J. Wehrle. Baltimore and London: The Johns Hopkins University Press.
    1981   *The Dialogic Imagination*. Ed. Michael Holquist. Trans. Caryl Emerson and Michael Holquist. Austin, TX: University of Texas Press.

Barthes, Roland
    1974   *S/Z*. Trans. Richard Miller. New York: Hill and Wang.
    1977   *Image Music Text*. Trans. Stephen Heath. New York: Hill and Wang.
    1975   *The Pleasure of the Text*. Trans. Richard Miller. New York: Hill and Wang.
    1981   "Theory of the Text." Pp. 31-47 in *Untying the Text: A Post-Structuralist Reader*. Ed. Robert Young. Boston: Routledge & Kegan Paul.
    1988   *The Semiotic Challenge*. Trans. Richard Howard. New York: Hill and Wang.

Bloom, Harold
    1973   *The Anxiety of Influence: A Theory of Poetry*. New York: Oxford University Press.
    1975   *A Map of Misreading*. New York: Oxford University Press.

Boyarin, Daniel
    1990   *Intertextuality and the Reading of Midrash*. Indiana Studies in Biblical Literature. Bloomington: Indiana University Press.

Buchanan, George Wesley
    1995   *Introduction to Intertextuality*. Lewiston, NY: Edwin Mellon Press.

Clayton, Jay and Eric Rothstein, eds.
    1992   *Influence and Intertextuality in Literary History*. Madison: University of Wisconsin.

Culler, Jonathan
    1975   *Structuralist Poetics: Structuralism, Linguistics, and the Study of Literature*. Ithaca: Cornell University Press.

1981 *The Pursuit of Signs. Semiotics, Literature, Deconstruction.* Ithaca: Cornell University Press.

Derrida, Jacques
1976 *Of Grammatology.* Trans. Gayatri C. Spivak. Baltimore: Johns Hopkins University Press.
1981 *Dissemination.* Trans. Barbara Johnson. Chicago: University of Chicago Press.

Draisma, Sipke, ed.
1989 *Intertextuality in Biblical Writings. Essays in Honour of Bas van Iersel.* Kampen: J. H. Kok.

Fewell, Danna Nolan, ed.
1992 *Reading Between Texts. Intertextuality and the Hebrew Bible.* LCBI. Louisville: Westminster/John Knox.

Godard, Barbara
1993 "Intertextuality." Pp. 568–72 in *Encyclopedia of Contemporary Literary Theory: Approaches, Scholars, Terms.* Ed. Irena R. Makaryk. Toronto, Buffalo, and London: University of Toronto Press.

Greimas, A.J., and J.Courtès
1982 *Semiotics and Language. An Analytical Dictionary.* Larry Crist, Daniel Patte, Gary Phillips, *et al.* Bloomington: Indiana University Press.

Hartman, Geoffrey H. and Sanford Budick, eds.
1985 *Midrash and Literature.* New Haven: Yale University Press.

Hays, Richard
1989 *Echoes of Scripture in the Letters of Paul.* New Haven: Yale University Press.

Kristeva, Julia
1980 *Desire in Language: A Semiotic Approach to Literature and Art.* Trans. Leon S. Roudiez. Chicago: University of Chicago Press.
1984 *Revolution in Poetic Language.* Trans. Margaret Waller. New York: Columbia University Press.

Morgan, Thais E.
1985 "Is There an Intertext in this Text?: Literary and Interdisciplinary Approaches to Intertextuality." *American Journal of Semiotics* 3/4:1–40.

Plett, Heinrich, ed.
1991 *Intertextuality.* Untersuchungen zur Texttheorie 15. New York: de Gruyter.

Peirce, Charles Sanders
1931–1958 *Collected Papers.* Ed. Charles Hartshorne and Paul Weiss. 5 Vols. Cambridge, MA: Harvard University Press.

Phillips, Gary A.
1991 "Sign/Text/Différance. The Contribution of Intertextual Theory to Biblical Criticism." Pp. 78–100 in *Intertextuality*. Ed. Heinrich Plett. Untersuchungen zur Texttheorie 15. New York: de Gruyter.

Rajan, Tilottama
1991 "Intertextuality and the Subject of Reading/Writing." Pp. 61–74 in *Influence and Intertextuality in Literary History*. Ed. Jay Clayton and Eric Rothstein. Madison: University of Wisconsin.

Riffaterre, Michael
1979 "Sémiotique intertextuelle. l'interpretant." *Revue d'Esthétiques* 1/2:116–28.
1983 *Text Production*. New York: Columbia University Press.
1985 "The Interpretant in Literary Semiotics." *American Journal of Semiotics* 3/4:41–55.

Thibault, Paul
1991 *Social Semiotics as Praxis*. Minneapolis: University of Minnesota Press.

Vorster, Willem
1988 "The Protevangelium of James and Intertextuality." Ed. Tjitze Baarda. Pp. 262-75 in *Text and Testimony. Essays on New Testament and Apocryphal Literature in honor of A.F.G. Klijn*. Kampen: J.H. Kok.

Worton, Michael and Judith Still, eds.
1990 *Intertextuality: Theories and Practices*. Manchester: Manchester University Press.

www.ingramcontent.com/pod-product-compliance
Lightning Source LLC
Chambersburg PA
CBHW020642300426
44112CB00007B/204